Adapting Western Classics for the Chinese Stage

Adapting Western Classics for the Chinese Stage presents a comprehensive study of transnational, transcultural, and translingual adaptations of Western classics from the turn of the twentieth century to present-day China in the age of globalization. Supported by a wide range of in-depth research, this book

- Examines the complex dynamics between texts, both dramatic and socio-historical; contexts, both domestic and international; and intertexts, Western classics and their Chinese reinterpretations in *huaju* and/or traditional Chinese *xiqu*;
- Contemplates Chinese adaptations of a range of Western dramatic works, including Greek, English, Russian, and French;
- Presents case studies of key Chinese adaptation endeavors, including the 1907 adaptation of *Uncle Tom's Cabin* by the Spring Willow Society and the 1990 adaptation of *Hamlet* by Lin Zhaohua;
- Lays out a history of uneasy convergence of East and West, complicated by tensions between divergent sociopolitical forces and cultural proclivities.

Drawing on disciplines and critical perspectives, including theatre and adaptation studies, comparative literature, translation studies, reception theory, post-colonialism, and intertextuality, this book is key reading for students and researchers in any of these fields.

Shouhua Qi is Distinguished Visiting Professor at the College of Liberal Arts, Yangzhou University and Professor and Chair of the Department of English at Western Connecticut State University.

Adapting Western Classics for the Chinese Stage

Shouhua Qi

Routledge
Taylor & Francis Group

LONDON AND NEW YORK

First published 2019
by Routledge
2 Park Square, Milton Park, Abingdon, Oxon OX14 4RN

and by Routledge
605 Third Avenue, New York, NY 10017

First issued in paperback 2020

Routledge is an imprint of the Taylor & Francis Group, an informa business

British Library Cataloguing-in-Publication Data
A catalogue record for this book is available from the British Library

Library of Congress Cataloging-in-Publication Data
A catalog record for this book has been requested

ISBN 13: 978-0-367-73382-7 (pbk)
ISBN 13: 978-1-138-21433-0 (hbk)

Typeset in Sabon
by Apex CoVantage, LLC

Contents

Acknowledgments   vi
Prologue   viii

1 First contact: early Chinese encounters with Western drama   1

2 *Black Slave's Cry to Heaven*, the birth cry of modern
   Chinese drama, and a group of post-'80s amateurs in
   search of a director   11

3 Guess who's coming: Brecht, Beckett, Miller, and the
   revival of modern Chinese drama   27

4 Tragic hero and hero tragedy: reimagining classic Greek
   drama as Chinese *xiqu* today   67

5 Old man Shakespeare, the all but forgotten Shaw, and
   the importance of being Oscar Wilde   86

6 An old "mentor and friend" from afar: adapting classic
   Russian drama for the Chinese stage   122

7 The tragic, the comic, the absurd, and the "grand feast"
   of French classics   152

Epilogue   184
Index   187

Acknowledgments

It is a distinct pleasure to express my heartfelt gratitude to all those who have helped at various stages of this study that I began in 2013, especially the following:

Angelique Richardson, Claire Concesion, Rossella Ferrari, Çiğdem Üsekes, Jinqi Ling, Jacqueline Padgett, Liang Luo, June Grasso, Aimin Chen, and Mingjian Zha for reviewing the project proposal when it was still at the drawing board and for offering thoughtful feedback and enthusiastic support, especially in the form of recommendation letters.

The two anonymous experts who reviewed the book proposal submitted to Routledge for their constructive feedback and many valuable suggestions that helped sharpen the topical and thematic focus, contextualize the discussions and analyses, and shape the organization of the book.

Wei Zhang for reading through the drafts of all the chapters and offering insightful commentary, and, particularly, for coauthoring a journal article on Chinese adaptations of classic Greek drama as *jingju* (Peking opera) that is incorporated into Chapter 5.

Elizabeth Bradburn, Lofton L. Durham, and Nick Gauthier of *Comparative Drama*; Frode Helland, Torhild Aas, and Kavitha Dharmaraj of *Ibsen Studies*; and Constanze Guthenke and Alison Hutchins of the *Classical Receptions Journal*, as well as the anonymous expert reviewers for reading the submissions to the three journals, respectively, and for their thoughtful feedback and constructive suggestions for revisions.

Zhixiang Zhuang, Jun Chen, Don Gagnon, Jiangchao Wang, and many others for their friendship and enthusiastic support as the study forged its tortoise way forward.

Librarians, staff, and student workers at the Hass Library of Western Connecticut State University for their warm professionalism, especially interlibrary loan staff for working diligently over the years to track down and secure for me many a hard-to-find book or journal article.

Martha Palanzo at the office of Macricostas School of Arts & Sciences, Kim Spinelli at the office of Institutional Advancement/Fiscal Affairs, and Gabrielle Jazwiecki at the office of Sponsored Research Administrative Services for patiently guiding me through the loop of paperwork for all my research travels.

Western Connecticut State University for research grants and released time for research, which made it possible for me to travel and conduct research and prepare the manuscript for this book.

Finally, Ben Piggott at Routledge for believing in this project and, along with Kate Edwards, Laura Soppelsa, Jennifer Bonnar, and Louise Peterken, for shepherding me through the entire process from proposal to book.

Prologue

On February 11, 1907, at the YMCA of China in Tokyo, a three-story building (of classrooms, dorms, a cafeteria, a bookstore, and a small shop) recently opened for young Chinese studying in the capital city of Japan, a group of Chinese students mounted the third act of *La Dame aux Camilias* (Alexander Dumas fils), which tells the tragic love story of Marguerite Gautier, a young *courtisane*, and Armand Duval, a young bourgeois from a "good" family.

The performance was to raise relief funds for flooding victims back in China, mostly in the southern provinces of Jiangsu and Anhui. It was attended by about 2,000 people, Japanese and Westerners, as well as Chinese, and was enthusiastically reviewed in the host country's newspapers.

A few months later, in early June that same year, riding the success of this maiden performance, members of the Spring Willow Society (*Chunliu she*), once again with the capable coaching of Fujisawa Asajiro (1866–1917), a well-known *shinpa*[1] actor, staged a full production of *Black Slave's Cry to Heaven* (*Heinu yutian lu*), a five-act play based on a 1901 Chinese translation of Harriet Beecher Stowe's *Uncle Tom's Cabin*, at a much more prestigious venue, Hongo-Za Theatre. The performance was once again successful and enthusiastically received; its artistic achievements were even more extensive and significant.[2]

The 1907 adaptations of *La Dame aux Camélias* and *Uncle Tom's Cabin* by young members of the Spring Willow Society in Tokyo have been hailed as a remarkable, momentous development in the history of Chinese drama although scholars disagree as to whether those bold performances should be credited as the birth cry of *huaju* (spoken drama) and, by extension, modern Chinese drama.[3] Since then over a century of reimagining Western classics[4] – to reinterpret, to relocate, and to recreate transnationally and transculturally, as well as translingually, mostly through adaptation endeavors – for the Chinese stage bespeaks a history of uneasy convergence of East and West complicated by tensions between divergent sociopolitical forces and cultural proclivities.

In the Chinese language and culture, there are two near equivalents for the term "drama" as typically understood in the West:[5] *xiqu* and *xiju*. In literary and artistic discourse, *xiqu* is generally used to refer to traditional Chinese drama such as *jingju* (Peking opera or Beijing opera), *kunju* or *kunqu* (kun opera), *yueju* (*yue* opera), *yuju* (yu opera), *chuanju* (Sichuan opera), and *qin-qiang* (qin opera), whereas *xiju* is used to refer to Western-style genres such as *huaju* (spoken drama), *geju* (song drama, opera), and *wuju* (dance drama, ballet), as well as more modern developments, although the distinctions between the two terms *xiqu* and *xiju* sometimes blur in everyday parlance.[6]

Chinese dramatic tradition can be traced back to the dawn of the Chinese civilization – to communal festivals featuring song and dance and to rites and rituals performed to exorcize evil spirits and to give thanks to the gods for their blessings. It continued to evolve and reached its first heyday in the Yuan and early Ming dynasties (1271–1550), especially in *zaju* (variety play), which claims some of China's greatest playwrights: Guan Hanqing (1241–1320) – often dubbed the Shakespeare of China, Wang Shifu (1250–1307?), and Ma Zhiyuan (1250–1321). Among other illustrious pre-twentieth-century playwrights are Tang Xianzu (1550–1616), Hong Sheng (1645–1704), and Kong Shangren (1648–1718).[7] Throughout the centuries, traditional Chinese *xiqu* had flourished in more than 300 local, regional, and national genres, the best known among them including the aforementioned *jingju, kunqu, yueju, yuju, chuanju,* and *qinqiang.*

Each genre of the traditional Chinese *xiqu* has its own rich history of gestation and development, although many are closely related through kinship of one kind or another. Take *jingju* (Peking opera), for example. Known to the outside world as a quintessential, representative *xiqu, jingju* is a relatively recent development during the Qing dynasty (1636–1911), having evolved from *huiju* (Anhui opera, popular in the southern province of Anhui) and *hanju* (popular in Shaanxi and other central provinces) in the decades from the late eighteenth century to the early nineteenth century. Similarly, each local, regional, or national genre of *xiqu* has its distinctive style of performance. *Huaguxi* (Flower drum opera, popular in Hunan and its neighboring provinces), for example, is characterized by its song and dance. *Tanhuang* (popular in Jiangsu and Zhejiang provinces during the late Qing period), which evolved into *huju* (Shanghai opera, popular in Shanghai) and *xiju* (popular in the Wuxi area of Jiangsu province), etc., typically had the actors (3 to 11) sitting around a table and singing. Indeed, many *xiqu* genres are known for blending singing (*chang*), acting (*zuo*, mix of dance and performance), speaking (*nian*), and fighting (*da*, mix of acrobatics and martial arts) in one theatric event and experience.[8]

Through its millennium-long trek of developments across vast stretches of time – e.g., from dynasties of Han (202 BC–AD 220) to Qing (AD 1644–1911) – and space – e.g., northern and southern regions of China – *xiqu* flourished and along the way acquired a few salient characteristics that, according to many Chinese drama scholars, would distinguish itself from Western dramatic tradition.[9] I would hasten to add that for the purpose of discussion here the term "Western dramatic tradition" is used in a most broad and general sense to refer to Western (European and American) drama from classical Greece to modern times without getting into even the most important historical developments and the artistic, as well as philosophical distinctions between various theatre forms and movements – e.g., medieval, Elizabethan, neoclassical, realism, naturalism, modernism, expressionism, post-modern, and, more recently, immersive/interactive theatre and "media intermultimodality"[10] – and without foraying into the long history of contact, interaction, and flow of ideas between East (e.g., India, China, and Japan) and West, especially since the West began to expand into Asia much more assertively in the nineteenth century. I am equally mindful of the fact that what Chinese drama scholars refer to as *xiqu*'s distinguishing characteristics may not be that unique after all. Take *zonghexing* or *zongyixing* (interfusion of arts) for example. Drama/theatre, East or West, is by its very nature an "intermultimodal" event. In classic Greek theatre, for instance, the chorus (a group of actors who provide necessary background information and comment on the dramatic action as it unfolds) would variously dance, sing, or speak their lines to help the audience follow and appreciate. They sometimes wore masks too. Neither is *xunixing* or *xieyixing* (symbolic representation) particularly unique to *xiqu* because drama/theatre, East or West, is symbolic and make-believe by its very nature. Nonetheless, interfusion of arts (*zonghexing*, *zongyixing*), symbolic representation (*xunixing*, *xieyixing*), and stylization (*chengshixing*) are regarded by many Chinese drama scholars as the three most distinctive characteristics of *xiqu*. These characteristics, when considered together (but without overlooking the differences between the many genres of *xiqu*), can still serve as a useful frame of reference for discussing the subject of this book: transnational, transcultural, and translingual adaptations of Western classics for the Chinese stage.

Interfusion of arts

This "intermultimodal" proclivity of many genres of *xiqu* can be traced back to the early days of the Chinese civilization when *yue* (art, entertainment) meant a composite performance of poetry, song, and dance. As noted in *Yueji* (Art records), a book from Spring, Autumn, and Warring States periods (*chunqiu zhanguo*, approximately 771 to 221 BC), and *Maoshi xu* (Mao poetry preface), written around the same time as that of the monumental *Shijing* (Book of Songs, the earliest collection of Chinese poetry dating from the eleventh to seventh century BC): poetry is an expression of *zhi* (soul, spirit); when *zhi* in one's heart and mind expresses itself in speech, it becomes poetry. Similarly, *qing* (emotions, sensibilities) originates from one's inner being and expresses itself in speech: when speaking does not express oneself fully, augment it with exclamations; when exclaiming does not express oneself fully, sing; when singing does not express oneself fully, dance. Indeed, it would take no less than all three – poetry, song, and dance, blended in one act – to give full expression to the human spirit.[11] This artistic and aesthetic ideal long upheld from antiquity, as applied to *xiqu*, would manifest itself in the amalgamation of all three – poetry, song, and dance – to give full, multimodal expression to the full range of human experiences.

Symbolic representation

Although the rise of the realist theatre in the West was very much a nineteenth-century phenomenon[12] and realism as a dominant mode in arts and literature has long since been deconstructed on philosophical and other grounds and challenged by many other theories and movements, especially post-modernism, *mimesis* remains an important concept for both theorists and practitioners to wrestle with even today, and realism as an important mode of representation remains intimately associated with a significant portion of Western arts and literature.[13] Much of the traditional Chinese dramatic art, in contrast, up till the first decades of the twentieth century when it encountered the much more realistic mode of theatre from the West, was minimalistic in the use of stagecraft such as scenery and lighting to invoke a sense of time, place, people, and event. Springing from another artistic and aesthetic ideal of the Chinese culture, which values capturing the "essence" and "spirit" rather than "replicating" the physicality of human experiences and nature (e.g., landscape), and constrained by the lack of advancement in the technology of stage design,[14] traditional Chinese *xiqu* was characterized by its breaking down of the "fourth wall" in presenting "life" for the audiences.

It is true that the "fourth wall" illusion in the West is more associated with the realistic/ naturalistic theatre in the decades between the late nineteenth century and early twentieth century, and that it was frequently broken for comic effect even back in the Elizabethan theatre by actors directly addressing and/or interacting with the audiences. However, its presence is as pronounced in much of the Western dramatic tradition as its absence in traditional Chinese *xiqu*.[15] Indeed, in much of *xiqu* there is no pretention that whatever is happening on the stage is real life in the physical and material sense, although the "essence" and "spirit" of human experiences, as played out by well-trained and talented actors, should be as authentic and intense. A few quick steps across the simple, makeshift stage would be enough to suggest a journey of 10,000 *li* and three or four actors tumbling in a carefully choreographed "sword and spear" play would convey a sense of armies at each other on an epic scale. Spring, summer, autumn, winter; rain, snow, thunderstorm; climbing a mountain; setting sail on swift waters; charging forward on horseback, etc., can all be invoked with a few simple but highly conventionalized (see the following) gestures, movements, and/or a quick declaration in the lyrics or speech, without resorting to elaborate audio-visual technology to achieve verisimilitude. All a traveling troupe needs are a few good actors, a minimal supply of costumes and cosmetics (whereby to paint the faces red, black, or white according to the roles), two or three simple string and percussion instruments, and a small set of "swords" and "spears."

Stylization

Highly conventionalized way of acting is another hallmark of *xiqu*, although stylization is inherent in all artistic – including dramatic – performances and is present even in the most realistic theatre.[16] As a language or grammar of sorts established from long tradition and understood by the audiences, stylization is an especially necessary condition for the minimalist and highly suggestive *xiqu* to work. Actors have on distinctive costumes, masks, or painted faces appropriate to the roles they play. The roles in *jingju* are typically organized in four major groups: *sheng* (male), *dan* (female), *jing* (painted face), and *chou* (clown), each of which then falls into secondary and even tertiary subcategories. Under the general category of *sheng* (male), for example, there are *xusheng* or *laosheng* (bearded male, old male), *xiaosheng* (young male), *hongsheng* (red-faced male), *wusheng* (martial male), and *wawasheng* (young boys), whereas under the *dan* (female) role, there are *qingyi* or *zhengdan* (bluish-dressed female, righteous female), *huadan* or *huashan* (lively, florally dressed female), *laodan* (old female), and *wudan* (martial female). Even music for traditional Chinese *xiqu* – its songs and melodies – is highly conventionalized both in composition and in performance with an elaborate system of arias, fixed tune melodies, and percussion patterns.[17]

The Chinese could claim great achievements in drama comparable to any other dramatic tradition in the world. If Voltaire (1694–1778) was impressed with the Confucian morality as embodied in the thirteenth-century Yuan play *The Orphan of Zhao* (despite its apparent violation of the neoclassical "dogmas" of unities of time, action, and place) and felt inspired enough to adapt it into French (*L'Orphelin de la Chine*),[18] and if Brecht (1898–1968) saw in *xiqu*, as exemplified in the performances of Mei Langfang (1894–1961), one of the greatest *jingju* actors, during his 1935 European tour, some inspiration or confirmation – possibly based on a "misreading" of the aesthetics of *xiqu* – for his theory of *Verfremdungseffekt* (alienation, defamiliarization, or estrangement effect) and indeed for the expansion of the Epic Theatre,[19] a generation of patriotic Chinese youths and intelligentsia living in the late Qing and early Republican[20] decades of China saw nothing but decadence and were "alienated" from it in highly charged political ways. In their eyes, *xiqu*, thanks to its mostly unrealistic stories and stylized acting, was every bit part of the old culture that had not served China well in the "brave new world" of modern times and would have to be reformed or reinvented if there were to be authentic, socially relevant drama and indeed if China were to be saved and renewed.[21]

To save China from its perceived moribund fate was what motivated the tens of hundreds of young Chinese, including those who would become the founding members of the Spring Willow Society alluded to in the opening paragraphs, to go abroad to study during the late Qing and early Republican era. Young members of the Spring Willow Society mounted their adaptation of Harriet Beecher Stowe's *Uncle Tom's Cabin* in Tokyo, far away from home, not just because they cared about the history of slavery and racial injustice in America, or because they were passionately interested in the make-believe world of theatre. More importantly, it was their way of living the *wen yi zai dao* (literature/art as a vehicle of the way) mantra upheld by the Chinese intelligentsia from time immemorial. It was their way of searching for *dao* – for ideas and ways to awaken and enlighten the people and to renew and reinvigorate the Chinese culture. What they found was a new Western way of storytelling on the stage; they took it up and experimented with it by mounting a bold and by all accounts successful adaptation of a Western classic, and that has made all the difference.

To awaken the spirit of the people and renew and reinvigorate the culture has been the motivating force behind much of the Chinese adaptation endeavors ever since. It was the inspiration for the 1918 special issue of the *New Youth* magazine that gave a full-throated introduction of Henrik Ibsen and "Ibsenism" as (mis)read by Hu Shi and like-minded contemporaries, which harbingered an era, and indeed a movement that appropriated the Western playwright as a champion of sorts, and Nora, the heroine of *A Doll's House*, as a rallying cry for the cause of women's liberation. It was the same quest for enlightenment and cultural renewal that took a new generation of intellectuals and artists to Western classics as represented by Brecht, Beckett, and Miller in the years immediately after the Cultural Revolution (1966–1976). Experimenting with expressionism, the Epic Theatre, the Theatre of the Absurd, and other ideas and ways of modern and post-modern Western drama/theatre has profoundly changed both the *what* and *how* in the contemporary Chinese theatre scene.

China has come a long way socioeconomically and as the second-largest economy in the world today the Chinese civilization has no real, imminent threat for its survival or vibrancy. Nonetheless, with the onslaught of technology and pop culture – e.g., television, film (especially in the form of Hollywood blockbusters, imported or pirated), and the Internet – drama/theatre is gradually losing its foothold in the cultural landscape. For example, as reported in a study completed in 2004, the year 1985 saw a total of 472,600 *xiqu* performances. By 2002, the number of performances had fallen to 239,000, a 49.4% drop. Similarly, the year 1985 saw a total of 57, 261, 000 people in the *xiqu* theatre. By 2002, the audience size had shrunk to 31,143,000, a 45.6% drop.[22]

Another alarming reality is the demographics of the *xiqu* audiences. The overwhelming majority, about 70%, are in the 50 and above age group. Indeed, there seems a schizophrenic split among the Chinese theatre population. The more modern, "Western" *huaju* (spoken drama), whose share of the market has been equally threatened by the onslaught of technology and pop culture, is fast becoming an all but exclusive club of the twentysomething college students. For example, a study of the Beijing *huaju* market published in 2003 found that the 18–30 age group claimed 63.9% of the Beijing People's Art Theatre audience and 62.8% of the Central Experimental Spoken Drama

Theatre (*Zhongyang shiyan huaju yuan*) audience, whereas the 50 and above age group took only 11.5% and 7.5%, respectively.[23] These findings are borne out by my own theatergoing experiences in Beijing, Shanghai, Hangzhou, Suzhou, Guangzhou, and elsewhere for the last several years. More often than not, I find myself the lone representative of the 50 and above age group in a theatre packed with young and lively college students who have come in groups of friends and classmates, smartphones at the ready to snap pictures and video record their favorite moments during the performance.

Feeling the mounting pressure of the marketplace, many of the drama troupes, whether they specialize in *xiqu* or the relatively modern *huaju*, invest much of their hope of survival and vibrancy in their adaptation endeavors.[24] In a way, adaptation of Western classics for the Chinese stage today takes on the same survival and renewal theme, albeit with some marked variation from most of the twentieth century. Much of the success or failure rides on how the Chinese theatre artists approach their adaptation endeavors, given the vast differences in history, culture, religion, customs, and language, as well as theatergoers' tastes, sensibilities, and habits. Typically, adaptation endeavors assume one of the four modes: fidelity (faithful to the original play in story, structure, and production), indigenization (appropriating the original play as inspiration and raw material to make a new Chinese play, especially in a traditional *xiqu* genre), hybridization (interfusing two distinctive dramatic traditions into the same theatric event), and experimentation (experimental in story, structure, and production, whether it takes the form of *xiqu*, *huaju*, or a mishmash of the two). Of course in practice, there is considerable fluidity among the four modes. For example, even the most faithful production of a Western classic can entail some level of experimentation (or "deviation" from the original) thanks to the complex nature and processes of such translingual, transcultural, and transnational undertakings. Indeed, it would be impossible to say definitively which of the four modes would be the most conducive to adaptation success. For example, Huang Zuolin's mostly faithful approach in his 1959 full-scale adaptation of Brecht's *Mother Courage and Her Children* turned out to be quite a failure, even by his own estimate. Yet his 1979 adaptation of Brecht's *Life of Galileo*, essentially in the same "fidelity" mode, turned out to be quite a success. Similarly, the 1983 production of *Death of a Salesman* mounted by the Beijing People's Art Theatre and directed by Arthur Miller himself, a full "fidelity" endeavor down to the running time, was quite a success too.

However, what would be the most sensible and universally acknowledged measure of success? Is it box office, market share, the opinion of professional reviewers and drama experts, or, for that matter, international recognition in the form of awards and invitations to perform at prestigious international drama festivals? Take, for example, traditional *xiqu* adaptations of Shakespeare at the 1986 and 1994 International Shakespeare Festivals in Beijing and Shanghai. They garnered mostly enthusiastic responses from Chinese drama experts. However, Murray J. Levith, a US-based Shakespearean scholar, in his 2004 book *Shakespeare in China*, keeps questioning the authenticity of *jingju*, *kunju*, *huangmeixi*, and *yueju* adaptations of Shakespearean plays: When King Lear assumes the Chinese name of *Li'er Wang* and when the story of Hamlet is relocated to a time and place in Chinese history and acted out in stylized performance and *yueju* arias, is it still Shakespeare? How far can one go "before Shakespeare is no longer really Shakespeare?"[25] Such questioning is a recurrent theme of the book although, as one Chinese reviewer of the book commented, Levith seems to have no qualms comparing Shakespeare and Confucius based on English translations that may not represent the real Chinese sage at all.[26] All the stars, so to speak, have to be perfectly aligned, more or less, to ensure the success of any such adaptation endeavors – success measured in box office as well as in the opinions of drama experts from both source and target cultures. Even the acoustics of a theatre could help derail a production, which was probably the case of the May 5, 1923, performance of *A Doll's House* by students of Beijing Normal College for Women. This failure engendered quite a bit of tension, in public display, among Ibsen enthusiasts.[27]

From the bold, albeit amateur, adaptations staged by young Chinese studying in Tokyo (1907) to *Search for Spring Willow Society* (*xunzhao chunliushe*), a post-modern play mounted by the storied Beijing People's Art Theatre (2007) to reimagine the rehearsing of *Black Slave's Cry to Heaven* with three present-day directors guided by contrary artistic visions; from the publication of a special Ibsen issue by the iconoclastic *New Youth* magazine (1918) and the first staging of *A Doll's House* (1924) in Shanghai, which inspired many a "Chinese Nora" to slam the door on unhappy homes and arranged marriages and to venture out and seek their own happiness, even at the peril of their lives, to a new adaptation mounted by Central Experimental Spoken Drama Theatre (*Zhongyang shiyan huaju yuan*, 1998) that has Nora following her Chinese husband to his ancestral home in the China of the 1930s, thus adding transcultural and interracial complications to the theme of gender equality; from the first translations of Charles Lamb's *Tales from Shakespeare* (1903) to International Shakespeare Festival held in Beijing and Shanghai (1986, 1994, and thereafter), with more than 20 of the Bard's plays having been adapted into *jingju*, *kunju*, *yueju*, *yuju*, *chuanju*, *qinqiang*, *bangzi*, and other genres as well as *huaju* (spoken drama), adaptations of Western classics[28] into *huaju* and various forms of *xiqu* have profoundly transformed the drama scene and experience and, for that matter, the cultural life of modern China and will continue to do so years and decades into the future.

This book is not an attempt to write another history of modern Chinese drama to add to the list of existing books in both Chinese and English.[29] Nor is it another book devoted to the reception history of a particular Western playwright in China – e.g., Shakespeare, Ibsen, or O'Neill.[30] Rather, it is a comprehensive, interdisciplinary study of transnational, transcultural, and translingual adaptation of Western classics from the turn of the twentieth century to present-day China in the age of globalization.

This study draws from critical perspectives of intertextuality – e.g., Julia Kristeva (whose theorization of intertextuality, in turn, draws from Bakhtin's concepts of dialogism and heterroglossia), Gérard Genette (whose concept of transtextuality encompasses intertextual, paratextual, hypertextual, as well as architextual connections), Harold Bloom (whose concept of "anxiety of influence" speaks to the ambivalence many Chinese feel about all things Western, including arts and literature), and post-colonialism (which shines light on the unequal relationships, among other things, between the dominant/source cultures and texts and the dominated/target cultures and texts).[31] It also draws from comparative drama[32] as well as comparative literature (especially its more recent focus on the intercultural aspects of literature in relation to history, politics/geopolitics, and globalization),[33] translation studies (e.g., the concept of "cultural translation" as outlined by Susan Bassnett and André Lefevere),[34] and reception theory (including the study of reception history).[35] Critical perspectives from these and other pertinent fields of inquiry, along with adaptation studies, have many points of both convergence and diversion between and among them (for example, translation and adaptation)[36] will lend this study an assortment of lenses, so to speak, to both see the big picture – broad contours and topographies – and sharpen the view of subtle nuances.

At its most raw and basic level, to adapt is to make suitable to or fit for a specific use or situation. The ability to adapt, in response to environmental challenges, is a fundamental property of life that distinguishes itself from nonliving matter. Adaptation, innate or involuntary, unconscious or deliberate, contributes to an organism or species' fitness and survival.[37] For the Chinese in much of the modern times since its door was blasted open by Western Powers in the mid-1800s, adaptation to the "brave new world" was more forced upon than voluntary and it was often a fitful and painful process. Through adaptation China, or rather, the Chinese civilization, has not only survived but also become fitter although much may have been lost in the process too.

The term adaptation, as applied to this study, such as drama, theatre, literature, culture, modernity, and almost all such terms and concepts, would resist any attempt at a simple and definitive definition in the post-modern world we live in today. For the purpose of this book, we can describe adaptations, as Julie Sanders does in *Adaptation and Appropriation* (2006), as "reinterpretations of established texts in new generic contexts or perhaps with relocations of an 'original' or source text's cultural and/or temporal setting, which may or may not involve a generic shift,"[38] and/or as Linda Hutcheon does in *A Theory of Adaptation* (2012), as "deliberate, announced, and extended revisitations of prior works" which should be approached as both product(s) and process(es), (re)creation and reception.[39] Since transcultural adaptations, which would entail a relocation in time, place, language, audience, and possibly dramatic/theatric genre and style, and would often occur, as in the case of China, against the backdrop of convoluted international as well as domestic politics, the study of the *what, who, why, how, when,* and *where* would be even more complicated and hence more rewarding.

In deciding what would fall into the scope of this study of transnational, transcultural, and translingual adaptations of Western classics, I choose to consider both processes and products and the totality of the basic questions of *what, who, why, how, when,* and *where* instead of giving undue weight to any one or two. For example, as will be discussed in the second chapter of this book, *Black Slave's Cry to Heaven* mounted by the young members of Spring Willow Society in 1907 falls well within the scope of this study although it was directed by a well-known Japanese *shinpa* actor and staged in Tokyo – far away from the native soil of China. Similarly, *Death of a Salesman* as mounted by the Beijing People's Art Theatre in 1983 fits well despite the fact that it was directed by Arthur Miller himself. From initiation of the project to choice of play (Miller initially recommended *The Crucible*) to translation (using the richly flavored Beijing dialect) to acting (the entire cast remained "Chinese" in their makeup, speech, and behavior) to decisions such as whether to cut "Requiem" (so the audience members could catch the last late night bus ride home), the entire production, from beginning to end, was a suspense-filled process of transcultural, translingual, and political "negotiations" in the context of post-Cultural Revolution China.[40]

Adaptation from another dramatic tradition (itself being polymorphous, fluid, and resistant to neat definitions), whether driven by necessity for survival or by a desire to break down walls and open up new vistas – to imagine anew, to recreate, to reclaim past glories real and imagined – has never been an easy convergence. This book, once again, is a study of transnational, transcultural, and translingual adaptations of Western classics – the complex dynamics between texts (dramatic and socio-historical), contexts (domestic and international), intertexts (Western classics and their Chinese reincarnations in *huaju xiqu*), and dominance and resistance (of culture and ideology) – across the rugged terrain of more than 100 years of modern Chinese history.

The first chapter of the book gives a brief overview of the early Chinese encounters with Western drama in the late 1800s. It is followed by two chapters, each devoted to a pivotal development pertaining to the subject under consideration. The remaining four chapters each focus on adaptations of Greek, Anglo-Irish, Russian, and French classics, respectively. The book concludes with an epilogue, a recap of the last 100 years (and counting) history of transnational, transcultural, and translingual adaptations.

Comprehensive as it is, this book is not meant to be encyclopedic and exhaustive, having a substantial discussion of every Western classic of which there has been a Chinese adaptation. Conspicuously absent, because of space limits, is a chapter on Henrik Ibsen (1828–1906), a towering figure in the annals of modern Chinese arts and literature whose impact is as much felt, studied, and, yes, debated today as it was in the much headier days of the early decades of the twentieth century.[41] Similarly, this book does not have a chapter on Chinese adaptations of American drama as represented by

Eugene O'Neill (1888–1955) and Tennessee Williams (1911–1983), although the presence of American drama, albeit relatively young, is as much felt, and its impact is just as profound as that of classic Greek, English, French, and Russian dramas. This notable absence is somewhat compensated by a section in Chapter 3 devoted to Arthur Miller in China. Regrettably, this book does not have a chapter on adaptations of German classics either, although Bertolt Brecht (1898–1956), an important Western playwright who both drew from traditional Chinese *xiqu* and in turn exerted catalytic influence on the revival of modern Chinese drama in the decade right after the Cultural Revolution, receives ample attention in Chapter 3. Other notable absences include adaptations of contemporary Western drama, although such adaptations – e.g., *Accidental Death of an Anarchist* (1998–present) by the 1997 Nobel Prize in Literature laureate Dario Fo (1926–2016) – are an important part of the drama/theatre scene in today's China. Finally, and perhaps most importantly, although this book has a rather broad scope, it does not include adaptations of Western classics on the stages in Taiwan or Hong Kong. They each have such a rich and vibrant history of adaptation endeavors shaped by their unique cultural identities, historical experiences, and socioeconomic conditions that only a full-length book study can hope to do justice to.

Notes

1 The term *shinpa* (new school), as opposed to *kabuki* (old school), refers to a movement in Japanese drama/theatre from the 1880s to the early 1900s that focused on contemporary topics and Westernized realistic performances, although it was *shingeki* (new drama), a movement following *shinpa*, that was the main force in modernizing Japanese drama/theatre by introducing and adapting Western classics such as Henrik Ibsen, Anton Chekhov, and Eugene O'Neill. See Siyuan Liu.

2 See Huang Aihua, "*Chunliushe yanjiu zaji*" (Research notes on Spring Willow Society); Yu Shiao-ling; and Siyuan Liu.

3 See Ding Luonan, 014–30; Wang Fengxia; Fu Jin; and Yuan Guoxing, 1–16.

4 For the purpose of this book, the term "Western classics" is used quite liberally. Its reference is not limited to dramatic works from antiquity (i.e., ancient Greece and ancient Rome); rather, it extends so far as to include some of the most important dramatic works of the twentieth century. The term "Western," as used in this book, mostly refers to Europe and the United States.

5 *The Oxford Dictionary of Literary Terms*, 3rd ed.

6 The near equivalents in English for *qu* in *xiqu* are music, melody, and song, whereas the near equivalents for *ju* are drama and play. The term "opera" has been used in translating names of traditional Chinese *xiqu* – e.g., Beijing opera (Peking opera) for *jingju* or *jingxi*, *kun* opera for *kunju* or *kunqu*, *yue* opera for *yueju*, and *huangmei* opera for *huangmeixi*. However, these genres of traditional Chinese *xiqu* are not exactly operas as understood in the West, which typically have all parts sung to instrumental accompaniment although they incorporate elements of the theatre such as acting and sometimes include dance too.

According to a recent study, the use of the term "opera" in reference to traditional Chinese *xiqu* can be traced back to Chen Jitong (aka Tcheng ki-tong or Chean Ki Tong, 1851–1907), a long-time Chinese diplomat in Europe who served, among other things, as an attaché in Paris. Chen took it upon himself to introduce and promote Chinese culture in Europe, and in doing so he, in his 1886 book *Le Theatre des Chinois* (written in French and published in Paris), he compared traditional Chinese *xiqu* to French operas and highlighted several notable similarities between the two, especially the central role of singing in both "operas." See Man Xinying.

7 Among the most acclaimed plays by these classic Chinese playwrights are *Dou' e yuan* (The Injustice to Dou E, aka Snow in Midsummer) and *Jiu fengchen* (Saving the Prostitute) by Guan Hanqing (1241–1320), *Xixiang ji* (The West Wing Story) by Wang Shifu (1250–1307?), *Hangong qiu* (Autumn in the Han Palace) by Ma Zhiyuan (1250–1321); *Mudan ting* (The Peony Pavilion) by Tang Xianzu (1550–1616), *Changsheng dian* (The Palace of Eternal Life) by Hong Sheng (1645–1704), and *Taohua shan* (The Peach Blossom Fan) by Kong Shangren (1648–1718).

8 See Wilt L. Idema, "Traditional Dramatic Literature;" and Ye Changhai.

9 This portion of the discussion on the salient characteristics of *xiqu* draws from Xu Muyun; Ye Changhai and Zhang Fuhai; and Ye Changhai.

  All English translations, paraphrases, or summaries from Chinese sources, when not otherwise noted, are provided by the author of this book.

10 See Andy Lavender.

11 Ye Changhai and Zhang Fuhai, 4.

12 The decades between the late nineteenth century and early twentieth century also saw several other developments in drama/theatre – e.g., symbolism (Maurice Maeterlinck), aestheticism (Oscar Wilde), and expressionism (August Strindberg and Eugene O'Neill). All of these movements were introduced to China in the early decades of the twentieth century, although none received the same intensity of attention as the realist drama embodied by Henrik Ibsen, Anton Chekhov, and Bernard Shaw, and none exerted the same extent of influence on the development of modern Chinese drama. See Shouhua Qi, "Misreading Ibsen."

13 For an in-depth discussion on "mimesis" as a central, seminal concept in Western arts and literature from Plato and Aristotle all the way to the modern times (despite its wide range of meanings that shift and evolve), see Gunter Gebauer and Christoph Wulf.

14 For centuries, until the early decades of the twentieth century, traditional Chinese *xiqu* had been typically performed in teahouses, gardens of the rich and powerful, and town or village squares with makeshift platforms. There was no Chinese equivalent for "the Globe Theatre" associated with William Shakespeare. Anything that resembles the proscenium or thrust stage is a recent, twentieth century development – a result of adapting from Western dramatic/theatric tradition.

15 For an in-depth discussion of the "fourth wall" in *xiqu*, especially in connection with Brecht's theory of *Verfremdungseffekt*, see Min Tian, "'Alienation-Effect' for Whom?" Ronnie Bai; and Haun Saussy, "Mei Lanfang in Moscow, 1935."

16 Vsevolod Meyerhold (1874–1940), when speaking of the art of Mei Lanfang (1894–1961, one of the most accomplished and famous *jingju* artists), went so far as to say, "It is a mistake to contrast stylized theatre with realistic theatre. Our formula is stylized realistic theatre." See Min Tian, *The Poetics of Difference and Displacement*, 65.

17 See Xu Muyun, 177–94.

18 See Liu Wu-Chi; Wilt L. Idema, "The Orphan of Zhao"; and Adrian Hsia.

19 See Min Tian, "'Alienation-Effect;'" Ronnie Bai, "Dances With Mei Lanfang;" and Haun Saussy, "Mei Lanfang in Moscow, 1935."

20 The early Republic (1912–1916) refers to the years following the 1911 revolution (led by Sun Yat-sen) that overthrew the Qing Dynasty (1644 to 1912).

21 See Ding Luonan, 532–46.

22 Guo Yanlin, 40–1, 44. See also Tao Ran.
23 Zhou Hong, 100–6.
24 For an example of traditional Chinese *xiqu* adaptation of *Antigone*, see Xu Lian and Fang Chen.
25 Murray J. Levith, 73, 75, 83, and 136.
26 Zhang Weiping, 21–2.
27 Qi, "Misreading Ibsen," 346–48.
28 For various definitions of the term "adaptation," see Julie Sanders, 17–25, and Linda Hutcheon, 1–27.
29 See Chen Baichen and Dong Jian; Xiaomei Chen; Ding Luonan; and Dong Jian and Hu Xingliang.
30 See He Chengzhou; Alexander C. Y. Huang; Murray J. Levith; Liu Haiping and Lowell Swortzell; and Xiao Yang Zhang.
31 For a fuller discussion of "intertextuality," see Graham Allen.
32 See Hu Xingliang; Huang Aihua, *Ershi shiji zhongwai xiju bijiao lungao*; and Yun-Tong Luk.
33 See Susan Bassnett, *Comparative Literature*; Charles Bernheimer; Haun Saussy, *Comparative Literature in an Age of Globalization*; Steven Tötösy de Zepetnek and Tutun Mukherjee; and César Domínguez; Haun Saussy; and Darío Villanueva.
34 See Susan Bassnett, *Translation Studies*, and André Lefevere. See also Anthony Pym; Douglas Robinson; and Lawrence Venuti.
35 See Susan Bennett; Robert C. Holub; and Charles Martindale and Richard F. Thomas.
36 See Laurence Raw and Katja Krebs for discussions of interdisciplinary tensions, as well as confluences between translation studies and adaptation studies.
37 See Gary R. Bortolotti and Linda Hutcheon for an in-depth discussion of adaptations from a biological perspective.
38 Sanders, 19.
39 Hutcheon, xvi, 1–32.
40 See Qi, *Western Literature*, 146–48.
41 For my discussions of Ibsen in China, see Qi, "Misreading Ibsen" and "Reimagining Ibsen."

Bibliography

Allen, Graham. *Intertextuality*, 2nd ed. New York: Routledge, 2011.

Auerbach, Erich. *Mimesis: The Representation of Reality in Western Literature*. Princeton, NJ: Princeton University Press, 2013.

Bai, Ronnie. "Dances With Mei Lanfang: Brecht and the Alienation Effect." *Comparative Drama* 32, no. 3 (Fall 1998): 389–433.

Baldick, Chris, ed. *The Oxford Dictionary of Literary Terms*. 3rd ed. Oxford: Oxford University Press, 2008.

Bassnett, Susan. *Comparative Literature: A Critical Introduction*. Oxford: Blackwell Publishers, 1993.

———. *Translation Studies*. Oxford: Taylor and Francis, 2002.

Bennett, Susan. *Theatre Audiences: A Theory of Production and Reception*, 2nd ed. New York: Routledge, 1997.

Bernheimer, Charles, ed. *Comparative Literature in the Age of Multiculturalism*. Baltimore, MD: Johns Hopkins University Press, 1994.

Bortolotti, Gary R., and Linda Hutcheon. "On the Origin of Adaptations: Rethinking Fidelity Discourse and 'Success' – Biologically." *New Literary History* 38 (2007): 443–458.

Chen, Baichen, and Dong Jian, eds. *Zhongguo xiandai xiju shigao* (1899–1949) (A History of Modern Chinese Drama) (1899–1949), 2nd ed. Beijing: China Drama Press, 2008.

Chen, Xiaomei. *Acting the Right Part: Political Theater and Popular Drama in Contemporary China*. Honolulu, HI: University of Hawaii Press, 2002.

Ding, Luonan. *Ershi shiji zhongguo xiju zhengti guan* (A Comprehensive Overview of Twentieth-Century Chinese Drama). Shanghai: Shanghai Baijia Press, 2009.

Domínguez, César, Haun Saussy, and Darío Villanueva. *Introducing Comparative Literature: New Trends and Applications*. New York: Routledge, 2015.

Dong, Jian, and Hu Xingliang, eds. *Zhongguo dangdai xiju shigao* (1949–2000) (A History of Contemporary Chinese Drama: 1949–2000). Beijing: China Drama Press, 2008.

Elam, Keir. *The Semiotics of Theatre and Drama*. New York: Routledge, 2002.

Fang, Chen. "*Cong Tebaicheng shuo qi*" (To Begin With *Antigone*). *Dawutai* (Big Stage) 2 (2003): 8–10.

Fu, Jin. "*Chongxin xunzhao huaju zai zhongguo de qidian*" (Search Again for the Starting Point of Spoken Drama in China). *Wenyi bao* (Art Paper), August 28, 2007.

Gebauer, Gunter, and Christoph Wulf. *Mimesis: Culture-Art-Society*. Translated by Don Reneau. Berkeley, CA: University of California Press, 1996.

Guo, Yanlin. "*Zhongguo xiju yu shichang liubian*" (Chinese Drama and Market Fluctuations). Master's thesis. Southeastern University, Nanjing, China, 2004.

He, Chengzhou. *Henrik Ibsen and Modern Chinese Drama*. Bergen, Norway: Akademika Publishing, 2004.

Holub, Robert C. *Crossing Borders: Reception Theory, Poststructuralism, Deconstruction*. Madison, WI: University of Wisconsin Press, 1992.

Hsia, Adrian. "*The Orphan of the House Zhao* in French, English, German, and Hong Kong Literature." *Comparative Literature Studies* 25, no. 4 (1988): 335–51.

Hu, Xingliang. *Dangdai zhongwai bijiao xiju shi lun* (1949–2000) (A Comparative Study of Contemporary Chinese and Foreign Dramas: 1949–2000). Beijing: People's Publishing House, 2009.

Huang, Aihua. "*Chunliushe yanjiu zaji*" (Research Notes on Spring Willow Society). *Xiju yishu* (Theatre Arts) 2 (1993): 76–83.

———. *Ershi shiji zhongwai xiju bijiao lungao* (A Comparative Study in Twentieth-Century Chinese and Foreign Dramas). Hangzhou: Zhejiang University Press, 2006.

Huang, Alexander C. Y. *Chinese Shakespeares: Two Centuries of Cultural Exchange*. New York: Columbia University Press, 2009.

Hutcheon, Linda. *A Theory of Adaptation*, 2nd ed. New York: Routledge, 2012.

Idema, Wilt L. "The Orphan of Zhao: Self-Sacrifice, Tragic Choice and Revenge and the Confucianization of Mongol Drama at the Ming Court." *Cina*. 21 (1988): 159–90.

———. "Traditional Dramatic Literature," in *Columbia History of Chinese Literature*. Edited by Victor H. Mair. New York: Columbia University Press, 2001.

Krebs, Katja, ed. *Translation and Adaptation in Theatre and Film*. New York: Routledge, 2014.

Lavender, Andy. "Modal Transpositions Toward Theatres of Encounter, or, in Praise of 'Media Intermultimodality'." *Theatre Journal* 66, no. 4 (December 2014): 499–518.

Lefevere, André. *Translation, History and Culture*. New York: Routledge, 2002.

Levith, Murray J. *Shakespeare in China*. New York: Continuum, 2006.

Liu, Haiping, and Lowell Swortzell, eds. *Eugene O'Neill in China: An International Centenary Celebration*. Westport, CT: Praeger, 1992.

Liu, Siyuan. "The Impact of Shinpa on Early Chinese Huaju." *Asian Theatre Journal* 23, no. 2 (Fall 2006): 342–55.

Liu, Wu-Chi. "The Original Orphan of China." *Comparative Literature* 5, no. 3 (Summer 1953): 193–212.

Liu, Yanjun. *Dongxifang xiju jinchen* (East and West Drama Developments), 2nd ed. Beijing: Wenhua Yishu Press, 2005.

Luk, Yun-Tong. *Studies in Chinese-Western Comparative Drama*. Hong Kong: The Chinese University Press, 1990.

Man, Xinying. "*Faguo geju zai wanqing de chuangbo yu jieshou*" (Introduction and Reception of French Operas in Late Qing China). *Yinyue yanjiu* (Music Research), no. 6 (2011): 48–65.

Martindale, Charles, and Richard F. Thomas, eds. *Classics and the Uses of Reception*. Oxford: Wiley-Blackwell, 2006.

Pym, Anthony. *Exploring Translation Theories*. New York: Routledge, 2010, 2014.

Qi, Shouhua. "Misreading Ibsen: Chinese Noras on and Off the Stage, and Nora in Her Chinese Husband's Ancestral Land of the 1930s – As Reimagined for the Present-Day Stage." *Comparative Drama* 50, no. 4 (Winter 2016): 341–64.

———. "Reimagining Ibsen: Recent Adaptations of Ibsen Plays for the Chinese Stage." *Ibsen Studies* 17, no. 2 (2017): 141–64.

———. *Western Literature in China and the Translation of a Nation*. New York: Palgrave Macmillan, 2012.

Raw, Laurence, ed. *Translation, Adaptation and Transformation*. New York: Continuum, 2012.

Robinson, Douglas. *The Translator's Turn*. Baltimore, MD: Johns Hopkins University Press, 1991.

Sanders, Julie. *Adaptation and Appropriation*. New York: Routledge, 2006.

Saussy, Haun, ed. *Comparative Literature in an Age of Globalization*. Baltimore, MD: Johns Hopkins University Press, 2006.

———. "Mei Lanfang in Moscow, 1935: Familiar, Unfamiliar, Defamiliar." *Modern Chinese Literature and Culture* 18, no. 1 (Spring 2006): 8–29.

Tao, Ran. "*Zhongguo xiju (huaju) shichang ji shichang yingxiao*" (Chinese Drama (Spoken Drama) Market and Marketing). Master's thesis. China Academy of Art, Beijing, China, 2006.

Tian, Min. "'Alienation-Effect' for Whom? Brecht's (Mis)interpretation of the Classical Chinese Theatre." *Asian Theatre Journal* 14, no. 2 (Autumn 1997): 200–22.

———. *The Poetics of Difference and Displacement: Twentieth-Century Chinese-Western Intercultural Theatre*. Hong Kong: Hong Kong University Press, 2008.

Venuti, Lawrence. *The Translation Studies Reader*, 3rd ed. Routledge, 2012.

Wang, Fengxia. "*Chongtan bainian huaju zhiyuan: zhongguo huaju bushiyu chunliushe buzheng*" (Revisiting the Origin of One Hundred Years of Spoken Drama: Additional Evidence Indicating that Chinese Spoken Drama Did Not Begin With Spring Willow Society). *Yishu baijia* (Hundred Schools in Art) 103, no. 4 (2008): 167–70.

Xu, Lian. "*Tebaicheng shi bu shi yi ji liangyao*" (Is *Antigone* a Good Medicine?). *China Culture Daily*, May 30, 2002, Section 002.

Xu, Muyun. *Zhongguo xiju shi* (A History of Chinese Drama). Shanghai: Shanghai Guji Press, 1938, 2001.

Ye, Changhai. *Zhongguo xijuxue shigao* (A History of Chinese Drama Studies). Beijing: China Drama Press, 2005.

Ye, Changhai, and Zhang Fuhai. *Zhongguo xiju shi chatu ben* (An Illustrated History of Chinese Drama). Shanghai: Shanghai Guji Press, 2004.

Yu, Shiao-ling. "'Cry to Heaven': A Play to Celebrate One Hundred Years of Chinese Spoken Drama by Nick Rongjun Yu." *Asian Theatre Journal* 26, no. 1 (Spring 2009): 1–53.

Yuan, Guoxing. *Zhongguo huaju de yunyu he shengcheng* (The Gestation and Growth of Chinese Spoken Drama). China Drama Press, 2000.

Zepetnek, Steven Tötösy de, and Tutun Mukherjee, eds. *Companion to Comparative Literature, World Literatures, and Comparative Cultural Studies*. New Delhi: Cambridge University Press India, 2013.

Zhang, Weiping. "*Zhongguo wutai shaweng zhi yangren guan: du Lieweisi de Shashibiya zai zhongguo*" (Shakespearean Plays on the Chinese Stage in the Eyes of Foreigners: Reading Levith's *Shakespeare in China*). *Shanghai xiju* (Shanghai Theatre), no. 2 (2005): 21–2.

Zhang, Xiao Yang. *Shakespeare in China: A Comparative Study of Two Traditions and Cultures*. Plainsboro, NJ: Associated University Presses, 1996.

"*Zhongmei xijuren xieshou dazao bailaohui jingdian Boli dongwuyuan*" (US-China Theatre Artists Join Hands in Re-creating Broadway Classic *Glass Menagerie*). *China News*, December 16, 2015. www.chinanews.com/cul/2015/12-16/7674489.shtml.

Zhou, Hong. "*Dangdai huaju guanzhong goucheng ji dui huaju fazhan de yingxiang*" (Contemporary Spoken Drama Audience Composition and Its Impact on Spoken Drama Development). *Wenyi yanjiu* (Art Research), no. 6 (2003): 100–6.

1 First contact

Early Chinese encounters with Western drama

The staging of the third act of *La Dame aux Camilias* (Alexander Dumas fils) by young student members of Spring Willow Society (*chunliushe*) in the winter of 1907 in Tokyo – far away from home – and especially the full production of *Black Slave's Cry to Heaven* adapted from Harriet Beecher Stowe's *Uncle Tom's Cabin* in June that same year marked a momentous development in the history of modern Chinese drama. Many scholars have hailed it as the birth cry of *huaju* (spoken drama), essentially a "foreign" and imported art form, and, by extension, the birth of *xiju* (modern Chinese drama).[1] Some scholars, however, have tried to turn the searchlight from outside the country back to the homeland, tracing the origin of *huaju* to certain elements of traditional Chinese *xiqu* centuries back in its early burgeoning days,[2] or to student performances in Shanghai and drama reform endeavors around the turn of the twentieth century in a quest to locate in the native soil an alternative starting point for *huaju* and, by extension, modern Chinese *xiju*.[3]

A more "balanced" view or, rather, a more meaningful approach than trying to pin down an exact date or event, at least as far as the subject of this book – transnational, transcultural, and translingual adaptation of Western classics – is concerned, is to see the birth of *huaju* and indeed modern Chinese *xiju* as a convoluted process of gestation catalyzed by forces from both within and the outside world.[4] The 1907 Spring Willow Society's reimagining of Western classics in Tokyo, a significant and arguably epochal event, didn't happen out of the blue; rather, it came about from the convergence of forces geopolitical and domestic, necessary and coincidental, literary, artistic as well as sociopolitical. This adaptation, which inspired the 2007 play *Search for Spring Willow Society*, mounted in Beijing to reimagine the rehearsing of *Black Slave's Cry to Heaven* 100 years ago, speaks volumes of the important agency adaptations of Western classics exert in shaping the development of modern Chinese drama, and indeed the social and cultural life of a country seeking to modernize and redefine itself in a "brave new world."

In the decades following the Opium War (1839–1842), as China was forced to open its doors for Westerners to come in and trade and proselytize and for the Chinese – albeit only a small handful, mostly imperial envoys and diplomats sent to Western countries to represent the Qing interest abroad – to go and see the outside world for themselves, exposure to Western drama as part of the transnational, transcultural, and translingual encounters became inevitable.

Since most of these early Chinese "innocents abroad," so to speak, spoke little or no languages of the Western countries they were visiting and, more importantly, since their primary concern was in science, technology, industry, and navy, which the Chinese believed had given Western countries the upper hand in their dealings with China, arts and literature would amount to little more than "sideshows" or occasional cultural excursions. Nonetheless, even from outside looking in, scratching no more than the physically observable surface, their experiences of Western drama – the differences as compared to traditional Chinese *xiqu*, from the imposing physical structures of theatres to the breathtaking verisimilitude ambience to the perplexingly respectable social status of actors – would register a level of responses that can only be described as cultural shock.

Early Chinese encounters with Western drama also took the form of "West cometh to East" through the agency of newspapers, Western expatriates in China, visiting drama troupes, and mission colleges in Shanghai and elsewhere.

Chinese "innocents abroad" and their chance encounters with Western drama

Li Shuchang (1837–1896), who at the age of 25 had had the audacity to send a "10,000-word" petition to Empress Dowager Cixi (1835–1908) advocating reform, was among the first batch of diplomats sent abroad in 1876, serving as an attaché of Chinese embassies in Britain, Germany, and Spain. During his five-year stint as a diplomat in Europe, Li visited as many as ten countries and recorded his observations in a book titled *Xiyang zazhi* (Western World Impressions). Here is what he had to say about the Opéra in Paris:[5]

> The Opéra in Paris is the best in the world, having no rival in its splendor and grandeur. All visitors to Paris would brag about having seen it. . . . Walking in, one sees two stories of building, the lower level boasting of seven big doors, the upper level a long, meandering corridor of marble and granite. In the back of the theatre are dozens of rooms – designated residential area for the actors – looking as grand as a royal palace. Once inside the theatre, one sees five levels of seating with a total of two thousand one hundred fifty-six seats. . . . The theatre has in residence a troupe of two hundred fifty actors, the best of them enjoying a wage of one hundred thousand to one hundred twenty thousand francs, the playwright five hundred francs per performance. . . . The Opéra in Paris receives an annual subsidy of eight hundred thousand francs from the government as part of its powerful financial backing.
>
> (*Ellipses mine*)

Li Shuchang's account, hyperbolic as it may sound, is echoed by similar firsthand observations from other Chinese visiting Europe around this time, such as Zeng Jize (1839–1890), the second son of Zeng Guofan (1811–1872) – a prominent figure in the late Qing decades, especially known for his role in the crackdown of the Taiping Uprising (1850–1864). While serving as ambassador to Britain and France, Zeng Jize was dispatched to Russia to renegotiate the "Treaty of Saint Petersburg" (1881), which he did as forcefully as he could to make the terms less punishing to China territorially. In his *Chushi ying fa e riji* (Diary of the Ambassador to Britain, France, and Russia), Zeng recorded his impressions of a Western theatre that appeared "more magnificent than a royal palace." More interestingly, ever mindful of the plight of his homeland since the Opium War and the potential social function of drama and theatre, Zeng observed,[6]

> In the past when the French were defeated by the Germans, they began the construction of a big theatre house once the Germans had left to awaken the spirit of the people. They also raised enormous funding to support galleries with paintings of how the French people suffered the shame of defeat and misery of homelessness to arouse the desire and hence resolve for national revenge. It all looked like play, but underneath it all was deep significance. I was told that both the theatre house and the galleries were ideas from people of powerful positions.

Zhang Deyi (1847–1918), another Chinese who had the privilege to travel abroad, was of much humbler pedigree. He earned a scholarship for the Tongwen Institute in Beijing, the first foreign language school in China, and later became foreign language teacher of the Guangxu Emperor (1871–1908). In 1866, at the age of 19, Zhang was chosen as a member of the first group of Chinese sent abroad to study the West – France, Britain, Belgium, Holland, Denmark, and Russia, among other countries and places. In his book series *Hanghai shuqi* (My Overseas Adventures) were such extensive observations of Western drama/theatre that he is sometimes accredited as the first Chinese to introduce Western drama to China. Among the shows he saw were *Tsar and Carpenter* by Gustav Albert Lortzing, *Faust* by Charles Gounod, *Rip Van Winkle* adapted from Washington Irwin's short story, *Around the World in Eighty Days* adapted from Jules Verne's novel, *Wilhelm Tell* by Friedrich Schiller, *The Count of Mount Cristo* adapted from Alexandre Dumas' novel, *Beauty and the Best*, *Don Juan or The Feast with the Statue* by Molière, *Emily* based on Charles Dickens' novel *David Copperfield*, and *Hamlet* and *Romeo Juliet* by Shakespeare. Some of his notes were short, while others were as elaborate as over 1,500 words long, quite detailed in documenting the ambience as well as "playbill" aspects of his Western theatre experiences.[7]

Indeed, these early Chinese "innocents abroad" were quite awestruck by the realistic ambience – the verisimilitude effect they experienced in Western theatres from lifelike furniture on the stage to vivid scenery in the backdrop thanks mostly to the use of superior stagecraft technology. Dai Hongci (1853–1910), one of the five cabinet level officials sent abroad by the Qing court in 1905 to study political systems in the West by way of preparing (reluctantly, of course) for "constitutional monarchy" (*xianzheng*), had this observation in his *Chushi jiuguo riji* (Diary of My Diplomatic Missions to Nine Countries):

> Western theatres excel in pictorial ornaments; buildings and balconies appear on stage in the blink of an eye. Rain or shine and weather changes feel so real, as if you the audience are right in it. It's amazing that such magic can happen in real life.

Wang Zhichun (1842–1906), an imperial envoy who traveled to St. Petersburg by way of Paris and Berlin, among other cities, to attend the funeral of Alexander III of Russia (1845–1894), couldn't help marvel either in his eight-volume *Shi e cao* (Diary of an Envoy to Russia):

> The oil painting of landscape in the backdrop looks so real that you seem to see mountains upon mountains stretching far into distance. If the backdrop is the painting of a city, you can see buildings and streets so clearly as if it is a real metropolis.

Even with "a telescope powerful enough to see 10,000 *li*," as other Chinese visitors to Western theatres had enthused, one would not be able to tell whether the scenery in the backdrop was real or unreal, and if one stares at it long enough, "the human figures (in the backdrop) would begin to move and the waters ripple."[8] In addition to being dazed by the magnificent architect and magical stagecraft of Western theatres, early Chinese "innocents abroad" sometimes found themselves perplexed by the apparent social status actors enjoyed in Western countries. Zhang Deyi, the self-made man alluded to earlier in this chapter who had taken extensive notes about Western drama, observed that it was the custom in Britain for theatre owners, managers, or directors to invite dignitaries to the opening night. He himself, an imperial envoy, had had the dubious honor of being the recipient of such invitations.[9] In his 1896 tour of Russia, Germany, Belgium, France, Britain, and the United States, Li Hongzhang (1823–1901)[10] was received as grandly as head of a state wherever he went. However, when he received an invitation from the general manager of a theatre house in London to attend one of its performances, members of Li Hongzhang's entourage were not so amused. Such a thing had been unheard of back in China: what thick-faced audacity for a mere theatre manager to even dream of hosting an almost royal personage such as Li Hongzhang? They soon realized, however, that, unlike back in China where acting was regarded as a rather lowly, disrespectable trade and where even talented actors (*youling*) were often treated as playthings of the rich and powerful, here in the West, actors were respected as artists (*yishi*) and had no problem mixing with high-ranking officials.[11] As it turned out, Li and his entourage were more than pleased with the grand reception at the theatre:[12]

> At eight o'clock, upon arrival at the theatre compound in his vehicle, the Imperial Envoy was greeted with an enthusiastic chorus of "Welcome, Your Excellency!" The theatre compound was brightly lit with electric bulbs, skirted with blooming flowers, its entrance flanked with flags. What dazzling magnificence. The Imperial Envoy was then greeted by the general manager himself and was led to a box especially prepared for him, more comfortable and extravagant than one could ever expect.

However, these early Chinese visitors abroad were not impressed by the content of Western drama they had seen – the stories being told on the stage, dismissing them as verging on "mythology and trickery, reminding one of the tall tales back home."[13] This lack of enthusiasm can perhaps be explained by language barriers and their unfamiliarity with Western dramatic tradition, which prevented them from being fully engaged intellectually as well as emotionally while their eyes were being dazzled. More significantly, however, it could have come from a much deeper place, from the same "Chinese learning for the foundation and Western learning for use" (*zhong xue wei ti xi xue wei yong*) attitude prevalent among the intelligentsia and even reformers around this time, a belief that all China needed from the West was its superior science and technology because Chinese culture (its arts and literature and philosophy) was as good as, if not superior to, that of the West – a belief or positioning that persists among many Chinese to this day.[14]

West cometh to East: drama performances by Western expatriates, visiting troupes, and mission college students

If what has been sketched in the preceding section can be described as "East goes to West" – early encounters with Western drama through eyewitness accounts by the handful of Chinese who traveled to Europe as envoys and diplomats during the post-Opium War decades when China, ever reluctantly, began to establish diplomat missions in Western countries – such early exposures and encounters also took the form of "West cometh to East" through the agency of newspapers, Western expatriates, visiting troupes, and mission colleges.

As far back as in 1857, the inaugural issue of a Chinese magazine *Liuhe congtan* (Zodiac Forums) published by Westerners in Shanghai (one of the five ports opened to foreign trade and settlement as a result of the Opium War) carried a short article introducing classic Greek playwrights such as Aeschylus, Sophocles, Euripides, and Aristophanes. This was followed by many other such short articles published in various newspapers and magazines about Western drama and arts and literature.[15] For example, the June 6, 1867, issue of *Shanghai xinbao* (Shanghai New Newspaper) on its first page carried a short article about William Shakespeare – his life, career, achievements, and influence, probably the first published introduction of Shakespeare in China. *Shanghai xinbao* then followed it up with a *Hamlet* series,[16] although it is not clear whether the series was an abridged or full-text translation of Shakespeare's play or a retelling of the story based on *Tales from Shakespeare* (1807) by the brother and sister team Charles and Mary Lamb.

By the 1860s, there were already performances of Western drama in Shanghai. The March 19, 1867, issue *Shanghai xinbao* reported the news of a foreign (*waiguo*) – meaning Western, although the brief news report did not specify – troupe coming to perform at *Man tin fang* (Full Fragrance Courtyard), the first Chinese drama house in the foreign concessions of Shanghai. It can be assumed that the repertoire of this Western country troupe would be Western drama (rather than traditional Chinese *xiqu*), that it would give more than one performance and would stay (for a tour?) for days and perhaps weeks, and that more than a few curious Chinese – e.g., compradors (*maiban*) who were more or less communicatively proficient in English – would be mixing in the audiences of primarily European and American expatriates. In the decades to come, many more Western troupes would travel half a globe over to visit again and again, as reported in the newspapers, bringing to Shanghai a rather different, "exotic" way of (re)presenting "life" and telling stories on the stage.[17]

Some of these early performances by Western troupes took place at Lyceum Theatre (*lanxin dajuyuan*), the first Western-style theatre in China that opened its doors in Shanghai in 1867. It was a theatre – a relatively simple wooden structure – built by Westerners (British expatriates) to stage Western plays performed by Westerners (visiting troupes from Western countries as well as amateur actors such as British "Shanghailanders" and members of the Amateur Dramatic Club of Shanghai) for mostly Western audiences, although gradually more Chinese would find themselves drawn into the theatre to see such performances. According to a newspaper report then, the theatre's debut was quite a success:[18]

> No one who saw the commencement of that timber bird-cage on the desecrated, once consular grounds, would have imagined that in two months it would have grown into the beautiful little theatre in which we sat last night. . . . every seat in the house was full before the last fiddle in the Orchestra had given its final premonitory scrape.

The theatre was burned down in a big fire in 1871. A few years later, a new and much grander building emerged in its place. Among the notable plays staged at Lyceum Theatre were *The Devil's Disciple* by Bernard Shaw (1902) – the playwright's debut in China, *Aida* by Giuseppe Verdi, *Madama Butterfly* by Giacomo Puccini, and, significant enough, *Black Slave's Cry to Heaven* mounted in October 1907 by Spring Sun Society (*Chunyang she*), arguably the first modern drama troupe inside China,[19] a few months after the Spring Willow Society performance of the same play in Tokyo.

Another important venue where early Chinese encounters with Western drama occurred was mission schools set up by Western missionaries in the post-Opium War decades when their proselytizing activities were protected by treaties and law. Although most of the early mission schools – hundreds of them established in various parts of China – provided only elementary education, by the late 1800s, the first group of mission colleges began to appear in Shanghai, Beijing, Tianjin, Guangzhou, and other big cities. In Shanghai alone, thousands of young Chinese were attending mission colleges. St. John's University (*Shengyuehan*), for example, a well-known Anglican university founded by American missionaries in 1879, provided a vibrant setting for the Chinese to experience Western drama both on and offstage.

One of the traditions at St. John's University was to have drama performances during its annual commencement exercises in July as the closing events and during the Christmas and holiday season near the end of the year. On July 18, 1896, for example, near the end of a full day of celebratory commencement events, a group of ten upper-class students performed Act IV of Shakespeare's *Merchant of Venice* – the trial of Shylock in a Venice "court of justice." Although by the time the show began, it was already early evening, so audiences in the not so well lit standing room only theatre couldn't see clearly what was unfolding on the stage, it was quite a success, as reviewed in a newspaper a few days later:[20]

> This group of student actors was so engrossed in the performance that they sounded authentic and succeeded in capturing the spirit of the play. They had spent so much time studying their character roles that there was no need for script prompters. Shylock, naturally the main character for the story, did a very good job. We found his acting excellent although his enunciation was somewhat lacking in clarity. We also found Antonio's farewell speech well delivered. Portia's voice remained clear throughout the performance, unlike the other actors whose voices we sometimes found it hard to hear thanks to their nervousness or low volume. The beard as a stage prop, when used adroitly to augment the effect, as in the case of both the Duke and Shylock, added in no small measure to the entertainment of the evening.

Subsequent annual commencement exercises at St. John's University saw students performing acts or scenes from *Julius Caesar* (1899), *Hamlet* (1901), *Merchant of Venice* again (1902), *Henry VIII* (1904), *As You Like It* (1906), and *The Taming of the Shrew* (1907). Performing Shakespeare had established itself as such a tradition at St. John's University that in 1905 its president started a "Shakespeare Club," which was open to all students and met every Saturday evening to read and discuss Shakespeare – in

English, of course, as were all the performances during the annual commencement exercises.

Although the primary purpose of such Shakespearean performances was to help students learn and improve their English, the main language for teaching and studying at the Anglican university, it also provided engrossing firsthand experiences of Western drama for both the Chinese actors and for the dominantly Chinese audiences – young students of the university as well as visitors and guests. Among the audience members was a young student Wei Yi (1880–1930), who later collaborated with Lin Shu (1852–1924) in translating some 50 titles of Western literature into Chinese, including Harriet Beecher Stowe's *Uncle Tom's Cabin;*[21] their translation provided the basis for Spring Willow Society's 1907 adaptation in Tokyo. Another young audience member was Song Chunfang (1892–1938), a St. John's University student when *The Taming of the Shrew, A Midsummer Night Dream,* and other Shakespeare plays were performed. Song later became an independent and forceful voice in the drama reform movement.[22]

The 1899 Christmas season performances at St. John's University found among the audiences a young boy named Wang Youyou (1888–1937). Although Wang was lost most of the time, as he recalled many years later, because the performances were in English and featured no singing or dancing (hallmark of *xiqu*), the novelty of it all left some undeletable imprint on his impressionable mind. Wang grew up to be an active member of the drama reform movement and acted, among other things, in the October 1920 production of Bernard Shaw's *Mrs. Warren's Profession* at New Stage (*xin wutai*) in Shanghai (a box office failure, as it turned out).[23]

All of these early Chinese encounters, through both the agency of late Qing Chinese diplomats traveling abroad and the agency of newspapers, Western expatriates, visiting drama troupes, and mission schools in the last decades of the nineteenth century, helped in no small measure in preparing the fermenting soil for Western drama to be adapted (and appropriated) in China to serve its dire cultural and sociopolitical needs in the early decades of the new century.

Notes

1 See Yuan Guoxing, 1–16, and Huang Aihua, *Ershi shiji* (A Comparative Study), 001–105.
2 See Ding Luonan, 014–30.
3 See Wang Fengxia; Jin Fu.
4 See Siyuan Liu for a full discussion of the emergence of a hybrid form of modern Chinese drama (in the early decades of the twentieth century) based on Western spoken theatre, classical Chinese theatre, and a hybrid form of modern Japanese theatre.
5 Zuo Pengjun, 53. See also "Li Shuchang."
6 See Sun Yixue, 38; Yuan Guoxing, 19; and "Zeng Jize."
7 Yi Dexiang; and "Zhang Deyi"
8 Sun Yixue, 36; Yuan Guoxing, 21. See also "Wang Zhichun" and "Dai Hongci."

9 Sun Yixue, 39.
10 A prominent, albeit controversial, much-maligned, figure in the second half of the nineteenth century thanks largely to his role as the chief negotiator for most of the "unequal treaties" with the West.
11 Yuan Guoxing, 20.
12 Zuo Pengjun, 54.
13 Yuan, 22.
14 See Shouhua Qi, 9–18.
15 This portion of the discussion about Chinese early encounters with Western drama draws in part from Yuan, 17–23.
16 Zhu Hengfu, 80–1.
17 Ibid, 79.
18 Quoted in Michelle Qiao.
19 Lyceum Theatre, the first of many such Western-style Theatres and cinemas in Shanghai, was to see many reincarnations in shape, site, and ownership, as well as identity through decades of wars and revolutions. Renovated in 2003 in Italian Renaissance architectural style and loaded with modern technology of sound and light and other stagecraft, the theatre today is a popular cultural landmark as well as a place to go and experience drama – adaptations of Western classics as well as traditional Chinese *xiqu*. See "*Yingyuan juchang guanli*" (Cinema and Theatre Management) and "*Lanxin dajuyuan*" (Lyceum Theatre).
20 Zhong Xinzhi, 18–19.
21 Qi, 40–6.
22 Zhong, 25.
23 See "Wang Youyou (1888–1937)" and "Wang Youyou."

Bibliography

"Dai Hongci." http://baike.baidu.com.
Ding, Luonan. *Ershi shiji zhongguo xiju zhengti guan* (A Comprehensive Review of Twentieth-Century Chinese Drama). Shanghai: Shanghai Baijia Press, 2009.
"*Lanxin dajuyuan*" (Lyceum Theatre). https://zh.wikipedia.org and http://baike.baidu.com.
"Li Shuchang." http://baike.baidu.com.
Liu, Siyuan. *Performing Hybridity in Post-Colonial China*. New York: Palgrave Macmillan, 2013.
Qi, Shouhua. *Western Literature in China and the Translation of a Nation*. New York: Palgrave Macmillan, 2012.
Qiao, Michelle. "Lyceum Building Named for Theater." February 18, 2014. www.shanghaidaily.com/.
Sun, Yixue. "*Wanqing xiqu gailiang he wanqing dashi*" (Late Qing Drama Reform and Late Qing Diplomats). *Xiju* (Drama). *Journal of China Central Drama Academy*, no. 4 (2006): 38.
Wang, Fengxia. "*Chongtan bainian huaju zhiyuan: zhongguo huaju bushiyu chunliushe buzheng*" (Revisiting the Origin of One Hundred Years of Spoken Drama: Additional Evidence Indicating that Chinese Spoken Drama Did Not Begin With Spring Willow Society). *Yishu baijia* (Hundred Schools in Art) 103, no. 4 (2008): 167–70.
"Wang Youyou (1888–1937)." *Shanghai tong* (All Things Shanghai). http://shtong.gov.cn.
"Wang Youyou." http://baike.baidu.com.

"Wang Zhichun." http://baike.baidu.com.

Yi, Dexiang. "*Wanqing shiguan de xifang xiju guan*" (Late Qing Diplomats' Views on Western Drama). *Chinese Comparative Literature*, no. 4 (2006): 147–8.

"*Yingyuan juchang guanli*" (Cinema and Theatre Management), *Shanghai tong* (All Things Shanghai). www.shtong.gov.cn.

Yuan, Guoxing. *Zhongguo huaju de yunyu he shengcheng* (The Gestation and Growth of Chinese Spoken Drama). Beijing: China Drama Press, 2000.

"Zeng Jize." http://baike.baidu.com.

"Zhang Deyi." http://baike.baidu.com.

Zhong, Xinzhi. "*Qingmo shanghai shengyuehan daxue yanju huodong jiqi dui zhongguo xiandai juchang de lishi yiyi*" (Drama Performances at Shanghai St. John's University Near the End of Qing Dynasty and Its Historical Significance for the Development of Modern Chinese Drama). *Xiju yishu* (Theatre Arts) 3 (2010): 18–26.

Zhu, Hengfu. "*Chunliushe zhiqian de shanghai xinju*" (New Drama in Shanghai Before Spring Willow Society). *Xiju yishu* (Theatre Arts) 6 (2006): 79–83.

Zuo, Pengjun. "*Zhongguo jindai shiwai zaiji zhong de waiguo xiju shiliao shulun*" (An Overview of Observations of Foreign Drama in the Diaries of Late Qing Diplomats and Envoys). *Journal of South China Normal University* (Social Science Edition), no. 2 (April 2001): 53.

2 *Black Slave's Cry to Heaven*, the birth cry of modern Chinese drama, and a group of post-'80s amateurs in search of a director

Members of the Spring Willow Society (*chunliushe*), who staged their adaptations of *La Dame aux Camilias* (Alexander Dumas fils) and *Uncle Tom's Cabin* (Harriet Beecher Stowe) in Tokyo in 1907, a momentous development in the history of modern Chinese drama, were among the waves of Chinese students that sailed across the sea to study in Japan in the years immediately after the first Sino-Japanese War (1894–1895). The defeat in the hands of its next-door neighbor, a much smaller country that had for centuries been treated as an apprentice of sorts but, having recently taken a crash course from the West, was more than eager to flex its new muscles, dealt China another big blow. In the spring of 1896, before the dust and smoke of the first Sino-Japan War had settled, 13 young Chinese students, all marked by their "traditional queues and long gowns," arrived in Tokyo, a vibrant metropolis of post-Meiji Restoration Japan. This first group was followed by another 100 in 1899, 400 or so in 1902, and 1,000 in 1903. By 1905–1906, right on the eve of the epochal Spring Willow Society performances, between 8,000 and 9,000 Chinese students were studying in Japan.[1] Many Chinese students chose Japan because of the perceived cultural and linguistic kinship, geographic proximity, and expenses (typically one-third of the expenses of living and studying in Europe or the United States).[2]

The early dawn of the twentieth century saw among the thousands of young Chinese studying in Japan future founding members of the Spring Willow Society such as Zeng Xiaogu (1873–1937), Li Shutong (1880–1942), Ouyang Yuqian (1889–1962), and Lu Jingruo (1885–1915), each carrying a dream for their own future and the future of their homeland. Zeng Xiaogu and Li Shutong were both artistically talented, Zeng having already graduated from a provincial normal school, Li having written and published prolifically on arts and literature. They were both enrolled in the Tokyo School of Fine Arts. It was there that they had firsthand experience of Western-style theatre via the agency of Japanese *shinpa* and *shingeki*.[3] Lu Jingruo came to Japan in 1900 at the tender age of 13 and stayed there for 12 years. This was a period during which *shingeki* was thriving via first adapting Western drama as exemplified by Ibsen, Chekhov, O'Neill, and Shakespeare, and then producing original Japanese works in the realist tradition. After graduating from high school, Lu entered Tokyo Imperial University (today's University of Tokyo) to study philosophy, psychology, and sociology, as well as aesthetics to prepare for more focused study of drama. English literature was also part of the required curriculum, which he took with Natsume Sōseki (1867–1916), probably the greatest writer in modern Japanese history and a patron and supporter of the Art Association formed in 1906 to spearhead arts reform and modernization. In a 1908 newspaper review of a Japanese play in which Lu acted (to the delight of Japanese audiences and critics alike), Lu was quoted as saying that "traditional Chinese *xiqu* was bound to die out, to be replaced by a new kind of drama like *shingeki* enthusiastically received by the populace," that traditional Chinese *xiqu* was immature and had been left behind by the tides of modern times, and hence had no value whatsoever and that he was resolved to return to China upon graduation to push for a new modern Chinese drama.[4]

In the winter of 1906–1907 Zeng Xiaogu and Li Shutong formed the Spring Willow Society much in the spirit of the Japanese Arts Society, of which Zeng was possibly a member, with a clear-eyed vision of remaking the Chinese drama in the image of Japanese *shingeki*, much as the latter was being remade in the image of the realistic tradition of Western drama. In the same vein as the Japanese Art Society, the Spring Willow Society states in its founding charter that the purpose of the society is to study various arts; that as a first step forward, the society forms a performing division to help spearhead drama/theatre reform and renewal back in the homeland; and that the society, when staging plays, whether old or new, aims primarily at enlightening and inspiring the people. It further states that what is at stake with drama/theatre is nothing short of the viability of a civilization.[5]

Black Slave's Cry to Heaven: the birth cry of modern Chinese drama?

Some scholars have argued that given the trajectory of "natural" development within traditional Chinese *xiqu*, especially with the increased presence of speech or dialog as opposed to singing and dancing, and the increased use of current events as subject matter, a kind of Chinese *huaju* or modern *xiju* would have evolved into being without the unsettling encounters with and hence influence from Western drama. Most scholars, however, find such what-if, alternative history mode of arguments both unproductive and untenable.[6] It is true that even before the 1907 Spring Willow Society performances in Tokyo, there had already been earnest efforts toward reforming *xiqu*, so it would better capture and hopefully help shape the sociocultural realities of the times. However, such dramatic reform was anything but "natural" evolution; it was much more a response to the series of national crises than the work of some innate proclivity for technical innovation. Chinese encounters with Western drama, whether in the form of "West cometh to East" or "East goes to West" (Chapter 1), helped pave the fermenting ground and proved more than catalytic in the drama reform movement during the late Qing and early Republic decades.

One of the first and most vocal advocates for drama reform – indeed, drama revolution – was Liang Qichao (1873–1929). A leading reformist during the late Qing period and a key figure in the failed Hundred Days' Reform (1898), Liang turned to "fiction" (*xiaoshuo*) – a general term for arts and literature, including drama – as a cure-all for the ills of China. He wrote in 1902,[7]

> To renew the people of a country, one has to first renew its fiction; to renew its morality; one has to first renew its fiction; to renew its religion, one has to renew its fiction; to renew its political system, one has to renew its fiction; to renew its customs, one has to renew its fiction; to renew its learning, one has to renew its fiction; to renew the spirit of its people and their character, one has to renew its fiction. Why? Because fiction has unimaginable power to influence and control the way of people.

Toward achieving moral, cultural, and, indeed, national renewal by means of fiction, Liang translated political novels (from Japanese), wrote a political novel titled *The Future of the New China* (*Xin zhongguo weilai ji*), a hybrid of political commentary and fantasy, and two plays, *Jie hui meng* (Dream of apocalyptic dust) and *Xin luoma* (New Rome). Liang speaks through a character in *Jie hui meng*:[8]

> Ever since the War of Jiawu[9] I've been so alarmed by what's going on in the world and felt as if I'd just awoken from a bad dream. I want to sing; I want to cry; I want to laugh; I want to curse – all to no avail. You see, during the time of Louis XIV in France people felt just as hopeless, right? Then, came a man of letters by the name of Voltaire, who wrote several novels and plays to awaken his people from their slumber and succeeded! Yours truly, a mere bookworm, neither a governor nor a warrior nor learned enough to write scholarly works for posterity, I figure I might as well pour all that has been heavy on my mind, the thoughts I've been pondering over and again in my heart, into a small romance (*chuanqi*)[10] to entertain the rich and powerful as well as the common folks and children in their leisure time. Such entertainment, unworthy as it is, should be a bit better than *Xixiang ji* (The West Wing Story) and *Mudan ting* (The Peony Pavilion).

A significant number of patriotic plays were indeed written soon after the rallying call from Liang Qichao to awaken the spirit of the Chinese people. Notable among the early drama reformists was Wang Xiaonong (1858–1918), a versatile dramatist (actor, director, playwright) who alone wrote more than 30 plays drawing subject matter from Chinese as well as Western histories to better reflect or, rather, impact the sociopolitical reality of his times. One of these is his 1904 play *Gua zhong lan yin* (Reap What You

Sow), aka *Bolan wangguo can* (Sorrows of Poland Lost). It is the first *jingju* play that experimented with Western subject matter with actors dressed in Western-style clothing. Although it still featured singing, hallmark of *xiqu*, the play incorporated much more speech (one of the impassioned speeches lasting for 500 words long) using the vernacular (everyday speech) instead of classical verse. Wang used the story of Poland suffering the shame of defeat in the hands of Turkey[11] not because he was interested in the history of another country in and of itself; rather, he was borrowing foreign history to serve the purpose of arousing patriot feelings of his own people.[12] Also of interest was the fact that in these more "experimental" plays of his the lines between traditional character roles such as *sheng* (male), *dan* (female), *jing* (painted face), and *chou* (clown) became somewhat blurred, and the stage-craft would be more "realistic" than "symbolic," using more stage props to have more true-to-life effect.[13]

All such early drama reform endeavors were taking place against the back-drop of the post-Opium War (1839–1842) geopolitical and sociocultural realities China found itself entangled in, marked by major historical events that threatened the survival of the country and its way of life – e.g., Taiping Uprising (1851–1864), whose leader Hong Xiuquan (1814–1864) claimed to have been driven, at least in part, by Christian Bible inspired visions; the Self-Strengthening Movement (1861–1895), which aimed at industrial and military modernization to better cope with the "brave new world" domi-nated by Western Powers armed with much superior science, technology, and military, especially the navy, etc. The First Sino-Japanese War (1894–1895) ended in the catastrophic defeat of the *Beiyang shuishi* (Northern Ocean Fleet), the crown jewel of the Self-Strengthening Movement and the largest naval fleet in Asia at the time, and hence the defeat of China and cessation of Liaodong Peninsula, Taiwan, and Penghu Islands to Japan "in perpetuity." The Hundred Days' Reform (1898), though blessed by no less than the Guangxu Emperor himself, ended with the young emperor put under house arrest, the execution of six of the leading reformists, and Kang Youwei (1858–1927) and Liang Qichao fleeing to Japan. Then, at the turn of the century, the Boxer Rebellion (1899–1901), an anti-imperialist uprising, was eventually crushed by the joint forces of Japan, Russia, Britain, France, the United States, Germany, Italy, and Austria-Hungary, and ended in the looting of Beijing and burning down of Yuanming Yuan (Gardens of Perfect Brightness), the old imperial summer palace in the northwest outskirts of the capital city, which has since become a historical site, a symbol for China's "national wound" suffered in the hands of Western Powers.

None of the early drama reform endeavors, however, were as self-conscious, extensive, and indeed revolutionary as those mounted by the young stu-dents of the Spring Willow Society in 1907. Indeed, members of the Spring Willow Society had an acute sense of mission to spearhead a revolutionar-ily new style of drama/theatre by way of helping to save and renew their home country. The patriotic mission of their drama reform endeavors were unmistakably stated in the advertisement for *Black Slave's Cry to Heaven* published in a dozen or so Japanese newspapers days and even weeks in advance of the event scheduled for early June to put the performance in the context of the plight of Chinese laborers in America much worsened by the Chinese Exclusion Act (adopted in 1882, renewed in 1892, made permanent in 1902, and not repealed until 1943) that singled out the Chinese for immigration restrictions. The advertisement included an excerpt from the preface Lin Shu wrote for his translation of *Uncle Tom's Cabin*:[14]

> (T)he yellow people (in the US) are probably treated worse than the blacks. But our country's power is weak, and our convoys are cowardly and afraid of arguing with the Americans. Furthermore, no educated person has recorded what has happened, and I have no way to gain factual knowledge. The only precedent I can rely on is *A Black Slave's Cry to Heaven* (Uncle Tom's Cabin). . . . In this book the miseries of the blacks are depicted in detail. This is not because I am especially versed in depicting sadness; I am merely transcribing what is contained in the original work. And the prospect of the imminent demise of the yellow race has made me even sadder.

Spring Willow Society's adaptation, based on Lin Shu's Chinse rendition of Harriet Beecher Stowe's novel, was just as bold, taking creative license – from plot to stagecraft to acting – to better serve the stated mission of "enlightening and inspiring" the people instead of aiming for 100% fidelity.[15]

In Stowe's novel, the main story line is that of Uncle Tom, a kind-hearted man and devout Christian who bears all the suffering and injustice stoically. That is why, despite its storied role in the antislavery, abolitionist movement, many later readers and critics of the novel, such as James Johnson (1871–1938) and James Baldwin (1924–1987) rejected the character of Uncle Tom as portrayed by Stowe for being too subservient to his white slave masters and that is why the term "Uncle Tom" has since acquired its share of negative connotation.[16]

In the Spring Willow Society adaptation, however, the plight of George and Eliza, the couple's struggle and flight to freedom, emerges as the main story line. Zeng Xiaogu, the principal writer for the adaptation, chose to rearrange the sequence of events and the appearance of main characters to help drive home the message the young actors wanted to get across: take up arms to fight against injustice instead of putting up with it quietly. Near the end of the original story, Tom is beaten to death for refusal to betray Cassy and Emmeline, the two slaves who have escaped. In Zeng's adaptation, however, Tom joins George and Eliza and other slaves in their run to freedom and becomes a freedom fighter too. Instead of crying out to heaven for salvation, the young Spring Willow Society members wanted to appeal to the Chinese people directly, trying to wake them up from their long slumber in the "iron house," to borrow from Lu Xun, who some years later did the very same via his writings such as *Call to Arms* (*Na han*) (1922).

In terms of dramatic art *Black Slave's Cry to Heaven* as staged by the Spring Willow Society also presented a marked departure from traditional Chinese *xiqu*, more radical than any Chinese drama performances around this time. As with the production of the third act of *La Dame aux Camilias* back in January, this production of a full five-act play benefited from artistic coaching by Fujisawa Asajiro (1866–1917), a well-known *shinpa* actor and a leading figure in the modern Japanese drama movement. The venue was now the much more professional and prestigious Hongo-Za Theatre located in the university district of the imperial capital, a powerhouse for the production of new *shinpa* plays. More significantly, it was primarily a *huaju* (spoken drama) featuring very little singing and dancing except for in Act II, which started with a celebratory party scene of spirited singing and dancing, including a few bars of *jingju* arias. In addition, the production featured elaborate realistic stagecraft – from makeup to costume to scenery in the backdrop.

Finally, this bold reimagining of a Western classic by a group of Chinese students in Tokyo, very much in the realist tradition of Western drama/theatre as introduced and experienced at the time, received extensive media attention both before and after the performance and was enthusiastically reviewed by leading Japanese drama/theatre critics, its impact rippling back to the homeland, and thus making it a landmark event in the history of modern Chinese drama.

Harriet Beecher Stowe's 1852 novel *Uncle Tom's Cabin*, by way of *Black Slave's Cry to Heaven*, Spring Willow Society's 1907 adaptation in Tokyo, would see at least two other reincarnations for the Chinese stage, one in 1958 and one in 2007. The 1958 re-adaptation of the story, written by Ouyang Yuqian (a key member of the Spring Willow Society) to commemorate the fiftieth anniversary of *huaju* or modern Chinese *xiju*, was titled *Black Slave's Hate (Heinu hen)*. Written ten years after the 1949 Communist victory in China, the play was a fiery embodiment of the domestic politics of class struggle as well as international geopolitics of the Cold War. The 2007 version of the story, titled *Cry to Heaven (Yutian)*, was reimagined by Yu Rongjun (Nick Rongjun Yu) for the centennial celebration of *huaju*. The absence of "black slave" reference in the title made it clear that this play would deviate considerably from the original story line. Indeed, *Cry to Heaven* was a trip in the rugged memory lane of modern Chinese *xiju*, each of its six acts devoted to a period from 1907 to the present. With a star-studded cast, the play was as much a celebration of the achievements in the last 100 years as a call (or, rather, cry to heaven) for artistic freedom.[17]

Some scholars have argued that student performances at Nankai University in Tianjin in the early decades of the twentieth century contributed significantly to the development of *huaju* and modern Chinese *xiju*.[18] It is true that drama endeavors at Nanking University from the formation of *Xin jushe* (New Theatre Society) in 1909 (blessed by the university president who had just returned from a study tour of colleges and universities in Western countries) all the way to the 1930s amounted to an important chapter in the history of modern Chinese *xiju*. Such new drama endeavors included translations, adaptations, and performances of Westerns classics by Shakespeare, Wilde, Ibsen, and O'Neill. Student enthusiasts of Nankai *Xin jushe* focused primarily on the art of drama/theatre rather than on its sociopolitical functions and were more interested in revealing the true nature of humanity than "enlightening and inspiring" the people, which, as noted earlier, was the stated mission of their Spring Willow Society forerunners. What young Nankai *Xin jushe* members saw in classic Western drama were powerful presentations of the inner realities – confusions and conflicts people experience when caught in the machines of modern times. As Cao Yu (1910–1996), a Nankai University student from 1920 to 1924 active in the drama society, wrote after reading Ibsen's plays,[19]

> It's amazing that the art of *huaju* turns out to be so rich and wide-ranging, its portrayal of characters so realistic yet complex, capable of portraying so many different types of men and women, each so vivid, lifelike. It is so versatile and dexterous, using simile, metaphor, symbolism, etc. with such ease . . . Then, his (Ibsen's) structural conception is so smart, clean, flawless, all parts so perfectly woven together, with no superfluous elements whatsoever that do not directly pertain to the central conflict. What an eye-opening!

Among Western classics adapted by Nankai University drama enthusiasts are Wilde's *Salome*, Hauptmann's *The Weavers*, Ibsen's *An Enemy of the People*, Molière's *Tartuffe* and *The Miser*, and Galsworthy's *Strife*. Aside from his translation and adaptation work for the campus drama society, Cao Yu proved to be a talented young actor – his performance in an adaptation of Molière's *The Miser* as the leading character Harpagon was well received. He went on to become one of the most important modern Chinese playwrights, best known for such masterpieces as *Thunderstorm* (1933), *Sunrise* (1936), *The Wilderness* (1937), and *Peking Man* (1940), signifying to the world that *huaju* or, rather, modern Chinese *xiju* had finally come of age. All of these important drama works by Cao Yu, although all rooted in and inspired by the sociopolitical and cultural realities of China, strike significant intertextual reverberations with Western classics from Greek tragedies to Ibsen and O'Neill.[20]

In addition to Nankai University, campus drama activities at quite a few other universities, such as Fudan and Jiaotong in Shanghai, Qinghua (Tsinghua), Yanjing (Yenching), and Peking Women's College of Education (now Beijing Normal University), Southeastern (*Dongnan daxue*) in Nanjing, and Soochow (*Dongwu daxue*) in Suzhou, all contributed to the growth of modern Chinese drama.

What young drama enthusiasts did on university campuses in the years and even decades of early twentieth century, however, was a *continuation* of the bold, pioneering work of their Spring Willow Society forerunners. The bold reimagining of Western classics in Tokyo back in 1907 by Zeng Xiaogu, Li Shutong, Ouyang Yuqian, and Lu Jingruo, who happened to be almost a generation older, might not be exactly spring thunder in the wilderness, but it did shine light for a new direction and new path for Chinese drama. Whether it amounted to the birth cry of *huaju* or modern Chinese *xiju* may be open to debate, their significance cannot be underestimated. Whatever followed, as members of the Spring Willow Society returned to China, would be a continuation of momentous albeit messy, uneasy developments until major modern Chinese playwrights such as Cao Yu came on the scene. Even then, encounters with Western drama continued and even many of the plays staged 100 years into the future, in the twentieth-first century, show the same Spring Willow Society spirit of adapting (as well as appropriating) Western classics for the Chinese stage, for use in China and, despite the range of variations, in the same quest for new ways to both represent and impact social and cultural realities.

Back to the future: a group of *balinghou* amateurs in search of a director to reimagine the reimagining of *Black Slave's Cry to Heaven* 100 years ago

Fast forward to the year 2007 in Beijing. April 27 exactly.

On the stage of the recently renovated 450-seat Jinfan (Golden sail) Music Hall in Beijing debuts a play titled *Xunzhao chunliu she* (Search for Spring Willow Society). In this play, a group of present-day Beijing college students, mostly *balinghou* (post-'80s), to use a term in popular parlance in China today, try to rehearse a play also titled *Search for Spring Willow Society* – their attempt to reimagine how the twentysomethings of the Spring Willow Society 100 years before in Tokyo rehearsed *Black Slave's Cry to Heaven* – by way of commemorating the centennial birthday of *huaju* in China.[21]

It soon becomes clear that what unfolds on the all but bare stage, with a simple backdrop of faded black and white pictures of Spring Willow Society members and their Tokyo performances, is a metadramatic, metatheatric event. Woven into the tapestry of this short play (about 110 minutes) framed by a well-known sentimental, nostalgic theme song "*Songbie*" (Fare Thee Well) are layers of reimagining – transnational, transcultural, and translingual – as well as temporal and spatial relocations: a group of Beijing college students in 2007 reimagining on the stage how a group of Chinese college students back in 1907 reimagined on a Tokyo stage the lives of black slaves in the pre-Civil War America, their reimagining being inspired by their patriotic passions and artistic aspirations, as well as Lin Shu's 1901 Chinese rendition of Harriet Beecher Stowe's novel *Uncle Tom's Cabin*, which, in turn, had been inspired by Stowe's own observations of slavery, her religious sentiments, and her abolitionist stance.

What holds all of these layers and strands together into a coherent story that presents a compelling theatric experience is its thematic thrust, the core question it never relents in asking what does *huaju* mean – for both the Spring Willow Society generation back in 1907 and for China today – in the twenty-first century? The play is a journey back to the past to search for meaning for today and to search for direction for the future.

This 2007 group of young Beijing college student actors have rehearsed for some time on their own, rudderless, haphazardly, unlike their 1907 Spring Willow Society older brethren who benefited from the professional guidance of a renowned Japanese *shinpa* actor. Frustrated, making no progress, they decide to get guidance from professionals, which, as it turns out, takes the form of three directors, each, from a different generation, embodying a different set of sociocultural ideologies as well as artistic visions.

The first professional director on the scene is 70-year-old Zhao,[22] a famed theatre artist and a walking (albeit with the assistance of a cane) museum of half a century worth of modern Chinese drama history. A passionate, unfaltering believer in in *huaju* as a serious art, Old Zhao is quite disappointed by the nonchalant, anachronistic way the student actors rehearse. To help the students find their correct moral compass, the 70-year-old "old-school" director launches into a big, heartfelt speech about the soul of *huaju*:[23]

> *Huaju* is a serious art that is about representing particular people in a particular situation. I repeat: particular people in a particular situation. That's the quintessential characteristic of *xiju*. There's no way to rehearse without understanding this; there's no way to perform on stage without living up to this. . . . Drama is religion in the minds of actors; where they rehearse is their church. . . . The soul of *huaju* is truth – truth of its time, truth of its circumstances, truth of its place, truth of its characters. You have to truly listen, truly see, and truly feel on the stage.
>
> (*Ellipses mine*)

All that earnest admonishment producing little improvement in the young student actors' rehearsal, and all but heartbroken by their inability to appreciate the history of slavery, of the plight of the early Chinese immigrants in America, and indeed the historical as well as artistic significance of Spring Willow Society's adaptation of *Black Slave's Cry to Heaven*, Old Zhao walks away, shaking his head.

His successor is a young, buoyant, and quite brash 30-year-old, US-educated, who, despite her expressed appreciation of the historical significance of Spring Willow Society, comes from a very different place. Barely able to contain her distain, Director Qian Qian[24] dismisses Old Zhao's quasi-religious piety toward drama as naïve and laughable:

> The soul of *xiju* is truth? Gosh, that's the way to interpret the soul of *xiju* is truth? You think you can truly recreate the truth of 100 years ago? You think it'd be a good play if you recreated the truth of 100 years

ago, and it'd attract audiences? . . . . So, what is put on stage in a play? It is *qingqu* (emotive experience). What do people come to see on stage? It is *qingqu*. . . . Let me tell you this: in the theatre, actors are lunatics, the audiences are fools.

(*Ellipses mine*)

And directors, as one of the young student actors finishes the thought for Director Qian Qian, are "con artists."

Under the guidance of a thirtysomething "con artist" director the group of twentysomething "lunatics" breathe through a hypnotically induced trance-like warm-up routine before turning a slave market scene from *Black Slave's Cry to Heaven* into a carnival of maddening disco, hip-hop, and twerking on and then offstage until Director Qian Qian disappears into a taxi and until it dawns on the young student actors that they have once again lost their way, lost touch with what the play *Black Slave's Cry to Heaven* is all about.

To get back on track, the group of twentysomethings now seeks guidance from 50-year-old Director Sun[25] who happens to have a PhD in theatre from a British university. As can be expected by now, Director Sun has yet another very different message for the young drama enthusiasts:

> Why did Chinese students in Japan back then start the Spring Willow Society to perform *huaju*? These students didn't go to Japan to study drama, yet they spent so much precious time organizing *huaju* perfor-mances. Why did the Spring Willow Society mount *Black Slave's Cry to Heaven*? It's because they were trying to cultivate *pinwei* (highbrow artistic taste). Because *Uncle Tom's Cabin* was the best known liter-ary works of its times. President Lincoln once said to Mrs. Stowe: So you're the little woman who wrote the book that made this great war! The theme song of the film adaptation of *Uncle Tom's Cabin* "Ol' Man River" is still the greatest Blacks' song today. That is the power of art; that is *pinwei*. Isn't that what we are searching for today?

Having succeeded in working up the student actors' passion about drama through his rallying call to defend it as our spiritual home, now under siege and under assault by pop culture, Director Sun leaves the twentysomethings to rehearse on their own; he does not want to be late for a pre-booked (pos-sibly lucratively compensated) guest appearance on a television show.

So the play throbs with three divergent energies, each pulling in a different direction, that prove to be both invigorating and perplexing to the young col-lege students in their existential quest for meaning not just in the theatre, but in life beyond the fantasy world of make-believe: truth (*zhenshi*) – fidelity to absolute, uncompromising socio-historical truth; play (*wan, qingqu*) – a take-no-prisoner post-modern, carnivalesque attitude toward just about everything and anything; and art (*pinwei*) – a variation of the "*l'art pour l'art*" theme that is not exactly in tune with the "art and literature as vehicle for serious moral purpose" (*wen yi zai dao*) mantra long held by Chinese intellectuals, writers, and artists from time immemorial, including the Spring Willow Society generation.

This 2007 play also pulsates with several sets of apparent incongruities blended into one uneasy yet somehow synergic theatric event:[26] armature playwright (Li Longyin, although his father Li Moran was a veteran actor and past president of Chinese Dramatic Artists Association) and critically acclaimed director (Ren Ming, who has directed several dozens of plays, including adaptations of Western classics such as *Hamlet*, *Desire under the Elms*, and *Waiting for Godot*); community theatre club (Chaoyang District) and storied national theatre (Beijing People's Art Theatre); serious topical and thematic concern (quest for meaning; history of slavery in America) interjected with ample moments of levity, of hilarious comedy produced by, in part, mixing different styles of music (Chinese, Japanese, American, and African); and registers of speech (quasi-classic Chinese used by Lin Shu for his rendition of *Uncle Tom's Cabin*, Japanese-flavored Chinese expressions, and colloquialisms of 1907 and 2007 China) – the humor produced by the mixing of such apparent incongruities was well appreciated by a packed audience on the debut evening, mostly a "who's who" in the drama/theatre scene in Beijing, and was rewarded with more than 20 big laughs from them.[27] The fact that each young actor plays several roles "traveling" in time, space, culture, and, sometimes, even gender at the snap of a finger, so to speak, adds to the comic, entertaining effect of the play too. Young actor Wang Lei, for example, who channels Li Hong'er, the 20-year-old college student drama club president, morphs in and out of several male and female roles during the 110-minute performance: Li Shutong of Spring Willow Society 100 years ago, the black female slave Eliza, the white plantation owner Arthur Shelby, and Eliza's husband George, as the flow of story demands.

Such dexterity in code (styles and registers) switching and fluidity in modality – e.g., realism and expressionism, seriousness and levity, art and entertainment, native and foreign, modern and post-modern, time and space – should come as no surprise to the knowing audience in the Jinfan Musical Hall.

After all, by 2007, 100 years after the Spring Willow Society's bold, epochal experiments in Tokyo, the drama/theatre scene in China had already trekked decades of transformative, oftentimes traumatic, experiences through wars and revolutions: the first 17 years (1949–1966) of the Communist rule and the ten years Cultural Revolution (1966–1976), especially the decade between late 1970s and late 1980s, when the whole country soul-searched while nursing the wounds in its psyche inflicted by the radical leftist Mao ideologies and policies in arts and literature as in every other facet of socio-economic, cultural, and political life of China.

By 2007, the drama/theatre scene had long busted out of the procrustean bed of the "eight model plays,"[28] the handiwork of Jiang Qing (Madame Mao), had already experienced firsthand Arthur Miller's *Death of Salesman* (staged in Beijing in 1983, directed by Miller himself), had been experimenting with various modes of drama/theatre other than (socialist) realism, which had held dominion since the early decades of the twentieth century, relishing what small, avant-garde theatre experiments[29] had to offer, and had gone well past the point of no return into the "sea" of commercial production.

In 2007, much as it is today, despite the runaway boom in economy, the apparent prosperity (for a sizable portion of the population), the newly found confidence, and the good time many seemed to be having, with a sort of vengeance and abandon (reminiscent of the Roaring 20s in America and much of the West), there was an acute sense of ennui, of angst, of being rudderless, without knowing where exactly they were going and for what purpose and good. China seemed, as it still seems now, a nation somewhat lost in its own recent success of adaptation. *Search for Spring Willow Society* – a play within play about how to adapt a Western classic – captures that sense of loss, existential crisis, and urgency felt by many to search anew for meaning and direction.

By the end of the 110-minute play, however, the "holy grail" of meaning and purpose remains as elusive as ever. Apparently, there is no simple, easy, and definitive answer to the questions raised about *huaju* and about just anything else China as a nation and indeed as a civilization is facing. Meaning, perhaps, lies in the quest itself.[30]

As alluded to earlier, what frames and sets the sentimental, nostalgic tone of *Search for Spring Willow Society*, despite the many intervals of comic relief, is the theme song "*Songbie*" (Farewell Thee Well), a song that is well known in China, especially among generations of the college educated, a sort of "Auld Lang Syne" that plays in the hearts and heads of millions, if not literally in the air, as they bid farewell to old friends upon graduation.[31] Li Shutong, a key member of the Spring Willow Society, when he was probably still in Japan, and certainly before he bid farewell to worldly pursuits and became a Buddhist monk in 1918, wrote and arranged the lyrics for the melody of "Dreaming of Home and Mother" by John Pond Ordway (1824–1880), possibly inspired by a popular Japanese song also set to the tune of this 1850s' American song. Thanks to Li Shutong, a Chinese student who found himself far away from home in Tokyo when the twentieth century was still young, and thanks in part to the 1964 film *Zaochun eryue* (Early Spring) and 1985 film *Chengnan jiushi* (My Hometown Stories), both of which featured this farewell song, the melody of a largely forgotten American song has found its home in the hearts of millions upon millions of Chinese. Quite a story of transcultural adaptation in and of itself, "*Songbie*" seems an apt theme song for a play about adaptation and re-adaptation, artistically and otherwise.

Equally worth noting is the venue for the debut event, Jinfan Musical Hall, formally known as *Bamian cao jiushijun zhongyang tang* (Octagon Trough Salvation Army Central Hall), the headquarters of the Salvation Army in Beijing built in 1917 when this quasi-military Christian organization first entered China. Its architectural style was (and still is) primarily Western, although it adopted some noticeable Chinese architectural elements – e.g., its clock tower. The building was turned into a Children's Palace in 1950, the year after Communist victory in China, and in 1997 renovated and retooled with modern audio-visual systems; it morphed into a state of the art performance center. The stated mission of Jinfan Musical Hall is music education for the young.[32] The chain of adaptation and appropriation that transformed the former Octagon Trough Salvation Army Central Hall to what it is today makes this storied place a fitting venue for an event loaded with transnational, transcultural, and translingual, as well as socio-historical significance.

In August 2007, still basking in the "afterglow" of the successful debut performance and performances at various Beijing university campuses and the biennial China Drama Festival, the show traveled to Japan for the Fourteenth BESETO (Beijing-Seoul-Tokyo) Drama Festival, a program established by artists of China, Japan, and South Korea back in 1994 to promote cultural and artistic exchange and cooperation between the three countries.[33] Spring Willow Society, in its latest, post-modern reincarnation, had finally returned "home," so to speak, after a 100-year journey across the rugged terrain of history in the home country of Zeng Xiaogu, Li Shutong, Ouyang Yuqian, Lu Jingruo, and other young, talented, and patriotic student actors.

The 2007 play *Search for Spring Willow Society* presents another testimonial of how the Chinese readapt themselves in the brave new, globalized world of the twenty-first century. It is a search for meaning and direction not just for *huaju*, for drama and theatre, for that matter, but, more significantly, for arts and literature, culture, and, indeed, the future of China: how far it has come and where it is going in another 50 to 100 years into the future. In that fitful and suspense-filled quest, adaptation of Western classics, as exemplified by *Black Slave's Cry to Heaven* and other such endeavors studied in this book, has a potent role to play.

Notes

1   This portion of the discussion draws from Paula Harrell, 1–2; Chen Qiongying, 1–2, 65–9; Shouhua Qi, 52–3.
2   See Qi, 58–63, 63–5.
3   See Note 1 in the prologue for more information on *shinpa* (new school) and *shingeki* (new drama).
4   See Wei Mingjie, "*Lun riben xinju yundong*" (On the Influence).
5   Huang Aihua, "*Chunliushe yanjiu zaji*" (Notes on Spring Willow Society Research), 79–80; *Ershi shiji zhongwai xiju* (A Comparative Study), 001–105.
6   Ding, 018; Ge Wu, 24–5.
7   Quoted in Wu, 26. See also Qi, 35–40.
8   Quoted in Wu, 26.
9   The first Sino-Japanese War (1894–95) that ended in China's defeat and the cession of Taiwan to Japan, among other things, under the Treaty of Shimonoseki.
10   The term "romance" (*chuanqi*), when used in the context of classical Chinese literature and drama, could refer to either a genre of short fiction that goes back to the Tang and Song dynasties or the kind of traditional drama popular in Southern

China during the Ming and Qing Dynasties as opposed to "variety play" (*zaju*) popular in Northern China around the same time. In this speech, the term is used self-referentially to mean a play. *Xixiang ji* (The West Wing Story) and *Mudan ting* (The Peony Pavilion) are well-known classical Chinese plays of heartrending love stories.

11 The historical basis for the play could be the Polish-Ottoman War of the 1600s. Wang, however, may have used the material quite freely to better serve the sociopolitical purpose he had set for almost all of his dramatic endeavors.

12 Bo Qiumin, 49. See also "Wang Xiaonong."

13 See "China's First Western-Style Theatre."

14 R. David Arkush and Leo O. Lee, 77–8.

15 This portion of the discussion draws from Wei Mingjie, "*Chunliushe*" (The Backstory), 72–88.

16 See James Weldon Johnson, 24, and James Baldwin.

17 See Yu Shiao-ling.

18 This portion of the discussion draws from Ku Huijun; Yang Hong.

19 Quoted in Ku, 38.

20 See Qi, 99–102; see also Joseph S. M. Lau.

21 This portion of the discussion draws from Yu Lie, Hong Hai, Ji Guoping, and Shi Jun.

22 Zhao is the first in the old Chinese *Hundred Family Names* (*baijiaxing*), implying perhaps that Director Zhao is old school.

23 All English translations of quotes from the play are based on the script available at the website of "Tufeng Drama Troupe."

24 This young director's last name, Qian, the second in the old Chinese *Hundred Family Names* (*baijiaxing*), means "money," and her first name Qian means "forward." Her full name, Qian Qian, implies a pop culture, box office oriented, post-modern attitude toward drama and theatre.

25 Although Sun also occupies a front-row seat in the old *Hundred Family Names* (*baijiaxing*), this director's age seems to suggest that he takes a position somewhere in between the "conservative" 70-year-old Director Zhao and the brash 30-year-old Director Qian Qian along the sociocultural and artistic spectrums.

26 See Li Gang, 128, and Tao Zi.

27 See Xu Shipi, and Wei Ruiyan.

28 The "eight model plays" include six Beijing operas (*The Legend of the Red Lantern, Shajiabang, Taking Tiger Mountain by Strategy, Raid on the White Tiger Regiment, Ode of the Dragon River,* and *On the Dock*) and two ballets (*Red Detachment of Women* and *The White-Haired Girl*), all featuring revolutionary characters and themes. Incidentally, during Richard Nixon's 1972 visit to China, he and the first lady, Patricia Nixon, were treated to an evening of the ballet *Red Detachment of Women*. See *Nixon in China*, an opera in three acts by John Adams (1987), for a dramatic reimagining of that historical event.

29 See Rossella Ferrari.

30 See Ji Guoping.

31 See "Songbie;" "John P. Ordway." For an English rendition of the song, see "Song Bie Ge."

32 See "*Jinfan yinyue ting*" and "*Bamian cao jiushijun zhongyang tang*."

33 See Tao Zi.

Bibliography

Arkush, R. David, and Leo O. Lee, trans. and eds. *Land Without Ghosts: Chinese Impressions of America From the Mid-Nineteenth Century to the Present*. Berkeley, CA: University of California Press, 1990.

Baldwin, James. "Everybody's Protest Novel," in *Notes of a Native Son*. Edited by James Baldwin. Boston, MA: Beacon Press, 2012, 13–24.

"*Bamian cao jiushijun zhongyang tang*" (Octagon Trough Salvation Army Central Hall). https://zh.wikipedia.org/wiki/.

Bo, Qiumin. "*Lun Wang Xiaonong de xiju gailiang huodong*" (On Wang Xiaonong's Drama Reform Endeavors). *Xiju yishu* (Theatre Arts) 3 (1988): 45–54.

Chen, Qiongying. *Qingji liuxue zhengce chutan* (Qing Government Study Abroad Policies Overview). Taiwan: Wenshizhe Press, 1989.

"China's First Western-Style Theater." www1.chinaculture.org/.

Ferrari, Rossella. *Pop Goes the Avant-garde: Experimental Theatre in Contemporary China*. Calcutta, India: Seagull Books, 2012.

Fu, Jin. "*Chongxin xunzhao huaju zai zhongguo de qidian*" (Search Again for the Starting Point of Spoken Drama in China). *Wenyi bao* (Art Paper), August 28, 2007.

Harrell, Paula. *Sowing the Seeds of Change: Chinese Students, Japanese Teachers, 1895–1905*. Stanford, CA: Stanford University Press, 1992.

Hong, Hai. "*Xiju de linghun daodi shi shenme: Li Longyin jiqi xinbian huaju Xunzhao chunliushe*" (What Exactly Is the Soul of Drama: Li Longyin and His Newly Completed Spoken Drama Search for Spring Willow Society). *Wenhua Yuekan* (Culture Monthly), no. 6 (2007): 14–15.

Huang, Aihua. "*Chunliushe yanjiu zaji*" (Notes on Spring Willow Society Research). *Xiju yishu* (Theatre Arts) 2 (1993): 79–80.

———. *Ershi shiji zhongwai xiju bijiao lungao* (A Comparative Study in Twentieth-Century Chinese and Foreign Dramas). Hangzhou: Zhejiang University Press, 2006.

Ji, Guoping. "*Huaju jingshen de dangdai xunzhao: Guan xunzhao chunliu she ganyan*" (In Search of the Spirit of Contemporary Spoken Drama: Thoughts on Search for Spring Willow Society). *Zhongguo xiju* (Chinese Drama) 6 (2007): 31–2.

"*Jinfan yinyue ting*." (Golden Sail Music Hall). https://zh.wikipedia.org.

"John P. Ordway." https://en.wikipedia.org/wiki/John_P._Ordway.

Johnson, James Weldon. *The Autobiography of an Ex Colored Man*. New York: W. W. Norton & Company, 2015.

Ku, Huijun. "*Ruhe pingjia nankai huaju huodong zai zhongguo huaju shi shang de diwei*" (How to Assess the Importance of Nankai University Spoken Drama Endeavors in the History of Chinese Spoken Drama). *Journal of Jianghan University* (Humanities and Social Sciences) 28, no. 4 (August, 2009): 37–42.

Lau, Joseph S. M. *Ts'ao Yu: The Reluctant Disciple of Chekhov and O'Neill*. Hong Kong: Hong Kong University Press, 1970.

Li, Gang. "*Cuowei de yishu: you gan yu Beijing renyi huaju Xunzhao chunliu she*" (Art of Incongruity: Reflections on Beijing People's Art Theatre's Search for Spring Willow Society). *Da Wutai* (Big Stage) 10 (2010): 128.

Qi, Shouhua. *Western Literature in China and the Translation of a Nation*. New York: Palgrave Macmillan, 2012.

Shi, Jun. "*Jiafeng zhong de jiewen: Guan huaju xunzhao chunliushe yougan*" (Quest Anew When Pushed Against the Wall: Thoughts After Watching Search for Spring Willow Society). *Shanghai xiju* (Shanghai Theatre), no. 10 (2011): 22–3.

"Song Bie Ge." https://en.wikipedia.org/wiki/Song_Bie_Ge.

"Songbie." www.baike.com.

Tao, Zi. "*Xunzhao Chunliushe: Zhuanye yishu yu qunzhong wenhua de shuang ying*" (Search for Spring Willow Society: Win-win for Professional Art and Mass Culture). *Zhongguo wenhua bao* (Chinese Culture), December 26, 2007, Section C.

"Tufeng Drama Troupe." http://blog.sina.com.cn/tufengjutuan.

"Wang Xiaonong." http://baike.baidu.com.

Wei, Mingjie. "*Chunliushe heinu yutian ji zai riben de shengcheng beijing*" (The Backstory of Spring Willow Society's Black Slave's Cry to Heaven in Japan). *Xiju yishu* (Theatre Arts) 6 (2014): 72–88.

———. "*Lun riben xinju yundong dui Lu Jingru de yingxiang*" (On the Influence of Japanese Shingeki on Lu Jingru). *Xiju yishu* (Theatre Arts) 4 (2014): 54–69.

Wu, Ge. "*Zhongguo huaju caochuang de duochong nuli: chongxie zhongguo huaju shi*" (Multiple Forces at Work in the Creation of Chinese Spoken Drama: Toward Rewriting the History of Chinese Spoken Drama). *Journal of Yunan Arts University*, no. 1 (2014): 24–36.

Xu, Shipi and Wei Ruiyan. "*Kaowen huaju gongzuozhe zenme kandai huaju yibai nian: Xunzhao chunliushe xixiao huixie zhong tanqiu huaju zhi hun*" (Questions to Spoken Drama Workers About How They See Spoken Drama's One Hundred Years: Search for Spring Willow Society Searches for the Soul of Spoken Drama through Laughter and Humor). *Zhongguo wenhua bao* (China Culture Paper), May 14, 2007, Section A.

Yang, Hong. "*Zaoqi xiaoyuan huaju zai zhongguo xiandai huaju shi shang de yiyi*" (The Significance of Early College Campus Spoken Drama Endeavors in the History of Modern Chinese Drama). *Sichuan xiju* (Sichuan Drama), no. 5 (2008): 26–8.

Yu, Lie. "*Li Longyin xinju Xunzhao chunliushe chuangzuo wangcheng*" (Li Longyin Completes New Play Search for Spring Willow Society). *Wenyi Bao* (Art Paper), March 27, 2007, Section D.

Yu, Shiao-ling. "*Cry to Heaven*: A Play to Celebrate One Hundred Years of Chinese *Huaju* by Nick Rongjun Yu." *Asian Theatre Journal* 26, no. 1 (Spring 2009): 1–53.

3   Guess who's coming

Brecht, Beckett, Miller, and the revival of modern Chinese drama

In the days and months immediately after the ordeal of the Cultural Revolution (1966–1976) was over, the theatre scene in China was alive with plays that tugged at the heartstrings of a nation still licking its deep psychological as well as physical wounds and have now earned their places in the annals of modern Chinese art and literature – e.g., *Shuguang* (Dawn), *Yu wu sheng chu* (Thunder in the Silence), *Danxin pu* (Loyal Heart Song), *Bao chun hua* (Primrose; Spring Harbinger), and *Jiaru wo shi zhen de* (If I Were for Real).[1] These plays were liberating in their subject matters given that political dogmas and ideological taboos such as *liangge fanshi* (the two whatevers: whatever decisions made by Chairman Mao we support unfalteringly; whatever instructions from Chairman Mao we follow all the way through),[2] though already being challenged, still held sway. In fact, the 1979 play *Jiaru wo shi zhen de* (If I Were for Real), enthusiastically received by audiences and striking emotional chords across the country, touched a nerve all the way to the politburo in Beijing, the highest echelons of the Communist Party, which summarily issued a decree to ban any more performances because it "smeared the Party" and could cause social unrest. A film based on the play made in 1981 met with the same fate in mainland China.[3] These bold plays were therapeutic and cathartic too for the badly scarred national psyche that had sustained long and horrific ordeal, having witnessed millions of people, from top national leaders and old revolutionaries to intellectuals, artists, teachers, and ordinary folks, being battered by physical, verbal, and emotional violence; many did not survive.

In terms of dramatic art, however, all of these plays still adhered to the realist mode, a blend of the nineteenth-century realism associated with Henrik Ibsen and the Stanislavski system that had dominated the drama/theatre scene in China for over half a century. For the May Fourth generation in the early decades of the twentieth century, Ibsenism represented "unwavering realism" that China direly needed to help cure many of its social ills and to create a new kind of drama that would reinvent itself.[4] Also introduced to China in the early decades of the twentieth century was the Stanislavski system (method) from the Soviet Union, a system of acting that aims at producing realistic characters on stage via techniques such as emotional memory to trigger in the actor the emotions of the role the actor is playing so the role is brought to life.[5] Since then, the realist mode of representation, drawing from Ibsen and Stanislavski, as they were (mis)read and oftentimes dogmatically applied, had been a dominant mode of theatre, a dominance that was buttressed, politically, by the brand of socialist realism ideology Mao Zedong promulgated in his 1942 "Talks at The Yan'an Forum on Literature and Art."[6]

When the immediate social and psychological needs were being met, people felt restless; they wanted more; they began to look elsewhere for new ideas and new ways of representing life on the stage. As has been often the case since the Opium Wars (1839–1860) decades, they turned to the West. After all, this was a time of paradigmatic shifts and seismic changes in China. The "Practice Is the Sole Criterion for Testing Truth" debate[7] was raging across the country and loosening up the old, ironclad ideological control, although the "Democracy Wall" movement, which challenged the Communist Party's monopoly of power, was cracked down fast enough. The floodgate to the outside world, once opened, could not be shut again. All kinds if ideas, isms, fads, and modern science and technology were gushing in, sweeping across the physical and cultural landscapes of a country thirsting for things new, different, modern, which, as it happens often, come from the West.

In 1979, less than three years after the curtain of the Cultural Revolution had fallen and one year before Madame Mao (aka Jiang Qing, who had presented a fiery Chinese reincarnation of Nora as a rebel on the stage in Shanghai in the 1930s and thereby launched her bid for stardom in modern Chinese political sphere) was put on trial, the China Youth Theatre troupe (Beijing) put on a *huaju* called *Cai yi cai shui lai chi wancan* (Guess who's coming to dinner), based on the 1967 American film starring Spencer Tracy, Katharine Hepburn, and Sidney Poitier. This production, the first play about contemporary American life ever performed on the Chinese stage,[8] was a relatively safe bet, politically speaking, thanks to its less than flattering portrayal of race relations in the United States. Besides, it is a story of romantic love that overcomes pernicious, deep-rooted prejudices to pursue its own course toward happiness and therefore would appeal to Chinese audiences.[9] In that same year, the China Youth Theatre mounted another Western play, a much more ambitious production and hence a much more "dramatic" event: Bertolt Brecht's *Life of Galileo*. The reintroduction of Brecht harbingered a decade or so of fervent experimentation that transformed the theatre scene in China by, among other things, erasing "walls" between actors and audiences, interfusing traditional Chinese *xiqu* and modern "Western" *huaju*, and removing the "masks" to show the interior world of the subconscious and the unconscious.

Indeed, the staging of the Brechtian play in 1979 was not an isolated event. It was part of a momentous, transformative development reminiscent of the New Culture Movement some 60 years ago. In the short span of just a couple of years after the Cultural Revolution was over (re)translations of many Western classics, old and modern, were published: Sophocles' *Oedipus at Cornish*; J. B. Priestley's *An Inspector Calls*; Eugene O'Neill's *Desire under the Elms, The Emperor Jones*; Henrik Ibsen's *Peter Gynt*; August Strindberg's *The Ghost Sonata*; Tennessee Williams' *The Glass Menagerie*; Arthur Miller's *Death of a Salesman, The Crucible, A View from the Bridge*; Eugène Ionesco's *The Bald Soprano, Amédée, or How to Get Rid of It, Rhinoceros*; Albert Albee's *The Zoo Story, The American Dream*; Samuel Beckett's *Happy Days*; Jean Cocteau's *Orphée*; Jean-Paul Sartre's *Dirty Hands, Morts sans sépulture, No Exit, The Respectful Prostitute*; Albert Camus' *The Misunderstanding*; and Luigi Pirandello's *Six Characters in Search of an Author*. In the second issue of the journal *World Literature* 1978, Zhu Hong, an eminent foreign literature scholar at the Academy of Social Sciences, published an article titled "An Overview of the Theatre of the Absurd,"[10] which was followed by many more articles and book-length translations on modern Western drama – e.g., *Brecht on Theater, Meyerhold Speaks, The Theatre and Its Double*, and *The Empty Space*. In the same year of 1978, the Central Academy of Drama organized a symposium, which featured a talk on Brecht by Chinese scholar Ding Yangzhong, a talk on the Theatre of the Absurd by a French scholar working at the magazine *China Reconstruct* then, and a demo performance of scenes from Eugène Ionesco's *The Bald Soprano* by the French scholar, his wife, and an English scholar also working in China at the time. In the year 1980 alone, over 22 adaptations of foreign plays, including *Romeo and Juliet, Macbeth, Merchant of Venice, La Dame aux Camilias, Sherlock Holmes, The Miser*, and *The Servant of Two Masters* were staged. Notable productions of Western plays in 1981 included Jean-Paul Sartre's *Dirty Hands* and Arthur Miller's *The Crucible* (under the title *Salemu de nüwu*, Salem's Witches). All of these, translations, studies, and productions of Western plays, especially the modern classics, exerted potent impact in reviving and reshaping the Chinese drama in the decade immediately after the Cultural Revolution.[11]

Bertolt Brecht in China: an epic story of requited love

In the history of Chinese reception and adaptation of Western classics, their fascination with Bertolt Brecht (1898–1956) is unique and unusual in that it is in no small measure a reciprocation of the German playwright's fascination with Chinese culture, philosophy, and *xiqu* – e.g., *jingju* as demonstrated by Mei Lanfang during his 1935 European tour. It is a story of requited love, so to speak, of mutual admiration, intellectual resonances, and intertextual reverberations in epic proportions.[12]

Brecht seemed a "natural" fit as well as a godsend for the Chinese when they began to look outward again at the end of the 1970s. The German playwright's fascination with China can be traced back to his middle school days when young Brecht came in contact with Chinese literature by way of translations of classic Chinese poetry such as the Tang poet Li Bai (701–762). In 1938, while in exile in Denmark, Brecht translated seven classic Chinese poems into German based on Arthur Waley's English translations and later, while in exile in the United States, he translated two more classic Chinese poems. When the WWII was over, Brecht translated Mao Zedong's "Snow" – to the tune of *qin yuan chun* (*Qin yuan chun·Xue*), a well-known Mao poem written in 1936 (when the Empire of Japan had just launched an all-out war against China) not only to sing the breathtaking, sublime beauty of the motherland, but also to give full-throated expression to his sense of his own grand destiny in the country's history. Exactly how much inspiration or confirmation Brecht drew from traditional Chinese *xiqu*, possibly based on a "misreading,"[13] is open to debate; however, this fascination of his did help shape his theory of *Verfremdungseffekt* ("alienation effect") and indeed the expansion of the Epic Theatre.[14]

His sustained interest in Chinese *xiqu* as well as Chinese culture is eloquently evidenced not only in his seminal article "Alienation Effects in Chinese Acting"[15] but also in his dramatic works such as *The Good Person of Szechwan* (1938), *The Caucasian Chalk Circle* (1945), and his unfinished play on the life of Confucius (551–479 BC).[16] *The Caucasian Chalk Circle*, for example, was inspired by the thirteenth-century Chinese play *The Story of the Chalk Circle* (*Huilan ji*) although variations of the same story of a wise judge adjudicating the claims of motherhood over a child can also be found in the Old Testament (Hebrew), the Quran (Arabic), and the Tipitaka (the Pali canon of Buddhism).[17] As far as the Chinese rediscovery of Brecht near the end of the 1970s is concerned, the fact that the German playwright was an unfaltering Marxist didn't hurt,[18] although, as he testified to the US House Committee on Un-American Activities in 1947, Brecht was never a card-carrying member of the Communist Party. No other Western playwright, classical or modern, has drawn so much inspiration from Chinese *xiqu* and has returned the favor by shining so much light on new paths for the Chinese when they were searching for ways to reshape and reinvigorate their drama/theatre for the new age. It is a near perfect "partnership" based on mutual admiration as well as benefit that treks across vastly different dramatic traditions.

Bertolt Brecht first came to China by way of a 1929 *Times Literary Supplement* article on German theatre and a 1930 book on modern world literature, both translated by Zhao Jingshen (1902–1985).[19] When his essay "Alienation Effects in Chinese Acting" was first published in 1936, it caught the eye of Huang Zuolin (1906–1994), who at the time was studying Shakespeare at the University of Cambridge and directing at London Academy of Music and Dramatic Art. This first Brechtian contact by the young Chinese student would prove to be the beginning of a long, impactful relationship as Huang in subsequent decades would become the most dedicated and thoughtful interpreter, promoter, and experimenter of the Brechtian ideals of theatre in China.

The Brechtian theatre on an epic scale (1950s–1960s)

Returning to the war-torn China in 1937, Huang Zuolin directed a number of notable plays and films and in 1950 he co-founded Shanghai People's Art Theatre, where in 1951 he directed a play titled *Kangmei yuanchao dahuobao* (Resisting the US aggressions and aiding Korea big skit). Its apparent politics (the Korean War was entering its second year at the time) aside, this was the first notable experiment in the Brechtian Epic Theatre on the Chinese stage.

The play opens with a prelude set on a Japanese warship in 1885, when the Sino-Japanese War (1894–1895) ended in the catastrophic defeat of the Chinese. In this prelude, an American envoy – a Mr. Dulles – "brokers" a peace treaty between the victorious Japan and the defeated China, or, rather, he conspires with the Japanese prime minister to force Li Hongzhang (1823–1901), the Qing representative, to sign on the Treaty of Shimonoseki, which essentially ceded the Liaodong Peninsula, Taiwan, and Penghu Islands to Japan "in perpetuity."

The bulk of the play consists of four acts. Act I is set on a university campus several years after the "9.18 Incident" (aka the Mukden Incident) in 1931 orchestrated by the Japanese army as a pretext to annex Manchuria, the northeastern provinces of China. In this act, university president Leighton schemes to undermine students' anti-Japanese activities by, among other things, offering one of its leaders, Liang Derui, a scholarship to study in America. Liang betrays his fellow activists and becomes a ruthless government agent. Act II is set in the 1940s Shanghai to expose how America floods Chinese market with all kinds of products and crushes the country's burgeoning domestic industries. Act III is mostly set in Nanjing, the capital city of China, in 1945 – the time of Japanese surrender. The Nationalist (Guomindang) government and Japan, once again "brokered" by the Americans, form some kind of alliance against the people and forces led by the Communist Party. Act IV, set along the China-North Korea border during the Korean War (1950–1953), is the titular story of the play: how the Chinese people, heroically, come to the aid of the North Korean people in their fight against aggressions from American imperialists and their long-time ally Japan.

The play ends with an epilogue set in two places: first in Tokyo where the Japanese prime minister, an American envoy, who happens to be a new generation of Dulles and a Taiwan government envoy scheme to form some kind of military alliance in the Far East, and then in Beijing where people from all over the world, Russian, Chinese, Korean, etc., join hands to sing and celebrate peace.

Apparently, this is a play that sprawls across expansive time and space with no central character or dramatic action, each of the four acts having its own setting and ensemble of characters/roles. What holds everything together is the overarching anti-Japanese and American imperialists theme, with ample use of signature Epic Theatre techniques such as slide projection and narration.[20]

Huang Zuolin had to wait until 1959 to mount a full-scale adaptation of a Brechtian play on the Chinese stage. It is not clear why Huang chose *Mother Courage and Her Children* (1939) for this challenging undertaking. By 1959, the first ten-year rule of the Communist Party had already been punctuated with one massive continued revolution or campaign after another: Three-Anti and Five-Anti (1951–1952), Land Reform (1947–1952), Agriculture Collectivization (1951–1953), Anti-Rightist (1957), and Great Leap Forward and People's Communes (1958). The year 1959 marked the beginning of the disastrous "Three Years of Great Famine" that would cost the lives of tens of millions of people. If Huang took up the undertaking as political theatre of sorts, as intended by Brecht, and indeed if he saw in the figure of Mother Courage – an unheroic heroine and ultimate survivalist who, having her mind set on profiting from war, doggedly drags her canteen wagon from one battle-scarred scene to another, unfazed even by the deaths of her own children – a trope or criticism, however implicit or opaque, of the Communist Party, or Mao Zedong, Huang did not let on. This experiment, a great leap attempted by Huang, because the Brechtian play did not exactly fit with the dominant Stanislavski-/Ibsenesque mode of realist theatre, fell short – far short. It earned Huang the dubious nickname of "Father Courage," not because, as one might suspect, it was censored by the government on account of any political satire, but because it proved too alienating for the Chinese audiences. As Huang himself would put it years later, his production of the play "alienated the audiences to the outside of the theatre."[21]

The failure of this 1959 Brechtian endeavor lies in two intertwined factors: Huang's uninspired directorial approach, based on a mechanical (mis)reading of Brecht, and the audiences' inability to appreciate Brecht. To achieve what he understood at the time to be the full "alienation effect," Huang studied video recordings of the play staged in Europe in the 1940s, from stage design to craft to costume, lighting, and music with a view toward effecting a replication, as close as possible, on the Chinese stage. What he did not anticipate was that the character of Anna Fierling, Mother Courage, not exactly a heroic mother figure, proved too confusing for the Chinese audiences who were used to portrayals of characters (or character types) as good or bad without any ambiguity, as made abundantly clear as by the role types in traditional *xiqu*. Indeed, even for the play's European audiences, including critics, back in the 1940s, Mother Courage had proved a bit too perplexing, so much so that Brecht had to fine-tune her characterization so audiences would not bestow too much uncalled for sympathy on her.[22] Besides, *Mother Courage*, a play with 12 scenes, sprawls over a vast canvas of time and space as Courage drags her canteen wagon across battlefields of the Thirty Year War (1618–1648) in Europe, an "alien" place with too many strange names (in Chinese transliterations) for the typical Chinese audiences to keep track of.

The irony is that Brecht had drawn from traditional Chinese *xiqu* in conceptualizing his theory of "alienation effect" and the Epic Theatre, yet the Brechtian theatre, as conjured up on the Chinese stage by Huang, proved too alienating for the Chinese. The Chinese, typically, don't go to the theatre to be enlightened, to have their political consciousness awakened although theatre, especially since modern times, has been used for political motivation and even mobilization.[23] Huang's failure in 1959 was reminiscent of the challenges experienced by the pioneers around the turn of the twentieth century striving to reform and reinvent Chinese drama/theatre by introducing and experimenting with realist theatre associated with Ibsen.[24]

Finally, although one does not have to be in the midst of a war to fully appreciate Homer's *Iliad* and *Odyssey*, reading Homer's epics while large armies are clashing night and day does create a sense of immediacy and urgent resonance one probably would not experience otherwise. *Mother Courage and Her Children* was written in 1939 and first staged in the 1940s when WWII was still raging on. The ongoing war, the most colossal and devastating hitherto in human history, created an unparalleled exigency as well as unimaginable backdrop, live, for the dramatic action to unfold. Similarly, the 2006 production of the play in Central Park, New York, owed much of its success not only to the talent and star power of Meryl Streep, who channeled Mother Courage, but also to the fact that the country and its allies were still deep in a controversial and seemingly unwinnable war.[25]

Life of Galileo *(1979)*

About 20 years later, in the winter of 1979, Huang Zuolin tried once again to mount a Brechtian play. This time it was meant as full-throated political theatre as intended by Brecht although politics in China had just experienced seismic changes and there would not be serious political risk for Huang and his team for mounting this Western play. This second full-scale Brechtian endeavor by Huang would be political theatre in the sense that *Shuguang* (Dawn), *Yu wu sheng chu* (Thunder in the Silence), *Danxin pu* (Loyal Heart Song), *Bao chun hua* (Primrose; Spring Harbinger), *Jiaru wo shi zhen de* (If I Were for Real), hit *huaju* plays of the late 1970s alluded to earlier, were as such and more: not only to provide the much-needed therapeutic remedy for the battered national psyche but also, more significantly, to inspire people to think, act, and right the human condition in China. As Huang put it in a 1979 article written to reintroduce Brecht and to educate the Chinese audiences as to how to "properly" experience his production of *Life of Galileo*:[26]

> While deliberating how to portray the character of Galileo so he will be regarded properly, we can't help but think of how the Gang of Four has persecuted the scientific workers all over our country: How much of him to praise and how much to criticize? If we answer this question with a beautiful quote from Galileo as created by Brecht – "Thinking is among the greatest pleasures of the human race" – then we should reserve this right-to-think to our audiences.

Huang meant not only the "right to think" about the character of Galileo, heroic yet not without human frailties, but also, by extension, the "right to think" about the plight of scientists, intellectuals, artists, teachers, veteran revolutionaries and millions of ordinary people during the Cultural Revolution, and, more significantly, the "right to think" and question why such a national tragedy, prolonged and on epic scales, could have happened: What in the Chinese culture, its sociopolitical system and structure, and indeed what in the character and psyche of the nation as well as the character and psyche of each individual theatergoer that had allowed this to happen? What could be done to effect changes and amend the human condition so similar tragedies would not ever happen again?

Among those persecuted during the Cultural Revolution was the Chinese translator of *Life of Galileo*, Ding Yangzhong (1932–),[27] who had studied Western drama in Lepzig, Germany (East Germany then) in the late 1950s and become fascinated with Brecht. In May 1970, at the height of the Cultural Revolution, Ding, along with all faculty and students of the Central Academy of Drama in Beijing, where he was a professor, was sent to a military farm to be re-educated through physical labor. Not long after that he was accused of being the "arsonist" for two fires on the farm and labeled a "counter-revolutionary." For the next six months, Ding was subjected to relentless condemnation sessions but refused to confess and plead guilty because he had not committed the crime. At one of the last condemnation sessions, infuriated by Ding's stubborn refusal to cooperate, the commander of the military farm pronounced an "execution by firing squad" sentence on him, which, fortunately, was not carried out.

During the most difficult days of his life then, Ding thought of Brecht's Galileo as channeled by Ernst Busch (1900–1980) in a Berlin Ensemble production he had seen while studying in Germany, especially how Galileo, when threatened with torture by the Vatican during the Inquisition, recanted his "heretic" teachings. Ding Yangzhong decided to translate *Life of Galileo* into Chinese, whose story, he believed, would resonate with and indeed inspire the Chinese intellectuals undergoing unimaginable test of their courage at the time. For this clandestine translation project, Ding camouflaged his copy of the play by Brecht, a Marxist, with a copy of *The Communist Manifesto* by Karl Marx, both in their original language: German. After a long day of hard labor cleaning up more than 20 makeshift outhouses and working in rice fields, when everyone else in the dorm had already gone to bed, he would resume the "covert operation" using a flashlight and the paper given him for writing his confessions. With the help of sympathetic roommates, who would keep an eye out at the door while he was at it and supply him with more paper stolen from the farm's command office, Ding completed the translation project seven months later, in the winter of 1971. After giving a talk on Brecht in 1978 at the aforementioned Central Academy of Drama symposium, Ding worked with Huang Zuolin, along with Chen Yong (1929–2004) of the China Youth Theatre, to bring the story of Galileo on stage in Beijing.[28]

Days before the opening performance on March 24, 1979, after four months of rehearsal (November 1978–March 1979), against the chills of early spring morning, long lines of people, old and young, men and women, waited outside the box office. Within two hours, tickets for the next two weeks were sold out. The show had a successful run of more than 80 performances in a packed thousand-seat theatre until the actor for an important role became seriously ill, which suggested that the Chinese, a long time coming, had finally embraced Brecht – enthusiastically.[29]

The success of this 1979 production of Brecht on the Chinese stage can be attributed to a few interrelated key factors: the right choice of play, the right directorial approach, and the right timing sociopolitically. When Huang Zuolin, based in Shanghai, was invited to travel up north to Beijing to direct the play, the lessons he had learned from the colossal failure of the 1959 production of *Mother Courage and Her Children* was acutely on his mind.[30] Why did he choose Brecht (his Waterloo, so to speak) again, for the first major production of a foreign play in the post-Cultural Revolution era? To this question from his anxious assistant Huang replied, borrowing a line from Galileo, "My aim is not to prove that I am right, but to find out whether or not I have been."[31]

To get it right this time – i.e., how not to "alienate the audiences to the outside of the theatre" – Huang and his team tried to find the right balance between keeping intact the spirit of the Brechtian play and effecting and maintaining interest from the Chinese audiences. Toward that first goal, Huang and his team compressed the original 15-scene script into a more compact 12-scene version, cutting scenes and dialogs deemed not so essential to the thematic development, characterization, and dramatic action of the original so that the whole performance could be completed in about three hours. Another major change, based on the lessons learned in 1959, was to blend what Huang understood as the Stanislavski system and the Brechtian theatre into the production instead of rigidly following the latter to interject excitement, arouse passion, inspire the audiences to think (which, Huang believed, is not the exclusive privilege and pleasure of the German people), and to act – to change the world for the better.

As Huang understood it, the story of Galileo is that of the dignity of *ren* (man, humanity).[32] To foreground this positive humanistic theme, Huang gave the play an upbeat tone from the moment the performance began. The curtain now rises to a sunlit morning wherein Galileo, basking in the warm sunshine, washes while chitchatting with the 11-year-old Andrea, their hearty laugh filling the entire stage. Instead of the children's choir, it is now the half-starved ballad singer and his wife, appearing only in Scene 10 in the original, who now function as the chorus for the entire play. Huang thus explained in his 1979 article to guide the audiences in how to see the play:[33]

> Typically, churches use children's choir to sign hymns and show the holiness of Heaven. *Life of Galileo* is filled with struggle against the

repression of religion and church authorities. Wouldn't using children's choir dilute this fighting spirit? The ballad couple in Scene 10 would be perfect representative of the people and what they sing – "Who wouldn't like to say and do just as he pleases?" – would eloquently express the wishes and aspirations of the people.

So for this 1979 production, Huang and his team created rigorous costume, music, and dance numbers for the couple to showcase the power and spirit of the people throughout the play.

In Scene 6 (Scene 7 in the original), to give another example of changes made to achieve the desired effect, Galileo, along with his daughter Virginia and her fiancé Ludovico, goes to the home of Cardinal Bellarmin ("the first cardinal since the plague") in Rome to attend a big party. Whereas in the original the dance party remains in the background, in Huang's adaptation the trio arrives near the end of one dance so Galileo encourages the young couple to join the festivity: they dance joyously, center stage, surrounded by the other revelers, as a beaming Galileo claps to cheer them on.

In the last scene of the play, some 20 years after the opening scene, the grown-up Andrea comes to visit Galileo, now much older, grayed, and under house arrest. After a big speech about what true courage it takes to be truly devoted to the profession of science, Galileo delivers this harsh verdict on himself:

> I betrayed my profession. A man who does what I did cannot be tolerated in the ranks of science.

Among the enthusiastic audiences in Beijing in the spring of 1979 were many scientists, scholars, artists, old revolutionaries, etc., including Ding Yangzhong, the translator; Huang Zuolin, the director; Hua Luogeng (1910–1985), the most famous Chinese mathematician; and Zhou Yang (1907–1989), a prominent figure in modern Chinese arts and literature, who had all suffered egregiously during the Cultural Revolution. Now, as the curtain fell, each of them teary eyed, applauding, had to search in his/her own soul for an honest answer to the question whether he/she had remained true to his/her profession, be it science or art, and true to his/her dignity as a human being and to the dignity of fellow human beings, especially when to be true would lead to more egregious suffering and could very well mean a premature, unnatural end of one's physical being. Zhou Yang, for example, would have to have some serious soul-searching to do for the leading role he had played in many harsh campaigns against artists and writers although he had had his share of egregious suffering in the hands of the Gang of Four.[34]

This production of the Brechtian play happened at a time not only of seismic sociopolitical change in China but also in the midst of a spirited debate of the so-called *xiju guan*, mission, vision, and direction of Chinese drama/theatre: Where should it go from here and how? Many at the time felt that the crisis in Chinese drama/theatre was caused by the decades-long relentless dominance of the Stanislavski/Ibsenesque realism (*xieshi*) ideology, so they advocated breaking away from it toward the more suggestive, symbolic (*xieyi*) theatre. For Huang Zuolin, the ideal model or mode for the Chinese theatre would be a good interfusion of the Stanislavski/Ibsenesque realism, Brechtian theatre, and traditional Chinese *xiqu*.[35]

The Caucasian Chalk Circle *(1985)*

If Huang Zuolin did not get a chance to interfuse *xiqu* into the adaptation of another Brechtian play, Chen Yong, his co-director for the 1979 production of *Life of Galileo*, was able to do so in 1985 when she mounted *The Caucasian Chalk Circle* for the inaugural "Brecht Week" in China. In December 1986, she took the show to Hong Kong for the International Brecht Festival there. As Chen Yong understood it, the challenge for any Chinese director to mount a Brechtian play for the Chinese stage was "to find a way to introduce Brechtian plays so Chinese audiences can accept and understand – not just accepted by a handful of drama experts or intellectuals, but by the broad ordinary theatergoers in China."[36]

To achieve that goal, Chen Yong had her actors, face painted (as in traditional *xiqu* such as *jingju*), double as ushers before the show began. When the curtain rises, one sees a three-screen backdrop (which changes from mountains to farmhouses, etc., as the dramatic action unfolds) and simple, mobile stage props such as a makeshift wood house structure (which actors, doubling as stage crew during the performance, quickly reorganize as needed). During the performance, the actors, as immersed in their roles as in any realist theatre, sometimes address the audiences directly through the "fourth wall" to augment the "alienation effect."

During the scene when Grusha Vashnadze, the heroine of the play, takes the governor's baby to flee into the mountains, with rebels hot on her heels, the actor performs a series of breathtaking dance and acrobatic feat – tumble, somersault, cartwheel – hallmark moves from traditional Chinese *xiqu*, with the "baby" in her arms, accompanied by drumbeats from electronic synthesizer, which sound like percussion instruments of *jingju* but with noticeable modern (Western) flavor, to intensify the dramatic action and heighten the theatric experience for the audiences.[37]

Did Chen Yong succeed? Drama experts in China were positive in their reactions, lauding the production for its "perfect interfusion of traditional *xiqu* and the Brechtian alienation effect," and its originality of injecting traditional *xiqu* into the more modern *huaju*. Xu Xiaozhong (1928–), who, among other things, had directed Ibsen's *Peter Gynt* in 1983 and would take on Goethe's *Faust* in 2008 at the age of 80, praised the production as the first authentic Brechtian play on the Chinese stage that perfectly blended two cultures and two traditions into one theatric event at even a higher level of achievement. Antony Tatlow, then International Brecht Society president, said that this production was something "I've waited for for the last 20 years" and that it pointed to a direction Chinese drama could take for future development. Drama experts based in Hong Kong, however, were not that generous in their reviews. They felt that the attempt to blend different cultural and drama elements into the production – e.g., Cossack dance, resulted in an uneven mishmash and that the entire show was more fast-paced excitement than thought-provoking empowerment.[38]

The Good Person of Szechwan *(2010s)*

Perfect, harmonious fusion or not, the same enterprising spirit persisted in two adaptations of *The Good Person of Szechwan*, each taking much more creative license to indigenize this Western (despite its title and names of characters and places) play for the Chinese audiences: *The Good Person of Beijing* (Beijing *haoren*, 2010) and *The Good Person of Jiangnan* (*Jiangnan haoren*, 2013).

For Shen Lin, the creator of the 2010 extreme remake of the Brechtian play, the primary goal was to make full use of the political theatre potential of such a production to inspire thinking about the socioeconomic realities of China in the twenty-first century and taking action to change things for the better. Shen, who has a PhD degree from a UK university, started this project in 2000 when his bold, ambitious Epic Theatre play *Che Guevara*, an in-your-face, full-blast assault on corruptions and injustice in China today from an unapologetically leftist vantage point, caused quite a stir.[39] In many ways, *The Good Person of Beijing* was a sequel that had taken ten years to make and in the process its politics had mellowed somewhat and become less edgy, but artistically it was in full experimental mode, so much so that *The Good Person of Beijing* became all but fully indigenized and a present-day Chinese play.

One audacious thing Shen Lin and his team did for this adaptation, not without some political risk, was to move the setting of the play from the early twentieth-century Szechwan (in southwest China) to the twenty-first-century Beijing. As home for the echelons of the central government and Communist Party since 1949, Beijing is more than the name for a city; it is a symbol vested with much political significance, as sacred as the heart and soul of the People's Republic. What is underneath all that glitters in this capital city? Are there egregious pollutions, corruptions, and injustices as millions of ordinary people, native Beijingers and migrant workers alike, left behind by the high-speed train of capitalism, so to speak, struggle to survive?[40]

To bring the play up to date, Shen Lin and team gave the whole cast of characters brand new identities of present-day Beijing: Wang (Wong), a water seller in the original, now still sells bottled water, but has morphed into a retired teacher of the night school of Plant 798, an electronics manufacturing plant in Beijing that shut down in 2002, its site having been converted to a booming art zone since; Shen Dai (Shen Te), the heroine of the play, is now a *xitoumei* (hair washing sister, hairdresser), a profession which in the parlance of today's China carries a dubious reputation being associated with prostitution; Yu Biao (Yang Sun), an unemployed pilot in the original, is a young man with frustrated dreams of going to America to pursue advanced study – his visa application having been denied by the US embassy despite his impressive TOEFL and GRE scores; and Su Haogu (Mr. Su Fu), a barber in the original, is now a man in his 50s, a moderately successful dealer in Chinese antiques, who walks around and parades his pride in Chinese culture – donning old Tang dynasty costumes, humming classical *kun* opera arias, sipping Dragon Well tea. These characters, cartoonish caricatures they may seem, are real people in the sense that they "strut and fret" among the theatergoers and just about anywhere in Beijing and across the country.[41]

The most audacious thing Shen Lin and team did, artistically, to bring the production even closer home for the audiences, was to remake the story into a Beijing *quju*, a local genre that has evolved from old Beijing folk tunes by drawing from both traditional *xiqu* such as *jingju* and modern *huaju*,[42] featuring simple music instruments such as *sanxian* (three-stringed banjo) and *bajiaogu* (octagon drum). Throughout the performance, a seasoned *quju* musician, a one-person band and chorus (in the sense of classic Greek theatre), a minstrel of sort, sings, narrates, and comments, as well as providing musical accompaniment to She Dai, Wang, and everyone else when they sing. Each air or aria they sing is chosen from the genre's rich repertoire of styles, "rediscovered" by Shen Lin and his team, to fit the lyrics (completely rewritten in quasi-verse forms typical of traditional Chinese *xiqu*, loaded with wit, humor, irony, and satire) to the character and the moment in the dramatic action.

Operating on a shoestring, Shen and team had to be ingenious and improvise. For the three gods, the production used clay figurines, projected onto a big screen, each a stand-in for an unnamed legendary leader in modern Chinese history, who descend on the opening scene accompanied by the song "*Dongfang hong*" (The East Is Red),[43] find themselves in the hustle and bustle of today's Beijing, and are rather dismayed that a good person is hard to find in this "utopia" they had dreamed of in their revolutionary days. Other simple, make-do stage props include an old bamboo stroller, an old bench, a big palm-leaf fan (to produce the sound effects of wind and rain), and two pieces of plywood (to produce the sound effects of thunder), earthy, elemental, no fancy electronic gadgets, all performed in the glaring eye of the audiences. The cost for the stage props, etc., for the early performances was less than 20,000 yuan (RMB), a bit over US$3,000.

If *The Good Person of Beijing* is political theatre in the true Brechtian sense, it exudes less optimism (or the fighting spirit of *Che Guevara*, ten years before, for that matter) and more melancholy, sarcasm, and a bit of resignation, as embodied in one of the lines from the play: "Just as the rich eats meat and the poor bites bones, so will a harmonious society last ten thousand years." The message that one gets from the existential, moral crisis

Shen Dai/Sui Da struggles with throughout the play cannot be as uplifting as one would hope for: If you can't beat them and remain good, what choices do you have other than joining in and beating them at their own game. Even the "bad" people, such as Shen Dai's love interest, the unscrupulous Yu Biao, and the hypocritical Su Haogu: Aren't they driven to behave badly in order to survive (and thrive) in this brave new world of state capitalism wherein there is no safety net to catch you if you happen to fall? Nonetheless, to be true to the Brechtian idea of political theatre, and to make one last pitch toward achieving what Shen Lin and his team had set out to do with this production, Shen Dai turns to address the audiences directly, through the "fourth wall," before curtain fall:[44]

Don't just look on, come and help me.

Produced in 2013 by Zhejiang Hundred Flower Yue Troupe (the same theatre company that produced the Yue adaptations of Ibsen's *Hedda Gabler* and *The Lady from the Sea* in 2006), *The Good Person of Jiangnan*[45] is also set in present-day China. For this Yue remake of the Brechtian play, Shen Dai, a sing-song girl (*geji*), with gift money from the three gods, buys herself a decent-sized silk store, a line of business fit for the new locale for the story – Jiangnan being known for its elegant silk products. Mao Weitao (1962–), a big star Yue actor with accolades, plays the role of Shen Dai while a very handsome actor plays her love interest, Yang Sengang (Yang Sun). The ambition of Yang, who appears to be a prince charming of sorts earlier in the play, is to fly the blue sky again, but, failing that, he shows his true colors fast enough: an ugly man, petty, manipulative, and dark. As the story unfolds, the Shen/Yang relationship assumes center stage and becomes the driving force of dramatic action – Shen's dizzying joy of falling in love, tender, delirious sweetness of having just tasted the forbidden fruit for the first time, acute disappointment when the hope she has placed on her man fails to materialize, and agonizing despair when she finally sees through him as what he really is. In short, *The Good Person of Jiangnan* becomes a romantic love story that has gone sour. Although not without its share of "alienation effect" – e.g., use of cards – actors speaking through the "fourth wall" to the audiences directly, this Yue remake of the Brechtian play presents the audiences with a feast of singing, dancing (mixing in rap, contemporary, and jazz moves), and costumes, traditional Chinese and Western-style suit and tie – gratifying, perhaps, but not nearly as provocative as *The Good Person of Beijing*. It is more entertainment than political theatre although the two are not necessarily mutually exclusive.[46]

"(T)he light gleams an instant, then it's night once more": to adapt Samuel Beckett for the Chinese stage

If the Brechtian Epic Theatre, which was in part inspired by traditional Chinese *xiqu*, proved somewhat too alien for the typical Chinese theatergoers, at least in the 1950s–1960s, and had taken years for it to win acceptance through courageous and persistent efforts of scholars and artists alike, what would it take to make Samuel Beckett (1906–1989) – the Theatre of the Absurd as exemplified by him – work for the Chinese stage? After all, even for many readers and theatergoers in the source culture, Beckett's plays, mostly black comedy loaded with apparently irrational characters, illogical, "gibberish" speeches, can be very challenging.

It is not that the Chinese is immune to absurdity in human condition. They have been questioning the meaning of human existence from time immemorial as evidenced in the entire body of Chinese philosophy, Confucianism, Daoism, Buddhism, etc., although these native belief systems do offer moral codes as well as rites and rituals to help guide human behavior and interaction. In fact, during the years when Beckett's most important, signature works came out – *Waiting for Godot* (1953), *Endgame* (1957), *Krapp's Last Tape* (1958), and *Happy Days* (1961), China was being caught in one catastrophic episode of political absurdity after another, and when Beckett was receiving his Nobel Prize in Literature award in 1969, the Cultural Revolution absurdity was just reaching its shrillest pitch. Beckett did flicker a few times on the Chinese radar, so to speak, in the early 1960s. They found him and the avant-garde theatre he represented "decadent," anti-realism,[47] anti-art, anti-social, and human progress, the last whimper "on the eve of the collapse of capitalist ideology and the death of capitalist system" and therefore did not have much use for him. In 1965, on the eve of the Cultural Revolution, a Chinese translation of *Waiting for Godot* was published, but was limited to internal distribution for research purpose only.[48]

In the days immediately after the Cultural Revolution was over, the Chinese needed plays such as *Shuguang* (Dawn), *Yu wu sheng chu* (Thunder in the Silence), and *Danxin pu* (Loyal Heart Song) to help heal the wounds. They also found Brechtian plays such as *Life of Galileo* not only therapeutic but also inspiring, which shone a new path out of the relentless dominance of the social realist ideology in the realms of art and literature. Beckett was reintroduced at a time when the Chinese also felt the need to turn inward, to gaze into the psyche, and to contemplate and question the meaning of being even although Beckett provided no answers, solutions, or rational explanations and although his minimalist black comedy could prove too perplexing and therefore too "alienating" for the typical Chinese theatergoers to be of any real help. The brave and restless among Chinese theatre artists, unfazed, were more than ready to try.

Waiting for Godot *(1987)*

As early as spring 1978, as alluded to in the opening section of this chapter, Zhu Hong, in an article on the Theatre of the Absurd, reintroduced Beckett and *Waiting for Godot* for the Chinese readers. Later that year, a symposium on contemporary Western drama organized by the Central Drama Academy included a talk on the French avant-garde, the Theatre of the Absurd, and a demo performance by foreign experts working in China then. In December 1980, Shanghai Translation (*Yiwen*) Press put out a collection of Theatre of the Absurd plays, including the translation of *Waiting for Godot* that had seen a restricted distribution back in the 1960s. Publications of translations of other dramatic (e.g., *Endgame*) as well as fictional works by Beckett followed suite. However, the production of any Beckett plays on the Chinese stage had to wait until 1987, eight years after the 1979 production of Brecht's *Life of Galileo*. It was a graduating class production of *Waiting for Godot* at the Shanghai Theatre Academy.

Chen Jialin, a professor at the academy, took on the project with a healthy dose of anxiety and trepidation. He had read somewhere that for the play's opening night in France only four people had stuck to the end when Vladimir and Estragon finally decide to go, although they do not move, and that in the early 1960s when the play was making its debut on Broadway in New York, the producers put out an advertisement calling for 600 cultural elites for the opening night, fearing that it might not go well with average, less "cultured" theatergoers. To make things even more daunting for Chen Jialin and his graduating drama students, the Chinese theatergoers have very different tastes and viewing habits and therefore would be even less likely to make any sense of what is unfolding on the stage, let alone enjoying it. So, as Chen understood it, the challenge for him and his students was, once again, how to make the Western play appeal to the Chinese theatergoers and to make this audacious undertaking a rewarding experience for the students as well.[49]

As befitting a college professor, Chen began methodically by first helping the student actors understand what the term "absurd," as in Theatre of the Absurd, means. The typical Chinese translations for "absurd," *huangtang* or *huangdan*, are closer in meaning to "ridiculous" in English and therefore far from expressing its full meaning as a philosophical view of human existence, a view, though introduced from the West, that should have universal resonance because absurdity of human condition is not exclusive to the West. Then Chen went on to try to "naturalize" the play, perhaps as much for himself as for the benefit of his students, to somehow fit it into the frames of "realism," which, though challenged, was still the dominant mode of drama/ theatre then: although the Theatre of the Absurd appears to be anti-realism, it is realism in a different, twisted form that dares to face the reality of today unflinchingly and to poke underneath the surface to detect what is not so reassuring in the deep recesses. What about the apparent lack of dramatic action and development? Chen tried to see this through the lens of "dialectics" (*bianzheng*). It is a worldview that draws from both traditional Chinese philosophy and the orthodox Marxism and therefore comes natural to the Chinese – i.e., to see dramatic action in apparent inaction and change and progression underneath apparent repetition and circularity. There is even suspense, an important dramatic element in conventional theatres, in this supposedly "anti-art" play that would help arouse and sustain interest from the audiences: Who is Godot? Whether and when will he come? Finally, Chen would like his drama students to see tragedy (something serious and highly respectable) embodied in this black comedy – its apparent farcical form.

Since his actors were mostly students of traditional *xiqu*, Chen Jialin asked them to draw from their training in acting and voice so their performance would be more engaging for the audiences. For example, Chen thought that Lucky's big speech in Act I about man and God (that man, try as he may, can never come to a logical, rational conclusion about God), a two-page long unpunctuated "stream of consciousness,"[50] is the heart and soul of the play, yet has the risk of being boring, confusing, and hence losing the audiences. To inject "drama" into this scene, Chen had Lucky don an imaginary leash (instead of a physical one, as befitting the suggestiveness of traditional *xiqu*), put on the hat, fall on his knees, and move like a puppet as he begins to deliver the big speech; a few lines into the speech, still on his knees, Lucky moves a big half circle on the stage; then he gets on his feet and moves in the manner of a midget (*guibu*, rapid knee steps); finally, as he comes to this part of the speech,

> and who can doubt it will fire the firmament that is to say blast hell to heaven so blue still and calm so calm.

Lucky lifts his head, thrusts his arms heavenward, then runs around the stage like a wild horse, dragging Pozzo, Estragon, and Vladimir with him, until he finishes the speech, exhausted both emotionally and physically, and is subdued by the others.

To further help "naturalize" the play for the Chinese audiences, Chen had a poem by the Tang poet Chen Ziang on a big scroll on the stage.

Ode on Youzhou Terrace

Ahead, no wise men of times past in sight
Behind, no sages of future on the horizon
Trekking alone between the endless heaven and earth
I can't help but let tears roll down my cheeks

Emotively, this poem does seem to strike a chord with the motif as embodied in the original play's opening scene although it may not fully capture its primal, archetypal theme:

A country road. A tree. Evening.

Another classical Chinese poem by the Yuan poet Ma Zhiyuan may come somewhat closer in both sentiment and sense:

Autumn Thoughts

A withered vine, an ancient tree, crows at dusk

A little bridge, a flowing stream, a few thatched huts
An ancient road, a gusty west wind, an emaciated horse
Sunset at sky's edge, a heart-broken man far away from home.

Despite the "bleakness" of the picture drawn in this poem, however, the lone traveler is not completely alone in the world: thoughts of home, or the hope of returning home one day, could still give him a purpose and sustain him as he wanders in the big wild world.

This 1987 production of *Waiting for Godot*, a first in China, caught considerable attention from news media (all major newspapers in Shanghai covered it) as well as theatre artists such as Cao Yu and Huang Zuolin, as well as the French Consul General in Shanghai and many foreign art and literature scholars in China. The first two performances filled two-thirds of the 1,000-seat Changjiang Theatre on the Yellow River Road, formally the Carlton Theatre founded by the British in 1923. It was full capacity, standing room only, afterward. The production had an impressive run of 20 public performances, not a small achievement for Chen and his student actors, and stopped only when his students had graduated and had to leave school[51]

Waiting for Godot *(1991)*

Four years later in 1991, a young aspiring theatre artist took on *Waiting for Godot* in a much more experimental, or rather, explosive frame of mind both artistically and otherwise. By then, Meng Jinghui (1964–), a 27-year-old graduate student at the Central Academy of Drama, had already played a leading role in Ionesco's *Rhinoceros* (1987), mounted by the freshly formed Frog Experimental Theatre, an independent, part-time theatre company,[52] as its inaugural production; Igor Stravinsky's *The Soldier's Tale* (1988), also mounted by the Frog Experimental Theatre; and Harold Pinter's *The Dumb Waiter* (1990), directed by Meng Jinghui himself at the academy. In 1991, Meng first directed a production of Ionesco's *The Bald Soprano* as part of the academy's "Fifteen Days in Experimental Theatre" program and then a production of *Waiting for Godot* as part of his master's degree program requirements. Whatever fiery, iconoclastic artistic (and political?) sentiments that fueled these audacious experiments with the Theatre of the Absurd in the days and months immediately before and after the events on Tiananmen Square (1989) can be felt palpably in this "Director's Words" piece written by Meng, a manifesto of sort, to preface this production of *Waiting for Godot*:[53]

Is there anyone who sincerely wants to go and see this performance, to join us in this adventure to destroy an unreal phantom, to rebuild our home etched in our memory so we can see clearly the vista as far as our eyes can reach? This is what we want to know. To rekindle whatever little passion still remaining inside us, to safeguard the only habitat we have to survive in, and to return the glances others cast toward us with more honest, clear-headed, and alert attitudes – this is what we can do. . . .

These days, we firmly believe in our existence, forging ahead without stopping for a second, resolved that we shall never try to find any excuse for falling prey to the temptations of servitude, that we shall never become an ornament in the scenery of falsehood and affectations, that we shall never let our body and soul suffer the plight of weakening as we run for life.

The stage design for this production, mounted on the stage of a small auditorium at the academy was a brightly lit room of white walls with tall windows on both sides. Scattered in this eerily illuminated space were a black piano, a white bicycle, a small tree hanging down from a fan in motion, and a segment of Sandro Botticelli's "Allegory of Spring" hanging backstage – perhaps to help conjure up some surreal dreamscape or, rather, a daydream. As the play draws toward the end, as Estragon and Vladimir banter about whether to leave or to hang themselves, the stage fades into darkness, with only a candlelight flickering on a birthday cake and a dead body on the floor,[54] reminiscent of "the evening is spread out against the sky/Like a patient etherized upon a table" tableau drawn in the opening lines of T. S. Eliot's "The Love Song of J. Alfred Prufrock" (1920), or, more fittingly, the gloom-filled view of the world in Thomas Hardy's "Darkling Thrush" (1899): "The land's sharp features seemed to be/The Century's corpse outleant, /His crypt the cloudy canopy."

For some performances Meng would invite the audiences onto the stage and have the actors perform down stage, thus turning the theatre upside down, or, to quote Meng, turning the world of the play into a "hospital," a madhouse of sort, where Estragon and Vladimir go round and round in their gibberish tug-of-war, in the midst of which Vladimir, out of despair and defiance, knocks a piece of real glass into pieces with his cane.[55]

In March 1992, per invitation, Meng took his *Waiting for Godot* to Berlin to be part of a program featuring Chinese avant-garde art.[56] Meng and his rather nimble team (the original cast and crew for the graduation production: a director, a stage designer, and five actors) traveled light, bringing with them a minimal amount of stage props. Once they stepped into the 398-seat theatre on the second floor of the House of the Cultures of the World (*The Haus der Kulturen der Welt*), established in 1989 to bring to Berlin presentation and discussions of contemporary art and culture from around the world,[57] they realized, to their surprise, that it was not exactly the same as they had seen in the video footage of the theatre. So they had to improvise and redesign their simple props to adapt to the long, narrow stage which had very little depth. After three successful performances in Berlin, Meng and his team traveled to a small town 150 kilometers outside of Berlin to perform in an even smaller 80-seat theatre. It turned out to be quite a success and memorable experience for Meng and the cast and crew: When the performance was over they had to do six or seven curtain calls to thank the enthusiastic audiences for their thunderous standing ovation.

Waiting for Godot *(1998)*

Then something happened a few years later, in the spring of 1998, when two well-established theatre artists, Ren Ming (1960–) and Lin Zhaohua (1936–), were both bitten by the Beckett bug, so to speak, and came up with a production that might look a bit "absurd" in the eyes of the original creator of the play and make him a bit uneasy.

For his remake of *Waiting for Godot*, Ren Ming (deputy director of the much storied People's Art Theatre then, having been appointed to the position at the tender age of 34 in 1994) cast two young female actors as Didi (Vladimir) and Gege (Estragon). Instead of a country road and a tree in the midst of nowhere, the play is now set in a bar in present-day Beijing. As curtain rises for this new small theatre production,[58] one sees a semidark stage, a hat propped up by a pole from a shiny cocktail glass, a bar stool, and a dead tree dangling from the ceiling, as a haunting, wordless song sung by a tenor expands in the air. Didi, short-haired, donning fashionable leather jacket, walks onto stage, slowly, as if in a trance, sits down on the stool, picks up the hat and puts it on her head, and begins to swing her body frenziedly to the rigorous beat of a new, disco-like music that has just kicked in. Then one sees Gege, donning a pullover shirt, suspender pants, and a big hat, who appears on the stage, gazing toward where Didi is. She treads slowly, trance-like, to Didi's side; tosses her hat; and watches as Didi, bent over the stool, continues to wiggle left and right, as if possessed. Then, Didi stops, slowly lifts her head, and says,

> I'm beginning to make up my mind. Yes, I am beginning to make up my mind. Making up my mind has never been easy for me. I'm constantly telling myself: Didi, be rational, there're so many things in the world you have not yet tried. So, I'm beginning to struggle (*fendou*) again. Yes, struggle. Struggle!

What was gained or, rather, lost, in Ren Ming's rendition of *Waiting for Godot* with a cast and setting that Beckett, known for jealously guarding every word of his plays, including stage directions, would certainly frown upon?[59] Perhaps resetting the play in a bar in present-day Beijing instead of a timeless, archetypal "country road" and turning Vladimir and Estragon into two rather hip young women would bring the abstract and "alien" play a bit closer home and therefore make it a bit more accessible for the young audiences. After all, Ren Ming's stated goal for the production was to present it from the point of view of *dangdai nianqingren* (today's youth), although, as one Chinese critic put it, there is no such a thing as a homogeneous, stereotypical *dangdai nianqingren* that would fit into the same demographic profile and have the same tastes and expectations in the theatre.[60] The potential loss with such a production, on the other hand, is several-fold and significant. For one, it could dilute the rich symbolic and interpretive potentiality of the play. It is true that the "bar" motif on the stage, minimally represented, can be construed as having serious symbolic potentiality. After all, there is this saying in Chinese: *zuisheng mengsi* (born drunk dead dreaming), which suggests not only stupor induced by excessive indulgence in alcohol but also a purposeless, decadent lifestyle. Didi starts the play by vowing to renew her struggle (*fendou*), go all out to achieve her life's dream; however, whatever symbolic potential the bar motif seems to embody, the play fails to tap into and develop to the fullest.

Is there anything homoerotic or homosocial (a preference for the company of members of one's own sex)[61] in the relationship between Didi and Gege in this production? Gege's warm gaze, full blast, on Didi in the opening scene as the latter, bent over the bar stool, wriggles her body frenziedly, the two gazing into each other's burning eyes, their faces inches apart in the other scenes, and the two dancing rather sensually together, neck to neck, etc., would seem to suggest something of the kind. In the original play, there is quite a bit of back and forth between Vladimir and Estragon over a carrot:[62]

> VLADIMIR: Do you want a carrot?
> ESTRAGON: Is that all there is?
> VLADIMIR: I might have some turnips.
> ESTRAGON: Give me a carrot. (*Vladimir rummages in his pockets, takes out a turnip and gives it to Estragon who takes a bite out of it. Angrily.*) It's a turnip!
> VLADIMIR: Oh pardon! I could have sworn it was a carrot. (*He rummages again in his pockets, finds nothing but turnips.*) All that's turnips. (*He rummages.*) You must have eaten the last. (*He rummages.*) Wait, I have it. (*He brings out a carrot and gives it to Estragon.*) There, dear fellow.
> (*Estragon wipes the carrot on his sleeve and begins to eat it.*) Make it last, that's the end of them.
> ESTRAGON: Fancy that. (*He raises what remains of the carrot by the stub of leaf, twirls it before his eyes.*) Funny, the more you eat the worse it gets.

Somehow, in the Ren Ming production, the carrot (whatever symbolic meaning it potentially carries in the original play is open to interpretation, of course) is replaced by an imaginary piece of banana shared by Didi and Gege, who chew slowly and deliberately as if to relish every bit of its taste and nourishment. Sometimes, a banana is just a banana, just as a carrot is just a carrot. In this case, though, the replacement of carrot with banana turns on the sensuality (or sexuality) of the scene full blast – whether it was intended or not and whether it was lost on the Chinese audiences or not.

A definite big loss in this production is Lucky being replaced by a female mannequin (missing her body from waist down), sitting in a bathtub, being dragged onto the stage by Pozzo. Lucky is now dumb throughout the play, and whatever thoughts she has in her head never get expressed. And gone is the important speech by Lucky in Act I, the heart and soul of the play perhaps, a scene in which the1987 Shanghai Theatre Academy production had invested quite a bit of energy and creativity to bring alive on the stage. The loss is hardly compensated by whatever symbolic meaning is gained by this mannequin Lucky, highly sexualized yet missing half of her sexual self, who seems to suffer from aphasia resulted from whatever trauma, physical, sociopolitical, or psychological this modern life – this modern city of Beijing – has inflicted on her.

This is how the play ends as envisioned by Beckett:[63]

> ESTRAGON: Well? Shall we go?
> VLADIMIR: Pull on your trousers.
> ESTRAGON: What?
> VLADIMIR: Pull on your trousers.
> ESTRAGON: You want me to pull off my trousers?
> VLADIMIR: Pull on your trousers.
> ESTRAGON: (*Realizing his trousers are down.*) True. (*He pulls up his trousers.*)
> VLADIMIR: Well? Shall we go?
> ESTRAGON: Yes, let's go. (*They do not move.*)

In the Ren Ming production, thanks to casting two female actors for the leading roles, the trousers falling down the ankles drama, whatever symbolic meaning it has (suggesting the naked vulnerability of humanity?) seems too provocative or downright titillating for the stage of the *fin de siècle* Beijing where the bold, the brash, and the shameless "strut and fret" just about anywhere. This is how the play ends in the Ren Ming extreme remake instead:

> DIDI: Everything of everything is dead. Except for the tree.
> GEGE: What kind of tree is it?
> DIDI: I don't know. Just a tree.
> GEGE: Why don't we hang ourselves.
> DIDI: With what?
> GEGE: You don't have a rope with you?
> DIDI: No.
>   (Gege pulls out an imaginary rope from the back pocket of her pants)
> DIDI: Too short.
> GEGE: You think we'll be here again tomorrow?
> DIDI: Yes.
> GEGE: Remind me then to bring a better rope.
> DIDI: Mmm.
> GEGE: Didi, we can't be like this any longer. It's better we went separate
>   ways.

DIDI: Let's hang ourselves tomorrow.
GEGE: What if Godot comes?
DIDI: Then we'll be saved.
GEGE: Let's go.
DIDI: Okay, let's go.
    (They return to their bar stools at opposite sides of the stage, sit down, and gaze toward each other.)
GEGE: Shall we go now?
DIDI: Okay, let's go.

And they do not go anywhere. They freeze in time and space as the same song sung by the same tenor that began the show shrills demonically accompanied by haunting, Halloween-like music, the dead tree hanging from ceiling spinning on.

A couple of months after Ren Ming's production, another, even more audacious, extreme remake of the Beckett play appeared on the stage in Beijing. Lin Zhaohua, never one to be afraid to push the boundaries, stated that his purpose for mounting this production was to "let the audiences hear the voices of *dashi* (big masters)."[64] In this case, it is a duet of two big masters or, rather, a "synquel" (synthesis sequel) of sort, for lack of a better term, that blends Chekhov's 1890 play *Three Sisters* (the story of Olga, Masha, Irina, who, feeling stuck in a small outlying town, forever talk about their dreams of returning to Moscow, but never do anything to make it happen) and Beckett's 1953 play *Waiting for Godot*. Did the Beijing theatergoers in 1998 hear, loud and clear, the voices of the two big masters in *Three Sisters· Waiting for Godot*, blended into one melodic and engaging duet?

As the curtain rises,[65] one sees a small island surrounded by water on all sides. On the island sit the three sisters, Olga, Masha, and Irina, with a metal frame overhead, suggesting of their home in this faraway place, or rather, metaphorically, an iron house, a prison of sort. The sisters talk about the first anniversary of their father's death and about their beloved Moscow, which they left 11 years ago in the month of May when beautiful flowers were blooming everywhere. About ten minutes into this reminiscing and commiserating, Vladimir breaks onto the scene through the water – kicking up quite a splash along the way – to switch on, so to speak, the Beckett half of the play. As if on cue, the light dims on the three sisters, who freeze into statuesque poses, buffered by an invisible cocoon from the outside world – from Vladimir who, center stage now, addresses an imaginary audience:

My whole life I can never make up my mind . . . now I have made up my mind. I say to myself: Vladimir, there are so many things you've not tried, so be rational. . . . I'll continue to struggle (*fendou*).

Light shines on stage right to reveal Estragon who sits on the floor, trying to remove his boots.

Five minutes into their bantering, Vladimir (played by well-known actor Pu Cunxin) and Estragon (played by Chen Jianbin) are interrupted by the 60-year-old army doctor Ivan Chebutykin (played by Wu Wenguang), who, perched on a tall platform stage right, calls out to Irina, the youngest of the Chekhovian sisters, to present her a gift for the anniversary of her christening. Irina thanks him for the gift but says it is too expensive. Then the army doctor (Wu) announces the arrival of Lieutenant Colonel Vershinin (also played by Pu Cunxin) from Moscow in the midst of a rather moody, lyric-less song. Lieutenant Colonel (Pu) talks to the three sisters *through* the bubble between the two parallel universes. He remembers them as little girls back in Moscow and now they are all grown up. As he carries on the affectionate conversation with the sisters, especially Masha, Lieutenant Colonel (Pu) moves around the island, making loud splashing noise in the water, but never crosses over and gets onto the island. Neither do the sisters ever attempt even one step off the island. Apparently, the wall that separates them is as real as is invisible.

A few minutes later, Estragon (Chen), after getting some sleep offstage, staggers back, interrupts, and, in a wink of eye, Lieutenant Colonel (Pu) is Vladimir (Pu) again, and the three sisters, once again, freeze into a statuesque tableau in the backdrop. Vladimir (Pu) and Estragon (Chen) hear music playing in the air and wonder aloud what it is. One of the sisters, as if having heard them talking, answers that it's their brother Andrey playing, who dreams of becoming a professor in Moscow.

This pretty much establishes the seesaw, back-and-forth pattern of dramatic action as the "synquel" unfolds: Pu Cunxin (Vladimir/Lieutenant Colonel), Chen Jianbin (Estragon/Baron Tuzenbach, a lieutenant hopelessly in love with Irina and later killed in a duel), and Wu Wenguang (60-year-old army doctor/ the boy messenger for Godot) trot between the two parallel universities in their dual roles, weaving tenuously (at the best) related characters – their dreams, frustrations, existential crises, and despair – into an absurd interstellar story around the motif (or theme) of "waiting." Occasionally, some of the lines spoken by the characters send echoes down earth with unmistakable references to morality and other social issues facing today's China – perhaps to reward, comfort, or placate audiences fidgeting in their seats, perplexed.

The "synquel" ends with Vladimir (Pu) and Estragon (Chen) downstage, discussing how to hang themselves (the trousers element was not sacrificed in this production): they stand there gazing at the two-foot small, dead tree and wonder aloud, "What exactly have we been talking about?" Behind them are the three sisters, statuesque, forever stranded in their little island. The same haunting voice of a tenor rises like a tidal wave submerging the Chekhovian and Beckett-esque universes, each continuing in its own orbit, as if they had never crossed paths.

Would compressing two classics, each considerably truncated (e.g., Pozzo and Lucky were cut from the *Waiting for Godot* portion of this production) into one "synquel" necessarily make it a classic in and of itself, or simply, a worthy experiment, at least? Beckett would most certainly not be pleased to see his play being intermixed into this audacious Chinese remake while what Chekhov would say could be anyone's guess. Some Chinese drama enthusiasts did hear the two big masters "dueling" it out loud and clear and were enchanted with the ingenuity of Lin Zhaohua and his team. They felt enlightened by the polyphonic, dialogic quest for the meaning of human existence as presented by this production.[66] Many others, however, scratched their heads and didn't know what to make of it.[67]

Some of those disenchanted and underwhelmed had come to the show out of sheer curiosity and regretted having come at all by intermission time, so they did not return to their seats. One of them, a high school student, said, when interviewed,

> I've heard in school how good the *Three Sisters* is, a Chekhov classic, and have heard of *Waiting for Godot* too, really famous. Now that I have seen it, I feel really bad. Perhaps *huaju* is just like that, but I couldn't sit there a minute longer. Perhaps my level is too low to understand such highbrow art. So perhaps I should not have come at all.

A much older man and long-time theatre enthusiast said, "I've seen many *huaju* performances by People's Art, but have never seen anything as baffling. Should not have bothered to come." One college student who had the benefit of having read both plays before couldn't help dozing off several times during the performance, but decided to stick to the end "to accumulate understanding of such new kind of *huaju*. . . . otherwise I would have come for nothing."

Hearing such comments relayed to him by journalists during the after-show discussion, Lin Zhaohua said he didn't want to pamper or cajole the audiences too much:

> I can't always be led by their tastes and habits. True this production is way ahead of the audiences. In art creations I am never fond of touchy-feely things. My drama works require audiences to use their brains. I am partial to works that let people think on their own.

However, even a Central Academy of Drama professor, who is supposed to be able to think competently about matters of drama/theatre, didn't quite get it either:

> What does it mean when a play does not engage the audiences? It means the audiences never get into the play and never communicate with you. A play propped up by sheer action can never have any impact on the audiences. That's why I feel we should establish connections with the audiences and give them a key for understanding.

Waiting for Godot *and* Endgame *(2000s)*

A thumbs-down for the Lin and other Chinese remakes of *Waiting for Godot* came a few years later from German theatre artist Walter D. Asmus who had worked with Beckett from 1974 until Beckett's death in 1989. Asmus felt that the Chinese adaptations, hip as they were in their modern, city, and hybrid versions, went for the excitement but missed the real, quintessential Beckett and therefore misled the audiences. For him, the most important thing in any Beckett adaptation and production was to convey the original intended meaning of the play and to lead the audiences into the spiritual world as envisioned and created by Beckett. Asmus recognized that Beckett is difficult even for Western theatergoers – some would leave too before it is over – let alone Chinese theatergoers with a very different language, culture, and drama traditions. However, Asmus felt that it'd be worth it even if only one among the 10,000 could truly appreciate and find emotive and intellectual resonances in the production. In this regard, at least, he and Lin Zhaohua are not that much different although one is an uncompromising purist when it comes to the classics and the other takes an "all is fair game" attitude.[68]

In 2005, Asmus took the Gate Theatre's *Waiting for Godot* to Beijing and Shanghai. It was an eye-opening experience for many Chinese theatergoers to see an "authentic" Beckett performed by artists from his hometown Dublin. It was also a "mind-boggling" experience too even for the well cultured among the audiences despite the aid of projected subtitles. Nonetheless, it gave them a frame of reference to look back on the Chinese adaptations of the play and found that audacious as those endeavors were they had merely scratched the surface of the play.[69]

Asmus visited China again in 2006 during the Beckett Drama Festival (Shanghai) as part of the program to celebrate the centennial birthday of a dramatist whose name is so well known in China by now but remains as impenetrable as ever before. The festival featured Gate Theatre's performances of Beckett's *Molloy* and *A Piece of Monologue*; *Deng dao geduo* (Godot Cometh, an extreme adaptation by students of Shanghai International Studies University, which attempts to address the question: What happens if Godot does come?);[70] *Waiting for Guotuo*, a *jingju* adaptation of *Waiting for Godot* produced by theatre artists from Taiwan;[71] and a Sino-German joint production of *Endgame* directed by Asmus with Chinese cast and crew.

If Becket's plays such as *Waiting for Godot*, even in their Chinese renditions, remain a puzzle for most Chinese theatergoers, Asmus did not seem to experience any difficulty directing a Chinese production of *Endgame* with a Chinese crew and cast. For Asmus, Beckett is like Bach, who is universal and therefore transcends languages, so much so that he could understand and appreciate the "notes," so to speak, even when they are embodied and delivered in a language he does not speak. During his stay in Shanghai, Asmus often wandered around in streets and alleys alone, without an interpreter, to see and feel the hustle and bustle of this colossal cosmopolitan city firsthand in its most raw and living present. When it was time for supper, he would find his way into a small, homespun eatery, order food from a menu he couldn't read and servers he couldn't understand by way of drawing cow, chicken, and a few leaves (not unlike the new leaves appearing on the tree for Act II of *Waiting for Godot*?), and then settle down to enjoy his the meal. Language seemed a luxury not necessary for survival and essential human interactions. However, when it came to rehearsal, Asmus was as particular and demanding as could be. Sometimes, to get a single line or dialog right, Asmus would ask the young actors to do it again and again, for 5 minutes, 10 minutes, 20 minutes, until it rang authentic and perfect in pitch to his ear – e.g., the dialog about the dog – whether he is white or not.

> HAMM: He's white, isn't he?
> CLOV: Nearly.
> HAMM: What do you mean, nearly? Is he white or isn't he?
> CLOV: He isn't.

"Rhythm, rhythm," Asmus would remind the young actors:

> Is he white or isn't he? Has to be clear and forceful. He isn't, don't drag it out, needs to be clean. And the tone, you have to pay attention to your tone, a mix of frustration and defiance.

Asmus was also concerned that the actors seemed to lose their focus every now and then:

> Our rehearsal is like the weather in Shanghai, unpredictable. Now it is fine and now it is cloudy. It sees extremely difficult for the actors to have sustained attention. Perhaps it's because everyone is so tense and nervous that they get tired easily. In reality rehearsing a play is just like playing a game, to get a feel of the play. You'll not lose your focus if you are really into playing the game.

He was not too pleased with Shanghai theatergoers either, who have a bad habit of leaving their smartphones on during the show: the frequent eruption of ring tones during the show disturbed the actors on stage and ruined the experience for those who didn't just show up, but wanted to enjoy the show. For one drama scholar at least, the musicality of this production directed by Asmus was as enchanting as its probe into the nature of being was honest and illuminating.[72] Asmus, and indeed, Beckett, would be pleased to know.

To rekindle the dream: Arthur Miller and *Death of a Salesman* in Beijing

In the fall of 1978, a group of American tourists were visiting China, one of the first such groups visiting from America for quite some time. Ying

Ruocheng (1929–2003), who had recently returned to the People's Art Theatre after a stint in jail and years of reeducation through labor during the Cultural Revolution (1966–1976), heard through the grapevine that Arthur Miller, an American playwright he had been fascinated with since his college days in the 1940s, was in this group of American tourists. Ying told the informant, "Track him down for me, and don't let him get out of sight." He then relayed this exciting news to Cao Yu (1910–1996), author of some of the most important modern Chinese plays such as *Thunderstorm* (1933), *Sunrise* (1935), and *Wilderness* (1936), who had suffered his share of ordeal during the Cultural Revolution and recently reassumed directorship of the People's Art Theatre. Ying and Cao began an earnest hunt for Arthur Miller all over Beijing and eventually found him (feeling a bit lost in a big city of eight million people) at the hotel where the American tourists were staying.[73]

This was not a scene from the heyday of the "ping-pong diplomacy" in the early 1970s that would lead to Richard Nixon's historical visit to China in February 1972 and open a new chapter in the US-China relations. Neither was Arthur Miller, along with his photographer wife, Inge Morath, sent to China by Jimmy Carter as a special envoy to finalize the exact terms whereby the two countries would reestablish formal diplomatic ties on January 1, 1979. Arthur Miller's was a visit by a private citizen with no official mission, covert or public. Nonetheless, this visit turned out to be quite a significant event – at least as far as the subject of this book is concerned.

Miller's interest in China went back to the 1930s when, as a young and aspiring theatre artist, names of Chinese Communist leaders such Mao Zedong, Zhou Enlai, and Zhu De "were like flares shot into the sky out of a human sea . . . prophesying the dawn of reason and liberty in Asia."[74] For a while, Miller also enjoyed friendship with Edgar Snow (1905–1972), read his 1937 book *Red Star over China* about Mao, other top leaders of the Chinese Communist revolution, and the Long March (1934–1935), and thought it was "the best single piece of reportage I have ever read, and surely among the most influential ever written." However, the promise of "a new stage in human development" never materialized thanks to, among other things, the fanatic "factionalism" that had never let up since the Communist victory in 1949. So Miller, disillusioned, had remained disengaged, leaving "Chinese politics to the Chinese," until this 1978 visit – to rekindle an interest that had long faded, to see firsthand, in his own eyes, and to listen, "how it was at the particular moment when the dust of the temple began to settle,"[75] and when China was picking itself up and trying to move forward again.

Did he pack with him any idea of writing a play about China, about the Cultural Revolution (along the lines of *The Crucible*), or one day returning to Beijing and mounting one of his plays on the Chinese stage? Whatever the answer might be, the unexpected new friendship with Ying Ruocheng and Cao Yu meant drastic change of itinerary: Miller, along with Inge Morath, left the tourist group and went on a special tour of the country on their own, "curated" by his resourceful new Chinese friends. Their one-week visit, as originally planned, stretched to almost a full month, filled with talks with Chinese writers and artists who had been deeply scarred by the Cultural Revolution and many chance encounters with ordinary Chinese. He even got to see a play written by Guo Moruo (1892–1978), an important figure in modern Chinese cultural history, and offered his honest and less than flattering opinion. It was during this visit that a general idea of cooperation, to mount an Arthur Miller play in Beijing, was seeded although the choice of play would have to be "negotiated" in 1980 when Cao Yu and Ying Ruocheng took Lao She's play *Teahouse* to the United States and again in 1982 when Ying Ruocheng was a visiting scholar at the University of Missouri-Kansas City.

The story of Arthur Miller and his *Death of a Salesman* in Beijing has been well told by Miller himself in his 1983 book *Salesman in Beijing*.[76] A few salient points pertinent to the subject of this book are worth revisiting here. Although the play was directed by Arthur Miller himself, the entire production, from beginning to end, from initiation of the project to choice of play to translation to acting to decisions such as whether to cut "Requiem," was a suspense-filled process of transcultural and translingual, as well as political "negotiations" in the context of post-Cultural Revolution China. It was as much a "magical confluence of history's unaccountable accidents" (to borrow from Miller) as a full-hearted partnership, of concerted endeavors of Ying, Miller, and the cast and crew that made *Death of a Salesman* a dream come true in Beijing in the spring of 1983.

Given what had happened during the Cultural Revolution, Arthur Miller at first suggested *The Crucible*, his 1953 play about the Salem witch trials (1692–1693) written as an allegory of McCarthyism (1950–1956). After all, like Bertolt Brecht before him, Miller had had to appear before the House of Representatives' Committee on Un-American Activities in 1956 and, for his refusal to betray like-minded artists, was convicted of contempt of Congress.[77] What happened in the Cultural Revolution, Ying told Miller, were bygones and had already had its share of artistic and literary expressions in the so-called wound literature and in domestic plays such as *Shuguang* (Dawn), *Yu wu sheng chu* (Thunder in the Silence), and *Danxin pu* (Loyal Heart Song), as well as Brecht's *Life of Galileo* alluded to earlier. Indeed, during his 1978 China visit, Miller had recommended *The Crucible* to Huang Zuolin in Shanghai, who took it on in 1981 and mounted it under the new Chinese title *Salamu de nüwu* (Salem's Witches). It had a successful run of 52 performances, with long lines at the box office stretching several blocks, its story striking a chord with so many Chinese theatergoers who had survived the nightmare of the Cultural Revolution.[78]

Ying Ruocheng, on his part, had dreamed of one day mounting *Death of a Salesman* on the Chinese stage since his college days at Qinghua University when he first read the play. For him, this play represented something new, especially in its artistic aspects – its use of expressionist techniques to effect fluidity of time and space to capture fully Willy Loman's dogged pursuit of the American dream. Interesting enough, that fluidity of time and space had worried Joshua Logan back in 1953, a financier for the original Broadway production, so much so that he "urged" Miller to "remove Uncle Ben and all the elements of Willy's hallucinatory life because the audience would be hopelessly uncertain whether they were in the past or the present."[79] Logan had probably forgotten that a similar expressionistic fluidity of time and space did not confuse the audiences of Eugene O'Neill's *The Emperor Jones* (1920) and hinder its successful run on the Broadway.

For Miller, the misgivings about *Death of Salesman* stayed with him two full weeks into the rehearsal:[80]

> Why was *Salesman* chosen? Was it as propaganda against the American way of life? Is it really possible for the Chinese to relate to the very American situation and to Willy Loman's character? Do Chinese actors work differently from Americans in creating their roles? Is the humor likely to register? Are there really any parallels in Chinese society? Will the production be closed to the public, and with "certain strata" let in and see it?

Like anything else between the United States and China, (geo)politics never leaves the room and if it does, occasionally, it never stays far away. On April 5, about three weeks into the rehearsal, an incident flared up that almost derailed the whole project: the United States government granted political asylum to Hu Na, a young Chinese tennis player who had defected a year before while touring California as member of a Chinese tennis team. In retaliation, the Chinese government announced it would sever all cultural and artistic ties between the two countries. On April 6, *Xinhua* (New China News) published a piece describing *Death of a Salesman* as "a condemnation of monopoly capitalism."

Fortunately, saner heads prevailed despite tough stands taken by both sides – e.g., some American politicians talking about "derecogniz(ing)" China. Miller's Chinese colleagues were supportive and steadfast despite the hoopla. He knew that "everyone around the production wants the play to be received and felt as a human document applicable to China." On April 22, two weeks before the opening night, another piece that appeared in *Beijing Daily* about the "press run-through" of *Death of Salesman* made no mention of "monopoly capitalism"[81] – an auspicious sign.

Outside of politics, one big, persistent concern of Miller's was "whether and how much the Chinese audience could understand Western plays after so many years of such complete isolation."[82] After all, over 90% of the Chinese had been living in an agrarian society and probably had never heard of terms such as salesman and insurance policies, let alone having experienced them as facts of life. Moreover, anything other than traditional Chinese or realistic theatre, such as expressionism, would appear and sound alien to most of them. Miller believed, paradoxically, that the way to make it work, "to make this play most American is to make it most Chinese." Instead of the political theatre and "alienation effect" aimed for by the Brechtian drama/theatre, Miller asked the actors to work on being "emotionally true" to their characters, so much so that they eventually arrived at a place where they were simply "the Lomans-as-Chinese-looking-people."[83] They should not "pretend" to look American with use of false big noses, wigs, or any such props. Willy's dream for his sons' success, as one young actor put it, is "very Chinese" because the Chinese father "always wants his sons to be 'dragons.'"[84] To help the Chinese Biff to effectively channel the full emotional intensity of the father-son relations, Miller evoked the Cultural Revolution ordeal, which he had heard so much about during his 1978 visit and was still hearing about it now:[85]

> It's like the dilemma of the Cultural Revolution. Jiang Qing's leadership was also full of self-deluded demands on you, wasn't it? . . . She also claimed to be acting out of devotion to China, and that may have been what she felt, for all we know. Just like Willy, who believes he is trying to help you, not himself.

Not a neat analogy, but it worked.

A key factor in mounting any foreign plays on the stage is translation of the script from the source language and culture to the target language and culture, with particular sensitivity and attendance to performance on the stage – i.e., speakability and adaptability.[86] In this regard, Miller, and indeed *Death of Salesman*, could not have found a more ideal translator than Ying Ruocheng himself, fluent in both English and Chinese and a talented actor himself, "a man of double consciousness," to quote Miller, "Eastern and Western, literary and show business."[87] Ying, who had grown up in Beijing, chose to render the 1940s Brooklyn speech of the Lomans into the 1940s speech of native Beijingers, reproducing the same lengths and rhythms, "the flows to the peaks and the slopes toward the silences."[88]

Despite precarious geopolitics, real and hyped socioeconomic and cultural differences (e.g., there was not "a salesman the length or breadth of China," as described in a *Newsweek* report, which Miller dismissed as sheer "American snobbery"),[89] and serious logistics challenges (e.g., electricity, lighting, sound system), let alone vastly different drama traditions and audiences' tastes and habits, *Death of Salesman* in Beijing turned out to be quite a success.

On the night of the first review, the audiences, mostly young people, some having brought their children, were noisy by Western standard, but they followed the performance, understood, and applauded before "dashing out of the theatre at high speed to catch the last buses of the night" home; otherwise, they would have to walk home, wherever home is in this colossal city of the nation's capital. The audiences for the second preview were more "sophisticated," mostly editors, authors, artists, and academics, including Cao Yu, who had "fought hard to bring *Salesman* here as an opening to the modern world for Chinese actors and audiences."[90] Nobody left when the performance was over. The audiences applauded enthusiastically, something the Chinese rarely do.

The opening night on May 7 was attended by eager Chinese as well as Americans (American ambassador, journalists, TV crews, etc.) and other Westerners in Beijing. Ying Ruocheng and his actors owned their roles. The Americans understood it: "It comes over in Chinese!," enthused Ambassador Hummel. The Chinese understood it too because, as a young man interviewed by the producer of the Bill Moyers television show about this production said, China is "full of Willys, dreamers of the dream" too.[91] Miller, who had been worried about possible "politicization" of this play, couldn't help register a mental note of the historical irony: back in the 1950s, the US State Department denied him a passport to travel to Europe for the opening of *The Crucible* in Belgium (on account of his alleged un-American activities), yet today one of his plays is the United States' sole cultural contact with China – a "communist" country with whom its relations are hitting a low.[92]

The significance of *Death of Salesman* in Beijing, of course, reaches far and beyond geopolitics and Sino-American relations. Along with Brecht, Beckett, and other Western classics adapted on the Chinese stage in the decades following the Cultural Revolution, it helped transform the drama/theatre scene of China and, indeed, cultural life forever.

The so-called Brechtian fever (*bulaixite re*) first hit China in a couple of wavelets in the 1950s–1960s, pushed by Huang Zuolin, who directed the 1959 adaptation of *Mother Courage and Her Children*. The tidal wave of this feverish development, however, came in the late 1970s and early 1980s, when the Chinese artists, driven by a sense of crisis, were looking for an alternative to the realist mode that had dominated in the arts and literature scene since the May Fourth (1919) era. They found Brecht a natural fit artistically and politically, and embraced him enthusiastically. "The Brechtian fever" began to cool off in the late 1990s as artists and scholars began to take stock and ask questions.[93] Some scholars argued that the Brechtian theatre, originated from a desire to challenge classic Aristotelian theatre (its ideals of mimesis and catharsis), is more sociological (political) than artistic, and that its application is not universal, as has been misunderstood, especially in China, but limited to comedy. The Chinese, these scholars argued, saw the Brechtian theatre as an intermediate link between the Stanislavski system and the traditional Chinese *xiqu*, or, rather, they used the Brechtian theatre as a tool to break through the ironclad dominance of a narrow, twisted version of the Ibsenesque, Stanislavski realism and to inject new life into the impoverished Chinese drama and theatre. They went in for the techniques while neglecting its essential critical attitude and social engagement and in the process turned the Brechtian theatre into a new dogma.[94]

Finding its way into this ferment development in the decade immediately after the Cultural Revolution, when Chinese drama/theatre was restlessly redefining and reorienting itself, was the so-called absurdity fever (*huang-dan re*) although what it offered was more a worldview than a new drama/

theatre "system," as had been the case with Stanislavski or Brecht. Fascinating as he is, Beckett will perhaps remain a puzzle to most Chinese theatergoers for a long time to come as he is elsewhere in other parts of the world, including the West.

Miller's *Death of Salesman* in Beijing, on the other hand, is as much a notable cultural event, as the United States and China were still learning how to live with their newly normalized relations as an eye-opening experience for the Chinese theatre artists as well as Miller himself. Just as Miller's play blends realism and expressionism in telling a story that is as universal as American, its successful mounting in Beijing in 1983 serves as a useful lesson in how to do it right when it comes to adapting Western classics for the Chinese stage, or adapting any foreign plays for domestic audiences.

Despite all the "misreading" and perhaps "misguided" appropriation, as suggested by some cool-headed scholars recently, it would be hard to imagine the drama and theatre scene in China in the decades following the Cultural Revolution without the introduction, translation, and, indeed, adaptation of Western classics such as Brecht, Beckett, and Miller on the Chinese stage. Indeed, it would be hard to imagine plays such as *Bus Stop* (*Chezhan*) (1983), *Uncle Doggie's Nirvana* (*Gouerye niepan*) (1986), *Pan Jinlian* (1986), *The Story of Sangshuping* (*Sangshuping jishi*) (1988), etc., notable accomplishments in the endeavors to revive modern Chinese drama/stage.[95]

Notes

1 *Shuguang* (Dawn): a 1977 six-act play about the legendary General He Long (1896–1969) during the difficult years of the early 1930s, his fight against both the Russia-supported ultra-leftist leadership of the Communist Party, and the Exterminating Campaigns of the Nationalist (Guomindang) government.

   Yu wu sheng chu (Thunder in the Silence): a 1978 play set in the early summer of 1976, right after the Gang of Four orchestrated crackdown of the April 5 Movement (tens of thousands of people gathered on the Tiananmen Square to mourn the death of Premier Zhou Enlai and voice their anger at the Gang of Four).

   Danxin pu (Loyal Heart Song): set in early 1976, this 1978 play features an old traditional Chinese medicine doctor who, inspired by the blessings from Premier Zhou Enlai, devotes himself to researching and finding the cure for coronary artery disease.

   Bao chun hua (Primrose; Spring Harbinger): a 1979 play featuring a newly appointed factory general manger and Party Secretary Li Jian, who, despite stubborn resistance from his deputy party secretary, sets his sight on real quality production by deemphasizing the old ideology of class struggle.

   Jiaru wo shi zhen de (If I Were for Real): in this 1979 play, based on a real-life event, Li Xiaozhang, a *zhiqing* (sent-down youth), returns to Shanghai to visit his pregnant girlfriend, and taking advantage of an opportunity that presents itself, pretends to be son of a high-ranking official from Beijing. When this impromptu scheme is exposed, and his luck runs out, Li is arrested and before he kills himself in jail, Li writes these words on the wall: "If I Were for Real."

2 "Two Whatevers." https://en.wikipedia.org/wiki/Two_Whatevers.

3 See Shi Yan, "*Zhengyi shi ruhe yinfa de*" (How the Controversy Started).

4 Shouhua Qi, "Misreading Ibsen," 344.

5 See "Stanislavsky system."
6 Shouhua Qi, *Western Literature*, 91–2.
7 See Zhang Ming'ai.
8 See Daniel Yang.
9 Two years later in 1981, students of Shanghai Theatre Academy also performed an adaptation of *Guess Who's Coming for Dinner*. See Ding Jiasheng.
10 See Zhu Hong.
11 This portion of the discussion draws from Hu Xingliang, 197–218.
12 For a study of the introduction and reception of Brecht in China from the 1930s to the late 1970s, see Adrian Hsia.
13 See Min Tian.
14 See Min Tian, Ronnie Bai, and Haun Saussy.
15 See Bertolt Brecht.
16 See Wei Zhang: "Adapting Brecht's *The Good Person of Szechwan*."
17 See Lin Kehuan.
18 See Zhang Li.
19 See Zhou Xian.
20 Summary of the play is based on Du Xuan.
21 See Yao Jiaying.
22 The role of Mother Courage is challenging even for actors as brilliant and accomplished as Meryl Streep when she channeled the "hyena of the battlefield" in a 2006 production in Central Park, New York, to fully achieve the desired political theatre effect as the Iraq War was still dragging on. See reviews by Ben Brantley and Jeremy McCarter, respectively.
23 See Xiaomei Chen.
24 See Chapter 2 of this book.
25 See Ben Brantley.
26 See Huang Zuolin.
27 Liu Minghou, 31–2, 56.
28 Ding's translation was published in January 1980 by Henan People's Press. The 231-page book includes photos from the 1979 production, a preface from Huang Zuolin, Ding's full-text translation of the play and Brecht's own notes, and two essays on the play and the German playwright respectively, both by Ding.
29 See Gao Yin, "*Xin shidai bujia fenshi de tuxiang*" (Unbeautified Pictures of the New Age).
30 See Huang Zuolin.
31 Gao Yin, "*Xin shidai bujia fenshi de tuxiang*" (Unbeautified Pictures of the New Age), 59.
32 See Lu Eng.
33 Huang Zuolin, 124.
34 Gao Yin, "*Xin shidai bujia fenshi de tuxiang*" (Unbeautified Pictures of the New Age), 59.
35 For more on this debate and Huang Zuolin's idea of new drama/theatre, see Hu Xingliang, 197–406.
36 Lin Kehuan, 70.
37 Gao Yin, "*Xin shidai bujia fenshi de tuxiang*" (Unbeautified Pictures of the New Age), 59; Cao Tiliang.
38 Lin Kehuan, 71.
39 See Qi Jianmin; Xiong Zhu.
40 See Tao Yu.
41 Apparent combination of two names, Yu Jie and Jiao Guobiao, two independent writers, and dissidents originally based at Beijing University, who were associated with the "Tonight I Am an American" (or "One night American") public hoopla thanks to their public expression of sympathy to America in response to the 911

terrorist attack (In one stanza of a Jiao's poem he says: If I can be born again, I'd want to be an American GI; If I am doomed to die in war, I'd like to be the ghost of American precision missiles.") See Zhao Zhiyong. This portion of the discussion also draws from Gao Yin, "*Beijing*" (The Good Person of Beijing's), and Shi Yan.

42 "*Beijing quju.*" http://baike.baidu.com/view/180607.htm.
43 A hymn-like song that idealizes and indeed idolizes Mao Zedong (1893–1976) as the savior of China. Written in the 1940s, this song reached its feverish pitch – enjoying the status of the *de facto* anthem of China – during the Cultural Revolution (1966–1976). It has since faded into museum archives although its tune and lyrics would still strike some nostalgic or other emotive chords with many people, especially those who lived through the turbulent, frenzied mid-century decades of modern Chinese history.
44 See Zhao Zhiyong and Shi Yan.
45 The term Jiangnan refers to the southern Yangtze River region, typically including Shanghai and large portions of Jiangsu and Zhejiang provinces.
46 This portion of the discussion draws from Zhao Zhiyong, Fang Qijun, and Chen Xiangyuan and Hu Cheng.
47 See George Lukacs; Terry Eagleton, 27–31.
48 This portion of the discussion draws from Wang Yangwen and Tian Depei, Chen Zengrong, and Song Xuezhi and Xu Jun.
49 See Chen Jialin.
50 Samuel Beckett, 42–3.
51 See Wang Yangwen and Tian Depei.
52 For a manifesto of sorts of Frog Experimental Theatre, see Meng Jinghui, "*Wa shiyan jutuan zhi guanzhong*" (To Theatergoers).
53 Meng Jinghui, *Xianfeng xiju dangan* (Avant-Garde Theatre Archives), 46–7.
54 Ibid, 405.
55 Ibid, 393.
56 See Meng Jinghui, "*Shiyan xiju Dengdai geduo zai Bolin*" (Experimental play *Waiting for Godot* in Berlin).
57 "*The Haus der Kulturen der Welt.*" www.hkw.de/en/hkw/ueberuns/Ueber_uns.php.
58 Based on DVD of the production published in 2011. See Ren Ming.
59 See Jiao Er.
60 Ibid.
61 See Yates.
62 Beckett, 21–2.
63 Beckett, 88.
64 See Qu Peihui.
65 Based on Lin Zhaohua, *Lin Zhaohua xiju zuopin ji* (Collection of Lin Zhaohua Dramatic Works). DVD, 2012.
66 See Qu Peihui and Yu Hua.
67 See Wang Lei.
68 This portion of the discussion draws from Chen Bing, Song Shi, and Wei Zhang.
69 See Tao Zi.
70 This adaptation tries to answer the question "what happens if Godot does come?" In this production, set in a park literature themed park, two college students, where two workers act in the roles of Vladimir and Estragon to entertain tourists. Then come a male and a female Godot respectively, perhaps, so the two young workers murder the two Godots in order to keep their jobs. Finally, "Samuel Beckett," arrives, there comes an old man with a cigar in his mouth, and he likes how the title *Waiting for Godot* sounds and decides it will be the next play he will write. See "*Dengdai geduo*" (When Godot Cometh) and Ran Li.
71 See Zhu Xuefeng.

72 See Wei Zhang, "*Ganchu Beikete.*"
73 See Ying Ruocheng and Claire Conceison, 157–69.
74 Miller, "In China," 91.
75 Ibid.
76 See also Claire Concesion.
77 Miller, *Timebends*, 328–35.
78 In 2006, to celebrate the centennial birthday of Huang Zuolin, Shanghai Dramatic Arts Center (formerly Shanghai People's ArtTheatre) mounted another production of *The Crucible* under the same Chinese title, directed by Huang's grandson Zheng Dasheng, a film director directing a stage play for the first time. See "*Chong pai Salemu nüwu*" (Remounting Salem's Witches). In 2002, The National Theatre of China (*Zhongguo guojia huaju yuan*) also mounted a production of the play and then again in 2015, with the same director (Wang Xiaoying) and cast members. One theatergoer who saw the 2015 production felt it still resonated today because "in this day and age we still have the same hysteria of the masses and the same groundless accusations." See Zhang Hui .
79 Miller, *Salesman in Beijing*, 24.
80 Ibid, 43–4.
81 Ibid, 171.
82 Ibid, vi.
83 Ibid, 5, 172.
84 Ibid, 7.
85 Ibid, 80.
86 See Kevin Windle.
87 Miller, *Salesman in Beijing*, 240.
88 Ibid, 19.
89 Ibid.
90 Ibid, 216.
91 Ibid, 245.
92 Ibid, 250.
93 See Chen Shixiong, 313–42.
94 See Wang Xiaohua; and Zhou Xian.
95 See Shiao-ling S. Yu.

Bibliography

Bai, Ronnie. "Dances With Mei Lanfang: Brecht and the Alienation Effect." *Comparative Drama* 32, no. 3 (Fall 1998): 389–433.

Bao chun hua (Primrose; Spring Harbinger). www.baike.com/wiki/%E3%80%8A%E6%8A%A5%E6%98%A5%E8%8A%B1%E3%80%8B.

Beckett, Samuel. *The Complete Dramatic Works*. London: Faber and Faber, 1990.

"*Beijing quju.*" http://baike.baidu.com/view/180607.htm.

Brantley, Ben. "Mother, Courage, Grief and Song." *The New York Times*, August 22, 2006. www.nytimes.com/2006/08/22/theater/reviews/22moth.html?_r=0.

Brecht, Bertolt. "Alienation Effects in Chinese Acting," in *Brecht on Theatre: The Development of an Aesthetic*. Edited and translated by John Willett. New York: Hill and Wang, 1964, 91–9.

Cao, Tiliang. "Guan Gaojiasuo huilan ji" (Seeing The Caucasian Chalk Circle). Xijubao (Drama Gazette) 6 (1985): 19.

Chen, Bing. "*Fei zhongju jiedu Bekete*" (Not an Endgame Interpretation of Beckett). *Xinmin zhoukan* (Xinmin Weekly), April 7, 2005.

Chen, Jialin. "*Gengxin xiju guannian, tuokuan daoyan jiaoxue lingyu: Huangdan-pai mingju Dengdai geduo paiyan jiaoxue xiaojie*" (Renew Xiju Concepts, Widen Directing Curriculum: Summarizing Thoughts on Teaching and Rehearsal of Famous Theatre of the Absurd Play *Waiting for Godot*). *Xiju yishu* (Theatre Arts) 2 (1987): 68–73.

Chen, Shixiong. *Sanjiao duihua: Sitanni, Bulaixite, and Zhongguo xiju* (Triangle Dialogues: Stanislavsky, Brecht, and Chinese Drama). Xiammen, Fujian: Xiamen University Press, 2003.

Chen, Xiaomei. *Acting the Right Part: Political Theater and Popular Drama in Contemporary China*. Honolulu, HI: University of Hawaii Press, 2002.

———. "A Stage in Search of a Tradition: The Dynamics of Form and Content in Post-Maoist Theatre." *Asian Theatre Journal* 18, no. 2 (Autumn, 2001): 200–21.

Chen, Xiangyuan, and Hu Cheng. "*Xiju gaige ying shenzhong 'Jianli': Cong yueju Jiangnan haoren fansi Bulaixite 'Jianli' lilun de zhongguo hua*" (Drama Reform Should Be Cautious: Reflections on Sinicization of Brecht's 'Alienation Effect' Theory as Evidenced in the *yueju* Remake *The Good Person of Jiangnan*). *Fujian luntan* (Fujian Tribune) 11 (2013): 117–21.

Chen, Zengrong. "*Huangdanpai xiju zai zhongguo de yijie, yanjiu yu chuanbo*" (Translation, Research, and Spread of the Theatre of the Absurd in China). *Xiju wenxue* (Drama Literature) 5 (2010): 15–19.

"*Chong pai Salemu nüwu: Liu tai ju jinian Huang Zuolin bainian danchen*" (Remounting *Salem's Witches*: Six Plays to Celebrate Huang Zuolin Centennial Birthday). *Shanghai Youth*, September 7, 2006. http://ent.sina.com.cn.

Conceison, Claire. "Introduction," in *Death of a Salesman' in Beijing*. Edited by Arthur Miller, 2nd ed. London: Bloomsbury Methuen Drama, 2015, viii–xxxii.

Danxin pu (Loyal Heart Song). www.baike.com/wiki/%E3%80%8A%E4%B8%B9%E5%BF%83%E8%B0%B1%E3%80%8B.

"*Dengdai geduo*" (When Godot Cometh). www.baike.com/wiki/%E7%AD%89%E5%88%B0%E6%88%88%E5%A4%9A.

Ding, Jiasheng. "*Beijing huamian de biaoxianxing*: Cai yi cai shui lai chi wangcan sheji gousi" (Expressiveness in the Backdrop: Stage Design for *Guess Who's Coming for Dinner*). *Xiju yishu* (Theatre Arts) 1 (1982): 101–6.

Du, Xuan, et al. "*Kangmei yuangchao dahuobao*" (Resisting the US Aggressions and Aiding Korea Big Skit). *Xin wenyi chubanshe* (New Art and Literature Press), 1952.

Eagleton, Terry. *Marxism and Literary Criticism*. Berkley, CA and Los Angeles, CA: University of California Press, 1976.

Fang, Qijun. "*Wunong ruanyu de Bulaixiete: Xin gainian yueju Jiangnan haoren guanhou*" (Brecht in Soft-speaking Jiangnan Accent: Thoughts on New Concept *yueju* Adaptation *The Good Person of Jiangnan*). *Ningbo tongxun* (Ningbo News Report) 8 (2013): 58–61.

Gao, Yin. "*Beijing haoren dui Bulaixiete de dangdai chanshi*" (The Good Person of Beijing's Contemporary Interpretation of Brecht). *Xiju yishu* (Theatre Arts) 6 (2011): 11–16.

———. "*Xin shidai bujia fenshi de tuxiang: Bei zhongguo yanchu de Jialilue zhuan*" (Unbeautified Pictures of the New Age: *Life of Galileo* as Performed in China). *Zhongguo xiju* (Chinese Drama) 9 (2012): 58–61.

"*The Haus der Kulturen der Welt.*" www.hkw.de/en/hkw/ueberuns/Ueber_uns.php.

Hsia, Adrian. "Bertolt Brecht in China and His Impact on Chinese Drama: A Preliminary Examination." *Comparative Literature Studies* 20, no. 2 (Summer 1983): 231–45.

Hu, Xingliang. *Dandai zhongwai bijiao xiju shilun* (1949–2000) (A Comparative Study of Contemporary Chinese and Foreign Drama: 1949–2000). Beijing: People's Publishing House, 2009.

Huang, Zuolin. "*Zhuiqiu kexue xuyao teshu de yonggan: Wei bulaixite de Jialilue zhuan shouci zai zhongguo shangyan erzuo*" (Pursuing Science Requires Extraordinary Courage: Thoughts on First Production of Brecht's *Life of Galileo* in China). *Wenyi yanjiu* (Literature and Art Studies) 1 (1979): 121–7.

Jiao, Er. "*Zhunque, ranhou chuangzao: Ping xiaojuchang huaju Dengdai geduo jiantan jingdian zuopin wutai quanshi zhong de wenti*" (Be Accurate, Then Creative: On Little Theatre Spoken Drama *Waiting for Godot* and Problems in Interpretations of Classics on the Stage). *Zhongguo xiju* (Chinese Drama) 5 (1998): 11–13. *Jiaru wo shi zhen de* (If I Were for Real). https://zh.wikipedia.org/zh-hans/%E5%81%87%E5%A6%82%E6%88%91%E6%98%AF%E7%9C%9F%E7%9A%84_(%E5%8A%87%E6%9C%AC).

Li, Ran. "*Huaju Dengdao geduo bianju daoyan Li Ran de hua*" (Remarks by Spoken Drama Godot Cometh Playwright and Director Li Ran), April 11, 2006. http://ent.sina.com.cn/x/2006-04-11/18041046299.html.

Lin, Kehuan. "'*Gaojiasuo huilan ji' guanxi zhaji*" (Thoughts After Seeing *The Caucasian Chalk Circle*). *Xiju wenxue* (Drama Literature) 1 (1988): 66–72.

Lin, Zhaohua. "*Lin Zhaohua xiju zuopin ji*" (Collection of Lin Zhaohua Dramatic Works). DVD. Lin Zhaohua Drama Studio. Beijing: Renmin University of China Press, 2012.

Liu, Minghou. "*Jialilue zhuan zai zhongguo dansheng ji*" (How Life of Galileo Was Born in China). *Shanghai xiju* (Shanghai Theatre) 6 (1993): 31–2, 56.

Lu, Eng. "Jialilue zhuan *pailian de tihui: Xuexi Huang Zuolin laoshi daoyan gongzuo de yixie xinde*" (Takeaway From *Life of Galileo* Rehearsals: What I Learned From Observing Director Huang Zuolin at Work). *Huajua* (Spoken Drama) 4 (2006): 40–3.

Lukacs, George. "The Ideology of Modernism," in *The Meaning of Contemporary Realism*. Translated by John & Necke Mander. London: Merlin Press, 1963, 17–46.

McCarter, Jeremy. "The Courage of Their Convictions: Meryl Streep Survives a War and an Ill-fitting Role in Tony Kushner's Timely Brecht Adaptation." *The New York Magazine*, August 22, 2006. http://nymag.com/arts/theater/reviews/19669/.

Meng, Jinghui. "*Shiyan xiju Dengdai geduo zai Bolin: Deguo Bolin yanchu guanju ji*" (Experimental Play *Waiting for Godot* in Berlin: Performing and Seeing Performances in Berlin). *Juben* (Stage Scripts) 8 (1993): 65–7.

———, ed. "*Wa shiyan jutuan zhi guanzhong*" (To Theatregoers From Frog Experimental Theatre). *Xianfeng xiju dangan* (Avant-Garde Theatre Archives). *Zuojia chubanshe* (Writers press), 2011, 3–5.

Miller, Arthur. "In China." *The Atlantic Monthly*, March 1979: 90–117.

———. *Salesman in Beijing*. New York: The Viking Press, 1983.

———. *Timebends: A Life*. New York: Grove Press, 1987.

Qi, Jianmin. "*Cong huaju* Qie·Gewala *reyan kan xiandai zhongguo de jieji yu boxue wenti*" (Seeing the Social Issues of Class Polarization and Exploitation in Modern China From the Play *Che Guevara*). *Shimei* 13 (2013): 169–84.

Qi, Shouhua. "Misreading Ibsen: Chinese Noras on and Off the Stage, and Nora in Her Chinese Husband's Ancestral Land of the 1930s – As Reimagined for the Present-Day Stage." *Comparative Drama* 50, no. 4 (Winter 2016): 341–64.

————. *Western Literature in China and the Translation of a Nation*. New York: Palgrave Macmillan, 2012.

Qu, Peihui. "*Lin Zhaohua de* San zimei·Dengdai geduo *tanxi*" (A Tentative Analysis of Lin Zhaohua's *Three Sisters Waiting for Godot*). *Xiju wenxue* (Drama Literature) 6 (2008): 43–5.

Ren, Ming. "*Ren Ming Xiao Juchang Xiju Ji*" (A Collection of Ren Ming Small Theatre Productions). DVD. Beijing People's Art Theatre, 2011.

Saussy, Haun. "Mei Lanfang in Moscow, 1935: Familiar, Unfamiliar, Defamiliar." *Modern Chinese Literature and Culture* 18, no. 1 (Spring 2006): 8–29.

Shi, Yan. "*Beijing haoren, haori duo mo*" (The Good Person of Beijing, Good Things Take Time to Grind). *Nanfang zhoumo* (Southern Weekend), September 22, 2011, E27.

————. "*Zhengyi shi ruhe yinfa de: Jiaoru woshi zhen de taiqian muhou*" (How the Controversy Started: Behind the Scenes of *If I Were for Real*). *The Southern Weekend*, December 11, 2008. www.infzm.com/content/20991.

Shuguang (Dawn). Written by Bai Hua. Beijing: People's Literature Press, 1978.

Song, Shi. "*Zhongju: You yici chuncui de xiju tiyan*" (*Endgame*: A Pure Theatre Experience). *Shanghai xiju* (Shanghai Theatre) 5 (2005): 21–2.

Song, Xuezhi, and Jun Xu. "*Faguo huangdanpai xiju zai zhongguo de fanyi yu yanjiu*" (Translation and Research on French Theatre of the Absurd in China). *Waiguo wenxue yanjiu* (Foreign Literature Studies) 2 (2004): 147–52.

"Stanislavsky system." *Encyclopedia Britannica*. www.britannica.com/art/Stanislavsky-system (Last Updated: 10-15-2014).

Tao, Yu. "*Yong chuantong jiyi jihuo Bulaixite*: Ping Shen Lin *gaibian de Beijing haoren*" (Enlivening Brecht With Traditional Drama Techniques: On Shen Lin's Adaptation *The Good Person of Beijing*). *Shanghai xiju* (Shanghai Theatre) 12 (2011): 18–19.

Tao, Zi. "*Dengdai geduo jiqi zai zhongguo de mingyun*" (*Waiting for Godot* and Its Fate in China). *Yishu pinlun* (Arts Criticism) 7 (2004): 33–5.

Tian, Min. "'Alienation-Effect' for Whom? Brecht's (Mis)interpretation of the Classical Chinese Theatre." *Asian Theatre Journal* 14, no. 2 (Autumn 1997): 200–22.

"Two Whatevers." https://en.wikipedia.org/wiki/Two_Whatevers.

Wang, Lei. "*San zimei·Dengdai geduo suo 'dengdao' de yilun*" (The Comments *Three Sisters Waiting for Godot* 'Waited for' and Received). *Guangming Daily*, May 7, 1998. www.gmw.cn/01gmrb/1998-05/07/GB/17685%5EGM6-0703.HTM.

Wang, Xiaohua. "*Dui Bulaixite xiju lilun de chongxin pingjia*" (Toward a Reappraisal of Brecht). *Xiju yishu* (Theatre Arts) 4 (1996): 44–52.

Wang, Yangwen, and Depei Tian. "*Zhongguo Bekete yanjiu zongshu*" (Overview of Becket Research in China). *Jianghuai luntan* (Jianghuai Forums) 6 (2010): 185–9.

Windle, Kevin. "The Translation of Drama," in *The Oxford Handbook of Translation Studies*. Edited by Kirsten Malmkjær and Kevin Windle. Oxford: Oxford University Press, 2011, 153–68.

Xiong, Zhu. "*Wangmei de ren fenlie de xi*" (Perfect Man Splintered Play). *Xiju zhijia* (Playwrights) 4 (2004): 39–40.

Yang, Daniel. "Theatre in Post Cultural Revolution China: A Report Based on Field Research in the Fall and Winter of 1981." *Asian Theatre Journal* 1, no. 1 (Spring 1984): 90–103.

Yao, Jiaying. "'*Danda baba' dui huanjue wutai de dianfu yu huanyuan: Huang Zuolin zhidao Danda mama he tade haizimen de zai sikao*" ('Father Courage' Subverting and Restoring Make-believe Theatre: Rethinking Huang Zuolin Directing Mother Courage and Her Children). *Dangdai xiju* (Contemporary Drama) 2 (2013): 14–16.

Yates, Andrea L. "Abandoning the Empirical: Repetition and Homosociality in *Waiting for Godot.*" *Samuel Beckett Today /Aujourd'hui* 14 (2004): 437–49.

Ying, Ruochen, and Claire Conceison. *Voices Carry: Behind Bars and Backstage During China's Revolution and Reform.* New York: Roman & Littlefield, 2009, 157–69.

Yu, Hua. "*Neixin zhisi: Huaju* San zimei·Dengdai geduo *bitan*" (Death of Heart: Written Comments on *Three Sisters Waiting for Godot*), March 27, 2012. www.kanunu8.com/book3/7200/159185.html.

Yu, Shiao-ling S. *Chinese Drama After the Cultural Revolution, 1979–1989: An Anthology.* Lewiston, NY: Edwin Mellen Press, 1996.

Yu wu sheng chu (Thunder in the Silence). https://baike.baidu.com/item/%E4%BA%8E%E6%97%A0%E5%A3%B0%E5%A4%84/2936422.

Zhang, Hui. "*Huaju Salemu de nüwu: Kaowen shidai de lixing*" (Spoken Drama Salem's Witches: Interrogating Times' Sense of Reason') *Youth Reference*, January 21, 2015: 21. http://qnck.cyol.com/html/2015-01/21/nw.D110000qnck_20150121_1-21.htm.

Zhang, Li. "*Yizhi wenming de duihua*" (Dialogue Between Civilizations). *Waiguo wenxue pinlun* (Foreign Literature Review) 1 (2007): 28–38.

Zhang, Ming'ai. "An Article Influences Chinese History." January 19, 2008. www.china.org.cn/2008-01/19/content_1240036.htm.

Zhang, Wei. "Adapting Brecht's *The Good Person of Szechwan*: Innovative *Chuanju* and *Yueju* in China's Transition." *Asian Theatre Journal* 33, no. 2 (Fall 2016): 420–31.

———. "*Ganchu Beikete Zhongju de jiezou*" (Experiencing Rhythms of Beckett's *Endgame*). *Dangdai xiju* (Contemporary Drama) 5 (2008): 47–8.

Zhao, Zhiyong. "*Shuwei haoren: Qianxi Bulaixite Sichuan haoren de liang chu zhongguo dangdai gaibian banben*" (What Is a Good Person: On Two Contemporary Chinese Adaptations of Brecht's *The Good Person of Szechwan*). *Wenyi lilun yu piping* (Criticism and Theory in Arts and Literature) 4 (2013): 124–7.

"*Zhongguo juxie juban xueshu baogaohui*" (China Drama Association Organized Symposium). *Renmin xiju* (People's Theatre) 10. 1978, 75.

Zhou, Xian. "*Bulaixite dui women yiwei zhe shenme? Bulaixite dui dangdai zhongguo xiju de yingxiang*" (What Does Brecht Mean to Us? Brecht's Impact on Contemporary Chinese Drama). *Xiju* (Drama) 4 (1996): 28–39.

Zhu, Hong. "*Huangdanpai xiju shuping*" (An Overview of the Theatre of the Absurd). *Shijie wenxue* (World Literature) 2 (1978): 213–42.

Zhu, Xuefeng. "*Dengdai geduo yu zhongguo xiqu jianyi xiqu de kua wenhua shiyan yu chuangxin*" (Waiting for Godot, Traditional Chinese Drama, Transcultural Experiments and Innovations in Drama). *Yishu baijia* (Hundred Schools in Art) 2 (2007): 29–31.

4 Tragic hero and hero tragedy

Reimagining classic Greek drama
as Chinese *xiqu* today[1]

Compared to classic Greek drama, traditional Chinese drama (*xiqu*) is a late bloomer. Although, like classic Greek drama, *xiqu* can be traced back to communal festivals featuring song and dance, and to rites and rituals performed to exorcize evil spirits and to give thanks to the gods for their blessings at the dawn of the Chinese civilization, it remained in that early, fetal state for centuries. By the fifth century BC, classic Greek drama had already reached its golden age in artistic forms and occupied a central place in Athenian cultural life, holding annual contests between major playwrights such as Aeschylus (c.525–c.456 BC), Euripides (c.480–c.406 BC), and Sophocles (c.497–406 BC), and by the fourth century BC, Aristotle (384–322 BC) had already written the *Poetics*, among other important works of his, which theorizes on various aspects of drama, a foundational text still relevant today. There were no comparable achievements in drama in China although Chinese culture had also reached its golden age of development during the Spring and Autumn (722–476 BC) and Warring States (476–221 BC) periods, which saw, among other things, the flourishing of Confucianism and Daoism (Taoism) and splendid achievements in arts and literature – e.g., *Book of Songs* (*Shijing*).[2]

When Alexander the Great (356 BC–323 BC), the young king of Macedonia, tutored by Aristotle during his formative years, expanded his campaigns from the Balkans eastward to Asia Minor, the Persian Empire, and the Indian subcontinent, he took with him the seeds and fruits of Greek culture, including drama, resulting in transcultural diffusion along the way that reverberated far and wide. For example, classic Indian drama, Sanskrit theatre, interacted with Greek dramatic art Alexander the Great had taken to the subcontinent, although it is not clear in what specific forms and to what degrees the Greek influence happened. What is clear is that China, poised at the far-eastern portion of the Eurasian landmass, felt the ripple effect of such transcultural interfusion albeit centuries later.

When Buddhism, which originated in India around 400–600 BC, began to spread to its South Asian neighbors such as Sari Lanka, Burma, and Thailand and eastward to China, Sanskrit theatre came along in the bandwagon, so to speak, which provided the catalyst for Chinese *xiqu* to bloom and flourish during the Northern Song and early Ming dynasties (twelfth to fourteenth century). It was during this period that *xiqu*, particularly *nanxi* (southern drama) along China's southeastern coast and *zaju* (variety play) in northern China, matured and acquired its distinctive characteristics – e.g., blending song, poetry, and dance in the same theatric event, stylized acting, elaborate system of roles for men, women, heroes, and villains.

Direct introduction of classic Greek drama in China did not happen until modern times, in the forms of published translations – e.g., Aeschylus' *Prometheus Bound* (1926), *The Persians* (1936), and *Agamemnon* (1937); Sophocles' *Oedipus the King* (1936) and *Antigone* (1937); and Euripides' *Medea* (1937) and *The Trojan Women* (1938). New translations or newer editions of earlier translations were published during the first 17 years of Communist rule in China between 1949 and 1966 before the Cultural Revolution (1966–1976). Like everything else in arts and literature,[3] classic Greek drama experienced a boom in the late 1970s and early 1980s as China reopened its door to the outside world. By 1983, the entirety of classic Greek tragedies, all 32 plays by Aeschylus, Euripides, and Sophocles combined had been translated into Chinese. Many studies of classic Greek drama, by way of translation (from English and other languages) or original scholarship, had been published too.

Other than a 1942 adaptation of Euripides' *Medea* by a drama school in Sichuan and a 1946 adaptation of Aristophanes' *Lysistrata* in Shanghai, under the Chinese title *Nüren yu heping* (women and peace), as China was plunging deeper into another civil war (1945–1949), performances of classic Greek drama on the Chinese stage had been rare before the early 1980s. In March 1986, theatergoers in Beijing saw the first public performance of *Oedipus the King* mounted by the Central Academy of Drama – adapted and codirected by Luo Jinlin, a scholar of classic Greek literature. The challenge, as Luo knew only too well, was how to make this Chinese production of a two-millennium old Greek classic relevant and appealing for the Chinese of the 1980s. Therefore, instead of aiming for complete fidelity or going into a full post-modern experimental mode, Luo and his team chose the middle way: streamlining the dramatic action and scene flow and injecting elements of *xiqu* into the production while trying to stay true to both the story and the spirit of the classic tragedy.[4] In the summer of the same year, per invitation from the European Cultural Center of Delphi, the academy took the adaptation to both Delphi and Athens. Since then, several classic Greek plays – e.g., *Oedipus the King, Antigone, Medea, The Trojan Women, Prometheus Bound, Thesmophoriazusae* (*Dimujie funü*) – have seen Chinese productions in the forms of modern *huaju* (spoken drama) or traditional *xiqu* such as *jingju* (Peking opera).

As with adaptations of any foreign classics, the challenge for adapting Greek classics is always how to make it work for the Chinese stage that has a very different dramatic tradition whose audiences have very different tastes and theatre habits. There are four different routes to go about it – i.e. fidelity (faithful to the original play in story, structure, and production), indigenization (appropriating the original play as inspiration and raw material to make a new Chinese play, especially in a *xiqu* genre), hybridization (interfusing two distinctive dramatic traditions into the same theatric event), and experimentation (experimental in story, structure, and production, whether it takes the form of *xiqu*, *huaju*, or a mishmash of the two). Luo Jinlin,[5] who has directed quite a few noteworthy adaptations of Greek classics since the 1980s, summed up his approach this way in 1995:[6] the key to capture and truthfully represent the tragic spirit as embodied in classic Greek plays is proper understanding and interpretation of the tragic heroes. For Oedipus, the emphasis would be on his defiance of fate and his heroism in self-punishment; for Antigone, it would be the beauty of her humanity in opposition to Creon, who embodies ruthless power; for Medea, it would be her anguish as an oppressed woman despite her unpardonable crime of filicide; for the Trojan women, it would be on their suffering and the anti-war theme. Luo believes that for production, from stage design to acting, the minimalist approach would be the best to capture the spirit of classic Greek drama. Luo, as well as many others, believes that traditional Chinese theatre, known for its symbolic suggestiveness, would be a "natural" fit for classic Greek drama. In practice, however, recent Chinese adaptations rarely go the "minimalist" route. In fact, Luo himself has been intimately involved in a few big budget extravaganzas in part to make classic Greek drama appeal to Chinese theatergoers today and to help revitalize *xiqu*.

This chapter studies recent Chinese adaptations of classic Greek plays in various genres of *xiqu* – e.g., the 2009 *jingju* adaptation of *Oedipus the King*, the 2002 Hebei *bangzi* adaptations of *Medea* and *Antigone*, and the 2014 *pinju* adaptation of the *Oresteia Trilogy*. These *xiqu* adaptations do not completely indigenize the Greek classics, but they tend to deemphasize the agency of gods and compress and retool the dramatic action so it would be easier for Chinese audiences to follow and appreciate and so there would be ample time to give full play to the art of *xiqu*. Although these adaptations should be viewed in the context of the old "whether China has 'true,' 'authentic' tragedy" debate, and although in trying hard to succeed, both artistically and financially, some *xiqu* adaptations run the risk of turning drama into melodrama and tragedy into spectacle, they do engender interesting and enriching intertextual reverberations across cultures.

Oedipus the King as jingju

One of the most popular Greek classics in China that has seen many notable adaptations since the 1980s is Sophocles' *Oedipus the King*. In 1986, the graduating class at the Central Academy of Drama in Beijing mounted an adaptation of this Greek classic directed by Luo Jinlin.[7]

Luo approached this production professorially, first with a scene-by-scene analysis of the play to have a good sense of the pulse of its dramatic action, character portrayal, choral arrangement, and strands of tensions and thematic development – e.g., fate and free will, individual and state, crime and punishment. The challenge, Luo and his team knew only too well, was how to make this Chinese production of a two-millennium old Greek classic relevant and appealing for the Chinese of the 1980s. Instead of aiming for 100% fidelity or going into a full post-modern experimental mode, they chose the middle way, or the hybridization approach: streamlining the dramatic action and scene flow, and injecting elements of traditional *xiqu* (albeit not any particular *xiqu* genre) into the production while trying to stay true to both the story and the spirit of the classic tragedy.

To minimize confusion on the part of Chinese audiences who are not familiar with Greek mythologies, Luo and his team assigned the same name, Apollo, to all the gods – Zeus, Ares, Dionysus – referenced in the original play. They also cut or compressed a few of the nonessential choral songs to quicken the pace of scene flow. Most notably, instead of having Oedipus blind his eyes offstage, in keeping with classic Greek drama conventions of not showing bloody scenes onstage, Luo and his team chose to move this act center stage and dramatize it fully for character portrayal (Oedipus as a tragic hero who, in defiance against fate – i.e., gods – chooses to sacrifice himself for the common good of his people) and the emotive impact on the audiences. Since this 1986 adaptation, moving what happens offstage or before the curtain rises – i.e., the backstory – in the original center stage to be acted out in full for the audiences, to demythologize and thus deemphasize the agency of gods, and, indeed, to highlight the "heroism" of the tragic heroes have been the all but standard approach in Chinese adaptations of Greek classics.

This is certainly the case of the notable 2009 adaptation of *Oedipus the King* mounted by Zhejiang Peking Opera Troupe in partnership with Shanghai Theatre Academy. In addition to emphasizing the heroism theme, this production tapped the full range of the artistic tools granted by *jingju*, *chang* (song), *nian* (speech), *zuo* (mix of dance and performance), *da* (mix of acrobatics and martial arts), to capture the emotive depth and intensity of the classic story and create an engrossing theatric experience for the audiences both at home and abroad. Weng Guosheng, director of the *jingju* troupe who would play the titular role, and his team took considerable creative license to naturalize the story for it to work for the Chinese audiences and to streamline and simplify the plot development so there would be ample time to give full play to the art of *jingju*. What emerges from this interfusion or hybridization endeavor is a powerful albeit compact (the actual performance time is about 60 minutes)[8] tragedy that can be characterized as both classic Greek and Chinese.

The Chinese title for this Peking opera adaptation is *Wangzhe edi* (King edi), *edi* (two syllables) as transliteration for Oedipus instead of the usual *edipusi* (four syllables and sounding much more "foreign"). Thebes becomes *Tiguo* (Ti country), one syllable *Ti* plus the familiar "morpheme" *guo* (country), instead of *Tebai*, the usual transliteration, and Corinth, likewise, becomes *Keguo* (Ke country). All the other main characters are known only by their relationships to *Edi* (Oedipus) – e.g., *Wanghou* (queen) for Jocasta and *Guojiu* (imperial brother-in-law) for Creon. Apollo, Zeus, oracles of Delphi, the blind prophet Tiresias, and the Sphinx are all gone to further demythologize and indigenize the story. In their stead are three Taoist fortunetellers, who appear at the beginning, middle, and end of the play to provide the necessary supernatural agency for the story to work and function as a chorus of sorts too. Gone also are the offspring from the doomed union of Oedipus and Jocasta, so there are no references to Antigone and Ismene as daughters and half-sisters of *Edi* (Oedipus) and no bidding them farewell before *Edi* goes into exile. The messenger who comes with the news of the death of the old Corinthian king is now *Nainiang* (nurse) for young *Edi*. She happens to be the same servant who, many years ago, is given the baby by a *Tiguo* man who turns out to be the only surviving eyewitness of the killing of the old king. From this extensive demythologization, combination, and compression emerges a much leaner story line that would not require knowledge of Greek mythologies to follow, but would require considerable willing suspension of disbelief (e.g., how a young outsider could have come and married the widowed queen and succeeded to the thrown is never explained) to appreciate. What is gained is ample time and space for the full artistic "arsenal" of *jingju* to create and deliver a straightforward yet powerful theatric experience for the audience.

Right before the curtain rises, a one-minute offstage narration gives a quick background, or rather synopsis, of the story to prepare the Chinese audiences for what is about to unfold on the stage. It presents *Edi*, the titular character, as a young king who has ruled *Tiguo* wisely for the last three years and is well loved by his people who have enjoyed peace and prosperity. Then a disastrous plague hits and *Tiguo* plunges into deep misery. At the end of the narration, amid cries of agony and ominous music (Chinese flute and percussion instruments), three Taoist fortunetellers, in clownish makeup and costumes (as befitting their *chou* roles according to Peking opera), arrive on stage and dance sinisterly, much in the same fashion as the Three Witches in *Macbeth* by Shakespeare. As the fortunetellers continue their ill-boding dance, a tenor aria arises backstage, as if far away, an overture to the play of man versus fate:[9]

> In the universe vast and infinite,
> All seems empty and preordained.
> Karma or fate, which carries more
> weight in deciding one's fortune?
> Having committed no sin or crime,
> Why am I feeling such apprehension,
> Arriving at this crossroads? I wonder
> which path to take and to go where?

As the song gets nearer, permeating heaven and earth, the fortunetellers, as if sensing trouble, exit. A *wusheng* (martial art) actor enters, doing a series of tumbling and other moves typical of the *wusheng* role, to clear the way for the entrance of *Edi*. The young king, in the leading *sheng* (male) role, dressed in royal blue and white, urges his horse (suggestively, of course) onto the stage, as he continues to sing and act for more than six minutes to give full-throated expression to his love for his people and his pain at their suffering. As a last resort, *Edi* comes to seek help from the fortunetellers who dwell at a place enveloped in otherworldly, ominous aura. After *Edi* swears that he is willing to die 10,000 times (*wansi buci*) to save his people, the fortunetellers reluctantly tell him the "heavenly secret" (*tianji*): to relieve *Tiguo* of the plague a murder mystery has to be resolved and then one person has to be punished.

Dramatic action intensifies when, about 30 minutes into the play, *Naini-ang*, *Edi*'s old nurse, arrives to deliver the news that the old king of *Keguo* has died and to ask *Edi* to return to succeed to the throne. The murder mystery begins to unravel, and suspecting the worst, *Wanghou* sings a big aria while dancing in excruciating agony:

> Lightning bolt from blue sky shakes heaven and earth,
> A thousand disasters and ten thousand misfortunes befall me.
> The ill-starred baby given to the guard to abandon long ago,
> How on earth could he return to send his father to the netherworld?

When the old servant/guard, the last strand in the mystery murder, is found and arrives on stage, *Wanghou*, on her knees, begs *Edi* not to press on. *Edi* pushes *Wanghou* away and then, struck by the pain he has inflicted on her, helps her back on feet. They support each other, gazing into each other's eyes, and then, as if hit by lightning, *Edi* finally gets it. However, there is no going back on his sworn oath, as the sinister laugh of the three fortunetellers in the background reminds him:

> *Wanghou*, please do not blame *Edi*,
> Please do not hate *Edi*.
> To save *Tiguo*, Your King
> is resolved to get to the bottom of it all today.

As the horrific truth is about to come out, and there is no way for her to remain by the young king's side and no place in this world for her to hide from the unspeakable shame, *Wanghou* bids one last farewell from *Edi* and jumps (front stage) to her death. Heartbroken, *Edi* presses on and forces the last strand of the unsolved mystery out of a horrified old man/guard, who kills himself, the *seppuku* style, on stage too.

The last segment of this production, its climax, begins with the reappearance of the three fortunetellers, dancing, vaulting, and tumbling, accompanied by heartrendingly intense drum and percussion instruments and spasms of thunderous lightning, to prepare the scene for the last heroic act by *Edi* in the epic battle between fate and free will, person and state, and crime (albeit committed unwittingly) and punishment. As the theme song alluded to earlier arises again, *Edi* enters, now dressed in white and blue, signifying his essential

innocence and purity of spirit. In a soliloquy worthy of a Shakespearean tragedy, *Edi* deliberates and decides on what his punishment should be:

> To die,
> for *Edi*, would be too shallow a penitence;
> To die,
> for *Edi*, would be too light a punishment;
> To die a thousand times,
> for *Edi*, would not be atonement enough for the ungodly sin;
> To die a thousand cuts,
> for *Edi*, would not be atonement enough for the crime of ten thousand
>   lifetimes.
> *Edi* today will blind both of my eyes,
> say goodbye to my king's court,
> bid farewell to my own people,
> take punishment for my crime in this world
> and leave forever the land of *Tiguo* that I have loved with my heart and
>   soul and my whole life!

In another big aria following this soliloquy, *Edi* recounts the tragic story of
his life ("More sinn'd against than sinning"), protests fate that inflicts so
much misery on his people, and reconfirms his resolve to punish himself for
a crime committed unwittingly:

> To blind these unenlightened eyes of mine as atonement and
> To banish myself in darkness never to return and see light again.

Center stage, back to the audience and besieged by the same three fortunetellers, *Edi* readies himself for the act of self-punishment: he turns around and
bursts through the siege, tossing two long red *shuixiu* (long sleeves) into the
air, signifying blood shooting forth from his pieced eyes. An anguished, gut-
wrenching dance ensues as *Edi* fights one last battle with the fortunetellers,
giving one last expression of defiance against fate and the excruciating pain
he bears body and soul. The play ends with a tableau of *Edi*, blindfolded,
standing tall on the stone steps in front of the royal court, ready to be led by
the fortunetellers – one leading in front, one on each side holding the long
red *shuixiu* sleeves – out of *Tiguo* into the land of darkness, never to return.

This much streamlined, hybridized *jingju* production of *Oedipus the King*,
a hypertext, to borrow from Gérard Genette, can stand alone for the enjoyment of Chinese theatergoers who are not familiar with the hypotext, the
original play as well as its mythological origins. However, some knowledge
of the hypotext and indeed Western culture and dramatic tradition would
certainly help enrich and deepen their theatric experience and appreciation.
Similarly, Western audiences – e.g., Westerners who attended earlier versions
of this *jingju* production performed at the Barcelona International Drama

Festival in 2008 and Shanghai International Small Theatre Festival and various drama festivals in New York and Washington, DC, in 2009, who are familiar with the hypotext – could also have a powerful theatric experience. Indeed, many were awestruck by the power of Peking opera in embodying both the spirit and the story of this Western classic on the stage.[10] Nonetheless, without knowledge of Chinese language, culture, and dramatic tradition (e.g., English subtitles for the production are functional, but far from capturing the elegance, cadence, and richness of the dialogs and arias – so much is lost in the translation), they would not be able to understand and appreciate the power and beauty of this production as fully as would be desired or critique it as informedly. Nonetheless, such adaptations are worthy endeavors toward promoting transcultural understanding and appreciation.

The old "authentic" tragedy debate

This *jingju* production, as well as the 1986 production alluded to earlier, which chooses to highlight the heroism of Oedipus in defiance of a dooming fate should also be considered in the context of a long contentious debate: whether there is "true," "authentic" tragedy in China as the term is understood in the Western dramatic tradition.[11]

The negative view on this question can be traced back to Jean-Baptiste Du Halde (1674–1743), a French Jesuit historian specializing in China (although he had never been to China and did not speak Chinese either), who concluded, after reviewing the few translations of Yuan plays such as *L'Orphelin de la Maison de Tchao* (The Orphan of Zhao) available then, that there is not much difference between fiction and drama in Chinese culture, and, for that matter, between comedy and tragedy, both of which purport to serve some overt didactic, moral purpose. Many of the luminary figures in modern Chinese cultural movements and prominent scholars in arts and literature, such as Wang Guowei (1877–1927), Lu Xun (1881–1936), and Zhu Guangqian (1897–1986), held such a negative view too, although they each did so from a different philosophical and/or political perspective and concern – Wang Guowei measuring traditional *xiqu* by the Aristotelian ideals of tragedy, Lu Xun out of a concern for culture and people renewal as China struggled with its existential crisis, and Zhu Guangqian from an aesthetic and psychological lens informed by Schopenhauer. Many of the naysayers blame their perceived absence of tragedy on the happy endings (*datuanyuan*) of classic Chinese plays, which, they contend, are symptomatic of a weakness (or flaw) in the Chinese national character – i.e., the Chinese propensity for easy way out thanks to their lack of courage to face the dark and ugly courageously, and act to remedy what is amiss in life.

This critical view of traditional *xiqu* has been challenged since the 1980s, parallel in time with the gradual rise of China's economic power and cultural self-confidence. Many of the new generation of scholars reject the "Eurocentric" theories of tragedy as unfit for classic Chinese plays and instead argue for a theory and definition for "Chinese tragedy," or, rather, tragedy with Chinese characteristics. Some even go so far as to embrace "happy endings" not as weakness or flaw, but strength and courage because those "happy endings" are not really "happy"; they, instead, rather ironically, serve to augment and drive home the tragic sense of the whole play. These scholars also argue for a more evolving and polymorphic definition of tragedy to replace the "monolithic," "Eurocentric" definition of tragedy (which itself has been evolving and is polymorphic anyway). They prefer to see not only Chinese tragedy (as opposed to Western tragedy) as a genre in and by itself but also many subgenres such as hero tragedy (*yingxiong beiju*), women tragedy (*nüxing beiju*), fate tragedy (*mingyun beiju*), political tragedy (*zhengzhi beiju*), love tragedy (*aiqing beiju*), common people tragedy (*shiming beiju*), etc.

To view the 2009 Zhejiang *jingju* adaptation of *Oedipus the King* in the context of the debate of whether China has "true," "authentic" tragedy as outlined earlier, one could say, with full awareness of the risk of oversimplification, that *Wangzhe edi* has translated a classic Western fate tragedy (*mingyun beiju*) into a Chinese hero tragedy (*yingxiong beiju*) to make it more appealing to the Chinse audiences and indeed to better meet the needs of a culture and people as they transform with ever increased confidence in the globalized world today.

Weng and team maintained the same "hero tragedy" approach as they expanded this *jingju* adaptation of *Oedipus the King* into a fuller, more expansive production, which debuted in Hangzhou in 2010 and then traveled to various places in the world, including Cyprus in 2011 for the Fifteenth International Festival of Ancient Greek Drama there.[12]

Medea as Bangzi

Three years after the 1986 production of *Oedipus the King* at the Central Academy of Drama in Beijing discussed earlier, Luo Jinlin, the renowned classic Greek literature scholar, partnered up with the Hebei Bangzi Troupe of Hebei Province in mounting an adaptation of Euripides' *Medea*. This he would follow-up with a 2002 *bangzi* adaptation of Sophocles' *Antigone*, in partnership with the Hebei Bangzi Troupe of Beijing this time, and a 2014 *pingju* adaptation of Aeschylus' *Oresteia* trilogy under the Chinese title *Chengbang enchou* (Love and Hate between Two Cities, or the Legend of Two Cities), in partnership with Chinese Pingju Troupe in Beijing. These adaptation endeavors are noteworthy, because Hebei *bangzi* and *pingju*, though well-established *xiqu* genres, are not in the same league as national treasures such as *jingju* or *yueju* and are not as well-known outside of China. Although the 1989 *bangzi* production of *Medea* remained partially true to the "minimalist" principle Luo Jinlin had laid out for adapting Greek classics (as alluded to earlier), both the 2002 *bangzi* production of *Antigone* and the 2014 *pingju* production of *Oresteia* went for full-scale, big budget extravaganza. The beauty of such ambitious endeavors – what is gained (e.g., in popularity and market share) or lost (e.g., the tragic spirit of the Greek classics) is, as one could say, very much in the eye of the beholder.

Hebei *bangzi* is a northern Chinese opera, whose origin can be traced as far back as the Qin dynasty (246–206 BC). It is popular in Hebei and its neighboring provinces of Shandong, Shanxi, and Henan, and its nearby cities such as Beijing and Tianjin. It is similar to Beijing opera in its blending of *chang* (song), *nian* (speech), *zuo* (mix of dance and performance), *da* (mix of acrobatics and martial arts), and its system of roles such as *sheng* (male), *dan* (female), *jing* (painted), *chou* (clown). Its song (style of singing), however, is more earthy than urbane and tends to conjure up the vast, sublime vistas of the timeless Loess Plateau in central and northwestern China. The artistic character of this style of Chinese opera would make it an interesting vehicle for retelling the stories of ancient Greek drama nourished by the Mediterranean Sea.

In addition to its mythological origin and the agency of – or rather the meddling of human affairs by – gods such as Eros, Helios, and Zeus, a major challenge for the 1989 *bangzi* adaptation of *Medea* was the titular character herself – i.e., the filicide she committed by way of revenge for Jason's betrayal.[13] The repertoire of Chinese literature and drama has its share of female characters who, betrayed by their men, seek revenge in the most punitive way they could come up with – e.g., Du Shiniang – by drowning herself after dumbing all her treasures into the river; Qin Xianglian, by seeking justice in court and winning; and Fanyi, a modern character (in Cao Yu's 1933 play *Thunderstorm*), by forcing out the family scandalous past, which leads to the death of her own son, her son's love, and her own lover. Only in the 1993 Hollywood film *Joy Luck Club*, based on the 1989 novel by Amy Tan, that one would see a young Chinese mother, Ying-Ying, drown her baby son in the bathtub to punish her wayward husband.

To make the character of Medea "palatable," so to speak, to the Chinese theatergoers, the Hebei *bangzi* adaptation begins the story from the backstory of Medea and Jason – i.e., how they meet and fall in love, how Medea helps Jason secure the Golden Fleece, etc. – instead of beginning at a mid-point of the story, as in the original play, when Medea is raging at Jason for having arranged to marry Glauce, the daughter of Creon, king of Corinth. Luo Jinlin and his team invested much time in the first three titled scenes, *qubao* (treasure hunting), *zhuyang* (ram boiling), and *lijia* (leaving home) to portray Medea first as a lovely young woman and then as a loving mother and wife by using the full range of artistic expressions of Hebei *bangzi*, *chang* (song), *nian* (speech), *zuo* (mix of dance and performance), *da* (mix of acrobatics and martial arts), and giving full play to the impressive prowess of Peng Huiheng who played the title role. All of this is to prepare the audiences for the next two scenes, *qingbian* (betrayal) and *shazi* (filicide).

Scene 5, *shazi* (filicide), for example, begins with a loud, anguished cry of Medea (Peng) offstage. Upon hearing the cry, the six-member women chorus, as if on cue, all dressed in *shuixiu* (long sleeves) gowns, sings and dances onto the stage. They sing about how innocent and helpless the two young sons are and, as Medea (Peng) enters, fall on their knees to plead for the young boys' lives. Medea (Peng) sings and dances a big aria, which lasts for five minutes, about her love, rage, and pain. When the two young boys enter, the production gives full play to their innocence and brotherly love and Medea (Peng)'s motherly love. The physical act of filicide, from the moment Medea(Peng) pulls out the lethal red magic fan to the young boys dropping dead, takes six minutes to complete, filled with heartrending singing, dancing, pleading (on knees by their nurse), to show her unfathomable agony and make her a sympathetic figure. She then crawls over and bends over the bodies of her children singing and crying for a good two minutes before their father, Jason, enters.

Did the production succeed? Did the full range of Hebei *bangzi* art – singing, dancing, and acting – soften Medea's image for Chinese audiences despite the horror of filicide she commits, or make her "metamorphosis" – from the lovely young woman and loving mother and wife of the first two scenes to the murderess of the last scene – believable? After all, the filicide was not an act of momentary insanity, but a deliberate, albeit not cold-hearted, act to punish and revenge. The production's successful run of over 90 performances in the early 1990s alone seemed proof enough of its broad popularity among the Chinese theatergoers. Drama critics were laudatory about the production as a worthy experiment in retelling the classic Greek tragedy in Hebei *bangzi*, using *bangzi*'s arias, stylized acting (e.g., for horse riding, sailing boats on the rough seas), and acrobatic and *kungfu* choreography. What was also notable was its simple, suggestive stage design (it did without the proverbial "a table and two chairs" stage props characteristic of many *xiqu* genres). There was no elaborate scenery, digitized sound, or visual effects. All it had was a deep, dark-red backdrop curtain to set the tone for the whole play – an ominous sense of things to come even for the livelier and more upbeat first two acts. Some drama critics, however, feel that the first three scenes, intended to establish a likable portrait of Medea to win over the audiences, are padded with too many story elements, trying to cover too much ground. This, they believe, sometimes leads to too much breathless running around for the actors and too much hurrying on and offstage to be really engaging for the audiences.[14] Some critics are concerned that in trying to make this Western classic work for the Chinese audiences, the *Hebei bangzi* production injected too much Chinese mores and sentiments into the story. As a result, the tragic sense of the Greek classic is so diluted that it fails to inspire any deep, philosophical reflections on the tragedy of Medea, her emotive universe, and, for that matter, humanity and destiny.[15]

In 2002, the Hebei Bangzi Troupe of Beijing mounted a revival production of this *bangzi* adaptation of *Medea*, codirected by Luo Jinlin. It garnered similar laudatory responses for its achievements in blending two dramatic traditions and arts, its creative use of six-women chorus for multiple functions (comment, narration, stage props – e.g., rough sea, cliffs), and the performance of Liu Yuling who played the titular role this time. Drama critics had similar concerns of whether some tragic sense is lost in the *bangzi* translation of the Greek classic to make it appeal to the Chinese audiences. An inherent contradiction in such hybridization endeavors is that traditional Chinese opera such as Hebei *bangzi* is all about singing, dancing, and acting, so there could be a tendency to insert a big aria whenever there seems a crack of opportunity. For example, in this *bangzi* remake of the classic Greek play, Medea cries and sings over the bodies of her young sons for two minutes when a minimalist approach – e.g., silence – might have been more eloquent in speaking of her heartbreaking pain. Some critics even suggested developing two versions of the *bangzi Medea*: one, very much like the version already mounted in China, for the consumption of domestic audiences, and one, more faithful to the original, to be taken to stages outside China.[16]

Antigone as Bangzi

The year 2002 seemed one of ambitious thinking and undertaking for the Hebei Bangzi Troupe of Beijing. In that year, it mounted another adaptation endeavor: Sophocles' *Antigone*,[17] which, under the Chinese title *Tebaicheng* (Thebes City), traveled to the Eleventh International Meetings of Ancient Drama in Greece and has since performed at various international drama festivals.

One bold, creative license taken by Guo Qihong, an award-winning playwright and writer based at the Beijing People's Art Theatre, was to incorporate Aeschylus' *Seven against Thebes* into Sophocles' *Antigone*. As a result, as with the *Hebei bangzi* adaptation of *Medea*, what is essentially a backstory – events that have happened before the curtain rises – is now part of the main dramatic action played out on the stage for the audiences to see. What is "appropriated" from the Aeschylean original, however, is not the long and rich dialogs between the citizens of Thebes and their king Eteocles as Polynices, his brother, along with six other captains, leads the Argive army against the seven gates of the city to retake the disputed throne. Instead, it is the battle itself wherein the two brothers kill each other.

Another significant step Guo Qihong took was to expand and foreground the theme of sibling love (between Eteocles, Polynices, Antigone, and Ismene), as well as romantic love (between Antigone and Haemon). As a result, what is assumed, understood, and very much muted in the Sophoclean original now takes a central place in the ethos and pathos of this *bangzi* adaptation and provides the main source of emotive appeal to the audiences. The *bangzi* Antigone chooses to bury Polynices, in defiance of the decree issued by Creon, the king of Thebes then, not just out a sense of duty and justice (according to the law of gods), but also out of unfathomable love for her fallen brother. By moving the backstory and offstage developments center stage and turning narration into dramatic action, Guo Qihong and Luo Jinlin, director of this *bangzi* production, remade the story of Antigone into a hero tragedy as well as a love tragedy reminiscent of *Romeo and Juliet*.[18]

To highlight the theme of sibling and romantic love, Guo and Luo created this moment for the combat scene as *Zhizhengwang* (king-in-power,

Eteocles) and *Liuwangwang* (king-in-exile, Polynices), fully armed and armored, each leading his army, fight to the death for the disputed throne. In the thick of battle, as swords and spears fly, and the two brothers go at each other for the kill,[19] there appears *Andi* (Antigone):

> *Andi* comes in calm steps, elegant, solemn, fearless, weaving through columns of the fighting armies.
>
> ZHIZHENGWANG and LIUWANGWANG (shocked): Sister! Don't come over!
>
> ANDI (continuing to come toward them): My elder brothers! (sing): My elder brothers I implore you to quit fighting and return to the family feast!
>
> ZHIZHENGWANG and LIUWANGWANG (embarrassed): No way!
>
> ANDI (sings): Ask yourselves: can you be happy in your heart again if our kingdom is destroyed? Just think for a moment, those peaceful and happy days vivid like yesterday, our childhood memories, joy of growing up together, playing among the tall palace columns, running up and down the moss-covered steps!
>
> LIUWANGWANG (suddenly): Would rather die in battle than give up! Either the victorious king atop the city wall or the corps of a bandit rotting in the wild! Fight!
>
> (Furious drums and battle cries arise again. *Andi* is caught in the crosshairs. Just then, *Haimeng*/Haemon, on horseback, bursts on the scene and snatches *Andi* away to safety. The two armies clash again as swords and spears fly, amidst thunderous drums and battle cries.)
>
> (The two kings wave for their warriors to stop and step aside; they then take on each other. They fight. They are hit at the same time and fall, breathing their last)
>
> ZHIZHENGWANG (with whatever strength still in him): Elder brother!
>
> LIUWANGWANG (crying out in the same manner): Younger brother!
>
> ZHIZHENGWANG and LIUWANGWANG (same time): I love you! (die).

One would encounter several more such emotively charged scenes, intended to pull the heartstrings of the Chinese theatergoers before the curtain falls. To show that it is out of sibling love that *Andi* decides to defy the decree issued by *Keruiweng* (Creon), Guo and Luo designed a big funeral scene for *Zhizheng*wang (king-in-power, Eteocles). During the ceremony, *Andi* "sees" scenes from a happy childhood and sings, as if in a trance. Then,

> (the bell tolls. Yisi/Ismene enters)
>
> YISI: Elder sister. Why are you still here?
>
> ANDI (still lost): I'm still thinking of our brother, the brother that has not received our tears, the brother that has not been covered by earth!

YISI (sad): I have been thinking too of the moment wild animals catch sight of his body . . .

ANDI (holding Yisi's hands): We have to do our sisterly duty!

The two sisters then get into an argument over who should go and bury the dishonored brother. *Andi* wins the argument when guards come and take *Yisi* away.

In another emotively charged scene, *Andi*, back to her maiden chamber after the funeral, dreams of a tender moment with *Haimeng* (Haemon):

(Enters *Haimeng*, wearing a garland, eighteen roses in hand, moonwalking)

HAIMENG (tenderly): *Andi*! *Andi*! My love!

ANDI (rapturously): *Harmeng*, my poet! (pointing at the roses) This. . . .

HARMENG: You've forgotten? It's your birthday today! (presenting her the roses and putting the garland on her head). *Andi*! (sings)

Eighteen roses for eighteen years of our love.
When I put this evergreen garland on your head,
Your natural beauty shines without any rouge.
A poet's hand is the best vanity set in the world
(relishing the sight of her beauty)

ANDI (shyly): *Haimeng*! You're so good! (putting her hand in *Haimeng*'s)

HAIMENG (helping *Andi* to her feet): My fiancée, our bridal bed is over there. Just follow me (sings) You and I, a young man and a young woman, our hearts afire with love. . . .

ANDI (half-willing, half-reluctant): No, no, *Haimeng*. . . .

HAIMENG (sings): Rose, rose, for whom are you blossoming? (picks up *Andi* and carries her to the inner chamber)

To theatergoers with Western sensibilities, such scenes, which one would expect to encounter in a Western or romantic comedy, would perhaps feel blatantly melodramatic, but they draw from the reservoir of classic Chinese literature such as the thirteenth-century variety play *The West Wing Story* (*Xixiangji*) and the eighteenth-century novel *Dream of the Red Chamber* (*Hongloumeng*). They would be reminiscent of similar scenes in Shakespeare's *Romeo and Juliet* and John Keats' "St. Agnes Eve" too.

The last big scene that Guo and Luo created was another funeral procession, this time for *Andi*. Among those in attendance are the spirits of her loved ones who have died during the play: her two brothers, Haemon, and his mother. As percussion and wind music resounds, a group of spirits takes out a wedding veil and fresh flowers to dress up *Andi*, the dear departed. Carrying *Andi*'s bridal sedan are *Zhizhengwang* and *Liukewang*, who hand a whip to *Haimeng* atop horseback: an underworld wedding ceremony presided by a heavenly god, in the midst of a choir singing.

All of these creative licenses – e.g. moving the backstory center stage and translating narration ("appropriated" from another play) into dramatic action on stage – were taken by Beijing Hebei Bangzi Troup to stake out a place for itself, for a traditional *xiqu* form which, like all media and artistic forms in China today, fight tooth and nail for survival. On the success of such adaptations rides so much hope for the future of the troupe and indeed for Hebei *bangzi*.[20] In trying so hard to succeed, the *bangzi Antigone* ran the risk of turning drama into melodrama and tragedy into spectacle. It ran the risk of gaining popularity and market share at the price of losing the quintessential artistic characteristics of traditional *xiqu* such as simplicity and suggestiveness and diluting important themes of the classic Greek tragedy such as individual versus dictatorial rule. For one moment in this *bangzi Antigone*, at least, thematic seriousness trumps theatricality. When Tiresias, the blind prophet, tells Creon that heavenly gods are angry and that he should not insult the slain because the dead has as much dignity as the living, Creon accuses him of misleading people with falsehoods and of failing to resist the temptation of money. Tiresias responds in an impassioned speech first and then a rousing aria:

> Arrogance makes tyrant,
> Despotism brings disasters.
> Since you insult me for telling you the truth,
> You're doomed by the curse of the prophecy!
> (sings):
> You don't allow the dead to go and rest in peace,
> Nor do you let the living stay and live in happiness.
> You have committed a crime against both heaven and earth.
> Yet you are so full of sound and fury,
> Think you are the mightiest in this world.
> There's a treasure called foolishness
> That wins a king's heart more than gold.
> Be forewarned that foolishness ferments misfortune
> And not all punishments are doled out by heavenly gods.

One can only hope that such important messages are not lost in the abundant feast of dazzling (melo)drama and spectacle.

Oresteia as Pingju

Guo Qihong and Luo Jinlin continued their creative adaptation endeavors a few years later with Aeschylus's *Oresteia* trilogy, this time with a different "new" Chinese bottle, so to speak, for the "old" Mediterranean wine. *Pingju*, an important traditional *xiqu* genre that originated in Hebei and developed by drawing from *bangzi* and *jingju*, is popular in the northern provinces of China. In rewriting the trilogy into a play that can be performed as one theatric event, Guo was fully aware of what Eugene O'Neill had accomplished with his twentieth-century American remake of the same story in *Morning Becomes Electra* (1931), which Guo thinks is a greater play (cycle) than the Aeschylean original. Instead of a trilogy (*Agamemnon*, *The Libation Bearers*, and *The Eumenides*) or play cycle (*Homecoming*, *The Hunted*, and *The Haunted*), Guo and Luo compressed the tragic family saga into a five-act play under the Chinese title *Chengbang enchou* (Love and Hate between Two Cities, or the Legend of Two Cities), each act with a one-word heading: Fire (*huo*), Blood (*xue*), Funeral (*dian*), Poison (*zhen*), and Trial (*shen*).[21]

This is a big budget multimedia production using both traditional Chinese and Western music instruments, and modern digitalized sound, light, and visual effects. For example, in Act I, Fire (*huo*), as an intense stream of red light cuts across the sky ominously, *Ajia wang* (King Ajia, Agamemnon), shocked, exclaims, "Bloody light a sign for disaster!" The light descends on earth like a dragon and floods the world in bloody red. In Act II, Blood (*xue*), when *Ajia wang* is being stabbed to death, bloody rain pours down from the sky and envelopes the world in scarlet read.[22] Very little is left to imagination.

What is most noteworthy is that through streamlining and compression, this *pingju Oresteia* turns Agamemnon into a fallen war hero and Clytemnestra into a villain by deemphasizing Agamemnon's share of the "blame" for the tragedy (his decision to sacrifice their daughter Iphigenia to appease the gods at the start of the Trojan War and to take the Trojan prophetess Cassandra as a concubine). A tragedy of moral complexity is now reduced to a simple morality play. In this remake of the story, when *Ajia wang* fights a war far away from home, *Ke Lüdai* (Clytemnestra) couldn't bear the loneliness and empty bed, so she takes on a lover. Then, driven by ambition, she murders *Ajia wang* when he returns and usurps the throne:

> For me, for my city-state, I've killed him. Now I'll lead my city-state onto the sun-bathed road forward to live a brand new life!

Loud cheers of "long live the Queen! Long live the Queen!" erupt and echo between heaven and earth.[23] Even the Chinese names *Ajia wang* (King Ajia) given to Agamemnon, which sounds endearing, and *Ke Lüdai* (Putting on a Green Hat) to Clytemnestra, which suggests of the Chinese equivalent of "cuckold," show quite a bit of gender bias.

In choosing to turn Agamemnon into a mighty hero and Clytemnestra into a villain, a she-devil, the *bangzi Oresteia* seems to fall into the centuries old tradition of vilifying women, from Yang Guifei to Cixi to Jiang Qing (Madame Mao). It also seems to lend credence to the May 4th generation's complaint about the Chinese propensity to avoid harsh realities and morally complex issues. The Chinese remake ends with a big song and dance that calls for peace and joy to the world.

Other noteworthy Chinese adaptations include *Thesmophoriazusae* by Aristophanes mounted by Wuhan People's Art Troupe in 2007.[24] Although

Aristophanes had been introduced and translated into Chinese almost at the same time as his tragedian contemporaries, the 2007 production, once again directed by Luo Jinlin, was the first time ever an Aristophanes play had been mounted on the Chinese stage. In July of that same year, the production traveled to Delphi, Greece to perform at the drama festival there. In 2010, Wuhan People's Art Troupe produced a revival production of the same play under the catchier Chinese title *nanren.nüren* (Men.Women) featuring exaggerated acting and catchphrases of today's China, which produced more than its share of laughter among the Chinese audiences. This production traveled to the Fourteenth International Festival of Ancient Greek Drama in Cyprus and had three performances there.

Much is lost in translation and perfect adaptations are far and few in between, yet for Chinese audiences to experience Greek classics, there is no getting around translation and adaptation. In 2008, as part of the Year of Greek Culture events in China, Greek Art Theatre took its production of Aristophanes' *The Birds* to the National Performing Arts Center in Beijing. It was a grand avant-garde production performed in Greek with Chinese captions. Throughout the performance, the Chinese audiences sat there politely but remained unaffected, failing to follow the basic story line, let alone appreciating the fantasy, gaiety, and topical references. The only time the audiences laughed was when a Greek actor inserted a simple Chinese expression *xiexie* (thanks) into a dialog. Not that the Chinese don't like birds. In fact, Beijingers are bird lovers, although they show their love by putting birds in cages and taking them to the parks. Back in 1993, Lin Zhaohua directed a popular play titled *Niaoren* (Birdman), mounted by the Beijing People's Art Theatre. It is a play about humans and birds, and about people Beijingers can recognize and easily identify with. So the challenges for adapting Western classics such as classic Greek drama remain: how to balance between making it appeal to the Chinese audiences today and remaining true to the spirit, if not the story, of the original.

Notes

1 An expanded version of the discussion on the 2009 *jingju* adaptation of *Oedipus the King*, coauthored with Wei Zhang under the title "Tragic Hero and Hero Tragedy: Reimagining *Oedipus the King* as *Jingju* (Peking opera) for the Chinese Stage," is published in the *Classical Receptions Journal* 12, no. 3 (2018).
2 See Victor Mair, 786–847. For a more in-depth discussion of classic Greek and Indian dramas on the development of Chinese drama, see Ben Liao, 3–29; Liu Yanjun, 100–7, 135–39; and Tan Zhifeng.
3 Tan Zhifeng, 46–50, and Shouhua Qi, 135–62.
4 See Luo Jinlin, "*Guanyu daoyan*" (Thoughts), 117–22.
5 His father, Luo Niansheng (1904–1990), was one of the foremost scholars and translators of classic Greek literature, including Homer's *Iliad*, Aristotle's *Poetics*, and plays by Aeschylus, Euripides, and Sophocles.
6 See Luo Jinlin, "*Gu xila*" (Ancient Greek) and "*Guanyu daoyan*" (Thoughts).

7　This portion of discussion draws from Jinlin Luo, "*Guanyu edipusi wang*" (Director's Analysis).
8　This portion of the discussion is based on *Jingju wangzhe edi* (Peking opera *Oedipus the King*) DVD published by Zhejiang Yinxiang Press, 2010.
9　Unless otherwise noted in this chapter, all English translations from Chinese adaptations of classic Greek drama are mine. They are more literal than expressive to give full flavor of the Chinese adaptations.
10　See *Wangzhe edi haiwai yanchu yu zhizuo huaxu* (Scenes from *Oedipus the King* overseas performances and productions).
11　This portion of the discussion draws from Jun Chen.
12　See Xiao Lin; and Zhe Jing.
13　This portion of the discussion draws from Sun Zhiying; Cai Yi; and Min Tian.
14　Sun Zhiying, 32.
15　Cai Yi, 69.
16　Ta Shan.
17　A *huaju* (spoken drama) adaptation of *Antigone* was mounted in 1988 by Haerbin Spoken Drama Troupe, which traveled to Greece for the Fourth International Meetings of Ancient Drama there.
18　See Wan Liu.
19　My translations based on quotes from Wan Liu.
20　See Xu Lian; and Fang Chen.
21　See Guo Qihong.
22　Zhou Chuanjia, 37.
23　Ibid, 38.
24　Chen Xi and Lin Wen. This portion of the discussion also draws from Niu Hongying.

Bibliography

Cai, Yi. "*Qiantan Hebei bangzi Meidiya gaibian de de yu shi*" (Tentative Study of Hebei Bangzi *Medea* Adaptation's Gain and Loss). *Dawutai* (Big Stage) 3 (1996): 68–9.

Chen, Jun. "'*Zhongguo wu beiju' mingti bainian huigu yu fansi*" ('China Has No Tragedy' Hypothesis One Hundred Years in Retrospect and Reflection). *Zhonghua xiqu* (Chinese Drama) 1 (2011): 22–53.

Chen, Xi and Wen Lin. "*Dimujie funü shouyan: Zhongguo jutuan paiyan diyi bu gu xila xiju*" (*Thesmophoriazusae* Premiers: Chinese Drama Troupe Mounts First Ancient Greek Comedy). *Hubei Daily*, July 17, 2007, Section 004.

Fang, Chen. "*Cong* Tebaicheng *shuo qi*" (To Begin With Tebaicheng). *Dawutai* (Big Stage) 2 (2003): 8–10.

Guo, Qihong. "*Wo xie chengbang enchou*" (How I Wrote Love and Hate Between Two Cities). *Yishu pinglun* (Arts Criticism) 7 (2014): 28–31.

"*Jingju wangzhe edi*" (Peking opera *Oedipus the King*) DVD. Hangzhou, Zhejiang: Zhejiang Yinxiang Press, 2010.

Liao, Ben. *Dongxifang xiju de duizhi yu jiegou* (Counterpoints and Structures of Eastern and Western Dramas). Shangai: Shanghai Cishu Press, 2007.

Liu, Yanjun. *Dongxifang xiju Jincheng* (Developments of Eastern and Western Dramas), 2nd ed. Beijing: Culture and Arts Press, 2005.

Luo, Jinlin. "*Guanyu edipusi wang de daoyan fenxi he gousi*" (Director's Analysis and Conceptualization of Oedipus the King). Central Academy of Drama 1986. Made available April 3, 2007. http://web.zhongxi.cn/xqzl/xxjj/zxjslxj/zyxjxyjsldy/2808.html.

————. "*Gu xila xiju zai zhongguo*" (Ancient Greek Drama in China: A Talk at the VIII International Meeting on Ancient Drama in Delphi, Greece, August 1995). Made available April 3, 2007. http://web.zhongxi.cn/xqzl/xxjj/zxjslxj/zyxjxyjsldy/2809.html.

Niu, Hongying. "*Alisiduofen zai Zhongguo de yijie yu chuanbo*" (Aristophanes Translation and Reception in China). *Journal of Anhui University of Technology* (Social Sciences) 28, no. 2 (2011): 71–3.

Sun, Zhiying. "*Shilun Hebei bangzi* Meidiya *de wutai siwei*" (Tentative Study of Hebei Bangzi *Medea's* Stage Conceptualization). *Dawutai* (Big Stage) 3 (1995): 32–4.

Ta, Shan. "*Meidiya yanchu chenggong yu yishu jiazhi: Beijing Hebei bangzi jutuan Meidiya yantaohui zongshu*" (*Medea* Successful Performance and Artistic Value: A Report on the Beijing Hebei Bangzi *Medea* Symposium). *Journal of College of Chinese Traditional Opera* 24, no. 1 (2003): 75–8.

Tan, Zhifeng. "*Gu xila xiju ruhua kaolun*" (Study of Ancient Greek Drama Entry in China). *Xiju wenxue* (Drama Literature) 11 (2011): 46–50.

Tian, Min. "Adaptation and Staging of Greek Tragedy in Hebei Bangzi." *Asian Theatre Journal* 23, no. 2 (Fall 2006): 248–64.

Wan, Liu. "*Chuanshen shiju yu kua wenhua gaibian: Cong xila beiju* Antigenie *dao gaojia xi* Andi gongzhu" (Impassioned Play and Transcultural Adaptation: From Greek Tragedy *Antigone* to Gaojia Opera *Princess Andi*). *Journal of National Academy of Chinese Theatre Arts* 35, no. 2 (2014): 107–13.

"*Wangzhe edi haiwai yanchu yu zhizuo huaxu*" (Scenes From *Oedipus the King* Overseas Performances and Productions). Video made available July 18, 2013. www.youtube.com/watch?v=CNe1fRrFWvc.

Xiao, Lin. "*Gu xila beiju haineng zheyang yan! Jingju* Wangzhe edi *Saipulusi gu juchang shouyan*" (Ancient Greek Tragedy Can Be Performed This Way! Peking Opera *Oedipus the King* Premieres at Ancient Theatre in Cyprus). *Guangming Daily*, July 20, 2011, Section 8. http://epaper.gmw.cn/gmrb/html/2011-07/20/nw.D110000gmrb_20110720_9-08.htm.

Xu, Lian. "*Tebaicheng shi bu shi yi ji liangyao*" (Is *Thebes* a Good Medicine?). *China Culture Daily*, May 30, 2002, Section 002.

Zhe, Jing. "'*Zhongguo Edi*' Zhenhan Saipulusi: *Zhejiang jingjutuan shiyan jingju Wangzhe edi fu Sai yanchu ceji*" ('Chinese Oedipus' Excites Cyprus: A Report on Zhejiang Peking Opera Troupe's Experimental Play *Oedipus the King* Performances in Cyprus). *China Culture Daily*, July 26, 2011, Section 7. http://news.idoican.com.cn/zgwenhuab/html/2011-07/26/content_2426575.htm?div=0.

Zhou, Chuanjia. "*Da jingjie da zhuiqiu: Xikan pingju Chengbang enchou*" (Big Vision Big Undertaking: Pingju Love and Hate Between Two Cities Accomplishments). *Yishu pinglun* (Arts Criticism) 7 (2014): 35–9.

5 Old man Shakespeare, the all but forgotten Shaw, and the importance of being Oscar Wilde

English classics, including its drama, occupy a uniquely prominent place in modern Chinese culture thanks to the uniquely potent way the English, or, rather, the British, impacted the development of modern Chinese history, especially during the decades from the Opium Wars (1839–1842, 1856–1860) to the early twentieth century. In a way, as one Chinese reviewer of Murray J. Levith's *Shakespeare in China* (2004) put it, rather sardonically, the British warships that sailed halfway around the world to blast open China and force more opium and trade on its people also brought Shakespeare to the far-eastern country – Shakespeare, along with many other English writers, for example (with dates of the first introduction and/or translation), Jonathan Swift (1782), Daniel Defoe (1898), Alfred Tennyson (1898), Alexander Pope (1898), William Wordsworth (1900), Lord Byron (1902), Oliver Goldsmith (1904), Robert Louis Stevenson (1904), Sir Walter Scott (1905), Percy Shelley (1906), Charles Dickens (1907), Oscar Wilde (1909), George Eliot (1911), George Bernard Shaw (1919), D. H. Lawrence, James Joyce, and H. G. Wells (1922).[1]

Of these, as far as the subject of this book is concerned, Shakespeare, Shaw, and Wilde stand out and are the most noteworthy: Shakespeare remains as illustrious as ever in a league of his own; Shaw is still enthusiastically celebrated and studied, but his plays have rarely shone on the Chinese stage; Wilde, whose fortunes in China rise and fall precipitously with the times, finds himself glittering brilliantly again in the "gilded age" of China today, his plays being adapted, or rather, appropriated, earnestly for much-needed comic relief as well as serious social satire.

Old man Shakespeare

Early encounters and adaptation ventures

The first time China swam into the ken of William Shakespeare, to borrow from John Keats ("On First Looking into Chapman's Homer"), it was perhaps on the sky of *The Twelve Night* (1601) in the form of an offhand reference of "Cataian" or "Cathayan."[2] It is a term with pejorative connotation ("thief," "scoundrel") for a native of Cathay used by the perhaps not so deep-browed Marco Polo in his book on his travels in that "wide expanse" in the orient – a term that is long obsolete, although the Cathay Pacific Airline based in Hong Kong, a former British colony, still proudly embraces it. Then China appears again in Shakespeare's 1604 comedy *Measure for Measure*,[3] albeit once again for only a fleeting moment, in an apparently more pleasing association with elegant gourmet. On the other hand, the first time ever for a Chinese to breathe the "pure serene" of the make-believe world conjured up by the Bard would have to wait for more than two-and-a-half centuries after his passing. That was in the early spring of 1879 when Zeng Jize (1839–1890),[4] while serving as ambassador to Britain and France, saw a production of *Hamlet* in London with Henry Irving (1838–1905) playing the titular role. Another two decades would have to lapse before Shakespeare himself landed in China, so to speak, and made his debut on a Chinese stage – on the campus of St. John's University (*Shengyuehan*), an Anglican university founded by American missionaries in 1879 – in the form of upper-class students performing, in English, the trial of Shylock from Act IV of *The Merchant of Venice* during the university's commencement celebrations.[5]

The first performance of Shakespeare on the Chinese stage by the Chinese, for the Chinese, and in the native Chinese language would be the 1913 production of *The Merchant of Venice* under the Chinese title *Rouquan* (Flesh Bond, Ransom). It was based on a retelling of the story in Charles and Mary Lamb's *Tales from Shakespeare* rendered into Chinese by Lin Shu (1852–1924), one of the most prolific translators of Western literature, although Lin himself didn't know any foreign languages and therefore had to rely on his language facilitators who had had the benefit of education in Western countries. Therefore, this 1913 production was at least twice removed from its source text, language, and culture, although it might have given a fair representation of the gist of the story.[6]

By 1916, several Shakespearean plays had "fretted and strutted" on the Chinese stage under various Chinese titles: *Hamlet* as *Qieguozei* (The Usurper), *Shaxiong duosao* (To Kill the Brother and Steal the Sister-in-law), *Cuanwei daosao* (To Usurp the Throne and Steal the Sister-in-law), *Guizhao* (Ghost's Command), and *Luanshi jianxiong* (Unscrupulous Hero in Troubled times); *King Lear* as *Zimei huangdi* (Sister Empresses); *Othello* as *Hei jiangjun* (Dark General), and *The Merchant of Venice* as *Jiezhai gerou* (Pay Debt with Flesh), *Nü lüshi* (Woman Lawyer), and *Rouquan* (Flesh Bond, or Ransom); and *Macbeth* as *Wuhuo* (Witch Trouble), *Qieguozei* (The Usurper), and *Xin nanbei he* (New North and South Unified, New Emperor Dream). All of these Chinese titles have a notable melodramatic ring to them that would reverberate in the architextual (Gérard Genette) world of traditional Chinese drama (*xiqu*). They smack of the sensationalism that many of the new generation around the turn of the twentieth century (including those responsible for introducing Shakespeare and other Western classics, and translating and mounting them on the stage by way of reinventing the Chinese drama and indeed renewing the Chinese people and culture) had denounced as old, corrupting, and useless for China in the post-Opium War brave new world.[7] To appeal to the Chinese theatergoers, then, the Chinese adapters of *The Merchant of Venice*, or rather *Nu lushi* (Woman Lawyer), put this advertisement in the newspaper:[8]

> This is a famous play by *Shaweng* (Old Man Shakespeare). It tells the story of paying debt with one's flesh and of a woman lawyer. It brims with style and sentiments and brings you joy from beginning to end.

The racial bias in this newspaper advertisement for *Othello*, or its Chinese reincarnation *Hei jiangjun* (Dark General), is as unsubtle as is unmistakable:[9]

> A beautiful young lady, with all the beautiful young gentlemen available, chooses to marry a dark general who is dark from head to toe, which leads to a sea of love, hate, and grief. The most heart-wrenching of all Shakespeare plays.

Despite the apparent propensity for melodrama, these early adaptation endeavors were mostly undertaken for "serious" cultural and sociopolitical causes. Indeed, Shakespeare was "appropriated," as was the case of Henrik Ibsen and others, not only to help remake the Chinese drama and theatre but also, sometimes, to be the voice of resistance and protest. The 1911 Xinhai Revolution, led by Dr. Sun Yat-sen, succeeded in overthrowing the last emperor of the Qing dynasty and establishing the Republic of China. However, in 1915, Yuan Shikai, a powerful warlord general who had supported the revolution, declared himself the Hongxian Emperor, essentially returning China to monarchy. This angered the Chinese people all over the country. To join the nationwide protest, young drama enthusiasts in Shanghai mounted an adaptation of *Hamlet* under the Chinese title *Qieguozei* (The Usurper). The newspaper advertisement to promote the play goes like this:[10]

> A minister usurps the throne and usurps the kingdom while carrying on with the queen; a brother steals his sister-in-law and steals all the power as well. To carry out revenge on this ungodly murder of his father when his mother is already wife of his father's murderer, he has to pretend and play mad to spare his mother. In the end none escapes death, hence the misery of all miseries.

Qieguozei (The Usurper) was quite a hit. It caught the attention of Yuan Shikai, who understood what it meant just as Claudius knows what the play-within-a-play *The Murder of Gonzago* orchestrated by Hamlet means. He had Gu Wuwei, the actor who played the titular role, arrested and sentenced to death. Gu escaped death only when Yuan Shikai himself was overthrown less than a year after he put the crown on his own head, so to speak.

Bardolatry?

From the earliest performances more than 100 years ago to the first Shakespeare Festival held in Beijing and Shanghai simultaneously (1986) in the post-Cultural Revolution (1966–1976) China, the 1994 Shanghai Shakespeare Festival – originally planned for 1990, but put on hold because of events on the Tiananmen Square in 1989 – and many other festivals thereafter, big and small, held to celebrate the Bard, and the numerous adaptations and remakes in *huaju* (spoken drama) and dozens of traditional *xiqu* genres, the history of Shakespeare in China has been well documented and studied. Notable among book-length studies published in English are Xiao Yang Zhang's *Shakespeare in China: A Comparative Study of Two Traditions and Cultures* (1997), Li Ruru's *Shashibiya: Staging Shakespeare in China* (2003), Murray J. Levith's *Shakespeare in China* (2004), and Alexander C. Y. Huang's *Chinese Shakespeares: Two Centuries of Cultural Exchange* (2009). These books address a myriad of issues of translation, reception, and adaptation of Shakespeare in China through the lenses of sociopolitical, translingual, and transcultural studies as well as moral and gender criticisms.

Shakespeare, or rather *Shaweng* (Old Man Sha), enjoys a cultlike status in China that has rarely been questioned. An American Shakespearean scholar who attended the 1998 "Shakespeare in China: Productions and Research" symposium held in Shanghai complained about a palpable level of "Bardolatry" in Chinese attitudes in general and a lack of interest in race issues in their adaptations of plays such as *Othello*.[11] Indeed, that criticism would also speak to the 1907 Spring Willow Society adaptation of *Uncle Tom's Cabin* under the Chinese title *Black Slave's Cry to Heaven*, a bold and ambitious undertaking that was more concerned with the plight of China, its people and culture, in the post-Opium war brave new world, than with the racial injustice in America. It is not that Chinese critics and artists are completely oblivious to the complex issues of Shakespeare's portrayal of the racial, religious "Other" as well as gender biases present in his plays, but that the Chinese have other more pressing priorities.[12] Nonetheless, Shakespeare is like a *budao weng* (never falling old man), an egg-shaped children's toy that will not fall no matter how one spins it, not only thanks to his genius, his poetic prowess, and artistic virtuosity but also, perhaps, thanks to his being not as much a polemist or social realist as critics such as Shaw would like to see.[13] In other words, Shakespeare, a man "not for an age but for all time," is politically a safe bet. He remains a towering figure that has eclipsed even the greatest of Chinese own theatre artists such as Tang Xianzu (1550–1616) known for his play *Mudan Ting* (The Peony Pavilion).[14]

The Merchant of Venice

Chinese adaptations of Shakespeare, like Chinese adaptations of other Western classics, typically assume one of the four modes: fidelity, indigenization, hybridization, and experimentation.[15] A good example of an adaptation in the "fidelity" mode would be *The Merchant of Venice* mounted by the China National Youth Theatre in 1980–1982. As noted earlier, *The Merchant of Venice* was the first Shakespearean play to have been performed on the Chinese stage, whether in English or in Chinese. Somehow, the play had an uncanny appeal to the Chinese in the early decades of the twentieth century, as can be seen in the various Chinese titles given the story since Lin Shu's rendition: *yibang rou* (one pound of flesh), *rouquan* (flesh bond, ransom), *gerou ji* (story of cutting one's flesh), etc.[16] Another appealing aspect of the play is its portrayal of Portia, a new woman who has everything to offer: beauty, brains, and wealth. Although Chinese literature, including drama, has its share of woman heroes – e.g., Wang Zhaojun and Cai Wenji[17] – Portia represents a different kind of women, as promoted in another Chinese title for the play, *Nü lüshi* (a woman lawyer). Lawyers and legal representation were largely unheard of in most of Chinese history, let alone "woman lawyer," although Portia is far from as polemic as Nora, the heroine of Ibsen's *A Doll's House*. Besides, the play celebrates romantic love as pursued by three pairs of lovely young people: Portia and Bassanio,[18] Nerissa (Portia's maid) and Gratiano (Bassanio's friend), and Jessica (Shylock's daughter) and Lorenzo (Bassanio's friend), each happily and appropriately matched according to his or her social status. Finally, the outcome of the play – Shylock, the bad, vicious moneylender, being punished and Portia, Bassanio, Antonio, and their friends, good and virtuous, being richly rewarded – reconfirms the traditional Chinese idea of karma, reward, and retribution, and satisfies their craving for happy endings.

Zhang Qihong (1931–), trained at the Lunacharsky State Institute for Theatre Arts in Moscow (1953–1959), as were quite a few other prominent drama directors such as Xu Xiaozhong (1928–), had a clear vision for what she wanted to achieve with this 1980–1982 production, only a few years after the curtain on the ten-year ordeal of the Cultural Revolution (1966–1976) had fallen.[19] She understood the challenges of adapting a play like *The Merchant of Venice* that had garnered many interpretations by critics and theatre artists alike. For her, the key was to find her own voice – i.e., giving her own interpretation through directing, acting, and stage design that would speak to her own times and culture while remaining true to the spirit of the original play. As she read it, the spirit of the play is virtue overcoming vice; it is triumph and celebration of *zhen* (truth), *shan* (kindness), and *mei* (beauty). Therefore, her purpose in mounting the play was to "let justice and kindness (as embodied in the play) cleanse our soul" that had been so battered and defiled during the Cultural Revolution. The underpinning of this "good versus bad" reading of the play was the Soviet-inspired, class-based dominant literary discourse that would read the play as a conflict between the new bourgeoisie (as represented by Bassino, Antonio, etc.) and the old feudalistic forces (as represented by Shylock), the former being virtuous and generous (as if the capitalistic bourgeois class is not interested in making money), and the latter being parasitic, greedy, and viciously vengeful.

It was based on this reading that Zhang took to streamline the dramatic action and downplay the racial and religious theme present in the original play. It is not that Zhang was not appreciative of the racial and religious prejudice that Shylock suffered, but in her estimate, the racial and religious theme is far less important than the humanistic theme of individuality, liberty, and human rights, as embodied by the lovely and lively characters of Portia, Jessica, and Gratiano. Indeed, Zhang's 1980–1982 *Merchant of Venice* opens with a scene of Bassino, Gratino (donning a guitar), and Lorenzo rowing a boat and singing jubilantly down the grand canal to set a buoyant, upbeat tone for the entire play – before Antonio enters and gives his "in sooth, I know not why I am so sad" speech, which opens the play in the Shakespearean original. For many in the audiences who, like Zhang herself, had lived through 1950s China, this opening scene must have reminded them of "*Rang women dangqi shuangjiang*" (Let's Row the Boat Down the River), the theme song of the 1955 film *Flowers of the Motherland* (*Zuguo de huaduo*), or the poem that preludes Wang Meng's 1953 novel *Qingchun wansui* (Love Live Youth), which was made into a popular film in 1983:[20]

> Let all the days, let all the days come,
> Let me weave you, with golden threads of youth,
> Let me weave you, with pearls of happiness.
> Those days of singing and laughing on the little boat,
> Dancing our heart out on moonlit schoolyard,
> Meandering in the trees on a drizzly spring day,
> Marching on a fresh snow-covered morning,
> Oh, don't forget the spirited debates, and warm hearts beating fast.

It harks back, nostalgically, to the "good ol' days" of the 1950s, more mythologized than real. If audience members did take a stroll in the memory lane they would have found that those years were plagued with their share of political campaigns, including the notorious Anti-Rightist Movement (1957–1958), in which so many outspoken intellectuals and artists had been persecuted, an ominous harbinger for what was to come in the 1960s. This buoyant and mirthful tone frames and permeates the 1980–1982 adaptation despite short interludes (or intrusions) of darker notes from dramatic action associated with Shylock.

Zhang was concerned that most Chinese audiences lacked the necessary historical and cultural knowledge to understand fully and appreciate the racial and religious aspects of the play. They knew very little, if anything at all, of the long tensions between Christians and Jews, and indeed how the Jews, historically, were mistreated in England and elsewhere in Europe. Therefore, to minimize possible confusion and indeed to maximize attention on what she perceived to be the dominant theme of the story, she cut most of the Jew-specific references and what she considered to be the "nonessential" dialogs and scenes. Throughout the production, Shylock is known by his name, unlike in the Shakespearean original where he is often addressed or referred to as "Jew" or "the Jew," his racial and religious identity. For example, although much of the impassioned speech Shylock gives when he and Antonio negotiate the terms for the moneylending deal survived the cut, the word "Jewish" ("You call me misbeliever, cutthroat dog, /And spet upon my Jewish gaberdine," I-3, 102–124) had been surgically removed. Toward the end of the original play, Portia (a lawyer, instead of a judge) doles out severe punishment for Shylock based on the laws of Venice against an "alien" who dares to "seek the life of any citizen." In the Zhang adaptation, the reference to Shylock's "alien" legal status, on top of him being a racial and religious "Other," was dropped. In the original play, Antonio, out of mercy, lays out this condition, so upon Shylock's death, the half of his estate awarded to him will be given "the gentleman/That lately stole his daughter" (Lorenzo): Shylock's immediate conversion to Christianity (IV-1, 375–385). This exacting and profoundly humiliating condition, whether it reflects the racial bias on the part of Shakespeare or his gift as a socially realistic artist,[21] was dropped in the Zhang adaptation too. As a result, the theme of Shylock as a racial and religious "Other," suggested only by way of his "exotic" costumes and manner of speech, was reduced to a minimum.

The Zhang adaptation had a successful run of 500 performances from 1980 to 1982,[22] ample evidence of how it met the cultural and emotive needs of the people then. Most of its tens of thousands of audience members probably did not notice the significantly reduced racial and religious theme and therefore was not bothered by it. One drama critic, Zhou Peitong, a Central Academy of Drama professor, did notice the conspicuous reduction and write rather critically about it in his published review. For Zhou, who in the 1950s was exiled to the outlying northwestern plateau of Qinghai to be reformed through labor as punishment for a political satire short story he had submitted for publication,[23] Shakespeare "idealized" Portia and almost every other character in the original play except for Shylock. In fact, as seen by Zhou, Shylock is a round, realistically portrayed character who has suffered from egregious racial and religious oppression, and chooses to use the weapon of law to fight back, although one can never condone his greed and his vicious, all-consuming desire for revenge. He is as much sinned against as sinned and therefore deserves our sympathy too.[24] It is rather encouraging to see, though, even from the vantage point of 2018, that Zhou's review, which contains seriously worded criticism of the adaptation's attempt to essentially "erase" the racial and religious theme of the Shakespearean play, was published in the same 1981 issue of a drama journal side by side with Director Zhang's article explaining her own vision for this adaptation and her response to the criticism.

What saved this adaptation, in terms of the racial and religious theme, was the actor who played Shylock, Wang Jinyu, who gave full-throated expression to the character's range of human emotions as father, moneylender, and victim, as well as an implacable revenger. His performance was heartfelt and theatrical but not histrionic or caricaturish. The humanity of Shylock, as channeled by Wang Jingyu, flawed as it is, anchors the story in considerable depths of pathos and ethos despite the dominant mood of buoyant optimism of romantic comedy the director had set for the production. Indeed, toward the end of the play, one cannot but feel for Shylock, as he prostrates in front of the duke, thanking him for the mercy bestowed on him, having lost everything – daughter, money, the entire estate, and, above all, dignity – excessive, cruel, and unusual punishment indeed.

Overall, though, this 1980–1982 adaptation achieved what the director had set out to accomplish – to give her own interpretation through directing, acting, and stage design, so the play would speak to her own times and culture, although whether her adaptation remained true to the full spirit of the original play is open to discussion. Even the extensive use of wigs and golden dust to evoke a sense of the sixteenth-century Venetian culture, people, and life did not seem such a false note. Zhang was a conscious artist, as was Cao Yu, the artistic advisor for the production. Cao Yu would be involved in the 1983 production of *Death of a Salesman* in Beijing directed by Arthur Miller, who, among other things, insisted that his Chinese Willy Loman, Biff, and other characters remain Chinese, donning no wigs or false noses.[25]

One of the creative licenses Zhang took was to personify the three caskets Portia presents to each of her suiters with three dancers. The gold casket ("Who chooseth me shall gain what many men desire," II-7, 73), chosen by the first suitor, the impassioned Prince of Morocco, is presented by a dancer dressed in shiny gold accompanied by exotic Arabian music; the silver casket ("Who chooseth me shall get as much as he deserves," II-9, 78–82), chosen by the arrogant but foolish Prince of Arragon (an ancient kingdom of Spain), is presented by a dancer dressed in shiny silver accompanied by lively tango music, and the lead casket ("Who chooseth me must give and hazard all he hath," II-7. 11–12), chosen by Bassanio, is presented by a dancer dressed simply with no exotic music or dance to make her more alluring. They each provide a rather lively and entertaining moment in the production, although the racial and cultural bias in the portrayal of the three suiters, present in the Shakespearean original, is hard to miss. Adding to the entertainment value of the production are some "racy" (by Chinese standard then) expressions that roll off the tongue of Portia, a lovely and well-cultured Venetian lady, toward the end of the play when she demands that Brassino show the ring she has given him earlier:[26]

> If you cannot show me the ring, I will never climb into your bed (*yongyuan bu shang ni de chuang*).
>
> Then, I swear on my still intact virtue that I will ask that PhD lawyer to come and sleep with me (*wo hui rang na ge boshi lai pei wo shuijiao*).
>
> It was with that ring in hand that that PhD lawyer slept with me last night (*zuowan yijing he wo shui guo jiao le*).

"*Shangchuang*" (climbing into bed), "*shuijiao*" (sleeping together), and such common-folk expressions with universally known sexual connotations, uttered publicly on the stage in Beijing, must have raised some eyebrows, but also provided the much-needed release for the long, puritanically repressed sexuality in the collective psyche, as evidenced in the hearty laughter in the audience.

Hamlet

For a more experimental Shakespearean endeavor in China, one could not do wrong with the 1990 adaptation of *Hamlet* directed by Lin Zhaohua who has been responsible for several noteworthy adaptations of Western classics discussed in this book.

To discuss this adaptation of Shakespeare, one would have to revisit the socio-historical and psychological context of 1990. Regardless of where one stood on the massive student movements in 1989 – with them (most Chinese people then) on the sidelines, or on the side of the government that eventually chose to crack down with a show of force – one could not help but feel the deep wound on the body politic and the national psyche. Why, then, did Lin Zhaohua take on Shakespeare's *Hamlet* when Beijing, and, indeed, much of China, were still nursing this deep, tender wound and squirming under the heavy poll of gloom and despair? Lin did not put out a manifesto as Meng Jinghui did around the same time to preface his audacious experiments with the Theatre of the Absurd, more particularly, Samuel Beckett's *Waiting for Godot* (see Chapter 3).[27] Nonetheless, Meng's loud musings about if anyone would care to join him and other artists "in this adventure to destroy an unreal phantom, to rebuild our home etched in our memory so we can see clearly the vista as far as our eyes can reach" (Chapter 3) can serve as a useful index into the scarred emotive and spiritual landscape of many Chinese at the time, including Lin Zhaohua. It would not be too farfetched to imagine a variation of the same "to be, or not to be" question reverberating in the mind of Lin and many others. Lin Zhaohua answered the question by mounting an adaptation of the play where the question, both ontological and urgently personal, was raised and pondered with so much at stake, and gave the Shakespearean classic an audacious remake centering on a "We are all Hamlet" theme.[28]

The curtain rises on this 1990 *Hamlet* in a small theatre in Beijing to reveal a half-dug grave in the foreground (downstage) that fills the length from stage left to stage right. Two gravediggers joke jovially, as befits their clownish roles, trading witty questions about "what kind of people are the most long lived" ("they are ones tilling the land and we gravediggers"), "what is he that builds stronger than the mason, the shipwright, or the carpenter?" ("the gallowsmaker, for that frame outlives a thousand tenants," or, rather, a gravedigger because "the houses he makes last till doomsday"). This graveyard motif, which appears only once in the Shakespearean original (V-1), sets the tone for and indeed frames the entire production so that "Denmark" feels even worse than a prison. It is a ghostly, life-and-death wasteland upon which a puppet show is enacted by zombies on borrowed time.

The second appearance of the graveyard motif preludes the scene where Ophelia reports to her father Polonius that Lord Hamlet, "his doublet all unbraced," "his stockings fouled," "pale as his shirt," acted to her as if he had just been "loosèd out of hell" (II-1, 76–82). Gravedigger 1, who is in the half-dug ditch, tries to make a phone call (anachronistically, by design, to give the story a more modern vibe) using a dial phone, while Gravedigger 2 (played by Liang Guanhua) tries to make a phone call in a corner above the ground. Failing to get through, the two begin to talk, nonchalantly, about the death of Ophelia, more specifically, whether she deserves a Christian burial because she has committed suicide. It is an eerie conversation, an eerily dark and prophetic (before Ophelia has killed herself) comment offered by a two-gravedigger "chorus." This line by Gravedigger 1 – "Nowadays the rich and powerful have more freedom than us ordinary people, even in how they choose to jump into a river and drown themselves" – must have struck some chords among the Chinese audiences then.

Not long after this, the two gravediggers insert themselves before the scene where Polonius (also played by Liang Guanhua) orchestrates another meeting between Ophelia and Hamlet to prove his madness to King Claudius. An old compact film projector by his feet, Gravedigger 1 rings a bell, picks up a skull, and gives this speech:

> See, it's this thing (pointing at the skull). It might have been a politician, an old hand at stealing the sky and usurping the sun, or perhaps an honest, virtuous intellectual who, how to put it, is full of worries about the country and the people, and has done lots of good deeds for the people; and then, after a lawsuit, before he knows it, falls into this hole I've dug. Ahhh, one can never predict what kind of storm is in store for us. The best policy is still that old folksy saying: It's always wiser to mind our own business than try to mind the sky or the earth. When I am fed, my whole family knows no hunger either.

That message, "mind one's own business" instead of minding the business of "the sky or the earth," must have been heard loud and clear in the Beijing of 1990, and its echoes can still be heard across China today, as evidenced by the fact that ever since the 1989 Tiananmen Square crackdown, most Chinese have been channeling their passions and energy much more toward personal pursuits – socioeconomic, cultural, educational, etc. – than socio-political engagements.

Framed by the gloom of the graveyard is a court that feels like it has just seen a nuclear blast: old gray drapery in the background, old gray and badly wrinkled carpet covering the floor, half damaged tools scattered here and there, and an old barber's chair, right center, functioning as a makeshift throne – perhaps the combined result of both Lin Zhaohua's artistic vision for this production and a shoestring budget that his recently formed drama studio had to make do with. Recent death of King Hamlet hangs depressively over everyone, particularly the young prince, no matter how eloquent and sincere Claudius and Gertrude manage to sound in trying to cheer him up.

It is in this early scene (I-2 of the Shakespearean original) that the most experimental feat for this production happens. In this scene, Laertes asks permission to return to studies in France, and King Claudius (Ni Dahong) and Queen Gertrude (Xu Fang) talk Hamlet (Pu Cunxin) into abandoning the idea of returning to Wittenberg. When it is time for the king and queen, satisfied that the young prince will stay in Denmark, to retire to their inner chamber, Pu Cunxin, stage left, who has been in the role of Hamlet, delivers these lines:

> This gentle and unforc'd accord of Hamlet
> Sits smiling to my heart; in grace whereof,
> No jocund health that Denmark drinks to-day
> But the great cannon to the clouds shall tell,
> And the King's rouse the heaven shall bruit again,
> Respeaking earthly thunder. Come away.
>   (I-2, 326–331)

Snapping out of a moment of confusion, one realizes that Pu/Hamlet has morphed into Pu//Claudius, just as Ni/Claudius has morphed into Ni/Hamlet. It is now Pu/Claudius who helps Xu/Gertrude off the makeshift throne; the two exit the stage, leaving behind Ni /Hamlet to deliver these famous lines:

> O that this too too solid flesh would melt,
> Thaw, and resolve itself into a dew!
> Or that the Everlasting had not fix'd
> His canon 'gainst self-slaughter! O God! God!
> How weary, stale, flat, and unprofitable
> Seem to me all the uses of this world!
>   (I-1, 333–363)

In that shocking switch of actors' roles, a thematic coup has been accomplished: Claudius/Hamlet, king/prince, murderer and usurper/the murdered king's son, husband/wife/mother/son, and, indeed, good/bad are all blurred into a confusing mishmash.

A few moments later, when Horatio comes on the scene, it is to Ni/Hamlet that he reports the sight of the Old Hamlet's ghost ("My lord, I think I saw him yesternight"), and it is Ni/Hamlet who delivers these lines:

> My father's spirit in arms! all is not well;
> I doubt some foul play: would the night were come!
> Till then sit still, my soul: foul deeds will rise,
> Though all the earth o'erwhelm them, to men's eyes.

Yet, a couple of scenes later, it is Pu/Hamlet who goes to see for his own eyes the ghost of Old Hamlet, who tells him of the murder ("O, horrible!

O, horrible! most horrible!"); it is Pu/Hamlet who vows revenge and swears his friends into secrecy upon his sword. And then, in Act II, Scene 2, Liang/Polonius comes in with the actors, and Pu/Hamlet asks one of the actors to perform a rendition of the story of "the rugged Pyrrhus." When that rendition is over, another role switching happens: Pu Cunxin becomes Polonius, whereas Liang Guanhua, now in the role of Hamlet, asks the players to put on the play "the Murder of Gonzago" with an inserted speech "of some dozen or sixteen lines" to be set down by him later.

The most dramatic and hence thematically potent instance of the role switching, or rather, blurring, happens in Act III, Scene 1, right after Liang/Polonius tells Ophelia to walk on and have another encounter with Hamlet to see if her "good beauties be the happy cause/Of Hamlet's wildness" and then disappears, along with Ni/Claudius behind the drapery. When Pu/Hamlet wanders on stage, however, Liang/Polonius and Ni/Claudius join him in giving this most important soliloquy together, marching in various formations across the stage:

PU/HAMLET: To be, or not to be,
NI/CLAUDIUS: To be, or not to be,
LIANG/POLONIUS: To be, or not to be,
PU/HAMLET: that is the question:
NI/CLAUDIUS: that is the question:
LIANG/POLONIUS: that is the question:
PU/HAMLET
    Whether 'tis nobler in the mind to suffer
    The slings and arrows of outrageous fortune,
    Or to take Arms against a Sea of troubles,
    And by opposing end them:
LIANG/POLONIUS
    to die, to sleep
    No more; and by a sleep, to say we end
    the heart-ache, and the thousand natural shocks
    that Flesh is heir to? 'Tis a consummation
    devoutly to be wished.
NI/CLAUDIUS
    To die, to sleep,
    To sleep, perchance to Dream; aye, there's the rub,
    for in that sleep of death, what dreams may come,
    when we have shuffled off this mortal coil,
    must give us pause.
                        (III-1, 1749–1783)

For a moment, Hamlet, Claudius, and Polonius all mesh into the same role of the young prince of Denmark, or, rather, all three separate characters, the good, the bad, and the "officious, garrulous, and impertinent" busybody,[29] muse aloud on the heavy existential question in the same breath. Thematically, especially for the "We are all Hamlet" theme that Lin Zhaohua sets for this production, it is the climactic moment for the entire play. In a blink of an eye afterward, Ni/Claudius and Liang/Polonius disappear behind the drapery again to listen in as Pu/Hamlet tells Ophelia to "get thee to a nunnery: why wouldst thou be a breeder of sinners?"

Despite all the blurring of roles and mishmash of good and bad, one important soliloquy by Ni/Claudius, passionately delivered in Act III, Scene 3, has unmistakable moral clarity and perhaps hard-to-miss political resonances for the audiences in the 1990 Beijing:

> O, my offence is rank. It smells to heaven.
> . . . .
> What if this cursed hand
> Were thicker than itself with brother's blood,
> Is there not rain enough in the sweet heavens
> To wash it white as snow? Whereto serves mercy
> But to confront the visage of offence?

During the play-within-the-play (III-2), Ni/Claudius, a "guilty creature" being "struck so to the soul" perhaps, as Hamlet has hoped, gets up from the makeshift throne, downstage right, as if hypnotized, walks into the "the Murder of Gonzago" story being reenacted center stage, takes the crown from "Gonzago," and puts it on his own head. This telltale sleepwalk that indisputably "proclaim'd" Claudius' "malefactions," is performed twice, in the fashion of the playback function of the VHS technology popular in the 1990s,[30] for the world to see.

The duel between Pu/Hamlet and Laertes results in everyone – Gertrude, Claudius, Laertes, and Hamlet – fatally poisoned. As they all lie on the ground, breathing their last, one last role switching happens: kit is Ni Dadong, now in the role of Hamlet, that struggles on his feet, tells the dying Laertes, "Heaven make thee free of it," and asks Horatio not to kill himself, but to "draw thy breath in plain" in this hard world and tell the story of the Prince of Denmark.

Hamlet's story did get retold on the Chinese stage in 1990, when the wound in the national psyche was still tender and footages of recent events on the Tiananmen Square were still vivid in the minds of the body politic. This experimental adaptation of *Hamlet*, absent the usual wigs and false noses to create an illusion of "exotic" foreignness, must have hit home and struck many chords, emotive as well as sociopolitical, with many in the audiences in Beijing then.

King Lear

Four years later, in 1994, the story of Leir of Britain, a legendary pre-Roman Celtic king, as retold by Shakespeare in his 1606 tragedy *King Lear*, was retold again by Hebei Shijiazhuang Sixian Troupe.[31] Although *sixian* (silk strings) is a traditional *xiqu* genre that goes back to the early Qing dynasty, it is not as popular as Hebei *bangzi*, let alone the quasi-national drama *jingju*. The *sixian* troupe of Shijiazhuang, a city in the Hebei Province, is not well known either. However, its 1994 production of *King Lear* is noteworthy as an interesting example of Chinese adaptations in the full "indigenization" mode.

The Chinese, artists and audiences alike, tend to see loyalty (*zhong*) and filial piety (*xiao*) at the heart of the pathos and ethos of *King Lear* – loyalty to the country (as embodied, literally, by the king, emperor, or government) and filial piety being two of the most important and celebrated virtues for the Chinese from time immemorial. Therefore, as noted by Dai Xiaotong, who adapted the Shakespearean play for the 1994 *sixian* production,[32] the story of an old king betrayed by two ungrateful, unfilial daughters resonates almost naturally with Chinese audiences, urban or rural. Very little background knowledge is needed to understand and appreciate. All that it takes to bring this Western classic home for the Chinese is naturalizing the characters, so they are easy to remember and compressing and streamlining the story, so there is ample time and space for singing, dancing, and acrobatics and martial arts, hallmarks of traditional *xiqu* such as *sixian*.

To naturalize the characters, King Lear becomes a Chinese monarch, *Li'er Wang*, Li being one of the most popular Chinese family names, right behind Zhao, Qian, Sun (the family name of the emperors of the Tang dynasty, 618–907, happens to be Li too). The three daughters, Goneril, Regan, Cordelia, now go by their Sinicized titles only: First Princess (*Da Gongzhu*), Second Princess (*Er Gongzhu*), and Third Princess (*San Gongzhu*), which are so much easier to say and remember than these "exotic" names' usual Chinese transliterations. Their husbands, Duke of Albany, Duke of Cornwall, and King of France (suitor and later husband of Cordelia) now assume their corresponding Sinicized titles too: First Royal Son-in-Law (*Da Fuma*), Second Royal Son-in-Law (*Er Fuma*), and Third Royal Son-in-Law (*San Fuma*).

Outside the royal family, characters and plot developments undergo considerable compression too. Earl of Kent, honest and loyal to the end, and Earl of Gloucester, an injudicious old man who eventually finds his humanity again, are combined into one character, Earl Ge (*Ge Daren*), Ge being another popular Chinese last name. Edmond, Gloucester's illegitimate and opportunistic son, becomes Earl Ge's Son (*Ge Gongzi*), whose portrayal draws from other characters from the original play: Oswald, Goneril's steward and eager accomplice, and Duke of Burgundy, a suitor who rejects Cordelia when he discovers that she has been disinherited by her father. Edgar, Earl Gloucester's legitimate son and heir, is eliminated from this adaptation. As a result, the secondary plot of the Gloucester father and sons, a foil for the main story of King Lear and his daughters, is reduced to the minimum.

For costumes, the production team chose the style of the Ming dynasty (1368–1644), with some ethnic twist (e.g., hats ornamented with shiny, long rooster feathers) to imply that the story takes place in a far-flung minority area (as opposed to the Han Chinese hinterland). As luck would have it, the Hebei Shijiazhuang Sixian Troupe, restrained by a shoestring budget, already had a set of Ming dynasty costumes from the production of another play.

To fit the Western classic further into the artistic mode of *sixian*, Dai Xiaotong rewrote the dialogs and lyrics based on existent Chinese translations, using simple, direct, easily accessible (albeit clichéish) stock phrases and figurative language drawn from the repertoire of traditional Chinese literature and drama. For example, when *Li'er Wang* (King Lear) asks the three daughters to express their love for their father, here is what each of them sings by way of response:

FIRST PRINCESS (*DA GONGZHU*)
My love for my Royal Father is extraordinary,
May heaven be witness as I outpour heartfelt feelings.
My love is as far and wide as the endless grasslands,
My love is as long and deep as the roaring river,
My love is as high as cloud-piercing mountain peaks,
My love is as boundless as the infinite blue sky.

SECOND PRINCESS (*ER GONGZHU*)
I have the same heartfelt feelings for my Royal Father as my big sister,
Infinite loyalty and love for you.
I love you, more than all the filial daughters from time immemorial,
I love you, unrivalled by anything in the world and far beyond.
If, god forbid, Your Majesty ever loses my love,
Oh, birds would not fly, water not flow, grass not germinate, trees
    not grow,
The world devoid of songs, laughter, and fragrant flowers,
The sun, the moon, and all the stars would lose their shine.

THIRD PRINCESS (*SAN GONGZHU*)
My Royal Father,
I am not heartless, disloyal, cold as ice and frost.
It's just that I am unwilling, unwilling to seek rewards with honey-
    talked talk.
. . . .
I will not say anything that is not from the bottom of my heart,
I can only love Your Majesty as much as I am duty bound.
Say how high the mountain is as it is,
Say how long the river is as it is,
Honest people have clear conscience,
Always tell it like it is, never exaggerate.

The highlight of this fully indigenized adaptation of *King Lear* is the storm scene, Act V, *Yewai chongfeng* (reunion in the wilderness), as restructured by Dai and his team. In this scene, Zhang Helin, who plays the title role, brings his versatile talents in *chang* (sing), *nian* (speech), *zuo* (mix of dance and performance), and *da* (mix of acrobatics and martial arts) to channel and give full-throated expression to the "tempest" raging in the mind of *Li'er Wang* as he staggers in the wilderness of the heath, betrayed, abandoned, and furious.

As the curtain rises for this act, revealing a wilderness enveloped in dim, ghastly light, an aria arises offstage, in the magnetic, powerful, *lao sheng* (old male role) voice of Zhang Helin, that expands and fills the world between heaven and earth:

> Dark clouds rumble, thunderous lightning flashes, sky dims, and earth glooms

The last note still lingering in the thunderous lightning and intense music from string and percussion instruments, a disheveled, trembling *Li'er Wang*, cane in hand, staggers on stage:

> Great misfortune has befallen *Li'er Wang*,
> Stomach empty, I can hardly walk,
> Dog tired after days of hurried journey,
> Chilled to the bone by a downpour of cold rain

For more than ten minutes, *Li'er Wang* continues to sing and recount his misfortune of having been deceived by his honey-tongued first and second daughters, having disowned the honest third daughter and the misery his foolishness has caused his kingdom and all the common folks. Then he breaks into another big number, singing, dancing, acting, his whole being a heartrending, explosive outpouring of feelings that lasts for more than seven minutes:

> How I wish to destroy and offer myself as sacrifice to Heaven
> Fire in my heart shoots up to the clouds and flashes with lightning,
> Fury in my chest joins gusty wind to rock the waves,
> . . . .
> It feels like sky and earth melts into one,
> My body breaks apart, my soul scatters, I am falling into bottomless hole.
> I am wind I am rain!
> I am thunder I am lightning!
> I am god and I am judge!

The celebrated storm scene, as remade in this *sixian* adaptation, ends on a high, resounding note, a rousing call for divine (or rather, earthly) justice, a far cry from the tragic, elemental sense of being in the Shakespearean original as King Lear all but slips into insanity. Indeed, toward the very end of this *sixian* remake of the Shakespearean tragedy, justice – at least some degree of justice – is achieved to the satisfaction of both those in the play and the audiences offstage. By now, the three daughters are dead. Earl Ge's Son (*Ge Gongzi*), an overzealous accomplice to the First Princess (*Da Gongzhu*) who has committed the double crime against the cardinal virtues of loyalty (to the king) and filial piety (to his father), is now surrounded by armored troops led by the good Third Son-in-Law (*San Fuma*). After several rounds of well-choreographed fierce fight, witnessed by his father and *Li'er Wang*, Earl Ge's Son is cut down and drops dead. Then, in the midst of heartrending music, the spirt of Third Princess (*San Gongzhu*) arises, downstage, up to midair, for a moment of reunion of father and daughter, living and dead, before she disappears into the night. Heartbroken, *Li'er Wang* dances center stage as the chorus sings:

> False pretenses honest feelings life and death regrets,
> Good and evil struggle both jade and stone destroyed,
> Right versus wrong the sorrow from time immemorial,
> Cautionary story sung to this day lesson for posterity.

At the end of the song, *Li'er Wang* staggers and falls on his back, dead.

Like many other plays by *Shaweng* (Old Man Shakespeare) – *Hamlet*, *Macbeth*, *Othello*, *Romeo and Juliet*, *The Merchant of Venice*, *Richard III*, *A Midsummer Night's Dream*, etc. – the story of King Lear has been retold many times again on the Chinese stage. Most recently, in January 2017, a *huaju* production of the play was mounted at the National Center for the Performing Arts, the title role being played by Pu Cunxin, 26 years after he played Hamlet in the Beijing of 1990.[33]

The all but forgotten Shaw

On August 10, 2013, *Wenhui*, an important newspaper in Shanghai, published an article titled "Let's Not Neglect Bernard Shaw" (*Buneng hulüe le Xiaobona*) to commemorate the 80th anniversary of Shaw's visit to Shanghai. The opening of this article, written by Lu Jun, a professor at the Shanghai Theatre Academy, goes like this:[34]

> Neglecting Bernard Shaw seems justifiable. Although he was the successor to Ibsen and forerunner of Brecht, we are more receptive to Ibsen and Brecht when it comes to his dramatic works.
>
> Neglecting Bernard Shaw is not justifiable. Shaw's greatest contribution is that in the 1890s he advocated the idea that drama should reflect social realities and human destiny, which helped turn the 20th century drama toward a more rational development and significantly impacted the development of drama in many countries. As far as China

is concerned, Shaw's impact in drama development and drama education is particularly significant. Therefore, Bernard Shaw should never
be neglected.

This pretty much sums up the awkward place George Bernard Shaw (1856–
1950), the Anglo-Irish playwright, finds himself in the history of modern
Chinese drama. His towering importance can be encapsulated in the fact
that he is one of the few Western writers who enjoy the endearment "*Weng*"
(old man) in popular parlance as well as in critical discourse – i.e., *Xiaoweng*
(Old Man Shaw) – generally reserved for a few rarified members of the most
elite league such as *Shaweng* (Old Man Shakespeare) and *Tuoweng* (Old
Man Tolstoy). New translations of his plays such as *The Man of Destiny*,
Great Catherine, and *The Doctor's Dilemma* are being published, and old
translations of *Saint Joan*, *Pygmalion*, *The Apple Cart*, *Major Barbara*, etc.,
are being reprinted. Book-length studies as well as numerous journal articles
on Shaw have been published too, although redundancy seems unavoidable
and originality in insight and approach few and far between.[35] However,
unlike Shakespeare, Ibsen, Brecht, Chekhov, O'Neill, and other important
Western artists, Shaw has rarely been mounted on the Chinese stage. This
seems incongruous to his massive body of dramatic works and the venera-
tion that has been accorded him ever since he was first introduced to China
as the most important living playwright in 1915 by Chen Duxiu, editor of
the *New Youth* journal that would put out an Ibsen special issue in 1918.
Other than the not-so-successful 1921 production of *Mrs. Warren's Profession* and the noteworthy 1991 production of *Major Barbara*, and many
performances of *Pygmalion*, etc,. on college campuses, Shaw has not seen
much of the Chinese stage by way of professional endeavors. The apparently
schizophrenic reception Shaw has experienced in China, both idolization
and neglect, has much to do with a confluence of factors, culture, history,
and stageability (or lack thereof) of his plays.[36]

By the time the *Empress of Britain* sailed into the harbor of Shanghai on
the morning of February 17, 1933,[37] Shaw, then 77 years old, accompanied
by his wife, Charlotte Payne-Townshend (1857–1943), had already visited
Naples, Athens, India, Hong Kong, etc., as part of his round-the-world cruise.
As one of the most important living writers at the time – a Nobel Prize in
Literature laureate (1925) – Shaw's opinions on everything, including literary,
sociocultural, political, and world affairs, were eagerly sought and quoted. His
feelings and views on things, however, especially his political sympathies and
philosophies concerning Irish Home Rule, democracy, fascism, and commu-
nism, had been filled with inconsistencies and contradictions.[38] Forever averse
to the intrusive attention of the reporters (perhaps not yet as intrusive as the
"paparazzi" of our own times) and the circus-like atmosphere on the streets,
Shaw would have been happy to stay on board. However, he couldn't turn
down Madame Sun (Soong Ching-ling, 1893–1981), the beloved, Western-
educated widow of Dr. Sun Yat-sen, founding father of the Republic of China.

She had come in person in a small steam boat to extend him an enthusiastic and persistent invitation. What Madame Sun, Lu Xun, and other left-leaning Chinese intellectuals were hoping for from Shaw was not exactly his views on arts and literature, but his support for the Chinese resistance to the aggressions of Japan, the next stop of Shaw's round-the world tour. Albeit an accidental, reluctant visitor, Shaw humored the Chinese hosts with his quick wit and some curious questions about Chinese arts and culture (e.g., how can one enjoy traditional Chinese *xiqu* with so much noise from percussion instruments going on) and the political situations (e.g., the size of the Communist Red Army controlled area), but did not give any direct, full-throated condemnation of imperial Japan that had already annexed northeastern China, turned it into the puppet state of Manchukuo, and was taking its aggressions to the rest of China. Shaw did have this to say in a letter to his good friend Nancy Astor, on March 21, 1933, about a month after the China stopover:[39]

> I have fallen in love with China, & am now passionately excited about the war and the question & the whole question – & hate the Japanese. . . .
> China is wonderful. I felt *at home* there. I belonged there!

Mrs. Warren's Profession

Shaw's post-visit euphoric feeling about China was well matched by how the Chinese felt about him well before the visit had taken place. In an article on Bernard Shaw published in 1919, Mao Dun (1896–1981), a prominent figure in the May Fourth Movement, praised Shaw's thinking and ideas (*sixiang*) as being ahead of his time by "a full century." It is in this year that a full-text Chinese rendition of Shaw's 1893 play *Mrs. Warren's Profession* was published. This was a time when the drama/theatre scene in China was witnessing tremendous fermentation as the old (traditional *xiqu*), the new (Western-style *huaju*), the haphazard mixture of both were jostling side by side, each struggling to stake out a place for itself.[40]

Mindful of the challenges of making a realistic modern Western play appeal to the Chinese audiences, Wang Youyou (1888–1937), a leading figure on the drama scene then, and a group of talented, like-minded young actors, Sinicized the proper names of characters – e.g., *Hua nainai* (Mrs. Hua) for Mrs. Warren – practiced and rehearsed for three full months, and placed ads in the newspapers to promote the show. In spite of all these earnest efforts, *Hua nainai zhi zhiye* (Mrs. Hua's Profession) turned out to be a disheartening failure. It had only a three-day run, was sparsely attended, and among those attending many complained loudly, demanded refund, and left well before *Hua nainai* (Mrs. Warren) went out of *Weiwei's* (Vivie's) room and slammed the door behind her.

This early adaptation endeavor was doomed to failure thanks to a conflux of factors, or, to use a Chinese expression, its inauspicious positioning in terms of *tianshi* (right time), *dili* (right place), and *renhe* (right people). In addition to the vast differences between the source and target cultures and dramatic traditions, Chinese theatergoers were not ready for a Western play like *Mrs. Warren's Profession*. Not that they were particularly prudish concerning the topic of prostitution, as some scholars have suggested. After all, *Jiu fengchen* (Rescuing the Fallen),[41] a classic Yuan variety play by Guan Hanqing (1219–1301), features a smart and brave prostitute (*Zhao Pan'er*) who rescues another prostitute friend from an abusive marriage; *Du Shiniang*, a well-known classic story by Feng Menglong (1574–1646), which has been adapted into *jingju*, *yueju*, *chuanju*, *pingju*, etc.,[42] features a beautiful and impassioned prostitute who, betrayed by the man she loves, fights back by tossing all her treasures into the river and then jumping in herself.

The fact of the matter is there is little in the story of Mrs. Warren that would rise to the level of moral clarity and satisfy the Chinese theatergoers then. Neither is there much in her character that would redeem and indeed elevate her to the status of a heroine as is the case of *Zhao Pan'er* and *Du Shiniang*. By all accounts, the early adaptations of Ibsen's *A Doll's House* were not much more successful either, but at least the character of Nora offered a rallying cry for the young and educated Chinese for the cause of individuality and women's liberation. Mrs. Warren, and for that matter, her righteous daughter Vivie, have little to offer in this important aspect. If the Chinese audiences then found the play's moral ambiguity puzzling, they would also likely be confused by the messy plot and relationship entanglements between and among the main characters, Mrs. Warren, Mr. Praed, Sir George Crofts, Reverend Samuel Gardner, Vivie Warren, and Frank Gardner. Their witty, rapid-fire talkfest would leave Chinese theatergoers in the dust, so to speak. Finally, there was no singing, dancing, and acrobatics to help enliven the theatric experience.

Major Barbara

From this and other such failures, Chinese artists did draw useful lessons, especially in how to adapt and create drama that would fit the needs of the Chinese people, culture, and society.[43] The benefit of such lessons shows itself in many of the adaptation endeavors since, regardless of which of the four modes they choose, fidelity, indigenization, hybridization, or experiment. It shows in the 1991 adaptation of *Major Barbara*, the only other notable adaptation of a Shavian play, when the stars of *tianshi* (right time), *dili* (right place), and *renhe* (right people) seemed much better aligned.

This Shavian adaptation had an impressive run from June 1 to June 23, 1991, barely two years after the events on Tiananmen Square 1989. During those two years, Meng Jinghui, a recent graduate of the Central Academy of Drama, had mounted *Waiting for Godot* and other absurdist plays, and Lin Zhaohua, as discussed earlier, had mounted an experimental adaptation of *Hamlet* loaded with subversive implications. Why did Ying Ruocheng, a key player in the successful staging of *Death of a Salesman* back in 1983, who had just served as deputy minister of culture (1986–1990), want to take on a Shavian play at this juncture in the sociopolitical and cultural life of China?

As it turns out, *Major Barbara* was another Western play Ying had wanted to stage since his college days in the late 1940s. Other than being a safe bet politically, admired by Lu Xun, Tian Han, and many others, and having been celebrated as a great realist writer ever since his introduction in China,[44] Shaw seemed to have something to say to the country at this time in history. "The issues dealt with" in *Major Barbara*, as Ying explained to his cast and crew, "such as war, armament, ethics,"[45] are important issues also confronting China today. Moreover, as Ying further explained why he was so interested in the play:

> Many of Shaw's arguments in the play have still not been fully examined and understood. The major character, Undershaft, a millionaire, is nevertheless portrayed as a hero by Shaw. Some of his views are still valid today.

War and armament, important as they were and have ever been, were not the most pressing issues facing China then, even though the post-Tiananmen, post-Berlin-Wall world was far from being friendly. The most important existential question for China then was to shut the door and isolate itself from the world again or to remain open and engaged. For the millions of people who had participated or had been sympathetic to the democracy movement, the pressing "ethics," or, rather, "moral" question would be where to go from here: to hold out, to decamp, or to join in. Barbara's struggle with ideals (of Christian charity) and reality (war, religion, money, poverty, conscience), and her final conversion to the alternative "religion" of wealth and war, as preached and embodied by her father (wealth is the only way to salvation and warfare is a necessary evil) must have left a profoundly unsettling impression on the audiences. Indeed, some of the "sermons" delivered by "St. Andrew Undershaft" must have sounded like gospels to many "hungry" intellectuals who would soon sell their souls, so to speak, and throw themselves into the "sea of commerce" to seek the glory of getting rich first:[46]

> I had rather be a thief than a pauper. I had rather be a murderer than a slave. I don't want to be either; but if you force the alternative on me, then, by Heaven, I'll choose the braver and more moral one.

Such "sermons" must have sounded like gospels to a generation of "captains of industry" too who have since Deng Xiaoping's 1992 "southern tour" (which answered the existential question alluded to earlier: China was to continue on the track of economic reforms) made tremendous fortunes, although not many of them are generous donors for charity causes.[47] For Ying Ruocheng himself, the pressing issue was not whether to join and cash in. After all, he had shared (albeit per policy then rather than voluntarily) most of the money he made for his role in the 1982 television miniseries *Marco Polo* (as Kublai Khan) and 1987 Bernardo Bertolucci's film *The Last Emperor* (as detention camp governor) with his colleagues at the Beijing People's Art Theatre.[48] Without any explicit statements from him, one can only speculate what Ying meant by asserting that some of Undershaft's views were "still valid" sociopolitically. At a personal level, the battles between religious ideals and grim realities as played out in *Major Barbara* must have resonated with him. After all, Ying had struggled with his own moral dilemmas from the beginning of his theatre career in the early 1950s. For example, although he later tried to justify his willingness to serve as a government informant on his foreign friends on the grounds of idealism and patriotic feelings, betraying personal trust and friendship must have bothered him in no small measures, as can be glimpsed from the "Forbidden City" dream he had in 1997 when he was gravely ill.[49]

Whatever the stated or subconscious motives for choosing the Shavian play for adaptation in 1991, Ying Ruocheng, a gifted translator and actor, was the ideal artist to take it on. To ensure the success of this adaptation, Ying provided a new translation of the play himself, as he had done with *Death of a Salesman* back in 1983, paying particular attention to the performability of his rendition, using expressions that the Chinese audience could understand.[50] For the roles of Undershaft and Lady Britomart, Ying drafted his long-time friends and collaborators Zhu Xu (Charley for the Arthur Miller play) and Zhu Lin (Linda), respectively, and Song Dandan, an upcoming young actor then, for the role of Barbara. The two-week run in June 1991 bespeaks the hope that even a Shavian play, when adapted by the right people at the right time and the right place, can overcome its "innate" challenges of stageability (or lack thereof) and be mounted successfully. Indeed, one can only hope that it would not take decades again for another major Shavian adaptation to happen because even a play such as *Mrs. Warren's Profession*, if done right – i.e., faithful to the spirit of the original play but bold in taking creative license to update the characters and the story – can speak poignantly to China today.

The importance of being Oscar Wilde

Unlike Bernard Shaw, a contemporary who lived to the ripe age of 94, Oscar Wilde (1854–1900) had his life cut short at the young age of 46 by illness, barely one full year into the new century. Unlike Shaw, whose status as a towering literary figure has never been questioned in China, although his plays have not been staged often, Wilde's literary reputation in China, since his first introduction by way of a 1909 translation of his short story "The Happy Prince" rendered by Lu Xun (Zhou Shuren) and his brother Zhou Zuoren, has experienced a wild ride of rise and fall.

From adulation in the early decades of the twentieth century to a long period of eclipse during the decades between 1940s and the end of the 1970s to resurgence ever since, Wilde's literary fortune in China somehow parallels his dramatic career on his native soil, his rise with the glorious success of *Salome* (1892–1895), despite the initial ban by the Lord Chamberlain's licensor of plays thanks to the sensitive nature of its biblical story, *Lady Windermere's Fan* (1892), and *The Importance of Being Earnest* (1895), his fall through the trials on account of his homosexual liaisons, his imprisonment (1895–1897), exile (1897–1900), and death of cerebral meningitis on November 30, 1900, and then a long path of reassessment of the man and his works through the lenses of queer criticism, political economics, postcolonial criticisms, and rehabilitation, which culminates, so to speak, in his posthumous pardon in 2017 by Queen Elizabeth II because homosexual acts are no longer crimes in the United Kingdom.[51] Indeed, Wilde's reputation and reception in China is as much about the man – a personality, an iconic, and maligned cultural figure – as about his works, perhaps more so than any other Western artist in China. And like almost everything else, the rise and fall of Wilde's fortune in China has its marked Chinese characteristics, symptomatic of the turbulent history of modern China since the early twentieth century.

Like Shaw, Oscar Wilde was introduced in China when the country was undergoing dramatic fermentation during the May 4th Movement. Chen Duxiu, editor of the revolutionary *New Youth* magazine saw in Wilde's plays subversive social criticism, whereas members of the Creation Society and New Moon Society[52] found the Wildean "art for art's sake" aesthetics liberating. Wilde's bold, outlandish public persona – his long hair, his in-your-face fashion statements, and his quick wit and outspokenness, as well as a mix of performance and expressions of personal philosophy perhaps – proved particularly refreshing for a young generation of college-educated Chinese who found the traditional Chinese cultural norms unbearably repressive. By the early 1920s, as a result of the fervent interest, most of Wilde's important plays had seen Chinese translations – e.g., *Salome, Lady Windermere's Fan, An Ideal Husband*, the *Importance of Being Earnest* – with some having several renditions.[53]

Lady Windermere's Fan

The first Wilde play ever mounted on the Chinese stage was *Lady Windermere's Fan* directed by Hong Shen (1894–1955) in 1924. One of the pioneers in modern Chinese drama, Hong Shen had the benefit of both Western education and traditional Chinese schooling. In spring 1919, while studying at Ohio State University on a Boxer Indemnity Scholarship, Hong Shen wrote and produced in English an original play titled *The Wedded Husband* (*Weizhi youshi*). In the fall of that same year, Hong transferred to Harvard University to study drama under Professor George Pierce Baker. When Hong Shen took on Oscar Wilde's *Lady Windermere's Fan* in 1924, he had already been back to China for two years and had been actively engaged in the new culture, new drama movement. In 1922, only two years after the success of Eugene

O'Neill's *Emperor Jones* on Broadway, which he saw while still in the United States and was profoundly shaken by its power, Hong adapted the play or, rather, rewrote it into a Chinese play titled *Zhao Yanwang* (Yama Zhao) to satirize the war-torn China. Hong's attempt at the modernist, expressionist mode of storytelling by way of commenting on the current sociopolitical realities failed disastrously (Chapter 7).[54] This, coupled with the recent failure of *Mrs. Warren's Profession* on the Chinese stage mounted by Wang Youyou, must have been heavy on his mind as Hong Shen contemplated the next adaptation project. Oscar Wilde's *Lady Windermere's Fan*, which had had a successful run in both London and New York in 1892–1893, seemed to have so much to offer for a fresh start.

It is not a talkfest like a typical Shavian play, although there is so much more talk than a typical Chinese *xiqu*. It is not audaciously experimental like O'Neill's *Emperor Jones*, whose use of expressionist mode of storytelling fascinated theatergoers in London and New York, but failed to engage the Chinese in Shanghai. And it is not overtly political either. Rather, it is a comedy of errors whose story line – of a young wife who, suspecting her husband is having an affair with another woman, decides to leave him and her child when the "bad" woman, who turns out to be her mother who abandoned her about 20 years ago, comes to the rescue of the young damsel in distress – would appeal to the middle-class, bourgeois Shanghai theatergoers immensely. The "fan" in the title of the play would grab their attention right away, reminding them of fans in such Chinese classics as *Honglou meng* (Dream of the Red Chamber) and the classic play *Taohua shan* (The Peach Blossom Fan) by Kong Shangren (1648–1718).[55] Despite its social satire, the play is lighthearted, suspenseful, and ends happily for all: suspicion cleared, love reconfirmed, and "bad" woman redeemed through a selfless, sacrificial act of love. In addition, the play's extravagant décor and fashion, and indeed its consumer, mass culture–based aesthetics,[56] would appeal to the Shanghai bourgeois, "petty-bourgeois" theatergoers in no small measures as in London and New York.

To ensure the success of this new adaptation undertaking, Hong Shen did a translation of the play himself, instead of using translations already available. Hong's rendition was free-spirited, aiming for performability instead of literariness or *ya* (elegance), the highest virtue of translation according to Yan Fu. In Hong's rendition, the Wildean play assumes the Chinese title *Shaonainai de shanzi* (Young Wife's Fan), which is much simpler and much more an attention getter than *Wendemier* (transliteration of Windermere) *furen de shanzi*, a mouthful but far from as suggestive. Lady Windermere is now Xu Shaonainai (Young Mrs. Xu), her full name Xu Yuzhen (Pearly Chaste). Other characters undergo similar linguistic and cultural "metamorphoses" too:

Lord Windermere: *Xu Ziming* (Bright Gentleman)
Mrs. Erlynne: *Jin nüshi* (Mrs. Gold),
Lord Darlington: *Liu Boying* (Big Brilliance)

Lord Augustus Lorton: *Wu Ba Daren* (Lord Wu Eight)
Cecil Graham: *Li Bulu* (Cool-Headed Li)
Dumby: *Zhang Yigong* (Also Just Zhang)

To illustrate how far Hong Shen took his creative license, let's see this dialog between Lord Darlington and Cecil Graham in Act III of the original play:[57]

> LORD DARLINGTON: What cynics you fellows are!
> CECIL GRAHAM: What is a cynic? [Sitting on the back of the sofa.]
> LORD DARLINGTON: A man who knows the price of everything and the value of nothing.
> CECIL GRAHAM: And a sentimentalist, my dear Darlington, is a man who sees an absurd value in everything, and doesn't know the market price of any single thing.

Hong's rendition is essentially a rewrite, with words put in different characters' mouths, naturalized for the understanding and enjoyment of his 1924 Shanghai audiences (back-translated next from Chinese to English for illustration purpose here):[58]

> LORD DARLINGTON (LIU BOYING): What smart, cynical bohemians[59] you all are.
> MR. DUMBY (ZHANG YIGONG): (deliberately) What is a bohemian?
> LORD DARLINGTON (LIU BOYING): A man who is always critical and never complimentary.
> MR. CECIL GRAHAM (LI BULU): In other words, a man who smells the gamy odor of raw lamb but not the fragrant aroma of lamb delicacy.
> MR. DUMBY (ZHANG YIGONG): Conversely, a man who smells only the aroma of lamb delicacy but never the odor of raw lamb is a sentimentalist.

In addition to the lively, free-spirited rendition of the text, Hong recruited a cast of well-known talents for the production, with he himself playing the important role of Lord Darlington as well as directing. This is a suspenseful, cliffhanging story well told for the enjoyment of the audiences. Despite some subtle, witty social commentary, there is little that is dangerously subversive to the dominant Victorian values or values just about anywhere. Instead, there is confirmation of love – romantic, spousal, and parental – and there is redemption. Stumbling upon the letter Lady Windemere has left behind for her husband to read, Mrs. Erlynne knows that she has to act fast to save her daughter. Upon finding Lady Windemere at a potentially compromising place, Mrs. Erlynne urges the young woman to go back home:

> Go back, Lady Windermere, to the husband who loves you, whom you love. You have a child, Lady Windermere. Go back to that child who even now, in pain or in joy, may be calling to you . . . Back to your house,

Lady Windermere – your husband loves you! He has never swerved for a moment from the love he bears you. *But even if he had a thousand loves, you must stay with your child. If he was harsh to you, you must stay with your child. If he ill-treated you, you must stay with your child. If he abandoned you, your place is with your child.*

(*Italics mine*)

Toward the end of the play, when she comes to bid her farewell, Mrs. Erlynne impresses on her unwitting daughter the idea of motherhood once more:

And never forget your child – I like to think of you as a mother. I like you to think of yourself as one.

This, however it was rendered by Hong Shen, must have sounded so much more reassuring for many of the bourgeois theatergoers in Shanghai than what Nora of Ibsen's *A Doll's House* (which had been mounted by students of Peking Women's College of Education in 1923)[60] has to say when Helmer plays the children and motherhood card in a desperate attempt to keep Nora from going out into the world.[61]

Although this successful adaptation – a five-day run with sold out audiences – did not have any sociopolitical impact anywhere near that of Ibsen's *A Doll's House*, it did offer some useful lessons for how to adapt Western classics for the Chinese stage, how to do the balancing act between "art for life" – the mantra for the Chinese intelligentsia from time immemorial – and art for art, or, rather, art-for-entertainment, and box office concerns. *Lady Windermere's Fan* was adapted into a film in 1939 and later Chinese *xiqu* genres such as *Huju* (Shanghai opera) based on Hong Shen's translation. It has remained in the *Huju* repertoire ever since.[62]

Salome

Another Wildean play that fascinated the Chinese in the early decades of the twentieth century is *Salome* (*Salome*, 1891), which saw the first Chinese translation in 1920. Among the several translations that came out in the short span of ten years, the rendition by Tian Han (1898–1968) proved to be the most popular.

Tian Han, another important figure in the cultural life, especially the drama scene, of modern China,[63] had exposure to Oscar Wilde while studying in Japan (1916–1922). In fact, he saw a Japanese adaptation of *Salome* there, which had a successful run of 127 performances from 1912–1925.[64] Tian Han and his Creation Society (formed by Tian Han and Guo Moruo while studying in Japan) kindred spirits were fascinated by the story of Salome, stepdaughter of Herod II (the ancient Herodian kingdom of Judaea): per her mother Herodias' request, Salome demands the head of John the Baptist as reward for dancing the dance of the seven veils and kisses the head delivered to her on a silver platter before being put to death herself by Herod II.

Postcolonial critics today may find disturbing orientalism in the Wildean appropriation of the biblical story in its portrayal of the exotic, oriental femme fatale.[65]

For Tian Han, Guo Moruo, and others, and indeed even for the Chinese today, regardless of its cultural origins, the Bible, holy book for the dominant religion of all European countries and the United States, is quintessentially, archetypically Western. Therefore, a biblical story as retold by Oscar Wilde would be as occidental, or rather, Western, as can be. Chinese fascination with *Salome* and indeed with Oscar Wilde was inspired by the same desire then to learn from all things Western to save China and renew its culture. It is a warped version of orientalism, or Occidentalism, if you will, as the Chinese looked at the world from the eastern-most – both geographically and culturally speaking – end of the Eurasian landmass. Indeed by the time of the 1929 adaptation, the Wildean play had already inspired many a Chinese Salome, male and female, on and offstage, and many a variation of "Salome's kiss" as motif or troupe in literary and dramatic works as well as mannerism in real life.[66]

Although members of the Spring Willow Society, upon returning to Shanghai, might have mounted an adaptation of *Salome*, it is the 1929 endeavor directed by Tian Han based on his own Chinese translation that garnered much attention. Once again, all the stars, *tianshi* (right time), *dili* (right place), and *renhe* (right people) seemed perfectly aligned for this production: an "exotic" Western story, a sexy Chinese title for Tian Han's rendition, *Shale-mei* (Sha pleasure beauty), and Yu Shan (1908–1968), a young actress known for her beauty and daring attitude, cast in the title role. On the opening night on July 7, 1929, in Nanjing, the capital city of China then, the theatre was packed to the brim. When the show moved to Shanghai in August the same year, however, the usually receptive Shanghai didn't seem too thrilled. It did not repeat the same success, partly because Yu Shan left the show because of pressure from her family. It was criticized by Liang Shiqiu (1903–1987), Harvard-educated professor of English and editor of the famous *Crescent Moon Monthly*, for its sentimentalism and hedonism (*rouyu zhuyi*).[67] A year later, Yu Shan would play the title role of Tian Han's adaptation of George Bizet's *Carmen*, another "notorious" oriental, or rather, Western femme fatale. As if fate would have it, both Yu Shan and Tian Han would suffer egregiously in the hands of Madame Mao during the Cultural Revolution; they died in the same year of 1968.

The Importance of Being Earnest

After enjoying much adulation and glamor in the early decades of the twentieth century, Oscar Wilde fell into a long eclipse from the 1940s all the way to the end of the 1970s. The dimming of his star during those years was overdetermined by the dominant political ideology and cultural and literary discourse that would find the Wildean aestheticism and indeed "decadenism" not only useless but also corruptive. There was much denunciation of the whole Wilde canon, although there was not a word of his homosexual encounters, the trials, etc. (homosexuality being a taboo in China for most of the twentieth century), until the 1996 publication of a Chinese translation of *Oscar Wilde, His Life and Confessions* (1916), a biography written by his friend Frank Harris.[68]

The rehabilitation began soon after the Cultural Revolution was over. Today, one would find Oscar Wilde just about anywhere, research articles, graduate theses, and books of all shapes, forms, and media, from his fairy tales, to *The Picture of Dorian Grey*, to his plays in English, Chinese translation, and bilingual, full-text, and simplified put out by all kinds of publishing houses. His plays have been performed on numerous school campuses too. However, unlike Shaw and just about every other major Western playwright, Oscar Wilde did not see a serious professional production in mainland China until 2015, 15 years into the new century. *The Importance of Being Earnest*, or rather, *Buke erxi* (Not a Child's Play),[69] had a run from June 4 to June 16, catching considerable critical and media attention. For a while, the lucky star shone its full glory on Oscar Wilde, or rather *Aosika Wang'erde*, the Chinese transliteration of his name. *Aosika* shares the same glamor with Hollywood's academy awards, whereas *Wang'erde* means "King and Virtuous" or "Virtuous King." Oscar Wilde would have been pleased.

The adapter of this play – in the capacity of both translator and director – is Zhou Liming (Raymond Zhou), a glamorous Wildean sort of character (minus all the "scandalous" baggage) himself on the cultural scene in China today:[70] columnist, cultural critic, executive editor in chief of ChinaDaily. com.cn, author of 20 books (three in English) and more than 200 articles annually (in English or Chinese), who makes about 100 media appearances each year, as interviewee, host, or special guest. Zhou chose Oscar Wilde for this 2015 endeavor because Wilde was one of his favorite Western authors when he was studying English in at the Sun Yat-sen University in Guangzhou and because the parallels between London of the late Victorian era and the 2015 Beijing "are uncanny in terms of class consciousness, upward mobility, and all the trappings of the gilded age." A sizable (albeit still small in percentage of the Chinese population) "leisure class," conspicuous in consumption and every facet of lifestyle,[71] has emerged in China, especially in major metropolis such as Beijing, Shanghai, and Guangzhou, since the dawning of the new century. China, for better or for worse, is finally ready for a "trivial comedy" for "serious" and perhaps not so serious people alike.

Zhou was fully aware of the creative license, the "latitude" he could (and perhaps would have to) take in adapting and directing this work for the Chinese stage, to give it "a uniquely Chinese twist." He knew that a "faithful" rendition of the play, faithful to both the spirit and the letter, even if done well, would be good for reading, but not good for the stage. All the culture-specific references in the original play, such as Tories, Anabaptists, Shropshire, would leave the typical Chinese theatergoers scratching their heads. So Zhou retooled the story, from character names to locale to culture-specific references to make it resonate with prospective audiences for this production. All of the main characters now have their easily recognizable Chinese reincarnations:

> John Worthing: *Lu Huaxing* (Lu, nickname for Shangdong province; Huaxing, China revival), CEO of a multinational corporation (Huaxing could be the name of any big enterprise in China, such as Huawei Technologies Co. Ltd.)
>
> Algy Moncrieff: *Meng Yuanji* (Meng, Mongolian; Yuanji, Yuan dynasty), a "fu'erdai" (rich second-generation, child of the *nouveau riche*), whose name suggests that he is a descendent of Genghis Khan, going back to the thirteenth century.
>
> Lady Bracknell: *Pu Furen* (Lady Pu), last name implying a link to Pu Yi, of the Manchu Aisin Gioro clan, the last Emperor of China; a male actor was cast for this role for comic effect.
>
> Gwendolen: *Guan Delin* (Delin: having virtue).
>
> Cecily Cardew: *Jia Xixi* (Jia, homophone to "falsehood" in Chinese).
>
> Cheveley: *Qian Feili* (Qian, Money), a character appropriated from Wilde's 1895 play *An Ideal Husband*.

The basic plot of *Buke erxi* (Not a Child's Play) still follows that of *The Importance of Being Earnest*, although the setting is now Beijing, 2015: Lu Huaxing, or his fictitious libertine brother Lu Daoren (Daoist monk), woos Meng Yuanji's cousin Guan Delin. The two are stopped in the tracks by Lu's would-be mother-in-law Lady Pu before they can pull off a "*shanhun*" (getting married at lightning speed). In the meantime, Meng Yuanji, assuming the identity of Lu Huaxing's fictitious brother, Lu Daoren, travels to the countryside and succeeds in winning the heart of Jia Xixi, granddaughter of Lu's foster father. To spice up things and give the play an unexpected twist before the curtain falls, Zhou Liming lifted Cheveley, an ambitious and self-serving character in *An Ideal Husband*, and inserted her and a blackmail scene into this production before curtain fall.

Some loss in this bold remake of the Wildean play is inevitable. For example, the rich meaning of the original title, *The Importance of Being Earnest* – the play's play with the term "earnest," a linchpin for character and plot developments, loaded with comic irony mocking both the characters and the façade of "earnest" respectability of the Victorian era – is simply untranslatable. *Buke erxi* (Not a Child's Play), a smart, attention-getting Chinese title, is no equivalent to the original, because it is imposed from outside and has little to do with the characters caught in comedy of manners very much of their own making. Nonetheless, by and large, Zhou's *Buke erxi* is faithful to the spirit of Wilde's *The Importance of Being Earnest*, a comedy of a bunch of *nouveau riche* leisure class characters conspicuously and indeed earnestly pursuing trivialities in the "gilded age" of twenty-first-century Beijing – a comedy that can be replicated in just about any major city across China today.

The question remains though, does such a comedy of trivialities provoke any serious thought other than hearty laughter? George Bernard Shaw, for one, found *The Importance of Being Earnest* "extremely funny" but "really heartless."[72] How would he find this 2015 Sinicized remake of the play, especially when compared to other Chinese remakes such as Lin Zhaohua's *Hamlet* (1990) and his own *Major Barbara* as mounted by Ying Ruocheng in 1991? Would he recommend a revival of *Mrs. Warren's Profession*, updated and Sinicized so it would speak directly to the "gilded age" of China today after nearly a full century of no show on the Chinese stage?

Notes

1 The Chinese enthusiastically embraced these English writers and many more, although some of them, such as Defoe, Johnson, and Shelley, did not always return the favor. Defoe, for example, dismissed China's social order as based on tyranny, its religion as "idolatrous devil worship," and its products such as tea and porcelain as needless, a drain of European silver (see G. A. Starr, 435). Johnson counted the Chinese among the "barbarians" and dismissed Chinese learning because its rather "rude" language, which does not use the alphabet, makes it difficult for learning to happen "as there is more labour in hewing down a tree with a stone than with an axe" (Boswell, 707). Shelley in the preface to *Hellas: A Lyrical Drama* thus declares, "We are all Greeks. Our laws, our literature, our religion, our arts, have their root in Greece. But for Greece – Rome, the instructor, the conqueror, the metropolis of our ancestors, would have spread no illumination with her arms, and we might still have been savages and idolaters; or, what is worse, might have arrived at such a stagnant and miserable state of social institution as China and Japan possess." And the gods of "China, India, the Antarctic islands, and the native tribes of America," Shelley goes on to say in a note for the play, are "monstrous objects of the idolatry," and their evil reign would have continued but for the revival of Grecian learning and arts (Shelley, viii–ix, 58).
2 MARIA: What a caterwauling do you keep here! If my lady have not called up her steward Malvolio and bid him turn you out of doors, never trust me.
SIR TOBY: My lady's a "Cataian" (Cathayan), we are politicians, Malvolio's a Peg-o'-Ramsey, and "Three merry men be we." Am not I consanguineous? Am I not of her blood? Tilly-vally-"lady!" "There dwelt a man in Babylon, lady, lady."
(2.3: ll. 65–71; William Shakespeare, 1784)
3 ESCALUS: (to Angelo) Do you hear how he misplaces?
POMPEY: Sir, she came in great with child, and longing – saving your honour's reverence – for stewed prunes. Sir, we had but two in the house, which at that very distant time stood, as it were, in a fruit dish – a dish of some threepence; your honors have seen such dishes; they are not China dishes, but very good dishes.
ESCALUS: Go to, go to, no matter for the dish, sir.
(2.1, ll. 86–93; Shakespeare, 2040)
4 The second son of Zeng Guofan (1811–1872), a prominent figure in the late Qing decades, especially known for his role in the crackdown of the Taiping Uprising (1850–1864).
5 See Chapter 1, pp. 7–8.
6 Ding Luonan, 12.

7 Would Shakespeare, or the ghost of "Schakspear" as imagined by Johann Friedrich Schink (1755–1835) in his short play *Shakespeare in der Klemme* be equally infuriated with these Chinese adapters as he was with Jean-François Ducis and other French adapters? See Ton Hoenselaars.
8 Translation based on advertisement in *Minguo bao* (Republican Daily), May 25, 1916.
9 Translation based on advertisement in *Minguo bao* (Republican Daily), July 17, 1916.
10 Translation based on advertisement in *Minguo bao* (Republican Daily), March 11, 1916. See also An Ling, *Chongxie yu guihua*, 27–8.
11 See Liu Minghou, 44–6.
12 See Li Hongquan, Yue Feng, and Wang Yujie.
13 See P. A. W. Collins, Albert H. Silverman, and Robert B. Pierce.
14 See Wu Fan.
15 See Prologue, p. xiv.
16 This portion of the discussion draws from Song Hongying and Fang Ping.
17 See "Wang Zhaojun" and "Cai Yan."
18 Typically, a good-looking young nobleman who places his future on wooing a beautiful and rich heiress would not fit the traditional Chinese love story mode of a young scholar of humble origin who tries to find his way upward and into the heart of a beautiful young woman through his talent and hard work. In this case, however, the Chinese theatergoers then and now are too engrossed in the love story to be mindful of the young nobleman's idleness.
19 This portion of the discussion draws from Zhang Qihong, Zhou Peitong, and Li Weimin, "*Qingchun langman.*"
20 Wang Meng.
21 See Warren D. Smith, D. M. Cohen, and David Nirenberg.
22 Li Weimin, "*Qingchun langman,*" 101.
23 Yuan Ling.
24 Zhou Peitong, 20–1.
25 See Chapter 3.
26 Li Weimin, "*Qingchun langman,*" 102.
27 Meng Jinghui, 46–7.
28 This discussion is based on Lin Zhaohua, *Hamlet*. DVD. It also draws from Sun Yanna; Ma Qianglin; and Li Weimin, "*Zhuandong wanghua tong.*"
29 William Hazlitt describes Polonius as a "sincere" father, but also "a busy-body, (who) is accordingly officious, garrulous, and impertinent." See "Polonius."
30 Sun Yanna, 42.
31 Discussion and translation based on video *Sixian Li'er Wang (Sixian King Lear)*. See Dai Xiaotong, "*Minzhuhua.*"
32 Dai Xiaotong, 53.
33 See *Li'er Wang* (King Lear), "*Guojia dajuyuan.*"
34 Lu Jun, "*Buneng hulüe le Xiaobona.*"
35 Du Juan, "*Shangdai fajue.*"
36 The stageability of Shaw's plays is still an issue that challenges artists in his home country even today. See, for example, John Wyver.
37 This portion of the discussion draws from Kay Li, "Globalization versus Nationalism"; Jiangnan Xie and Xiangjun Zhang, "*Xiaobona yu zhongguo*"; and Lu Xun and Qu Qiubai, eds., *Xiaobona zai Shanghai.*
38 See H. M. Geduld, Eric Russell Bentley, and Piers J. Hale.
39 J. P. Wearing, 51.
40 See Siyuan Liu, *Performing Hybridity.*
41 "*Jiu Fengchen*" (Rescuing the Fallen).
42 "*Du Shiniang.*"

43 See Kay Li, "*Mrs. Warren's Profession.*"
44 See Lu Xun, "Six Essays" and Wendi Chen, "A Fabian Socialist."
45 Wendi Chen, "G. B. Shaw's Plays," 39–40.
46 Bernard Shaw, 148.
47 See Nisid Hajari and Mary Duenwald.
48 Ying Ruocheng and Claire Conceison, 178–81.
49 Ibid, xx–xxiv, 49–55, 189–91. Claire Conceison rightly interpreted the dream as symbolic of Ying's subconscious grappling with his impending death although the gate of the Forbidden City, the military maneuvering of Russian and Chinese armies and tanks, and his own role in all of this, confused, unsure of the strategies ("Is this wise"?), etc., could be read as Ying trying to come to terms with the important choices he had made in his life.
50 See Lu Xiaohong, "*Cong 'shilling' dao "tongzi'er.*"
51 See Peter Dickinson, Yeeyon Im, David Schulz, and Paul L. Fortunato.
52 See Yin Zhiguang, *Politics of Art.*
53 See Li Zhi and Sun Shengcun, "*Ershi niandai.*"
54 See Zhu Xuefeng, "*Wenmingxi wutai.*"
55 An Ling, "*Chanshi he chuangzao,*" 120. See also "Dream of the Red Chamber" and "The Peach Blossom Fan."
56 See Paul L. Fortunato.
57 Oscar Wilde, 95–6.
58 Quoted in An Ling, "*Chanshi he chuangzao,*" 119–20.
59 The Chinese expression is *Mingshipai*, referring to a type of people, educated, unconventional, and anti-establishment, around this time.
60 See Chapter 2. Hong Shen himself had published in *Fiction Monthly* (*Xiaoshuo yuebao*) a two-page synopsis of *A Doll's House* under the Chinese title *Jiaoqi* (Lovely Wife).
61 Henrik Ibsen, 119.
62 See "*Shaonainai de shanzi*" (Young Wife's Fan; 1939 Film), "*Shaonainai de shanzi*" (Young Wife's Fan; Shanghai opera repertoire play), and "Shanghai opera."
63 Among other things, Tian Han's poem "March of the Volunteers" written in 1934 as the Japanese were expanding its aggressions from Manchuria to the rest of China was adopted in 1949 as the lyrics for the national anthem of the People's Republic.
64 Zhou Xiaoyi, "*Shalemei zhi wen,*" 71.
65 See Yeeyon Im.
66 Zhou Xiaoyi, 71–2.
67 Li Zhi and Sun Shengcun, 37.
68 Hou Jingjing, "*Shiqi nianjiang,*" 143–44. Homosexual sex in China was not legalized until 1997, which was followed by homosexuality being removed from the official list of mental illnesses in 2001. See John Gittings.
69 This portion of the discussion draws from Raymond Zhou, "A Wild Retake on a Wilde Classic," and Liming Zhou, "*Gaibian shi hanghuo.*"
70 See "Raymond Zhou to Inaugurate Lecture Series of PKU News."
71 See Thorstein Veblen.
72 See Karl E. Beckson, 190.

Bibliography

An, Ling. "*Chanshi he chuangzao: Lun Hong Shen dui Aosika Wang'erde Wendemi'er furen de shanzi de gaiyi*" (Interpretation and Creation: On Hong Shen's Rewrite of Oscar Wilde's *Lady Windermere's Fan*). *Journal of Central Academy of Drama* S1 (2008): 48–58.

———. *Chongxie yu guihua: Yingguo xiju zai xiandai zhongguo de gaiyi he yanchu* (1907–1949) (Rewrite and Naturalization: Rewrite and Performance of English Drama in Modern China 1907–1949). Ji'nan University Press, 2015.

Beckson, Karl E. *Oscar Wilde: The Critical Heritage*. London: Routledge & Kegan Paul Books, 1970.

Bentley, Eric Russell. "Bernard Shaw, Caesar, and Stalin." *The Antioch Review* 3, no. 1 (Spring 1943): 117–24.

Boswell, James. *The Life of Samuel Johnson*. London: Penguin Classics, 2008.

"Cai Yan." https://en.wikipedia.org/wiki/Cai_Yan.

Chen, Wendi. "A Fabian Socialist in Socialist China." *Shaw* 23 (2003): 155–66.

———. "G. B. Shaw's Plays on the Chinese Stage: The 1991 Production of *Major Barbara*." *Comparative Literature Studies* 35, no. 1 (1998): 25–48.

Cohen, D. M. "The Jew and Shylock." *Shakespeare Quarterly* 31, no. 1 (Spring 1980): 53–63.

Collins, P. A. W. "Shaw on Shakespeare." *Shakespeare Quarterly* 8, no. 1 (Winter 1957): 1–13.

Dai, Xiaotong. "*Minzuhua, xijuhua, dazhonghua: Wo gai Li'er wang*" (To Indigenize and Popularize a Western Drama: My Adaptation of *King Lear*). *Dawutai* (Big Stage) 8 (1996): 53–5.

Dickinson, Peter. "Oscar Wilde: Reading *The Life After The Life*." *Biography* 28, no. 3 (Summer 2005): 414–32.

Ding, Luonan. "*Zhongguo huaju xuexi waiguo xiju de lishi jingyan*" (A Historical Overview of Chinese Spoken Drama Learning From Foreign Drama). *Zhongguo xiju chubanshe* (Chinese Drama Press), 1983.

"Dream of the Red Chamber." https://en.wikipedia.org/wiki/Dream_of_the_Red_Chamber.

Du, Juan. "*Shangdai fajue de 'Xiaobona shi' xiju: Guonei Xiaobona jieshou shi*" ("Shavian" drama yet to be explored: reception history of Bernard Shaw in mainland China). *Journal of School of Chinese Language and Culture Nanjing Normal University* 4 (December 2011): 84–8.

"Du Shiniang." https://zh.wikipedia.org/wiki/.

Fang, Ping. "*Fanpu guizhen: Weinisi shangren yanchu de shexiang*" (Return to Simplicity and Truth: Ideas for Production of *The Merchant of Venice*). *Foreign Literature Studies* 4 (1981): 10–21.

Fortunato, Paul L. "Wildean Philosophy With a Needle and Thread: Consumer Fashion at the Origins of Modernist Aesthetics." *College Literature* 34, no. 3 (Summer 2007): 37–53.

Geduld, H. M. "Bernard Shaw and Adolf Hitler." *The Shaw Review* 4, no. 1 (January 1961): 11–20.

Gittings, John. "China Drops Homosexuality From List of Psychiatric Disorders." *The Guardian*, Wednesday, March 7, 2001. www.theguardian.com.

Hajari, Nisid, and Mary Duenwald. "China's Superrich Could Spare a Yuan." *Bloomberg*, May 2, 2014. www.bloomberg.com.

Hale, Piers J. "The Search for Purpose in a Post-Darwinian Universe: George Bernard Shaw, 'Creative Evolution', and Shavian Eugenics: 'The Dark Side of the Force'." *History and Philosophy of the Life Sciences* 28, no. 2 (2006): 191–213.

Hoenselaars, Ton. "Between Heaven and Hell: Shakespearian Translation, Adaptation, and Criticism From a Historical Perspective." *The Yearbook of English Studies* 36, no. 1 (2006): 50–64.

Hou, Jingjing. "*Shiqi nianjiang (1949–1966) Wanger'de xiju zai zhongguo yijie de 'quexi' yanjiu*" (Translation Studies of Wilde Plays 'In Absentia' During the 17 Years 1949–1966). *Yingmei wenxue luncong* (English and American Literature Studies Forums) 5 (2009): 137–46.

Ibsen, Henrik. *A Doll's House*. Translated by William Archer. Boston, MA: Walter H. Baker & co., 1926.

Im, Yeeyon. "Oscar Wilde's *Salomé*: Disorienting Orientalism." *Comparative Drama* 45, no. 4 (Winter 2011): 361–80.

"*Jiu Fengchen*" (Rescuing the Fallen). http://baike.baidu.com/view/293524.htm.

Li, Hongquan. "*Shashibiya yu youse renzhong*" (SHAKESPEARE and the Colored Races). *Journal of Inner Mongolian University* (Social Sciences Edition) 4 (1994): 106–12.

Li, Kay. "Globalization Versus Nationalism: Shaw's Trip to Shanghai." *Shaw* 22 (2002): 149–70.

———. "*Mrs. Warren's Profession* in China: Factors in Cross-Cultural Adaptations." *Shaw* 25 (2005): 201–20.

Li, Ruru. *Shashibiya: Staging Shakespeare in China*. Hong Kong University Press, 2003.

Li, Weimin. "*Qingchun langman yu shiyi meixue fengge de chengxian: Zhang Qihong dui Shashibiya jingdian Weinisi shangren de wutai xushi*" (Expressions of Youthful, Romantic, and Poetic Aesthetics: Zhang Qihong's Stage Narration of Shakespeare's Classic the Merchant of Venice). *Sichuan xiju* (Sichuan Theatre) 7 (2014): 101–5.

———. "*Zhuandong wanghua tong: zai yinyu zhong kandao le xianfengxing – Lun Lin Zhaohua gaibian de Shashibiya xiju Hamulaite*" (Turning the Kaleidoscope: Avant-garde as Seen in Metaphors – On Lin Zhaohua Adaptation of Shakespeare's *Hamlet*). *Journal of Southwest University* (Humanities and Social Sciences Edition) 33, no. 2 (March 2007): 163–8.

Li, Zhi, and Shengcun Sun. "*Ershi niandai zhongguo xiju yu weimei zhuyi xiju guanxi zai bian*" (Chinese Drama and Aestheticism in the 1920s Reexamined). *Lun Xun Studies Monthly* 12 (2007): 36–44.

Li'er Wang (King Lear). "*Guojia dajuyuan xin zhizuo Shashibiya huaju Li'er wang*" (National Center of Performing Arts New Production of Shakespeare Play *King Lear*). www.chncpa.org/subsite/lew2017/.

Lin, Zhaohua. "Hamlet." DVD. *Lin Zhaohua xiju zuopin ji* (Collection of Lin Zhaohua Drama Works). Beijing: Remin University of China Press, 2012.

Liu, Minghou. "*Shashibiya zai zhongguo: 'Yanchu yu yanjiu' guoji yantaohui zongshu*" (Shakespeare in China: 'Production and Research' International Symposium Report). *Zhongguo xiju* (Chinese Drama) 11 (1996): 44–6.

Liu, Siyuan. *Performing Hybridity in Colonial-Modern China* (Palgrave Studies in Theatre and Performance History). New York: Palgrave Macmillan, 2013.

Lu, Jun. "*Buneng hulüe le Xiaobona: Jinian Xiaobona fangwen Shanghai 80 Zhounian*" (We Should Not Neglect Bernard Shaw: Commemorating the 80 Anniversary of Bernard Shaw's Shanghai Visit). *Wenhui Daily*, August 10, 2013: 6.

Lu, Xiaohong. "*Cong 'shilling' dao 'tongzi'er:' Lun Ying Ruocheng yi Babala shaoxiao de dongtai biaoyanxing yuanze*" (From 'Shillings' to 'Tong Zier:' On Ying Ruocheng's Performability Principle in the Translation of *Major Barbara*). *Kejiao daokan* (Journal of Science Education Guide) 6 (2015): 154–5.

Lu, Xun. "Six Essays in Defense of Bernard Shaw." *Shaw* 12 (1992): 61–78.

Lu, Xun, and Qu Qiubai, eds. *Xiaobona zai Shanghai* (Bernard Shaw in Shanghai), 1933. Reprint. Chengdu, Sichuan: Sichuan People's Press, 1983.

Ma, Qianglin. *"'Jijian' he 'hunda' de xianfeng changshi: Tan Lin Zhaohua bang Hamuleite Dajiangjun Kouliulan wumei sheji"* ('Minimalism' and 'Mashup' as Avant-garde Experiment: On Stage Design for Lin Zhaohua Adaptation of *Hamlet* and *Coriolanus*). *Juying yuebao* (Stage and Screen Monthly) 3 (2014): 70–1.

Meng, Jinghui. *"Xianfeng xiju dangan"* (Avant-Garde Theatre Archives), 46–47.

Minguo bao (Republican Daily), March 11, May 25, July 17, 1916.

Nirenberg, David. "Shakespeare's Jewish Questions." *Renaissance Drama, New Series* 38 (2010): 77–113.

"The Peach Blossom Fan." https://en.wikipedia.org/wiki/The_Peach_Blossom_Fan.

Pierce, Robert B. "Bernard Shaw as Shakespeare Critic." *Shaw* 31, no. 1 (2011): 118–32.

"Polonius." Britannica.com. Retrieved 2014-07-10.

"Raymond Zhou to Inaugurate Lecture Series of PKU News." http://english.pku.edu.cn/News_Events/News/Campus/7243.htm.

Schulz, David. "Redressing Oscar: Performance and the Trials of Oscar Wilde." *TDR* 40, no. 2 (Summer 1996): 37–59.

Shakespeare, William. *The Norton Shakespeare*. New York: Norton, 1997.

"Shanghai opera." https://en.wikipedia.org/wiki/Shanghai_opera.

"Shaonainai de shangzi" (Young Wife's Fan; 1939 Film). www.youtube.com/watch?v=Jn1k0b-iby0.

"Shaonainai de shangzi" (Young Wife's Fan; Shanghai opera repertoire play). http://baike.baidu.com/item/%E5%B0%91%E5%A5%B6%E5%A5%B6%E7%9A%84%E6%89%87%E5%AD%90/9611709.

Shaw, Bernard. *Major Barbara*. New York: Brentano's, 1920.

Shelley, Percy Bysshe. *Hellas: A Lyrical Drama*, 2nd ed. London: Reeves and Turner, 1886.

Silverman, Albert H. "Bernard Shaw's Shakespeare Criticism." *PMLA* 72, no. 4 (September 1957): 722–36.

Sixian Li'er Wang (Sixan King Lear), video. www.tudou.com/programs/view/XTjEqJSMTwI/.

Smith, Warren D. "Shakespeare's Shylock." *Shakespeare Quarterly* 15, no. 3 (Summer 1964): 193–9.

Song, Hongying. *"Xiju Weinisi shangren lüyan bushuai de yuanyin"* (Why the Stage Appeal of *The Merchant of Venice* Never Fades). *Dawutai* (Big Stage) 9 (2012): 11–12.

Starr, G. A. "Defoe and China." *Eighteenth-Century Studies* 43, no. 4 (Summer 2010): 435–54.

Sun, Yanna. *"Renren doushi Hamuleite: Lun Lin Zhaohua dui Hamuleite de zhuti zaichuang"* (Everyone Is Hamlet: On Lin Zhaohua's Re-creation of Hamlet's Themes). *Sichuan xiju* (Sichuan Drama) 1 (2010): 39–42.

Veblen, Thorstein. *The Theory of the Leisure Class* (Oxford World's Classics), Reissue Edition, Oxford: Oxford University Press; Reissue Edition (July 26, 2009).

Wang, Meng. *"Qingchun wansui"* (Long Live Youth). www.vipreading.com/novel-read-1317-24125.html.

Wang, Yujie. *"Shashibiya: Yuanchu nüxingzhuyizhe haishi yannüzhuyizhe – Shashibiya nüxingguang tanyi"* (Shakespeare: A Proto-feminist or a Misogynist? A Study of Shakespeare's Views on Women). *Journal of Lanzhou University* (Social Sciences Edition) 5 (2013): 142–7.

"Wang Zhaojun." https://en.wikipedia.org/wiki/Wang_Zhaojun.

Wearing, J. P., ed. *Bernard Shaw and Nancy Astor (Selected Correspondence of Bernard Shaw)*. Toronto: University of Toronto Press, 2005.

Wilde, Oscar. *Lady Windermere's Fan*. Paris, 1903.

Wu, Fan. "*Weishenme Shaoweng zai zhongguo dare, Tangweng que zai yingguo yinxing?*" (Why Is Old Man Sha So Hot in China While Old Man Tang Is Invisible in Britain?). *Shanghai Arts Review* 2 (2016): 43–5.

Wyver, John. "How TV Fell out of Love With George Bernard Shaw." Wednesday 30 April 2014. www.theguardian.com/stage/2014/apr/30/george-bernard-shaw-reinvention-shakespeare-chekhov.

Xie, Jiangnan, and Xiangjun Zhang. "*Xiaobona yu zhongguo: Shidai de xiangfeng yu wudu*" (Bernard Shaw and China: Encounters of Time and Misreading). *Zhonghua dushu bao* (China Reading Daily), June 5, 2013.

Yin, Zhiguang. *Politics of Art: The Creation Society and the Practice of Theoretical Struggle in Revolutionary China*. Leiden, Netherlands: Brill, 2014.

Ying, Ruocheng, and Claire Conceison. *Voices Carry: Behind Bars and Backstage During China's Revolution and Reform*. New York: Rowman & Littlefield, 2008.

Yuan, Ling. "*Ta de yihan zhishi yi ben shu*" (His Dying Wish is Only a Book). www.360doc.com/content/15/0821/08/9065871_493776210.shtml. Originally published in Zhong Sheng, *Dandu shi: Jiaolu de niandai* (Exclusive Read 10: Age of Anxiety). Guilin, Guangxi: Guangxi Normal University Press, 2015.

Yue, Feng. "*Cong Aosailuo kan shaju zhong de feizhouren xingxiang goujian*" (Shakespeare's Portrayal of Africans as Seen in *Othello*). *Journal of Xinjiang University* (Philosophy, Social Sciences and Humanities Edition) 6 (2014): 93–6.

Zhang, Qihong. "*Zai shijian he tansuo zhong de jidian tihui: Shitan Weinisi shangren de daoyan chuli*" (Experience From Practice and Exploration: On Directing *The Merchant of Venice*). *Renmin xiju* (People's Theatre). 1 (1981): 17–19.

Zhou, Liming. "*Gaibian shi hanghuo, zai haolaiwu yidian ye bu diuren*" (Adaptation Is Mainstream Practice, no Loss of Face Even in Hollywood). Interview, June 27, 2015. www.vmovier.com/46965.

Zhou, Peitong. "*Jiyao dadan chuangxin, yeyao zhongshi yuanzuo: Ping zhongguo qingnian yishu juyuan yanchu de Weinisi shangren*" (Be Both Audaciously Creative and Faithful to the Original: On China Youth Art Troupe Production of the Merchant of Venice). *Renmin xiju* (People's Theatre) 1 (1981): 19–21.

Zhou, Raymond. "A Wild Retake on a Wilde Classic." *China Daily*, June 02, 2015. www.chinadaily.com.cn.

Zhou, Xiaoyi. "*Shalemei zhi wen, xiaofeizhuyi yu zhongguo qimeng xiandaixing*" (Salome's Kiss: Aestheticism, Consumerism and Modernity of Chinese Enlightenment). *China Comparative Literature* 2 (2001): 67–89.

Zhu, Xuefeng. "*Wenmingxi wutai shang de Zhaoyanwang: Hong Shen, Aoni'er yu Zhongguo zaoqi huaju zhuanxing xiju yishu.*" (*Yama Zhao* on the Stage of 'Civilized Drama:' Hong Shen, O'Neill and the Art of Early Chinese Spoken Drama During Transformation). *Xiju yishu* (Theatre Arts) 3 (2012): 48–58.

6 An old "mentor and friend" from afar

Adapting classic Russian drama for the Chinese stage

Looking at any map of the world one could easily see an enormous landmass looming above the Asian continent, including China, which is not a small country by any measure. The sheer size of Russia (or the former Soviet Union),[1] its geographic proximity, and its economic and industrial might (relative to the much weaker China in much of the nineteenth and twentieth centuries) would translate into direct and profound influence from China's northern neighbor in the realms of (geo)politics and socioeconomics. On June 30, 1949, on the eve of Communist victory in China, Mao Zedong (1893–1976), in an important article that would pretty much set the tone (politics and policies) for the new People's Republic to be established in just a couple of months, gave special acknowledgment to "the roar of the canon firing from Russian October Revolution" (1917) that "brought us Marxism-Leninism."[2] Although a hyperbole perhaps, because the introduction of Marxism (not Leninism per se) in China had taken a more convoluted course than being described in Mao's sweeping attribution,[3] it encapsulates the enormous importance of Russia in the sociopolitical life of modern China.

The introduction of Russian literature in China, however, was somewhat late, relative to the introduction of other Western literatures thanks[4] in part to the fact that Moscow and St. Petersburgh, the cultural and historical heart of Russia, are tucked far away in the Eastern European half of the empire and that its Asian half manifests itself mostly in the vast, unforgiving Siberia that stretches from the Ural Mountains to the Pacific Ocean.[5] The first notable Chinese translation of Russian literature, in the form of *The Captain's Daughter* by Alexander Pushkin, did not happen until 1903. Within a decade after the publication of the Pushkin novel, however, works by Leo Tolstoy, Ivan Turgenev, Anton Chekhov, Maxim Gorky, etc., had been translated into Chinese, mostly "free" translation in the "quasi-classical" style and mostly secondhand work too, by way of existent Japanese and English translations.[6]

The first tidal wave of interest in Russian literature would come during the New Cultural Movement (1910s–1920s), especially after the Russian October Revolution, when young Chinese intellectuals and writers began to look upon Russian literature, as Lu Xun (1881–1936) put it, as "mentor and friend" (*daoshi he pengyou*), a source of inspiration and example to admire and emulate. Many of the leading revolutionaries and prominent figures in modern Chinese culture were Russian literature enthusiasts: Liang Qichao (1873–1929), Wang Guowei (1877–1927), Mao Dun (1896–1981), Guo Moruo (1892–1978), and Ba Jin (1904–2005), to name just a few. For decades, from the late 1940s to the late 1970s, Russia-originated ideologies such as class-oriented socialist realism dominated arts and literature discourse in China. Similarly, the "system" of Konstantin Stanislavski (1863–1938) shaped more than a generation of Chinese thinking and practice of actor training, and loomed over the theatre scene until the early 1980s when Bertolt Brecht (1898–1956), Samuel Beckett (1906–1989), and other modern and post-modern Western dramatists were (re)introduced.[7]

Even though since the late 1980s the star of Russian arts and literature in China has dimmed somewhat, so to speak, relative to that of its Western European and American cousins, its influence has never faded away. There has always been a soft spot in the minds and hearts of a generation of Chinese theatre artists, especially those who studied drama in Russia or with Russian teachers at the drama academies in Beijing and Shanghai in the 1950s and 1960s. Each time the Russian production of a classic or a relatively new play travels to China and tours the country – e.g., Gorky's *The Lower Depths* by the Gorky Moscow Art Theatre in May 2014, Gogol's *The Government Inspector* by the Alexandrinsky Theatre (aka. Russian State Pushkin Academy Drama Theatre) in August 2015, and *Brothers and Sisters* by the St. Petersburg Maly Drama Theatre, based on a 1958 novel by Fyodor Abramov (1920–1983) and directed by Lev Dodin (1944–), an eight-hour-long drama about the harsh life on a Soviet collective farm during WWII, etc. – it would fascinate and indeed "shock and awe" the Chinese with its artistic honesty, power, and beauty, forcing them to think and reflect on how much the old "mentor and friend" still has to offer.[8]

The reception of classic Russian drama in China and indeed the relative success or lack thereof that classic Russian dramatists such as Aleksandr Ostrovsky (1823–1886), Maxim Gorky (1868–1936), Nikolai Gogol (1809–1852), and Anton Chekhov (1860–1904) have experienced, respectively, on the Chinese stage bespeaks the complex dynamics between texts (dramatic, cultural, and socio-historical), contexts (domestic and international), intertexts (Western classics and their Chinese reinterpretations), and tradition and innovation entailed in such transcultural endeavors. For example, the story of Katerina, the heroine of Ostrovsky's 1859 play *The Storm*, her caged-bird-like existence in a small town on the Volga, her longing for happiness and love that ends in her death, resonated with the young Chinese in the early decades of the twentieth century. Similarly, the popularity Gorky's 1902 play *The Lower Depths* enjoyed in China in the 1940s can be attributed to the fact that through transcultural relocation and reinterpretation Chinese theatre artists made the story speak directly to the socioeconomic and emotive realities of the downtrodden in China at the time and appeal to their sense of social justice.

Like Ostrovsky and Gorky, Gogol has enjoyed long, enduring popularity in China. His satirical comedy, a mix of conventional (suspense, mistaken identities, hilarious characters, surprise ending, etc.) and new (its "surrealistic, dreamlike essence")[9] has never failed to deliver because it appeals to the Chinese, theatre artists, and ordinary theatergoers alike, both topically and artistically. The kind of poetic justice rendered in the play satisfies the Chinese desire for social justice even if it lasts for only two or three hours in the imaginary world of theatre. In the meantime, the suspenseful unfolding of story on the stage, despite, or rather because of, dramatic irony, one hilarious scene coming on the heels of another, not only arouses their interest but also sustains it all the way to the end.

In contrast, Chekhov's brand of drama, as is known to all Chekhov enthusiasts, defies an easy labeling of tragedy or comedy. It has no clear-cut heroes and villains as the terms are understood in both dramatic literature and in everyday life. It does not follow a discernable narrative arc (from exposition to climax to denouement) propelled by apparent conflicts of personalities, politics, or psychologies. Rather, it flows like a stream-of-ordinaries of daily life albeit presented with amusement, empathy, piercing insight of the human soul, and calm resignation of existential conundrum. Unlike Ostrovsky, Gorky, or Gogol, who could be "easily" drafted for pungent social commentary or sociopolitical satire, Chekhov remains noncommittal and evasive, although he believes in "absolute freedom."[10] It seems that as far as the Chinese are concerned, Chekhov the playwright, with his artless art and profound yet indeterminate interpretive possibilities, is better fit for scholarly studies than for dramatic presentation on the stage.

Ostrovsky and Gorky: to lift up the oppressed and the downtrodden

Like much of Western drama, early Russian drama was religious, taking the form of mystery and miracle plays. These shows gradually moved onto the secular scenes to tell stories of and, mostly, satirize through humor and comedy, history and contemporary life. Such performances, which would include adaptations of Molière – e.g., *Le Médecin Malgré Lui* (The Doctor in Spite of Himself) and *Les Précieuses Ridicules* (The Pretentious Young Ladies), performed at the Moscow academy, the Cadet School in St. Petersburg, and elsewhere – would shape the growth of a generation of young Russian enthusiasts of arts and literature. One of them, Alexander Sumarokov (1717–1777), who wrote tragedies in imitation of Racine (1639–1699) and Voltaire (1694–1778), and in strict adherence to the (neo)classical rule of "unities," would become the founder of classical Russian theatre. From then onward, there emerged quite a few great Russian playwrights, among them, Aleksandr Ostrovsky (1823–1886).[11]

Of all the plays by Ostrovsky, a highly prolific writer, *The Storm* (1859) was the first to see a Chinese translation, published in 1921 under the Chinese title *Leiyu* (Thunderstorm). It has since the 1930s acquired a different

Chinese title, *Daleiyu* (Big Thunderstorm), to distinguish from *Leiyu* (Thunderstorm, 1938) by Cao Yu (1910–1996), one of the greatest modern Chinese plays that drew inspirations from Ostrovsky as well as Eugene O'Neill, Henrik Ibsen, and Greek classics.[12] The year 1922 saw two more Ostrovsky translations, *Poverty Is No Vice* (1854) under the Chinese title *Ping fei zui* and *Sin and Sorrow Are Common to All* (1862) under the Chinese title *Zui yu chou*. An adaptation of *Sin and Sorrow* (*Ai yu hen*, Love and Hate) was mounted in Shanghai in 1936. Other plays by Ostrovsky that were translated into Chinese in the early decades of the twentieth century include *Without a Dowry* (1878; *Meiyou peijia de nüren*) and *Enough Stupidity in Every Wise Man* (1868; *Zhizhe qianlü biyou yishi*). *Without a Dowry* was adapted into a play by Chen Baichen (see the following) in 1946 titled *Xuanya zhi ai* (Love on the Cliff). A production of *Enough Stupidity* was mounted in 1962 and 1990, both by the Beijing People's Art Theatre, and as recently as 2006 by visiting Russian theatre artists as part of the "Year of Russian Culture" celebration.[13] His 1884 play *Guilty without Guilt* was adapted into a film in 1947 titled *Mu yu zi* (Mother and Son).

The most notable of all the cultural afterlives Ostrovsky's dramatic works have enjoyed in China has to be that of *The Storm*, or *Daleiyu*, as it is fondly known in China. The story of Katerina, the heroine of this five-act play, her suffocating life in a small town on the Volga, entrapped between a manipulative, despotic mother-in-law (Old Dame Kabanova) and a good-hearted but spineless mama's boy of a husband (Tihon Kabanov), and her longing for happiness and love that ends in her death (guilt stricken after meeting her lover Boris Grigorievitch in the garden, Katerina confesses her "sin" and then out of despair throws herself into the Volga) must have resonated with the young Chinese in the early decades of the twentieth century as they were struggling for women's liberation. There is no slamming the door and leaving the husband and children to go out into the big world as her Norwegian cousin Nora in Henrik Ibsen's *A Doll's House* (1879) would do 20 years later. Katerina's fatalistic sense of doom and indeed her suicide would hardly earn her admiration as a champion for the women's liberation cause.[14] However, Katerina seemed so real and relatable as if she had just stepped out of the pages of classic Chinese literature such as the eighteen-century novel *Dream of Red Mansions*. She could still be drafted as a loud protest against the repression of the old, intransigent patriarchy. That is perhaps why in the 1930s and 1940s *Daleiyu* (*The Storm*) was staged not only in Shanghai, the most Westernized city in China, but also in Chongqin, the war time capital of the country (1937–1945), and many other cities across the country. Indeed it was one of the most popular and frequently staged Western classics in China before 1949.[15]

In 1936 in Shanghai, the role of Katerina was channeled by Lan Ping (1914–1991), before she became Jiang Qing and Madame Mao, with Zhao Dan (1915–1980) playing her husband Tihon Kabanov (the two having paired up for Ibsen's *A Doll's House* earlier in the same year), and Shu Xiuwen (1915–1969), another gifted actor, playing her despotic mother-in-law Madame Kabanov. Both Zhao and Shu would pay dearly for their connections with Lan Ping, Shu with her life during the Cultural Revolution (1966–1976).[16] In the autumn of 1939 in Yan'an, "red capital" of the Communist forces (1936–1949), theatre artists planned to stage *Daleiyu* as part of the New Year's celebration. Halfway through the rehearsal, Mao Zedong, who had secured his leadership at the end of the Long March (1934–1935) and married Jiang Qing a year earlier, got wind of it, talked to Zhang Geng (1911–2003), the director, and suggested that they perform Cao Yu's *Sunrise* (*Richu*) instead. It is not clear why Mao Zedong did so, although it is suggested that at the time Mao thought highly of the New Culture Movement that had begun from the May 4, 1919 event, including the new drama, of which *Sunrise* was regarded as the best, even better, more progressive than Cao Yu's *Thunderstorm*.[17] About three years later, in 1942, the Ostrovsky play did get staged as part of the Army Day (August 1) celebration.[18]

Fast forward to July 9, 1959, when a centennial celebration of *Daleiyu* (The Storm) was held in Beijing with a performance by the Central Experimental Spoken Drama Theatre (*Zhongyang shiyan huaju yuan*), attended by the embassy and other Soviet Union representatives in the capital.[19] It was an interesting, or rather "stormy," time in the Sino-Soviet relationship as the "Big Old Brother" (*laodage*), led by Nikita Khrushchev (1894–1971), was undergoing de-Stalinization and seeking detent with the United States, which alarmed and upset Mao.[20] The "party" was still going on, though, at least in appearance and on the less contentious cultural scene, until the ultimate split in 1963. It was also an interesting, or rather difficult, time in China's domestic politics when the Chinese Communist Party leadership gathered in Lushan (Mount Lu), a renowned summer resort in the Jiangxi province, to take stock of the Great Leap Forward (1958–1962), given that a catastrophic outcome was already showing its ugly head. It was during this Lushan Conference (July 2 to August 1) that Mao fought back against critics such as Marshal Peng Dehuai (1898–1974) and punished them harshly, another prelude to the much worse that was to come during the Cultural Revolution.[21]

All of these would make the critical yet measured tone of a published review of the Central Experimental Spoken Drama Theatre production of the Ostrovsky play stand out. After a few approving words, the review, published in *Xiju bao* (Drama Gazette), a monthly whose editor in chief was Zhang Geng (alluded to earlier), went after the production critically, albeit as gently and constructively as the author Hong Gu (Red Girl, apparently a penname for an individual or team of writers) could manage. Through the lens of class struggle, the dominant ideology in arts and literature discourse in China then, the review saw Katerina as a fighter for women's liberation cause against a backward and cruel "dark kingdom" (*Heian wangguo*) and Madame Kabanov as its oppressive ruler. Such a heavy-handed political reading of the play, however, doesn't necessarily mean that one would be willing to lower the artistic expectations. Indeed, the review found the production's character portrayal unsatisfactory – flat, one-dimensional, not as nuanced as embodied in the source text by Ostrovksy:[22]

> The director and actors tended to emphasize one aspect of a charac-
> ter while overlooking the other aspects, e.g., emphasizing Katerina's
> kindness while overlooking her strong will and resistance; emphasizing
> Madame Kabanov's viciousness while overlooking her inner vulnerabil-
> ity; emphasizing Boris' weakness while overlooking his guilt-stricken
> feeling; emphasizing Kudriash being a "lady-killer" while overlooking
> him being a "bold and lovable young man."

The review thus concludes,[23]

> The overall performance was honest and relatable, but flat and color-
> less, with no powerful impact on the audiences. I would be most content
> if the views expressed herein, misplaced they might be, had any refer-
> ence value for the comrades of this production.

If only such a civil tone could have been maintained by everyone during the Lushan Conference that was going on at the time and in the years to come, especially during the Cultural Revolution.

Another Russian writer "drafted" to help lift up the oppressed and the downtrodden in China was Maxim Gorky, one of the most beloved foreign writers admired by the Left-Wing writers and intellectuals in the 1930s and 1940s. Gorky's works such as the novel *The Mother* (1907) and autobiog-raphies *My Childhood* (1913–1914), *In the World* (1916), and *My Univer-sities* (1923) were among the most popular in China, each seeing several translations and many reprints. From 1928 to 1949 alone, over 270 editions of Gorky's fiction and dramatic works and more than a dozen collections (in Chinese translations from Russian or by way of existent English and Japanese translations) had been published. *The Lower Depths* (1902), the best known of Gorky's plays, saw several translations under various Chinese titles: *Yedian* (Night Shelter, also translated as Night Inn, Night Lodging), *Shenyuan* (The Abyss), and *Diceng* (Rock Bottom). It would take the Chi-nese many more years, though, after these publications, to finally mount a production of *Yedian* (*The Lower Depths*) on the stage, more than 40 years after its successful premiere in Moscow directed by Konstantin Stanislavski.[24] This 1947 production in Shanghai, cowritten by Ke Ling (1910–1988) and Shi Tuo (1909–2000), and directed by Huang Zuolin (1906–1994), followed by a film adaptation in 1948, also directed by Huang Zuolin, presented an interesting case of transcultural relocation and reinterpretation, whereby the Chinese theatre artists remade the Russian classic so it would speak more directly to the socioeconomic and emotive realities in China as the coun-try plunged deeper into another civil war right after the War of Resistance against Japan (1937–1945) was over.[25]

To begin with, *Yedian* relocated the story told in *The Lower Depths* from Russia to China so all the characters assumed new Sinicized identities: Kostylyoff, the night shelter owner, becomes Wen Taishi (Big Master Wen); Vassilisa, his wife, Sai Guanyin (Out-Guanyin Guanyin, the Goddess of Mercy); Vasya Pepel, a young thief, Yang Qi (Seven Yang); Natasha, Vassilisa's younger sister, Shi Meimei (Younger Sister Shi); Luka, an old sage, Quan Laotou (Old Man Quan), etc. It also cut the ensemble of characters from 18 to 15 (dropping Satin, the murderer, and the two proletarian dock hands), redrew their socioeconomic profiles and behavior, and reshuffled their relative importance so that there would be less confusion about characters and that, more importantly, there would be less ambiguity in moral judgment.

As an important play known for its social realism, *The Lower Depths* has a naturalistic feel as the characters – a greedy landlord; his jealousy-consumed and vicious wife; a young thief, burdened by his past and struggling to begin anew; a pretty, egregiously abused young woman yearning for love and dignity; a gambler, an ex-artist, a prostitute, and other members of the low and downtrodden that gather in the dark, cramped cellar – drift in and out of the dramatic action without clear, morally satisfactory developments. *Yedian*, on the other hand, took it up a notch, so to speak, and sharpened the dramatic action with central characters and central conflict between the oppressors on the one hand – Wen Taishi (Kostylyoff), known as "single-eyed devil" in the play, and Sai Guanyin (Vassilisa), as selfish and sadistic as in the original, but having acquired a new biographical backstory: she had been sold to her husband by her parents to pay off the debt – and the oppressed on the other hand: Yang Qi (Vasya Pepel) and Shi Meimei (Natasha), etc. If *The Lower Depths*, as written by Gorky, is a portrayal of human condition, of people, beaten down, struggling to rise from the lower depths of existence, *Yedian* is much more a sociopolitical commentary, and – given the left-leaning political sympathy of all three theatre artists responsible for this production – an indictment of the social conditions under the corrupt and repressive Nationalist (Guomindang) Government. In sharpening its sociopolitical criticism, however, *Yedian* suffers in character portrayals. For example, toward the end of the Gorky play, Natasha chooses to leave the dark and cramped cellar and go out into the world on her own whereas Shi Xiaomei, her Chinese reincarnation, places all her hope on the man in her life, Yang Qi (Vasya Pepel), and hangs herself to preserve her last shred of dignity when her sister Sai Guanyin (Vassilisa) sells her to a much older rich man. She becomes a weaker character as a result of the transcultural relocation and reinterpretation.

Huang Zuolin and his team went further in reshaping the story and simplifying the morality for their 1948 film adaptation based on the *huaju* rendition of the Gorky play. The spotlight of *Yedian* the film now shines almost exclusively on two characters, Yang Qi (Vasya Pepel) and Sai Guanyin (Vassilisa). The young thief is now transformed into a hero of sorts: handsome, righteous, resourceful, and well-liked by the other tenants of the night shelter, not unlike a *xiake*, a popular Robin Hood type of character one would encounter in classic Chinese fiction and drama such as the *Shuihu zhuan* (*Water Margin,* also translated as *Outlaws of the Marsh* and *All Men are Brothers*). *Sai Guanyin* (Vassilisa), on the other hand, still charming in her own ways, is now viciously evil, who, along with her husband Wen Taishi (Kostylyoff), rules the night shelter like a tyrant. The love between Yang Qi (Vasya Pepel) and Shi Meimei (Natasha) is purer and even redeeming: it inspires Yang Qi to give up stealing and find an honest job instead. It is Yang Qi who raises funds among the tenants to bury Lai Saozi (Anna) when she dies of illness. The film ends with Sai Guanyin (Vassilisa) being arrested for the crime of having poisoned Wen Taishi (Kostylyoff) to death and Yang Qi being released from jail – he didn't beat Wen Taishi to death after all. Justice is served, although it comes too late for Shi Meimei: she has been sold to a rich old man and hanged herself out of despair.

Gorky's star continued to shine brightly in China until the second half of the 1960s when the Cultural Revolution began. There was a revival of interest in Gorky in the 1980s, primarily to take stock and remedy the distorted reception (adulation) by way of gaining a more complete appreciation of the Russian writer. As recently as 2007, theatre artists in Wuhan staged a revival production of *Yedian* to commemorate the fiftieth anniversary of the production of the play by Wuhan People's Art Theatre.[26] The cast for this production was mostly the same for the "original" 1957 production. Just imagine the now much grayed septuagenarians and octogenarians (the average age for the cast was 74 years old) playing the young characters as described by Gorky: Vasya Pepel, 28, Natasha, 20, Vassilisa, 26, etc. The year 2007 also saw a production of *The Lower Depths* by the graduating class of the Central Academy of Drama in Beijing. The co-directors of *Diceng* thus interpret the Gorky play, which shows how far they have traveled from the theatre artists who (re)made *Yedian* in the 1940s:[27]

> What touches and shakes us profoundly today is its embodiment of the power of human nature: the characters' longing for family, friendship, love and their longing for warmth, kindness, and a healthy life. This longing is the indispensable quintessence of being human. It is the force that propels us forward in life. What touches and inspires us are their thoughts on life, their faith in the future, and their dogged quest. "The purpose of life is to live better." To live a fulfilling life, a beautiful life, is what calls upon us to keep trying hard and never give up.

Gogol: satirical comedy that never fails to deliver

Very few writers enjoy so much fame in another country that they have a street named after them. Nikolai Gogol (1809–1852) is one of the fortunate few. In the northeastern city of Harbin, China, there is a Gogol Street, which opened in 1901 to mark the importance of Russian trade, culture, and diaspora in the socioeconomic life of this part of the Asian country. During an inspection tour here in 1958, as the Great Leap Forward raged on, Mao Zedong bestowed a new name onto the street: *Fendou* (struggle, strive). Gogol did have to "strive" to achieve the kind of literary fame he had longed for from childhood, although he came from a pedigree less humble than that of Maxim Gorky (who became an orphan at age 11). Forty-five years later, in 2003, the historical name was reinstated to honor the Russian writer and to promote cultural and socioeconomic exchange across the Sino-Russian borders. It is now a favorite tourist attraction alive with an interesting, uneasy mix of olden Russian architecture such as orthodox churches and brash new high-rises.[28] Despite the snub from Mao, perhaps to take a jab at the "Big Old Brother" (*laodage*) as de-Stalinization and other ideological and geopolitical disagreements were causing the alliance between the two Communist powers to crack, Gogol has remained an old favorite, especially Gogol the playwright, as represented by *The Government Inspector* (1836). Indeed, ever since the first Chinese translation of the play was published in 1921, *The Government Inspector* has seen many a successful adaptation and inspired quite a few notable Chinese dramatic works too.

As it happened, the first Chinese translation of Gogol is his best-known work *The Government Inspector* under the Chinese title *Xun an* (Emperor Sent Inspector) published in 1921. Not long after that, an adaptation of the play, based on this translation, was staged by the Nankai New Drama Troupe (*xinjutuan*) in Tianjin and by students of the newly established *Shenzhou nüxiao* (Shenzhou Girls School) in Shanghai. A few years later, in 1935, Shanghai *Yeyu juren xiehui* (Shanghai Armature Dramatist Association) mounted a production of the play, which, from 1935 to 1937, traveled to Tianjin, Nanjing, Xi'an, Ji'nan, Taiyuan, and other cities in China. The Gogol play was also adapted into a film in 1936 with a different Chinese title: *Kuanghuan zhi ye* (Carnival Night). Directed by Shi Dongshan (1902–1955), this film adaptation relocated the story to a small southern Chinese town in the 1920s. All the characters and places assume Chinese names and identities; the government inspector is now supposed to be the brother of the internal minister and Khlestakov a playboy from Shanghai instead of St. Petersburg. The film ends not only with announcement of the arrival of the real inspector but also the report that *geming jun* (the revolutionary army) is now attacking the guards for the town's corrupt officials[29] – an apparent reference to the war against the warlords in the 1920s of China.[30]

Gogol's *The Government Inspector*, now typically translated as *Qinchai dachen* (Emperor Sent Big Minister) inspired a 1945 play by Chen Baichen (1908–1994), *Shenguantu* (Map of Officialdom). The title of the three-act play refers to a century-old game whereby contestants go through an elaborate labyrinth of official positions to race to the highest echelon in the center of the map.[31] The dramatic action of the play centers on two bandits whose attempt to make their "officialdom dreams" (*shengguan meng*) come true leads to hilarious situations in a small town. On the run from authorities, the two bandits hide themselves in an ancient residence, fall asleep, and begin to dream. In their dreams, they take advantage of the aftermath of a local uprising by pretending to be the two incapacitated officials, the seriously injured county commissioner (*zhixian*) and the now dead secretary general (*mishuzhang*). The infighting among the corrupt officials that ensues leads to the county commissioner's wife marrying the province governor and everyone else (police superintendent, director of schools, postmaster, judge, warden of hospital, etc.) getting promoted. On the night of the wedding celebration, crowds of angry masses rush in, tie up all the corrupt officials, and take them away for justice. It is at this juncture that the two bandits wake up from their dreams. The intertextual reverberations between *Shenguantu* (Map of Officialdom) and *The Government Inspector*, both in story and in spirit, are significant, although the dream structural frame for Chen's play is inspired by the Tang dynasty fictional story *Zhenzhong ji* (Story of the Pillow) and the Ming dynasty play *Handan ji* (Story of Handan) by the well-known play-wright Tang Xianzu (1550–1616), often dubbed the Chinese Shakespeare. Set in the early days of the Republic (1910s–1920s), Chen's play was written to satirize the corruptions of the Guomintang (Nationalist) government ruling the country at the time. It was staged in Shanghai, Chongqing, and other cities in China in 1946.

The popularity of Gogol's *The Government Inspector* in China during the early decades of the twentieth century can be explained not only by its appeal to the sensibilities of Chinese audiences (theatre and film alike) but also, more importantly, by its "take-no-prisoner" satire directed at govern-ment corruption, which was rampant in China then as it is today. Corruption, although not peculiar to China, has its deep cultural roots (e.g., emphasis on kinship and familial ties) and systemic sociopolitical causes (e.g., *renzhi*, rule of people, instead of *fazhi*, rule of law).[32] Despite anti-corruption campaigns launched during the Republican China (1911–1949), including the 1948 *Dahu* (hit tigers – big corrupters) campaign mounted by Chiang Ching-kuo (Jiang Jingguo, 1910–1988) in Shanghai to save the Nationalist (Guomin-dang) Government from all but certain defeat by the Mao-led Communist forces, corruption, so entrenched, proved invincible. It costed the government general support from the people, which led to its flight to Taiwan in 1949.[33]

Similarly, despite manifestos and pledges institutionalized in the Commu-nist Party's charter and repeated national mobilizations – e.g., the Three-Anti (1951, *sanfan*, anti-corruption, anti-waste, anti-bureaucracy) and Five-Anti (1952, *wu fan*, anti-bribery, anti-theft of state property, anti-tax evasion, anti-cheating on government contracts, and anti-stealing state economic infor-mation) campaigns, corruption was never fully contained, let alone annihi-lated, in the 1950s and 1960s. It has gotten much worse since the end of the 1970s when China reopened its door and began experimenting with "socialist market economy with Chinese characteristics."[34] This sociopolitical reality of China largely explains why Gogol, as exemplified by *The Government Inspec-tor*, remains topically relevant as well as theatrically appealing.

The first production of *The Government Inspector* after the Communist victory in 1949 took place in May 1952. Sun Weishi (1921–1968), who had studied drama in the Soviet Union (1939–1946), mounted a production of the Gogol play, which, by all accounts, was a success although there is no known published review of the production. More interestingly, Gogol's play found another Chinese reincarnation in a 1956 play written by Lao She (1899–1966), *Xiwang chang'an* (Westward to Chang'an),[35] which was also inspired by real people and real events that had just happened in the mid-1950s. A young imposter invented a story dressing himself up (he did literally dress himself in old army uniform) as a hero from the recent Korean War and cheated his way to fame, fortune, and officialdom.[36] However, the play's criticism of corruption among officials of the recently established People's Republic was considerably tamed: Lao She turned the real-life, rough-hewn imposter into a sophisticated con artist, so to speak, so that the play became much more a humorous cautionary tale about government officials' gullibility than satire directed at government corruption. Despite the "caution" with which he wrote this play and other works of his after 1949, Lao She suffered egregiously during the Cultural Revolution, which claimed him as one of its earliest victims. A revival production of the play was mounted in Beijing in 2007 (starring Ge You) as part of the *huaju* centennial celebration.[37]

Another Gogol-inspired Chinese play that speaks directly to the contemporary sociopolitical life of the country is *Jiaru wo shi zhen de* (If I Were for Real), written in 1979 when the scars from the Cultural Revolution, both psychic and sociopolitical, were still tender and when Jiang Qing (Madame Mao) and her Gang of Four cohorts were yet to be put on trial, nationally televised (1980). In this play, also based on a real life event, Li Xiaozhang, a *zhiqing* (sent-down youth), returns to Shanghai to visit his pregnant girlfriend. One day, he goes to see a stage performance of Gogol's *The Government Inspector* and is mistaken for a *gaogan zidi* (son of a high-ranking official) from Beijing. Taking advantage of the opportunity that presents itself, Li plays along (to get himself transferred back to Shanghai) and is ingratiatingly received by the municipal officials. When this impromptu scheme is exposed, the young man is arrested. This six-act play was staged by Shanghai People's Art Theatre in September as *neibu yanchu* (internal performance, with limited, controlled admission, as opposed to public performance). This "internal performance" then traveled to several major cities across the country, striking a chord with packed audiences emotively, as well as socio-politically, and causing heated debates in intellectual circles as well as the echelon of the country's leadership. The official verdict that soon came down was that the play *mohei* ("smeared") the Party, so it was put on hold and never performed again.[38] The real and potentially subversive question for the audiences and indeed for the country, is raised by Li, the young impromptu imposter, before curtain falls, a variation of the "fourth wall" breaking line from Gogol's *The Government Inspector* ("Who are you laughing at? Laugh at yourselves."):

My mistake lies in me being an imposter. If I were for real, all I have done would be perfectly legal.

One would have to wait until 1999 (ten years after the 1989 Tiananmen Square events, which had started in part as protests against corruption and demands for equality in the post-Mao era)[39] for another notable production of *The Government Inspector*. It was mounted by the Chinese Youth Art Troupe, directed by Chen Yong (1929–2004), who had also studied drama in the Soviet Union in the 1950s.[40] Not a big fan of extreme remake of Western classics, Chen Yong believed that Gogol's play has universal reference that transcends time and space. Therefore, for her production, Chen aimed to be faithful to both the spirit and the story of the original play while interjecting some new vitality and fluidity into the performance by borrowing from other art forms such as film. The production was presented at the small theatre of the Chinese Youth Art Troupe which had a small thrust stage and could seat 397 people. To give the production a palpable Russian vibe, the stage had in its backdrop a Russian Orthodox Church dome basking in golden light and Russian music and songs. Chen also borrowed the "freeze-frame" technique from film to augment the dramatic effect. For example, in Act IV, Scene 1 (of the original play),[41] at the Mayor's home, as the county officials conspire to cover up their corruption, they are startled by Khlestakov ("the government inspector") waking up suddenly; they all dash to exit, almost falling on each other in the stampede, and are caught in a "freeze-frame" halfway on the stairway. The production ends in the last "Scene without Words,"where all the characters, minus Khlestakov and his servant Osip, are "frozen" on stage for a full minute, as if turned to stone. Chen hoped that this production would "interrogate the numbed soul of the people today . . . and awaken the conscience of mankind."[42] While some critics found the production richly classical, others found it lacking in invoking something deeper inside each of "us" other than apparent social criticism. After all, we are all Khlestakov, as one critic said, or rather, we have all been Khlestakov at one time or another.[43]

In June 2006, another production of *The Government Inspector* was mounted by students of the School of Television and Film Art, Communication University of China, directed by Zhao Ningyu, associate professor at the school. In 1999, a doctoral student at the Central Academy of Drama then, Zhao had seen Chen Yong's production of the Gogol play.[44] Like Chen Yong before him, Zhao Ningyu felt that Gogol's play belongs to all time and that underneath its sharp exposé of corrupt officials is the interesting history of a group of twisted, alienated human souls.

To deliver the universal "alienation of human souls" theme, Zhao and his team designed a stage that was essentially "empty," where characters with abbreviated Chinese transliterations of Russian names (e.g., *He Lida* for Khlestakov, the "government inspector"; *An Demu* for Antonovich, the mayor; *An Furen* for the mayor's wife; *An Qiqi* for the mayor's daughter) and characters with fully Sinicized names (e.g., Big Sister Zhang/*Zhang Dajie* for the director of schools: Three-Cannon He/*He Sanpao* for the police superintendent, Patriot Li/*Li Aiguo* and Paternal Li/*Li Aimin* for the two merchants, and Fat Liu/*Liu*

Pang for the charity commissioner and warden of the hospital) popping up from passageways underneath the stage to encounter each other, which led to many a hilariously comic situation. All of these characters are "foreign" (from another country and another time) yet feel awfully familiar, even familial at the same time as if they were among "us," or, simply, they are "us," as some critics put it, if only for some of the actions and for some of the time. To further shorten the distance from "us," from the ordinary people, Zhao Ningyu and his team set the ticket price at 30 to 120 yuan (RMB) to make access to the theatric event and experience much more affordable than the usual charge (five or six times more expensive) for such performances. The production went on for eight performances (June 10–18) and then traveled to quite a few cities in the country.[45]

Four years later, in 2010, Shanghai Theatre Academy and Jiao Huang Art Studio mounted another production of *The Government Inspector*. This is a dream come true half a century in the making. In 1959, the graduating class at Shanghai Theatre Academy rehearsed and was all but ready to perform the Gogol play when it was canceled (for unknown reasons, although the larger geopolitical context was that by then the Sino-Soviet split had worsened and reached the point of no return). Half a century later, a group from that class, septuagenarians by now, staged a "revival" production of the play.[46] Most of the actors had studied with Russian or Russia-educated drama teachers while in college and had been drilled in the Stanislavski system. The stage design and costumes were as "realistically" nineteenth-century Russian as possible. Jiao Huang, 74 years old then, who played the leading role of Khlestakov, dressed in red tailcoat, white pants, and donning a head of blond hair, was as energetic and lively on the stage as someone half his age. Perhaps his age, and indeed the "old" age of the cast (with the exception of Yang Kun, a young actor playing the mayor's daughter) proved a source of mirthful comic effect while adding a sense of history and gravitas to the performance. They performed in Shanghai and at the National Center for the Performing Arts in Beijing (five performances, April 14 to 19). Chen Mingzheng, a young teacher at the academy half a century before who had guided the young students' rehearsal then, served as the director. In many ways, this 2010 revival production of *The Government Inspector* was as much a tribute to their beloved Gogol as to the days when the cast members were still young.[47]

The most interesting and extraordinary Chinese rendition of *The Government Inspector*, however, has to be the 2004 puppetry production mounted by Quanzhou Puppetry Troup, Fujian Province.[48] Although the puppet production stays true to the spirit of the original, it undergoes full relocation in language, culture, and time, as well as mode of presentation. Instead of Tsarist Russia, the story now takes place in a fictional Nowhere County (*Wuyou xian*) in an unspecified pre-modern time of China. All the characters assume Chinese names – e.g., Money Three (*Qian San*) for the mayor, False Four (*Jia*

Si) for Khlestakov, and Zhu Five (*Zhu Wu*) for Osif – and are all dressed in colorful traditional Chinese costumes. The script is streamlined and compressed for an 80-minute performance.

As the curtain rises, we see Money Three (*Qian San*), the mayor, reclined in a chair, smoking Hookah, a maid fanning him by the side. As he falls asleep and snores, the official hat (*wushamao*) heaving on his chest, Money Wife (*Qian Qi*) and Money Daughter (*Qian Nü*) tiptoe over, search in his hat, and find a long string of corruption money hidden in it, thus unfolding the dramatic action for the show and a series of delightful comical scenes.

One of the memorable scenes happens before False Four (Khlestakov) has been mistaken for the government inspector. Having pawned everything, including his clothes, for food, a wretched False Four, along with Zhu Five, his servant, climbs a tall ladder to the top of the inn's kitchen wall, from where arises aroma of delicacies being cooked. They try to fish up food with a stringed hook, succeed in catching a mouthwatering well-cooked pig's paw, and then, as luck would have it, are discovered by the lady innkeeper. A delightful hide-and-seek play ensues between the wronged innkeeper and the two culprits. Then the mayor's steward (*Shi Ye*) arrives with a gang of guards looking for the "government inspector" visiting incognito and stumbles upon the scene. Startled by being "caught" again, this time by the government, False Four faints and falls crashing down with the tall ladder, to the joy of the mayor's steward who, confident that he has finally found the "government inspector," directs his men to carry the fainted False Four on the long ladder, like a jolly wedding procession, back to the compound of Nowhere County government. The agility and expressiveness of puppets, drawn from the rich repertoire of puppetry in China that goes back for at least 3,000 years, enable them to perform stunts where it would be impossible for their human counterparts to even try. The puppetry show has since performed in many cities in China and traveled abroad too.

The popularity of *The Government Inspector* has also been borne out by recent adaptation endeavors in traditional *xiqu* genres such as *Gezaixi* (aka. *jianghudiao*, river lake airs, the name referencing to its traveling minstrel origin) and a *huaju* production by Zhejiang *Huaju* Troupe in 2015. This latest *huaju* production relocates the story to the 1940s, when China was governed by the Kuomintang (Nationalist) Government with a twist for the Chinese title: *Qinchai mei dachen* (Emperor Sent No Big Minister).[49] It was a safe move politically (to put some respectful distance between the production and the politics of today's China), although artistically it was bold, creative, and entertaining. The promotional pitch by the Zhejiang theatre artists for the production, however, makes its barbed wire political satire as clear as broad daylight:

"Dark Society" of Power, "Deep Dark-ology" of Officialdom
(*quanli "hei shehui," guanchang "hou heixue"*):

> This is perhaps the most cowardly production of the play: we don't talk about politics;
> This is perhaps the boldest production in China today: we only want to see corrupt officials fall.
> If you say we are only interested in tabloids and gossip, we also enjoy the spectacular spectator sports of "tiger fighting";[50]
> If you say we only talk about family and sentimental things, we also care about the truth of the "anti-corruption" campaign.

It is followed by a disclaimer not unlike the "Notice" Mark Twain put up front for his novel *Huckleberry Finn*:[51]

> Never to put Zhang's hat on Li's head; never to use ancient past to satirize present-day:
> Subvert presentation on realist theatre; sharpen structure of century-old literary classic.
> 120 minutes of "Heavy Lifting with Ease"; hearty laugh runs through the whole show;
> Hit directly at the "Deep Dark-ology" ecology of modern officialdom; extrapolate a world of absolute absurdity.

By keeping a "respectful distance" from present-day sociopolitical realities in name only, the Zhejiang theatre artists were able to deliver a night of hilarious comedy, of hearty laughter, and pungent satire at the here and now.

Chekhov: the "quixotic" quest of the ever elusive

In the 1920s, when Chekhov was first introduced to China, Ibsen (1828–1906) was the rage of the day, answering the urgent sociopolitical and cultural needs of the time.[52] However, in the 1930s, Chinese writers and young intellectuals began to pay more attention to Chekhov's plays that offered a different, less "dramatic" way of presenting life on the stage. ("Things on stage should be as complicated and yet as simple as in life. People dine, just dine, while their happiness is made and their lives are smashed.")[53] The Chekhovian dramatic art influenced a generation of Chinese playwrights from Cao Yu to Lao She. Cao Yu, for example, after his *Thunderstorm* (1933) and *Wilderness* (1936), which show heavy influence of Ibsen, O'Neill, and Greek classics, was drawn to Chekhov and wrote his *Peking Man* (1940) in the Chekhovian style of artless art.[54] Lao She's *Teahouse* (1957) is another Chekhovian play of scenes and moods, an "uneventful" stream-of ordinariness that presents an ensemble of characters, from all walks of life, who come and go and drink tea and commiserate as big events, half a century worth of modern Chinese history (1898–1949), play out in the backdrop.[55] However, unlike Gogol, an old favorite of Chinese theatre artists and general theatergoers alike who almost always delivers, the well-beloved Chekhov has proved to be particularly fickle and unpredictable when it comes to how adaptations of his plays are received, which many a Chinese theatre artist has learned the hard way.

Uncle Vanya

The first production of a Chekhov play was mounted in May 1930 by the Shanghai Xinyou Drama Society. In 1928, the recently formed drama society issued a call to stage "difficult plays" (*nanju*), plays that are artistically challenging, instead of popular plays intended for entertainment of average theatergoers. One of the "difficult plays" the society took on was *Uncle Vanya* directed by Zhu Rangcheng, one of the drama society's founders, starring a young actor Yuan Muzhi (1909–1978) for the title role. To make this "difficult" foreign play that has no apparent plot development accessible and indeed appealing to prospective audiences, Zhu and his team gave their adaptation a new Chinese title that cut the more cumbersome three-syllable Chinese transliteration of Vanya, *wanniya*, to a simple one-syllable *wen*, hence, *Uncle Wen* (*Wen Jiujiu*). Also, striving for a realistic and credible representation of the title character, Yuan Muzhi went to a cheap Russian restaurant for several Saturdays and Sundays to observe Russian diners there, their clothing, their speech, their mannerisms, to look for "Uncle Wen" among them. The young cast and crew rehearsed for three months. All the careful and hard work paid off: Yuan, a gifted actor, turned out to be a very good Uncle Wen on stage, and the performance was quite a success.[56]

This early success with Chekhov was repeated more than 20 years later. In 1954, two years after mounting *The Government Inspector* in Beijing, Sun Weishi took on *Uncle Vanya* with a Russian co-director, P. V. Lesli (1905–1972), a student of Stanislavski who was teaching drama in China at the time. For this production, Sun cast her husband, Jin Shan (1911–1982), for the title role. Dubbed "Emperor of Spoken Drama" (*huaju huangdi*),[57] Jin Shan had played leading roles in *Nola* (Nora, an adaptation of Ibsen's *A Doll's House*, 1935, also starring Lan Ping, before she became Jiang Qing, Madame Mao),[58] *Xun'an* (*The Government Inspector*, 1936), and its film version *Carnival Night* (*Kuanghuan zhi ye*, 1936). Sun and Jin had fallen in love back in 1950 when Sun cast Jin for the title role in her production of *Pavel Korchagin (Baoer kechajin)*, adapted from the Russian novel *How the Steel Is Tempered* by Nikolai Ostrovsky (1904–1936) popular in China for much of the twentieth century. The couple paid dearly for having crossed paths with or, simply, having somehow crossed Lan Ping. In the early days of the Cultural Revolution, Sun Weishi was accused of being a spy for the Soviet Union and arrested per order of her erstwhile friend. Jin Shan did not know that his wife, a gifted theatre artist, had died (of foul play) in jail until he was "liberated" when the Cultural Revolution was over.[59]

One would have to wait for another 60 years, in 2013, to see another notable production of *Uncle Vanya* on the Chinese stage again. It was mounted by Shanghai Dramatic Arts Center, formerly Shanghai People's Art Theatre, directed by Adolf Shapiro (1939–), a critically acclaimed theatre artist known for mounting Russian classics, including Chekhov's plays, on Russian as well as international stages.[60] For some Chinese drama critics, Shapiro coming to direct a Chekhov play would present a golden opportunity to showcase once again serious drama production and the power and beauty of the Stanislavski system[61] at a time when melodrama and farce seem to rule the day.

True to form, Shapiro proved to be a serious (and very demanding, for that matter – see the following) theatre artist, although he was not afraid to incorporate multimedia into the production. For instance, audiences see lightning strike across the sky when the argument between Serebryakov, the retired professor, and his young wife, Yelena, heats up at the beginning of Act II, and the sky darken repressively as Vanya's frustration with life deepens. In the original play, when Astrov, the doctor, talks to Yelena about the woods in Act III, he shows her a map ("that is a map of our country as it was fifty years ago"). In this 2013 production, Shapiro had the map projected on the screen for the audiences to see too. Shapiro didn't even mind interjecting some "Chinese" elements into this Russian play: in a scene in Act II when Serebryakov acts up and complains of pain again, Yelena and Sonya, like a traditional Chinese wife or maid, respectively, wash his feet as the retired professor carries on. Then Marina, the old maid, takes over the feet washing "remedy" ("What's the matter, master? Does it hurt? My own legs are aching too, oh, so badly") and finally quiets him down.[62]

As expected, the power and beauty of this 2013 production of the Chekhov play would be in the eye of the beholder. While some critics were thrilled by this production,[63] others were quite disappointed, and even harsh in their reviews complaining that the actors had not truly mastered the Stanislavski system of acting and failed to capture and represent the full range of emotive texts and subtexts.[64] Also, there seemed a disconnect between the Russian director and Chinese actors, and for that matter a generational gap among Chinese cast members who had mixed perceptions from working with the Russian director, as evidenced in their post-performance "debriefings."[65]

Lü Liang (1957–), who played the title role, felt a dissonance with the "authoritarian" Russian director who expected absolute adherence to his instructions. According to Lü, the director did not talk about his interpretation of the play and his visions for the production; he did not walk the cast through the script or encourage the actors to ask questions. Lü had many questions, especially concerning the character of Uncle Vanya, yet never had a chance to discuss with the director. Another actor, Lü Liang (a different "Liang" in Chinese), a 1993 graduate from the Shanghai Theatre Academy cast for the role of the doctor in the production, had the same complaint about Shapiro. He posed this interesting question (challenging Shapiro's interpretation of *Uncle Vanya*): Who is misinterpreting the play? Lü even went so far as to question if Shapiro was a true Stanislavskian theatre artist, because he didn't encourage the actors to think and feel like their characters. Instead, Shapiro, according to Lü, instructed by demonstration and then expected the actors to replicate. In contrast, Cao Lei (1940–), who graduated from the same theatre academy in 1962 and had training in the Stanislavski system, loved the whole experience. As Cao, cast for the role of Marina, put it, Shapiro inspired her to get into the heart and soul of the old nurse in order to channel it credibly. Interesting enough, Chen Jiaoying, a young actor who graduated from the academy in 2002, felt a natural affinity with the Stanislavski system, a reconnection of sorts, from the first day of rehearsal ("Stani, long time no see!"). As it turned out, her portrayal of Sonia won the most positive reviews, and she attributed her success to the Russian director who had encouraged her to find the Sonia inside herself – the full range of emotions and psychology of the character.

Uneventful as *Uncle Vanya* is (despite the quiet tensions of unrequited love – i.e., Vanya/Yelena/Astrov, Sonya/Astrov, and a shot fired, etc.) and unspectacular as the success or failure of this and other productions is in the eye of the beholder, life must go on in its most mundane ways ("On the 2d of February, twenty pounds of butter; on the 16th, twenty pounds of butter again.") because, as Sonya puts it to her very "miserable" uncle,[66]

> What can we do? We must live our lives. [A pause] Yes, we shall live, Uncle Vanya. We shall live through the long procession of days before us, and through the long evenings; we shall patiently bear the trials that fate imposes on us. . . . Ah, then dear, dear Uncle, we shall see that bright and beautiful life; we shall rejoice and look back upon our sorrow here; a tender smile – and – we shall rest. I have faith, Uncle, fervent, passionate faith.

And faith ("fervent, passionate") the Chinese theatre artists must have – faith in drama as an art form, in Chekhov, and in themselves – to continue to try and mount Chekhov on the stage despite the risk of having their hopes dashed. Two years after the 2013 endeavor, another production of *Uncle Vanya* was mounted by the Beijing People's Art Theatre.[67] This 2015 adaptation was directed by Li Liuyi, who believes that the play is about Russian life as well as the whole human race. "Spiritual frustration," as Li put it, is universal, not something "only the Russians can experience." Going in, Li Liuyi was acutely aware what this undertaking meant:[68]

> staging Chekhov is a risky adventure; Beijing People's Art Theatre staging Chekhov is an even riskier adventure. Mediocracy would be safe, but an insult to Chekhov.

For this theatric adventure, Li Liuyi intended to be faithful to the original, or, rather, to the Chinese translation of *Uncle Vanya* rendered by Tong Daoming, a scholar of Russian literature, without changing a single word while striving to put his personal stamp on the production: "This production of the play belongs to China, to the world, and to me."

To be "faithful" and have Russian flavor for his production, Li Liuyi used full Chinese transliterations of the characters' names – e.g., *Wanniya* (Vanya), *Yelianna* (Yelena), *Asiteluofu* (Astrov), *Suoniya* (Sonya), *Xielieboliyakefu* (Serebryakov), *Maliya* (Maria), *Malina* (Marina), and *Yiliya* (Ilya). All of these multisyllabic, "tongue-twisting" Chinese transliterations of Russian names, "authentic" as they sounded, would prove challenging, even for those who have more than nodding acquaintance with Chekhov and this particular play, adding to the confusion and unenthusiastic response, if not downright boredom, many in the audiences experienced.[69]

The curtain rises to reveal a big "empty" boxed-in stage, a big brick wall (which will soon be covered by a black curtain) with a small door in the background, high-back white chairs of various sizes, and all the characters scattered on the stage, in their various statuesque postures. It has the effect of a watercolor painting with a motif suggestive of Ezra Pound's poem "In a Station of the Metro" ("The apparition of these faces in the crowd:/Petals on a wet, black bough."). For the first four or five minutes into the show, not a word is uttered. Then *Yelianna* (Yelena) walks around slowly, makes a full tour (which takes her two full minutes) of the stage, strikes a "freeze-frame" pose in the spotlight, and, finally, walks to the side. Apparently, this production shines its spotlight on *Yelianna* (Yelena), although in the original play Uncle Vanya, the titular character, and Sonya occupy the emotive, psychological, and philosophical center of the dramatic universe.

This slow and quiet beginning sets the tone and tempo for the entire performance. About ten minutes into the play, actors simply walk across and all over the stage, pause (as in freeze-frame), and talk (or rather, soliloquize) without listening to each other, so much so that for many in the audience, the production felt more like a "staged reading" (*juben langdu*) than actual performance. Most of the time, for the duration of the play, *Wanniya* (Vanya), perplexed, suspicious, and frustrated, nestles in a corner and dozes off. And for the first hour of the three-hour performance, despite the star-studded cast, many audience members dozed off, too, and by halftime, some had left and did not return.

Not that this production did not draw any enthusiastic responses. Some reviewers saw it as a bold, promising artistic quest that is lyrical and shows Chekhov in all his psychological and philosophical depth and complexity. The naysayers, however, seemed louder and more passionate. They saw this production as overreach by a director who doesn't really understand Chekhov, who imposes his own interpretation above the spirit of the Chekhov play, and who puts (novelty of) form above content. One independent drama reviewer, Bei Xiaojing, has this scathing comment in his review with a scathing title that would grab anyone's eyeball: "Form Violates Literature; Director Kills Vanya." It is worth quoting in full this independent critic's own interpretation of what the character Uncle Vanya means to him (or her):[70]

> What does Uncle Vanya ultimately represent? What does he have to do with us today? If we look back on our lives, we can easily see that

Vanya is not just a "little man" ("*xiao renwu*") created by Chekhov; he is a double for every one of us. When we discover that the ideals we have cherished are nothing but empty dreams; when our stubborn fight is finally disarmed by despair; when we are caught in the deep tide of mediocracy day after day with no hope of ever breaking out, we will see Vanya standing in our hearts.

It seems one either loves this production or hates it. There is not much room for fence-sitters.

The Cherry Orchard

Unfazed by the "negative" responses from many theatergoers, Li Liuyi pushed on from *Uncle Vanya* to *The Cherry Orchard* in 2016, once again garnering a mixed bag of reviews. As with the *Uncle Vanya* production, Li seemed more interested in showing thoughts and mindscape on the stage than telling a compelling story. The real challenge, as understood by Li, is how to present *The Cherry Orchard* as comedy:[71]

> Traditional comedy depends on external plot, external action. Chekhov's comedy marks a new expression of the modern art. It expresses itself in the absurdity of human nature and its literary humor. This is comedy in its truest sense.

To present this "modern" Chekhovian comedy for the Chinese audiences as part of the International Festival of Arts held in Shanghai, Li Liuyi once again designed (Li wears three hats for this production: stage designer, costume designer, and director) a boxed-in stage: rectangular, empty space bleached into a few shades of white. A few chairs are scattered here and there upstage left. A big "magic carpet" is placed center stage (which morphs into a nursery, a sitting room, or a dance floor, in the twinkling of an eye, as in *One Thousand and One Nights*). Fiers' last words (in English) before curtain falls, "Life's gone on as if I'd never lived," are painted on the wall in the backdrop upstage right. All the characters, as in *Uncle Vanya* a year before, are dressed in white, statuesque. The whole setup once again evokes a watercolor painting: modern, lyrical, and abstract. There is not a single physical reference to the cherry orchard itself – a motif loaded with sociopolitical, psychological, and philosophical significance. For some critics, this – Li Liuyi's latest pursuit of "pure drama made in China" – presents a welcome sharp, refreshing contrast to the sound and fury that rages on stage in many theatres across the country today.[72] Some critics, amazed by the power and beauty of this production, declare that "this time we've finally nailed it with *The Cherry Orchard*."[73]

The challenge for mounting this play on the stage, as with other Chekhov plays, is that this "fable" is a three-hour stream-of-ordinariness that does not follow a conventional narrative arc leading to a clear moral or maxim at the end. Indeed, the same "eventless" stream of ordinary life, punctuated with many long "pauses," proved too much for the sensibilities of other critics and the patience of the general theatergoers. It caused them many a groan, if not a grunt. Many enthusiasts came to the theatre with their own "Chekhov" in mind, gleaned from reading his fictional works, seeing his plays produced by Russian directors, etc., and found him absent or distorted in this 2016 Li Liuyi production. For them, this production is another instance of overreach by a director who is more interested in putting his stamp on the production than getting it right. They found the stage design and costume a *déjà vu* deplete of meaning. Even the red leather shoes Li put on Lopakhin (while everyone else is barefooted, implying a much closer connection with earth, with the cherry orchard) proved a jarring eyesore. For them, it suggested a simplistic "class-struggle" interpretation (Lopakhin representing the upstart bourgeois newcomer, etc.) reminiscent of the era when a brand of the Soviet critical realism dominated literary and artistic discourse in China. After all, the portrayal of Lopakhin in the original play is much more nuanced. More-over, all the actors sound the same to these critics, regardless of the social status (landowner, maid, nurse, etc.) they are supposed to portray. They all speak the same literary language with a twist of translation flavor instead of channeling anything from their hearts. The overall effect for these critics is another staged reading of Chekhov and not much more. Many general audience members, who were not necessarily Chekhov enthusiasts and came mostly for the star-studded cast, seemed to agree. They were so bored that they left early.[74] Although mediocracy for Li Liuyi would be "an insult to Chekhov," he was accused of mediocracy for this production. "Mediocratic creators," one critic stated, "not only waste their own time; they waste oth-ers' time too."[75]

That sounds a bit too harsh. Li Liuyi should perhaps take comfort in knowing that the same mixed responses also greeted the 2009 production of *The Cheery Orchard* directed by Lin Zhaohua (1936–), a veteran theatre artist active on the theatre scene since the early 1980s. It was criticized for being not properly "acclimated" (*shuitu bufu*)[76] despite its star-studded cast. For this production, Lin Zhaohua condensed the script for a 100-minute performance, changing many dialogs into soliloquies. Although this is sup-posed to be comedy for him ("the heart of this play is laughter; not tears"), Lin chose a gloomy, graveyard-like color tone for the entire production, reminiscent of the *Hamlet* production he mounted in fall 1989, barely a few months on the heels of the Tiananmen Square events that had ended in bloodshed.[77] The floor of the stage is covered with gray coarse fabric, with many lights hidden underneath. The low ceiling is also covered with the same gray fabric, arranged in the shape of clouds. Center stage is a withered cherry. In this gloomy, graveyard-like crawl space, the characters wander around, mumbling to each other or to themselves, like homeless souls. Some critics see this production, which presents the world of the cherry orchard as a spiritual wasteland, as being true to the original in spirit, although it deviates considerably in form.[78]

Other Chekhovian endeavors

Chinese theatre artists have also tried to adapt other Chekhov plays in the last couple of decades. In 1991, the Beijing People's Art Theatre mounted *The Seagull*, directed by Oleg Yefremov (1927–2000) from the Moscow Art Theatre, the first time a Russian theatre artist came to China and directed a Russian play since the 1960s. In 1998, Lin Zhaohua experimented with merging Chekhov's *Three Sisters* and Beckett's *Waiting for Godot* into a new play titled *Three Sisters Waiting for Godot*, with Pu Cunxin, the leading actor, shuttling between two imaginary worlds by juggling the roles of Vladimir (Didi) and Lieutenant Colonel Vershinin. In 2004, the National Theatre of China (*Zhongguo guojia huaju yuan*) mounted Chekhov's early play *Platonov* (written in 1878 and not published until 1923), directed by Wang Xiaoying, as part of an international drama festival held in Beijing, its theme "The Eternal Chekhov" (*yongyuan de qikefu*).[79]

Two Chekhov-themed original plays, both written by Tong Daoming (alluded to earlier), have also been mounted. The first is *I Am Seagull* (*Woshi haiou*),[80] produced in 2010 as part of the Chekhov 150-year anniversary celebration. This is a play-within-a-play that tells the story of two young actors, Dawei and Xiaoqian, who fall in love while rehearsing *The Seagull*. Dawei, cast for the role of Konstantin Treplyov, and Xiaoqian, cast for the role of Nina Zarechnaya, struggle with their conflicted feelings, values, and aspirations, only to end up as the characters they portray despite their best efforts. In a society where ideals have been cheapened, as Dawei and Xiaoqian find out, two idealists cannot form a happy family together. They cannot fly freely, like a seagull. The other original play is *Chekhov in Love* (*Ailian Qikefu*) mounted by the National Theatre of China in 2015 as part of the Chekhov 155-year anniversary celebration. It is a play about Chekhov's romantic relationship with Lydia Mizinova (1870–1939).[81]

Li Liuyi and other Chinese theatre artists can also take comfort in knowing that Chekhov the playwright proved a precarious undertaking even for Stanislavski, who had great success with *The Seagull* in 1898 at the Moscow Art Theatre, did reasonably well with *Uncle Vanya* in 1899, had mixed reception for his production of *Three Sisters* in 1901 (which Chekhov found a bit too "exuberant"), and really upset Chekhov with his 1904 production of *The Cherry Orchard* (having "ruined" it for Chekhov by turning a "comedy" into a "tragedy").[82] More recently, in her 2006 adaptation of *The Seagull*, Katie Mitchell, Britain's greatest living stage director in the eyes of many, tried to bring the story up into the twentieth century (with electric lighting and phonographs, etc.). For this and her other bold reinterpretations of world classics (such as retelling the story of *Hamlet* from Ophelia's point of view), Mitchell has been accused of being "a vandal smashing up the classics."[83] If Cate Blanchet won praise for her leading role in *The Present*, a reimagined version of *Platonov*,[84] Diane Lane did not have the same luck: the 2016 revival of *The Cherry Orchard* on Broadway, in which she played Lyubov Ranevskaya, met with near universal disapproval.[85]

Indeed, not all Chekhov adaptations, experimental or otherwise, are created equal, or, rather, equally enthusiastically received. What Virginia Woolf said about Chekhov's fictional stories should apply to his dramatic works too:

> But is it the end, we ask? We have rather the feeling that we have overrun our signals; or it is as if a tune had stopped short without the expected chords to close it. These stories are inconclusive, we say, and proceed to frame a criticism based upon the assumption that stories ought to conclude in a way that we recognise. In so doing we raise the question of our own fitness as readers. Where the tune is familiar and the end emphatic – lovers united, villains discomfited, intrigues exposed – as it is in most Victorian fiction, we can scarcely go wrong, but where the tune is unfamiliar and the end a note of interrogation or merely the information that they went on talking, as it is in Tchekov, we need a very daring and alert sense of literature to make us hear the tune, and in particular those last notes which complete the harmony.[86]

The Chinese should not be so discouraged that they begin to doubt their own "fitness" as theatre artists and give up on Chekhov. Neither should they feel complacent given their "success" with the more "easily" adaptable Ostrovsky, Gorky, and Gogol because these "old favorites" have so much more to offer than as represented by one or two masterpieces of theirs, and because it is always a daunting task to try and update old classics, even seemingly more "adaptable" classics such as *The Storm, The Lower Depths*, and *The Government Inspector*, and to make them resonate more with the sociocultural and emotive realities of the here and now. Indeed, transcultural adaptation endeavors, no matter who have the artistic vision and courage to take them on, will always encounter and entail tensions between texts, contexts, intertexts, and tradition and innovation. "Success" is never guaranteed. Every drama enthusiast goes to the theatre with a "tune" of *The Storm, The Lower Depths, Uncle Vanya, The Seagull, Three Sisters*, or *The Cherry Orchard*, etc., in his or her head. Would he or she, would most of the audiences, be pleased when hearing the "tune" (the dramatist's reinterpretation, boldly experimental or otherwise) played out on stage? One would never know for sure until curtain falls. The reward, perhaps, is in the quest itself: daring, creative, and thoughtful. Indeed, the reward is in our collective, dogged (albeit "quixotic" it may seem at times) quest for beauty, truth, and a better world for all to live in.

Notes

1 For the purpose of this chapter, the term "Russian," as in "classic Russian plays," "Russian literature," etc., is used to refer to the Russian-language culture (including

drama and literature) of today's Russian Federation and several independent nations once a part of the historical Russian Empire or the former Soviet Union.

2 See Mao Zedong. Unless otherwise noted, all translations from Chinese sources are mine.

3 See Hong Lijian, 1–22, and Adrian Chan.

4 For the purpose of this chapter, "Western," as in "Western literature," "classic Western drama," etc., is used mostly as a broad cultural term that includes Russian culture in its reference.

5 Liu Wenfei.

6 Ibid. See also Shouhua Qi, *Western Literature in China*, 41–5.

7 For an in-depth discussion on this topic, see Chen Shixiong, *Sanjiao duihua* (Three-Sided Dialogue). See also Song Xuezhi and Jun Xu, 147–52.

8 See "*Gao'erji xiju daibiaozuo*" (Gorky's Representative Dramatic Work). www. chinanews.com/cul/2014/05-06/6140632.sht, Xiao Yu'er, and Pan Yu.

9 Julia Listengarten, 27, 37.

10 "My holy of holies is the human body, health, intelligence, talent, inspiration, love and absolute freedom – freedom from violence and falsehood, no matter how the last two manifest themselves." Simon Karlinsky, ed., Michael Henry Heim, trans, 109.

11 See Robert Leach and Victor Borovsky.

12 Yu Li, "*Cao Yu he Aositeluofusiji*" (Cao Yu and Ostrovsky), 54–60.

13 This portion of the discussion draws from Yang Yang and Tong Daoming.

14 See Shouhua Qi, "Misreading Ibsen," 341–64.

15 Shi Man, 84, and Qian Liqun et al., 471.

16 See Zhang Dinghua.

17 Lai Huhong (Hiroshi Sato).

18 Tian Benxiang et al., 262–64.

19 "*Beijing jinian Daleiyu*" (Beijing Commemorating Centennial Anniversary), 33.

20 See Lorenz M. Lüthi.

21 "Lushan Conference."

22 Hong Gu, 17.

23 Ibid, 19.

24 Wang Qinren, 120–22, and Wu Xiaodong, 6–10.

25 This discussion of *Yedian* draws from Paul G. Pickowicz, 7–31, and Lu Weili.

26 "*Wuhan renyi*" (Wuhan People's Art Theatre), 31–2.

27 "*Zhongxi Gao'erji*" (Central Academy of Drama). See also "*Zhongxi 04 ji*" (Central Academy of Drama Class 2004).

28 "*Guogeli dajie*" (Gogol Street).

29 "*Kuanghuan zhi ye*" (Carnival Night).

30 See "Northern Expedition."

31 This portion of the discussion draws from "*Shenguantu*" (Map of Officialdom) and Zhao Jian.

32 See Adam Y. C. Lui, Chong-chor Lau and Rance P. L. Lee, and Jean-Louis Rocca.

33 See, for example, Wesley Marvin Bagby, 50–6.

34 See Yan Sun, Yong Guo, 349–64, and Julia Kwong.

35 Chang'an, historical name for the city of Xi'an in Shaanxi province, often used in classical literature as a stand-in for capital city of China. In this case, it could be a subtle reference to Beijing.

36 "*Xiwang chang'an*" (Westward to Chang'an).

37 See Lu Shuang and Huang Aihua, 16–19.

38 See Zhai Yejun and Shi Jun, 63–70.

39 See Peter Li, ed.

40 This discussion draws from "*Shijie jingdian huaju*" (World classic The Inspector General); and Qiao Zongyu, 38–9.

41 References to the original play are based on Nikolai Gogol, 1–108.

42 Pei Pei, 14.
43 Ibid, 14–15.
44 This discussion draws from A. Mang and Zhao Ningyu, "*Qinchai dachen*" (The Government Inspector).
45 Zhao Ningyu, "*Quanxin yanyi*" (Brand New Reinterpretation).
46 This portion of the discussion draws from Chen Mingzheng, ed.
47 Ibid, 96–7.
48 This portion of the discussion draws from Chen Shixiong, "*Qinchai dachen*" (The Government Inspector), and Zhuang Naizhen and Chen Xinying, "*Kuilei xi Qinchai dachen*" (The Art of Puppet Show), 183–85.
49 "*Baoxiao huaju Qinchai mei dachen*" (Hilarious Spoken Drama). This brief discussion is also based on the performance I saw on May 21, 2016, at Zhejiang Spoken Drama Art Theatre in Hangzhou.
50 A catchphrase in the sociopolitical life of China today referencing the campaign to fight corruption of high-ranking officials.
51 "PERSONS attempting to find a motive in this narrative will be prosecuted; persons attempting to find a moral in it will be banished; persons attempting to find a plot in it will be shot." Mark Twain, xix.
52 See Shouhua Qi, "Misreading Ibsen."
53 Ilia Gurlyand, "Reminiscences of A. P. Chekhov," quoted in Donald Rayfield, 203.
54 See Wang Wenying, 17–30.
55 See Zhang Zhiming and Chen Shan, 104–6.
56 Guo Xueqin, 24–6.
57 See Xian Jihua.
58 Shouhua Qi, *Western Literature*, 350–52.
59 See Yan Liu, "*Sun Weishi de huoyan*" (Sun Weishi's Fiery Spirit).
60 "Adolf Shapiro" (Biography).
61 Yajiasha 1966, "*Zhege shijie hui hao ma? Huaju Wanniya jiujiu*," 14.
62 Guo Chuanzhong, 24–5.
63 Ibid.
64 Yajiasha 1966, 15–16.
65 See A. Dong, 8–11.
66 Anton Chekhov, 216.
67 The year 2015 saw several productions of Russian drama, including *The Seagull* by Taiwan director Lai Shengchuan and *The Cherry Orchard* by the Central Academy of Drama, etc.
68 Pan Yu.
69 This discussion also draws from Na Xiaoyan and Deng Wei.
70 Bei Xiaojing.
71 Li Jihui. This portion of the discussion also draws from Zhang Bing.
72 Mei Sheng.
73 Li Jianming.
74 Zhang Bing.
75 Zhang Dalu.
76 Wang Lei.
77 This discussion is based in part on Lin Zhaohua, *Lin Zhaohua xiju zuopin ji* (DVD Collection of Lin Zhaohua Drama Works).
78 Li Weiyu.
79 Tian Lan.
80 "*Woshi haiou*" (I Am Seagull).
81 "*Ailian Qikefu*" (Chekhov in Love).
82 David Allen, 11–46.
83 Charlotte Higgins.

84 Ben Brantley, "Cate Blanchett and Chekhov," and Michael Paulson.
85 Ben Brantley, "All's Not Well in This *Cherry Orchard*"; Matt Windman; and Joe Dziemianowicz.
86 Virginia Woolf, 172.

Bibliography

"AdolfShapiro"(Biography).www.bolshoi.ru/en/persons/people/3502/."*AilianQikefu*" (Chekhov in Love). www.ntcc.com.cn/hjy/alqkf/201501/c21b21a1755b4f0b95bc 66ac54765f2f.shtml.

Allen, David. *Performing Chekhov*. London: Routledge, 2000, 11–46.

Bagby, Wesley Marvin. *The Eagle-Dragon Alliance: America's Relations With China in World War II*. Newark, NJ: University of Delaware Press, 1992.

"*Baoxiao huaju Qinchai mei dachen*" (Hilarious Spoken Drama: Emperor Sent No Big Minister). www.228.com.cn/ticket-89921265.html.

"*Beijing jinian Daleiyu shangyan yibai zhounian*" (Beijing Commemorating Centennial Anniversary of *The Storm*), *Xijubao* (Drama Gazette) 7 (1959).

Bei, Xiaojing. "*Xingshi qiangbao wenxue, daoyan shasi wanniya*" (Form Violates Literature; Director Kills Vanya), January 30, 2015. http://weibo.com/u/2641162085? is_hot=1.

Billington, Michael. "The Seagull." *The Guardian*, June 28, 2006. www.theguardian. com.

Brantley, Ben. "All's Not Well in This *Cherry Orchard*." *The New York Times*, October 16, 2016. www.nytimes.com.

———. "Cate Blanchett and Chekhov, Together on Broadway." *The New York Times*, September 13, 2016. www.nytimes.com.

Chan, Adrian. *Chinese Marxism*. London: Bloomsbury Academic, 2003.

Chekhov, Anton. *Ten Plays*. Mineola, NY: Dover Publications, 2008.

Chen, Mingzheng, ed. *Wushi nian de shouwang: Chidao de Qinchai dachen* (Fifty Years Waiting: Belated Arrival of *The Government Inspector*). Guilin, Guangxi: Guangxi Normal University Press, 2010.

Chen, Shixiong. "*Qinchai dachen: Cong huaju dao muou*" (*The Government Inspector*: From Spoken Drama to Puppet Show). *China Culture Daily*, June 15, 2016, Section 8.

———. *Sanjiao duihua: Stani, Bulaixite yu zhongguo xiju* (Three-Sided Dialogue: Stanislavski, Brecht, and Chinese Drama). Xiamen, Fujian: Xiamen University Press, 2003.

Deng, Wei. "*Wanniya Jiujiu zuowan dengtai maoxian*" (*Uncle Vanya* Ventured onto the Stage Last Night).*BeijingDaily*,January21,2015.http://news.ifeng.com/a/20150121/ 42977911_0.shtml.

Dong, A. "*Wengu Zhixin: Huaju Wanniya jiujiu bufen yanyuan fangtan*" (Review and Learn From Past: Spoken Drama *Uncle Vanya* Cast Members Interview). *Shanghai xiju* (Shanghai Theatre) 8 (2013): 8–11.

Dziemianowicz, Joe. "Diane Lane Leads a Fruitless *Cherry Orchard*." *New York Daily News*, October 16, 2016. www.nydailynews.com.

"*Gao'erji xiju daibiaozuo Zai diceng zhongguo shouyan*" (Gorky's Representative Dramatic Work *The Lower Depths* Debuts in China). *China News*, May 6, 2014. www.chinanews.com/cul/2014/05-06/6140632.shtml.

Gogol, Nikolai. *Gogol Three Plays: The Government Inspector; Marriage; The Gamblers* (World Classics). London: Methuen Publishing, 1999.

Guo, Chuanzhong. "*Jingdian huaju meili yongcun: Wanniya jiujiu guanshang zhaji*" (Classic Drama Charm Forever: Spoken Drama *Uncle Vanya* Review). *Shanghai xiju (Shanghai Theatre)* 7 (2014): 24–5.

Guo, Xueqin. *Qianmian ren: Yuan Muzhi zhuan* (Man With a Thousand Faces: Biography of Yuan Muzhi). Hangzhou, Zhejiang: Zhejiang People's Publishing House, 2005.

Guo, Yong. "Corruption in Transitional China: An Empirical Analysis." *The China Quarterly*, no. 194 (June 2008): 349–64.

"*Guogeli dajie*" (Gogol Street). https://baike.baidu.com/item/%E6%9E%9C%E6%88%88%E9%87%8C%E5%A4%A7%E8%A1%97.

Gurlyand, Ilia. "Reminiscences of A. P. Chekhov," quoted in Donald Rayfield, *Anton Chekhov: A Life*. Evanston, IL: Northwestern University Press, 1997.

Higgins, Charlotte. "Katie Mitchell, British Theatre's Queen in Exile." *The Guardian*, January 14, 2016. www.theguardian.com/.

Hong, Gu. "*Daleiyu xin yanchu tansuo*" (New Performance of *The Storm* Review). *Xijubao* (Drama Gazette) 8 (1959): 17–19.Hong, Lijian. "Studies in the Introduction and Adaptation of Marxism in China 1890–1920." *Australian Journal of Politics and History* 36, no. 1 (April 1990): 1–22.

Karlinsky, Simon, ed. Michael Henry Heim, trans. *Anton Chekhov's Life and Thought: Selected Letters and Commentary*. Evanston, IL: Northwestern University Press, 1997.

"*Kuanghuan zhi ye*" (Carnival Night). http://baike.baidu.com/item/%E7%8B%82%E6%AC%A2%E4%B9%8B%E5%A4%9C/3430696.

Kwong, Julia. *The Political Economy of Corruption in China*. New York: Armonk, 1997.

Lai, Huhong (Hiroshi Sato). "*Shilun Cao Yu zuopin zai Yan'an de yanchu*" (On Staging of Cao Yu's Plays in Yan'an). *China Cao Yu*, July 12, 2016. www.cncaoyu.com/show-9-263-1.html.

Lau, Chong-chor, and Rance P. L. Lee. "Bureaucratic Corruption in Nineteenth-Century China: Its Causes, Control, and Impact." *Southeast Asian Journal of Social Science* 7, no. 1/2 (1979): 114–35.

Leach, Robert, and Victor Borovsky. *A History of Russian Theatre*. Cambridge: Cambridge University Press, 2000.

Li, Jianming. "*Zheyici women zhongyu jiayu le Yingtaoyuan*" (This Time We've Finally Nailed It With *The Cherry Orchard*). *Wenhui Bao* (Wenhui Daily), November 9, 2016. www.whb.cn/zhuzhan/jujiao/20161109/74979.html.

Li, Jihui. "*Li Liuyi de Yingtaoyuan bu jiang gushi*" (Li Liuyi's *The Cherry Orchard* Does Not Tell Story). *Beijing Daily*, May 25, 2016, Section 12. http://bjrb.bjd.com.cn/html/2016-05/25/content_37056.htm.

Li, Peter, ed. *Culture and Politics in China: An Anatomy of Tiananmen Square*. New York: Routledge, 2007.

Li, Weiyu. "*Lin Zhaohua de Yingtaoyuan daodi li yuanzhu you duo yuan?*" (How Far Is Lin Zhaohua's *The Cherry Orchard* From the Original Play). *Beijing Evening*, September 29, 2012. www.chinanews.com/cul/news/2009/05-25/1706695.shtml.

Lin, Zhaohua. *Lin Zhaohua xiju zuopin ji* (DVD Collection of Lin Zhaohua Drama Works). Beijing: Remin University of China Press, 2012.

Listengarten, Julia. *Russian Tragifarce: Its Cultural and Political Roots*. Selinsgrove, PA: Susquehanna University Press, 2000.

Liu, Wenfei. "*Eluosi wenxue zai zhongguo de jieshou he chuanbo*" (Reception of Russian Literature in China). *Zhonghua dushu bao* (Chinese Reading Weekly), May 17, 2006, Section 3, 1.

Lu, Shuang, and Huang Aihua. "*Xiwang chang'an yu Qinchai dachen de xijuxing bijiao*" (The Comedy of *Westward Chang'an* and *The Government Inspector*: A

Comparative Study). *Journal of Zhejiang University of Technology* (Social Sciences Edition) 01 (2010): 16–19.

Lu, Weili. "*Cong Diceng dao Yedian: Lun Zhongguo sishi niandai xiju wenhua fazhan de dongle yu qianzai pianxiang*" (From *The Lower Depths* to *Yedian*: On Forces at Work and Potential Bias in Chinese Drama Culture Development in the 1940s). *Zhonghua xiju xuehui wenyi huixun* (Chinese Drama Association Art and Literature News), June 2009. www.com2.tw/chta-news/2009-6/chta-0906-03.htm.

Lui, Adam Y. C. *Corruption in China During the Early Ch'ing Period, 1644–1660.* Hong Kong: University of Hong Kong Press, 1979.

"Lushan Conference." https://en.wikipedia.org/wiki/Lushan_Conference.

Lüthi, Lorenz M. *The Sino-Soviet Split: Cold War in the Communist World.* Princeton, NJ: Princeton University Press, 2008.

Mang, A. "*Guogeli Qinchai dachen liuyue deng jiefangjun gejuyuan wutai*" (Gogol's *The Government Inspector* Performs on PLA Opera House Stage in June), May 30, 2006. http://yule.sohu.com/20060530/n243470742.shtml.

Mao, Zedong. "*Lun renmin minzhu zhuanzheng*" (On the People's Democratic Dictatorship), June 30, 1949. http://cpc.people.com.cn/GB/64184/64185/66618/4488978.html.

Mark Twain. *Adventures of Huckleberry Finn.* New York: Random House, 1996.

Mei, Sheng. "*Yu Qikefu gekong xiangxi? Xiangdangran er*" (Channeling Chekhov Across Space? Fanciful Thinking), July 13, 2016. http://culture.china.com/art/drama/11170655/20160713/23037093.html.

Na, Xiaoyan. "*Qikefu de bugan he fankang: Ping Beijing Renyi huaju Wanniya Jiujiu*" (Chekhov's Displeasure and Resistance: Review of Beijing People's Art Theatre Spoken Drama *Uncle Vanya*), January 30, 2015. http://中国文艺网.com/xw/bwyc/201501/t20150130_282824.html.

"Northern Expedition." https://en.wikipedia.org/wiki/Northern_Expedition.

Pan, Yu. "*Ba xiaoshi de eluosi xiju Xiongdi jiemei rang zhongguo huajuren kandao le chaju*" (Eight-Hour Long Russian Play *Brothers and Sisters* Let Chinese Theatre Artists See How Far They are Behind). *Pengpai Xinwen* (The Paper), March 8, 2017. www.thepaper.cn/newsDetail_forward_1634355.

———. "*Beijing Renyi Wanniya jiujiu pingjia liangji meiyou zhongyongpai*" (Beijing People's Art Theatre *Uncle Vanya* Polar Opposite Reviews: No Room for Middle Ground). *Dongfang zaobao* (East Morning Express), February 4, 2015. www.chinanews.com/cul/2015/02-04/7035245.shtml.

Paulson, Michael. "Cate Blanchett's Star Power Lifts *The Present* on Broadway." *The New York Times*, January 18, 2017. www.nytimes.com.

Pei, Pei. "*Women xiao shenme: Ganshou zhongguo qingyi xinban eguo huaju qinchai dachen*" (What Are We Laughing at: Experiencing Chinese Youth Art Troupe Edition of *The Government Inspector*). *Zhongguo xiju* (Chinese Drama) 5 (2000): 14.

Pickowicz, Paul G. "Sinifying and Popularizing Foreign Culture: From Maxim Gorky's *The Lower Depths* to Huang Zuolin's *Ye dian*." *Modern Chinese Literature* 7, no. 2 (Fall 1993): 7–31.

Qi, Shouhua. "Misreading Ibsen: Chinese Noras on and Off the Stage, and Nora in Her Chinese Husband's Ancestral Land of the 1930s – as Reimagined for the Present-Day Stage." *Comparative Drama* 50, no. 4 (Winter 2016): 341–64.

———. *Western Literature in China and the Translation of a Nation.* New York: Palgrave Macmillan, 2012.

Qian, Liqun, et al. *Zhongguo xiandai wenxue sanshi nian* (First Thirty Years of Modern Chinese Literature). Beijing: Beijing University Press, 1998.

Qiao, Zongyu. "*Qing yi: Qinchai dachen*" (Youth Art Troupe: The Government Inspector). *Xiju zhijia* (Playwrights Home) 6 (2000): 38–9.

Rocca, Jean-Louis. "Corruption and Its Shadow: An Anthropological View of Corruption in China." *The China Quarterly*, no. 130 (June 1992): 402–16.

"*Shenguantu*" (Map of Officialdom). http://baike.baidu.com/item/%E5%8D%87%E5%AE%98%E5%9B%BE/3710549.

Shi, Man. *Chongqing kangzhan jutan jishi: 1937 nian 7 yue-1946 nian 6 yue* (The Theatre Scene in Chongqing During the War of Resistance: July 1937 to June 1946). Beijing: China Drama Press, 1995.

"*Shijie jingdian huaju Qinchai dachen (Guogeli) Zhongguo qingnian huaju yuan*" (World Classic The Inspector General (Gogol) by China Youth Art Troupe). www.youtube.com/watch?v=szSAqcDk4Z4.

Song, Xuezhi, and Jun Xu. "*Faguo huangdanpai xiju zai zhongguo de fanyi yu yanjiu*" (Translation and Research on French Theatre of the Absurd in China). *Waiguo wenxue yanjiu* (Foreign Literature Studies) 2 (2004): 147–52.

Sun, Yan. *Corruption and Market in Contemporary China*. Ithaca, NY: Cornell University Press, 2004.

Tian, Benxiang, et al. *Zhongguo xiju lunbian* (Debates in Chinese Drama). Nanchang, Jiangxi: Baihuazhou Art and Literature Press, 2007.

Tian, Lan. "*Puladongnuofu wei xijujie jiemu*" (*Platonov* Opens the Drama Festival), August 18, 2004. www.people.com.cn/GB/wenhua/25806/2719956.html.

Tong, Daoming. "*Aositeluofusiji yu Zhizhe qianlü biyou yishi*" (Ostrovsky and *Enough Stupidity in Every Wise Man*), *Xiju wenzhai* (Drama Digest), May 22, 2009. http://blog.sina.com.cn/s/blog_59dc7a600100dcr2.html.

Wang, Lei. "*Lin Zhaohua ban Qikefu mingzuo Yingtaoyuan 'Shuitu bufu'*" (Lin Zhaohua Production of Chekhov Classic *The Cherry Orchard* Not Properly Acclimated). *Xinmin Evening*, May 26, 2009. http://gb.cri.cn/27504/2009/05/26/4145s2520840.htm.

Wang, Qinren. "*Gaoerji zuopin zai zhongguo de chuanbo*" (Introduction and Reception of Gorky in China). *Guowai wenxue* (Foreign Literature) 2 (1997): 120–2.

Wang, Wenying. "*Cao Yu yu Qikefu de xiju chuangzuo*" (Cao Yu, Chekhov, and Their Playwriting). *Wenxue pinglun* (Literary Review) 4 (1983): 17–30.

Windman, Matt. "*The Cherry Orchard* Review: Diane Lane Stars in Disjointed Revival." *AM New York*, October 16, 2016. www.amny.com.

Woolf, Virginia. *The Common Reader*. Fort Washington, PA: Harvest, HBJ Book, 2002.

"*Woshi haiou*" (I Am Seagull). https://baike.baidu.com/item/%E6%88%91%E6%98%AF%E6%B5%B7%E9%B8%A5.

Wu, Xiaodong. "*Gaoerji zai zhongguo yu 'zhongguo de Gaoerji'*" (Gorky in China and 'China's Gorky'). *Wenyi zhengming* (Literature and Art Forum) 5 (2015): 6–10.

"*Wuhan renyi lao yishujia yanchu Yedian*" (Wuhan People's Art Theatre Old Artists Perform *The Lower Depths*). *Zhongguo yanyuan* (Chinese Actors) 6 (2008): 31–2.

Xian, Jihua. "*Huaju Huangdi: Jin Shan zhuan*" (Emperor of Spoken Drama: Biography of Jin Shan) (China Writers Association Press, 1987).

Xiao, Yu'er. "*Qinchai dachen gei zhongguo xijuren shang le yi ke*" (*The Government Inspector* Taught the Chinese a Lesson). *Dongfang zaobao* (Oriental Morning Post), August 20, 2015. http://cul.qq.com/a/20150820/020884.htm.

"*Xiwang chang'an*" (Westward to Chang'an). www.baike.com/wiki/%E3%80%8A%E8%A5%BF%E6%9C%9B%E9%95%BF%E5%AE%89%E3%80%8B%5B%E8%80%81%E8%88%8D%E4%BD%9C%E5%93%81%5D.

Yajiasha 1966. "*Zhege shijie hui hao ma? Huaju Wanniya jiujiu*" (This World Will be Okay: Spoken Drama *Uncle Vanya* Review). *Shanghai xiju* (Shanghai Theatre) 8 (2013): 14.

Yan, Liu. "*Sun Weishi de huoyan*" (Sun Weishi's Fiery Spirit), Centre for Contemporary Cultural Studies, October 6, 2013. www.cul-studies.com.

Yang, Yang. "*Jingdian huaju Zhizhe qianlü biyou yishi wei eluosi nian jiemu*" (Classic Drama *Enough Stupidity in Every Wise Man* Opens Year of Russian Culture). *Jinghua shibao* (Beijing Times), February 23, 2006. http://ent.sina.com.cn/h/2006-02-23/1130995044.html.

Yu, Li. "*Cao Yu he Aositeluofusiji: Cong Leiyu tanqi*" (Cao Yu and Ostrovsky: To Begin With *The Thunderstorm*). *Foreign Literature Studies*, no. 4 (1991): 54–60.

Zhai, Yejun, and Shi Jun. "*Wei zhengzhi fuwu: Xiwang chang'an yu Jiaru wo shi zhen de*" (To Serve Politics: A Comparative Study of *Westward Chang'an* and *If I Were for Real*). *Shanghai Culture* 4 (2009): 63–70.

Zhang, Bing. "*Li Liuyi ban Yingtaoyuan weihe piruan*" (Why Li Liuyi Production of *The Cherry Orchard* Feels Listless), October 29, 2016. www.douban.com/note/589262413/.

Zhang, Dalu. "*Jingdian chongpai de ganga: Ping renyi ban Yingtaoyuan*" (Dilemma in Classic Drama Revival: Review of People's Art Theatre's *The Cherry Orchard*), July 12, 2016. www.chinawriter.com.cn/n1/2016/0712/c404033-28548621.html.

Zhang, Dinghua. "*Shi wutai wei shengming de Shu Xiuwen*" (Shu Xiuwen Sees the Stage as Her Life). *Wenhui bao* (Wenhui Daily), April 27, 2009. www.360doc.com/content/09/0428/11/111031_3298744.shtml.

Zhang, Zhiming, and Chen Shan. "*Xiaoshuojia de xiju: Qikefu juzuo yu Laoshe juzuo bijiaolun*" (Fiction Writer as Playwright: A Comparison of Plays by Chekhov and Lao She). *Xiju wenxue* (Drama Literature) 5 (2014): 104–6.

Zhao, Jian. "*Qinchai dachen yanchu shihua*" (*The Government Inspector* Brief Performance History), June 13, 2006. http://ent.sina.com.cn/j/2006-06-13/17151121417.html.

Zhao, Ningyu. "*Qinchai dachen he chuli fennu de xiju*" (*The Government Inspector*: A Play that Transcends Anger), May 27, 2006. http://bbs.tianya.cn/post-no01-243868-1.shtml.

———. "*Quanxin yanyi Qinchai dachen jiefangjun gejuyuan di piaojia yan*" (Brand New Reinterpretation of *The Government Inspector* Discount Ticket for PLA Opera House Performance), June 6, 2006. http://yule.sohu.com/20060606/n243591889.shtml.

"*Zhongxi 04 ji biye daxi yanyi Gaoerji mingzhu Diceng*" (Central Academy of Drama Class 2004 Graduation Performance Gorky's Famous Play *The Lower Depths*), December 4, 2007. http://ent.sina.com.cn/j/2007-12-11/18481830466.shtml.

"*Zhongxi Gaoerji mingju Zai diceng*" (Central Academy of Drama Perform Gorky Famous Play *The Lower Depths*), December 4, 2007. http://blog.sina.com.cn/s/blog_4830327001000dx1.html.

Zhuang, Naizhen, and Chen Xinying. "*Kuilei xi Qinchai dachen yishu tese zhi chuyi*" (The Art of Puppet Show *The Government Inspector*: A Tentative Discussion). *Jiannan Wenxue* (Jiannan Literature) (August, 2013): 183–85.

7 The tragic, the comic, the absurd, and the "grand feast" of French classics

By the time Voltaire (1694–1778), a towering figure of the eighteenth-century Enlightenment movement in France, took a fancy to the Chinese story centered on the survival and eventual revenge of an orphan (originated from the Spring and Autumn period, 771 to 476 BC) and turned it into his *L'Orphelin de la Chine* in 1753, the story had already traveled a long tortuous journey of transcultural relocations and reinterpretations from the mysterious Middle Kingdom in the orient.

The journey began in 1731 when Joseph Henri Marie de Prémare (1666–1736), a Jesuit missionary to China, took on the daunting task of translating the thirteenth-century Yuan *zaju* (variety play) *The Great Revenge of the Orphan of Zhao* (*Zhaoshi guer da bao chou*) into French under the title *L'Orphelin de la Maison de Tchao*, the first known European language translation of any Chinese play. Father de Prémare's, however, is more a truncation than translation because it cut all the songs and poetry from the original six-part play – five acts (*zhe*) and a wedge (*xiezi*). He felt that these songs and poetry, loaded with allusions and tropes drawn from the Chinese culture and long history, and therefore insurmountably difficult to render into French, were not essential to the telling of the story. This truncated version of the play found its way into the voluminous *Description de la Chine*, an encyclopedia compiled by Jean-Baptiste du Halde (1674–1743), a Jesuit historian who had never set foot in the Middle Kingdom, and published in 1735. From there and then the story of the Chinese orphan took off in Europe, morphing into several English, Italian, and French renditions. After all, this was a time when Europe was feverishly fascinated with all things Chinese, arts, literature, and architecture.[1]

What Voltaire saw in the story, as retold in Father de Prémare's *L'Orphelin de la Maison de Tchao*, was the Confucian morality (of loyalty and selfless personal sacrifice – borne out by the heroism of several characters, especially Cheng Ying, a physician who would rather die and sacrifice his own child than betray the last survivor of the family of Zhao), which he wanted to appropriate as an enlightening example for Europe. Nonetheless, Voltaire found the play "very deficient with regard to all other beauties" of the dramatic art and had to remold it through the stringent (neo)classical unities (of action, time, and place) to satisfy his own artistic sensibilities as well as those of his fellow Parisians.[2] *L'Orphelin de la Chine* was successfully staged in August 1755 at the grand *Comédie-Français* in Paris.[3]

In a letter to "The Most Noble Duke of Richelieu" that prefaces his *L'Orphelin de la Chine*, Voltaire thus laments about the Chinese (and the rest of the Asiatics):[4]

> These people, whom we take so much pains and go so far to visit; from whom, with the utmost difficulty, we have obtained permission to carry the riches of Europe, and to instruct them, do not to this day know how much we are their superiors; they are not even far enough advanced in knowledge to venture to imitate us, and don't so much as know whether we have any history or not.

If indeed the Chinese people did not know much about France and Europe (how they had not only caught up but also surpassed them in modern times), it would soon change in the decades following the Opium War (1839–1842) when China was forced to open its door to the brave new world, especially to the Western powers. Despite the success of Voltaire's *L'Orphelin de la Chine* and the other cultural afterlives *The Orphan of Zhao* assumed in Europe, it did not leave any significant imprint on either the moral philosophy and temperament or the development of dramatic arts in France or any other European country. It proved to be mostly an exercise to satisfy fancy, although the intellectual and cultural fascination with the Confucian Middle Kingdom as experienced by Voltaire and others was genuine and noteworthy, especially in terms of historiography of cultural interchange. Before long, the Europeans would find the Chinese culture "deficient," or worse. Montesquieu (1689–1755), for example, saw China as "a despotic state" based on the principle of fear.[5] Jean-Jacques Rousseau (1712–1778) dismissed the Chinese script as that of "a barbaric people."[6] Both Montesquieu and Rousseau, along with Voltaire, would be ardently admired as well as eagerly appropriated by the Chinese for their enlightening sociopolitical philosophies. The vogue, indeed, the *chinoiserie*, like any other such vogues, would eventually cool down and taper off.

In contrast, when Lin Shu (1852–1924) took on the daunting task of translating *La Dame aux Camélias by* Alexandre Dumas fils, in 1899, it would prove a much more momentous development that would have a much more tangible, long-lasting impact on the development of modern Chinese drama. Although the immediate occasion for Lin Shu, an old school man of letters, to embark on the extraordinary undertaking was perhaps personal – his friends having suggested the idea to help him cope with the loss of his wife to illness, its exigency, given the socio-historical and geopolitical context of the late Qing, post-Opium War decades, was not lost on him. It was very much part of a larger cultural renewal campaign spearheaded by the likes of Liang Qichao (1873–1929) and Yan Fu (1854–1921, who introduced

Huxley, Smith, Mill, and Spencer by way of annotated translations, in their quest for ways to strengthen and save China. Indeed it was a matter of national and cultural survival.[7]

Like the early French translations of *The Orphan of Zhao*, Lin Shu's rendition of *La Dame aux Camélias* (and all of his 180 or so titles of Western literature) was far from being "faithful." His is a "secondhand" translation because Lin Shu didn't know any foreign languages and therefore had to rely on his linguistic collaborators who had studied in Europe. Nonetheless, *Bali chahuanü yishi* (The Story of The Lady of the Camellias of Paris, the Chinese title for the Demas novel) turned out to be a huge success. The tragic love story of Marguerite Gautier and Armand, retold in Lin Shu's elegant quasi-classical style (classical Chinese mixed with colloquial expressions and neologisms) charmed the Chinese readers immensely. Lin Shu's *Chahuanü* (The Lady of the Camellias), as his rendition of the Dumas novel is popularly known, became the basis for a stage production mounted by a group of Chinese students in Tokyo in February 1907. In June of the same year, members of the Spring Willow Society mounted another significant production, *Black Slave Cry to Heaven*, based on Lin Shu's rendition of Harriet Beecher Stowe's *Uncle Tom's Cabin*. These two 1907 bold adaptation endeavors by Spring Willow society in Tokyo have since been celebrated as the birth cry of spoken drama and, for that matter, modern Chinese drama.[8]

Two years later in 1909, members of the Spring Willow society mounted another significant production in Tokyo, this time based on *La Tosca* (1887) by Victorien Sardou (1831–1908), under the Chinese title *Relei* (Hot Tears), later *Rexue* (Hot Blood). By the time Lu Jingruo, Ouyang Yuqian, and a few other like-minded young Chinese staged their *Relei* in Tokyo, Sardou's novel had also already traveled a long, tortuous journey of transcultural and even transgeneric relocations and reinterpretations from its debut in the Théâtre de la Porte Saint-Martin in Paris (November 24, 1887) to the *shinpa* production in Tokyo in 1907. One of the Japanese productions, adapted by Fukuchi Gen'ichirō (1841–1906) and staged at Kabuki-za (the principal theatre in Tokyo for the traditional kabuki drama form) in 1891, relocated the story to Tokyo right after the 1837 rebellion against the Tokugawa Shogunate led by Ōshio Heihachirō (1793–1837), a neo-Confucianist scholar. Members of the Spring Willow Society saw a production of the play in Tokyo in 1907 and, inspired, created an adaptation of their own in 1909. This 1909 Chinese production of *La Tosca* in Tokyo, under the Chinese title *Relei* (Hot Tears), and the excitement it generated, amounted to a palpable prelude to the 1911 Xinhai Revolution which, led by Dr. Sun Yat-sen, succeeded in overthrowing the Qing dynasty and establishing the republic.[9]

The lopsided, asymmetric attribution of importance in the early days of Sino-French intercultural relations as manifested in arts and literature – e.g., dram – was largely determined by the imbalance of power and status in the world from the mid-1800s to the early decades of the twentieth century. It is not atypical of what happens between a dominating conqueror's culture and that of a dominated, conquered culture.[10] Following the successful debut of French literature in China, in the form of Lin Shu's 1899 translation of *La Dame aux Camélias*, works by Molière, Verne, Hugo, Balzac, Flaubert, Romain Rolland, Stendhal, Zola, de Maupassant, Baudelaire, etc., were soon translated into Chinese, mostly secondhand by way of existent Japanese and English translations at first and later from French directly.[11] Added to the list of French cultural and literary figures introduced into China were Diderot, Montesquieu, Voltaire, Descartes, Rousseau, Monet, Cezanne, Degas, etc. The fascination with French arts and literature continues to this day, with many more new names from the twentieth century added: Sartre, Camus, Ionesco, Beckett, Foucault, Lacan, Derrida, Kristeva, etc. Indeed, from the tragic and the comic to the absurd, French dramatic classics, the topic of this chapter, remain as appealing to the Chinese – especially the drama scholars and theatre artists – as ever, like a "grand feast" that will never end, although their adaptation endeavors do not always produce the same impactful outcomes as did Lin Shu's translation of *La Dame aux Camélias* by Alexandre Dumas fils, or for that matter, Spring Willow Society's adaptation of *La Tosca* (1887) in the first decade of the twentieth century.

Corneille, Racine, and Molière: the triumvirate

If Corneille, Racine, and Molière dominated the theatre scene in France in the 1700s and have been devoutly revered in France ever since, they have commanded much admiration and scholarly attention from the Chinese too ever since they were introduced by way of translation in the early decades of the twentieth century. Of the three, Molière has seen the most adaptations while Corneille and Racine have been more studied than performed on the stage. As a matter of fact, there is no known noteworthy performance of Corneille on the Chinese stage other than the 2009 production of his best-known play *Le Cid* (1673), and there is no known performance of Racine other than a 2013 production of *Phèdre* staged by French expatriates in Beijing.

Corneille

In 2009, the National Peking Opera Company (*Guojia jingju yuan*) mounted a *jingju* adaptation of Corneille's *Le Cid* under the Chinese title *Qingchou jian* (Love Hate Sword), which has a quasi-classical ring reminiscent of a typical traditional Chinese *wuxia xiaoshuo* (martial arts fiction). This production is particularly noteworthy because it was a "spec production," non-commissioned, with no contract or even letter of intent, developed with the sole hope of being signed up by some French entertainment agency to take it to France and elsewhere for international performances. It was a bold and risky move undertaken to spread and promote traditional Chinese culture outside its borders and to expand the market share of traditional Chinese *xiqu* such as *jingju* that has faced a shrinking market in China in recent decades.[12]

This *jingju* version of the story follows the basic plot of *le Cid*: Long Dike (Don Rodrigue, Le Cid) and Gao Shimei (Chimène), both from powerful families, are in love with each other. Their fathers Long Fu (Father Long, Don Diègue) and Gao Fu (Father Gao, Don Gormas) get into a feud as a result of the former being appointed the royal tutor for the prince. Gao Fu slaps Long Fu, and to revenge the public insult on his father, Long Dike kills Gao Fu in a duel. Gao Shimei, torn between love for Long Dike and filial duty to her father, asks the king to put Long Dike to death. Long Dike, equally miserable, asks Gao Shimei to kill him with the sword bestowed on him by the king for his valor as a brave and victorious warrior. The conflict between love (personal) and duty (both personal and national) is resolved when Long Dike is sent to the battlefield again to lead a fight the invading Moors, returns triumphantly again, and wins back Gao Shimei's love. Full-blown tragedy is avoided and the play ends happily for the two main characters.[13]

The venue for the *jingju* adaptation performance was the recently renovated experimental theatre *changhe yuan* (Happy Harmony Garden), 475 square meters, 196 seats, classical Chinese garden architecture (blue and red motifs, pavilions, and long corridors), and equipped with current theatre technologies of sound, lighting, and multimedia.[14] It seemed a perfect setting for a play, a tragicomedy, as Corneille himself had envisioned it in the first place, wherein tensions, which could otherwise have led to catastrophic outcomes, are finally resolved, so too are love, duty, and honor all be preserved (although Gao Fu has to be sacrificed, a price to pay, inevitably). Before the public performances scheduled for June 26–29, a dress rehearsal, or rather a demo performance, was staged for the French embassy personnel as well as art and entertainment agency reps to see if it was good enough to travel to France for public (commercial) performances. There was no published or publicized follow-up after the performance by a star-studded cast. Even the official website of China National Peking Opera Company that mounted the production does not include any information – pictures, video clips, or news reports – about it or any subsequent trips to France or elsewhere, as if this demo performance had never happened.

Three years later, another *jingju* adaptation of *Le Cid*, under the same Chinese title *Qingchou jian* (Love Hate Sword), was staged by Fuzhou Peking Opera Company for public performance – free admission. Apparently, "Transcultural Peking Opera" (*kua wenhua jingju*) is not an easy path whereby to overcome the challenges of cultural changes at home and cultural differences abroad.[15]

Racine

Plays by Racine (1639–1699), Corneille's contemporary and rival, well-wrought, perfectly pitched neoclassical plays (following the rules of unities), did not fare well on the theatre scene in China either. His best-known play, *Phèdre* (1677), a tragedy of unrequited love and unresolved conflict between reason and feelings, has seen only one known public performance. It was staged in 2013 by Denglong Jutuan (Lantern Theatre Company), an amateur theatre troupe formed in 2005 by French expatriates in Beijing. The amateur theatre troupe's box office receipts are donated to help children of poverty-stricken areas realize their dreams of going to school. The performance was part of Croisements Festival 2013 (*Zhongfa wenhua zhi chun*, Sino-French Cultural Spring), an annual program established in 2006 to promote cultural exchanges, or "Franco-Chinese cultural spring," between the two countries.[16]

Molière

Of the triumvirate from the neoclassical age, Molière (1622–1673) proves to be the most beloved whose star on the Chinese stage remains as bright as ever before. If the kind of satirical comedy presented by Gogol, as exemplified by his *The Government Inspector*, appeals to the Chinese both artistically and sociopolitically – e.g., their need for social justice (see Chapter 7) – then Molière's comedy shines biting insight deep into human nature. His popularity sustained even during the 1950s in part because the Soviet-Russian critics saw Molière as a peak in the achievements of comedy and the Chinese simply followed their Soviet-Russian "Big Brother," as they did in almost everything else during those years, including in arts and literature.[17]

Variously translated as *Qianlin ren* (The Stingy Man) and *Linse gui* (The Stingy Devil), *The Miser* (1668) saw Chinese translations as early as 1914. It remains the most staged of all Molière plays since its debut in China in the 1920s. Back then, amateur drama troupes set their sights on *The Miser* and other Molière plays not exactly because they fit the political platforms of the May 4th generation, but because they would have a broad appeal among the ordinary theatergoers and therefore have a better chance of balancing the books. One of the notable early Chinese adaptations of *The Miser* was mounted in 1939 in Shanghai.[18] Written by Gu Zhongling (1903–1965) under the Chinese title *Shengcai you dao* (All Roads Lead to Money) and directed by Zhu Duanjun (1907–1978), this production relocated the story from Paris of the seventeenth century to the 1939 Shanghai, which had recently fallen to the invading Imperial Army of Japan.[19] This transcultural relocation would mean that all the characters would assume Chinese identities and the production would have a much more direct and urgent sense of immediacy to the theatergoers, although the basic story line followed that of the Molière play.

The main action of *Shengcai you dao* (All Roads Lead to Money) takes place in the sitting room of the residence of Hua Binggang (Harpagon). The backstory of Valère saving Élise from drowning in a shipwreck acquires a Sinicized immediacy in this adaptation: while fleeing Nanjing (Nanking), the besieged capital of China then, as the Rape of Nanking (Nanjing Massacre,

December 1937) was happening, Hua Yingmei (Élise) was saved by Fan Lihan (Valère) when her boat capsized. After they escaped to Shanghai together, Fan Lihan assumed the alias Zhang Yongqin and found employment at the Hua residence in order to stay closer to Hua Yingmei. Toward the end of the play, when he has to reveal his real identity, the young man says his line of work does not allow him to use his real name. As it turns out, his father, Fan Yunsheng (Anselme, Don Thomas D'Alburcy), has joined the underground resistance movement since the fall of Nanjing. Other indigenizing elements of this production include the décor of the Hua residence, which is of classical Chinese motifs – e.g., scrolls of calligraphy brushwork. When Hua Yingde (Cléante) orders four kinds of dessert from Guanshengyuan, a well-known brand in Shanghai and other cities in China, to treat Fan Liqiong (Marianne), Hua Binggang (Harpagon), the miser, who also wants to marry the young woman, is so pained by how much the desserts cost him, as if hit by a brick:

> Ten thousand brand new banknotes. All freshly minted by the three biggest banks of China. Not even one corner is wrinkled!

More significantly, instead of the ending in the original where Harpagon insists on seeing his "dear casket" as everyone else relishes the wedding (Valère and Élise) arrangement, the Chinese adaptation ends with Fan Lihan (Zhang Yongqin, Valère) making this proposition:

> Let's donate all the money we would have spent on the wedding and the dowry to our country!

All the audiences for this production would understand this as a call to donate for the war of resistance against Japanese invasion. All in the play, except for Hua Binggang (Harpagon), cheer "Hurray! Hurray!" This 1939 adaptation would be the basis for a number of other Chinese productions in the 1940s.

Several other popular Molière plays have seen productions on the Chinese stage, too – e.g., *Don Juan, The Imaginary Invalid, The Doctor in Spite of Himself*, and *The School for Wives*. In the 2009 and 2010 Croisements Festival, a Chinese production of *Don Juan* (Tang Huang) was staged by the drama students of the Communication University of China in Beijing. The production was based on a new translation by Ning Chunyan, who returned to China in 2005 after having studied and worked (as a professor and director) in France for many years.[20] This is an interesting production faithful to the original in plot development and using baroque stage design, yet the actors/characters speak present-day Chinese sprinkled with dialectal and catchy colloquialisms.[21] One could not have imagined a Western classic that features a habitual, unscrupulous adulterer and seducer of women being staged in China, although Ning, the translator and director, justified this by saying that Don Juan is a complex character who has a streak of anti-feudal spirit in him. Through the story of Don Juan, according to Ning, Molière intended this play as a jab at the hypocrisy of the ruling class of its times.[22]

This was followed by a production of *The Imaginary Invalid* under the Chinese title *Wubing shenyin* (Moan without Being Sick), staged by visiting actors from the Comédie-Française (Théâtre-Français) during its first visit to China to give the Chinese the full flavor of the play as it was staged in Molière's own times, in story as well as stage design, costumes, and props, including the chair for Argan, the hypochondriac. Although not a Chinese adaptation endeavor, this was an interesting theatric event, a performance in French with English and Chinese captions. The audiences took it in stride. As Xu Xiozhong, artistic director of the National Centre for the Performing Arts in Beijing, the venue for the performance, said, the play transcends time and space and cultural differences and, despites its "strangeness," speaks to us because human nature remains largely unchanged. People are prone to the same anxiety and stress, especially given the pace and pressure of modern life.[23] As if to prove the popularity of this play, Serbian theatre artists brought their modern reinterpretation of *The Imaginary Invalid* to the Inaugural Shanghai International Festival of Comedy (2015).[24] This is a condensed 80-minute production, which ends on a much more somber note than the original. Instead of the happy ending in the original play when Argon finally approves his daughter Angélique's marriage with Cléante and is made a doctor by way of a ceremony performed by gypsy dancers, the Serbian production ends with Argon being abandoned by everyone and murmurs,

Nobody will stay. I'll die alone.

In June 2011, the Denglong Jutuan (Lantern Theatre Company) staged another Molière play, *The Bourgeois Gentleman*, under the Chinese title *Guiren mi* (Nobleman-iac). This production mixed in hip-hop and *jingju* to maximize humor and dramatic effect.[25] It should speak to the Chinese who often complain about the newly rich who have acquired extraordinary amount of wealth but remain "uncultured."[26] A few years later, in 2015, French theatre artists from the *Théâtre des Bouffes du Nord* performed the same play at the National Center for the Performing Arts in Beijing with Chinese subtitles.[27]

In fall 2013, a production of *The Doctor in Spite of Himself* (1666) was staged in the small experimental theatre of Beijing People's Art Theatre under the Chinese title *Qudachenyi* (wrongfully beaten to be a doctor), to a packed audience.[28] This production stayed "faithful" to the original in the story and spirit although it took some creative license to update and make it speak to China today. It had a simple stage design: three floor screens, which are rearranged as the dramatic action unfolds. The actors played dual roles for humorous effect – e.g., Martine (Sganarelle's wife) and Jacqueline (Lucas's wife and Géronte's nurse), Lucinde (Sganarelle's patient, daughter of Géronte), Valère (Géronte's servant), Léandre (Lucinde's lover), and Géronte (Lucinde's father). This deliberate "blending" of roles create confusion in identity, class, and sexual politics, and hence hilarious comic scenes, which leads to many a hearty laugh by the audiences.[29]

Another interesting change for this production is the trade of the protagonist Sganarelle. Instead of being a woodcutter in Molière's original play, he is now a Chinese pancake (*jianbing*) maker, which creates more moments for comedy as the pancake maker tries to cook up some "panacea," literally, for his patient's illness. Also, to deliver what is promised in the Chinese title, this production makes Sganarelle a less complex and sympathetic figure and subjects him to so many beatings in the hands of Géronte's servants and even from Léandre. In fact, Léandre beats the "doctor" so hard that he begs for mercy:[30]

> You beat me when I say I am not a doctor. You beat me when I say I *am* a doctor. What on earth should I say? I'm just whatever you say I am.

Similarly, Perrin, a young peasant in the play, is changed into a "dimwit" who actually sees more sometimes. For example, when Sganarelle, the "doctor," drags his feet in giving his diagnosis of Thibaut, his father, Perrin points out the obvious: "Pop, he's waiting to get paid first."

In 2014, another play by Molière, *The School of Wives* (1662) was mounted by Shanghai Drama Art Center to commemorate the fiftieth anniversary of Sino-French diplomatic relations.[31] It was directed by Didier Bezace with a Chinese cast and crew, starring Zhou Yemang in the role of Arnolphe (Anuofu). For this production, the story is relocated to the France of the 1960s, when France, led by De Gaulle (1890–1970), was experiencing intense geopolitical developments and social unrest, including officially recognizing the People's Republic of China (1964), and the student protests (1968). The stage design is more like a film set, and all the main characters are dressed in typical 1960s French fashion style – e.g., Arnolphe (*Anuofu*), dressed in fedora and trench coat, a look-alike of Jacques Tati (1907–1982); Agnes (*Aniesi*), a look-alike of young Catherine Deneuve (1943–); Chrysalde (*Kelisade*) in shiny yellow suit and tie; and Horace (*Helasi*) both donning wigs of blonde hair.[32]

In the summer of the same year, Shao Sifan, who, like Ning Chunyan, returned to China after receiving education and working in France and elsewhere as an actor, directed a play titled *Juedui gaoji* (Absolutely Fashionable), a blend of Molière's *The Ridiculous Précieuses* (1659) and *The Versailles Impromptu* (1663). According to Shao, he was inspired by popular dating game shows in China (such as *Fei cheng wu rao* (Not Sincere? Don't Bother; If You Are the One)).[33] The young women in this show reminded Shao of Magdelon and Cathos, two provincial young women in Molière's *The Ridiculous Précieuses* who come to Paris in search of love and *jeux d'esprit* and reject two upper-class young men for being unrefined, and the biting comedy that ensues. This is a play-within-a-play with elements drawn from *The Versailles Impromptu* as the framing play and *The Ridiculous Précieuses* as the play to be staged within.[34]

As the curtain rises, the director instructs the actors to rehearse one last time before the show begins, but the actors do not understand the roles they are playing or the story the director wants to tell on the stage. The director begs the actors, but to no avail. Seeing the confusion and commotion on the stage, the audiences begin to fret impatiently in their seats. Just then the curtain rises for the show, *The Ridiculous Précieuses*, to begin – haphazardly.

While it is good theatre (for comic effect) to ridicule pretentious people, men or women, this production chooses to cast the Chinese Magdelon and Cathos as two country girls going to the big city looking for love and *jeux d'esprit*. This is problematic, even offensive, on several levels – i.e., gender, class, and city verus country. Although the biases are "preordained" by the original play, they are made much worse in Shao's production given the socioeconomic and cultural realities in China, especially for the last few decades, when tens of millions of country folks, especially young men and women, migrate to the booming cities in search of opportunities. In so many ways, the modernization of China's cities, emblematized by the new cityscapes of flashy high-rises, is built on the back of these millions of migrant workers who have been treated less than second-class citizens, who have been exploited egregiously and denied access to the same education (for their children) and health care, etc., enjoyed by the city residents. Young female migrant workers (*dagongmei*), whether they work in textile factories, fashion shops, smartphone assembly lines, or as domestic help, or escort service (which many have fallen into for survival), have fared even worse than their male counterparts as they suffer additional discrimination, including sexual harassment.[35] Indeed, Shao's *Juedui gaoji* (Absolutely Fashionable) is comedy at the expense of people who do not have much agency in the society – comedy that ridicules the weak and the disadvantaged for their cultural and romantic aspirations when they are too busy trying to make it in the world to have the luxury (time and money) and join the hearty laughs (albeit directed at themselves) in the theatre.

The existential and the absurd: Sartre, Camus, and Ionesco

Existentialism came to China by way of translations as early as the 1940s when it was still in its heyday in France and elsewhere in the West. The first Chinese translation of Jean-Paul Sartre (1905–1980) was his short story "Room," published in 1943, which was followed by the publication of another Sartre translation, "The Wall." At the time, Albert Camus (1913–1960) had just published *The Stranger* (1942) and *The Myth of Sisyphus* (1942), Sartre *The Flies* and *Being and Nothingness* (1943), and Sartre was probably putting finishing touches on *No Exit* (1944) and Camus was probably still working on *The Misunderstanding* (1944). Eugène Ionesco (1909–1994) was still years away from publishing his best-known dramatic works such as *The Bald Soprano* (1950), *The Chairs* (1952), and *Rhinoceros* (1959).

In autumn 1955, per invitation from the Chinese as part of their people's diplomacy (to eventually establish official relations with the guests' countries) strategy, Sartre, along with Simone de Beauvoir, made a two-month visit to China, a highly programmed tour to showcase the new People's Republic. The distinguished French guests had tea with Mao Zedong (1893–1976), although no substantive conversation happened. They also had the honor to join Mao on the Tiananmen podium during the National Day celebration and went on to tour Shengyang, Shanghai, Hangzhou, and Guangzhou.[36]

Although a translation of *The Stranger* was published in the 1960s,[37] Sartre, Camus, and all Western literature suffered the same fate of being condemned as decadent bourgeois poison during the Cultural Revolution (1966–1976). They would have to wait until the end of the 1970s to final a new life when China reopened its gate to the outside world and experienced another cultural and intellectual revival. It began with published translations of Camus's "The Adulterous Woman" (1957) and *The Plague* (1947) and Sartre's *Dirty Hands* (1948) in 1980, which was soon followed by other publications: *Plays by Sartre* (*Sate xiju ji*), *Novellas and Short Stories by Camus* (*Jiumiu zhongduan pian xiaoshuo ji*), *The Stranger*, *The Myth of Sisyphus*, and Simone de Beauvoir's novel *All Men Are Mortal* (1946). As early as in 1981, Sartre's *Dirty Hands* was staged in Shanghai (directed by Hu Weimin). The year 1986 saw a production of Beckett's *Waiting for Godot* in Shanghai (directed by Chen Jialin). The following year, Ionesco's *Rhinoceros* was staged in Beijing (directed by Mu Sen).[38] The theatre scene in China has never been the same ever since.

The cultlike Sartre fever (*sate re*) hit the college campuses the most. Now that the old leftist ideology and continued revolutions of Mao, which had caused deep psychic as well as physical wounds to the nation had lost its grip, college students – many of them being *zhiqing* (returned youths), or former Red Guards, Red Little Guards, or many having scarred memories of seeing their parents and grandparents being persecuted egregiously during the Cultural Revolution – were anxiously looking for a new "faith" to embrace, to fill the spiritual void, to give meaning to their existence. Maxims such as "existence precedes essence" were eagerly embraced. This was also a time of the big "Practice is the Sole Criteria for Testing the Truth" debate,[39] the Democracy Wall, the new era of Reform and Opening Up (*gaige kaifang*, 1978–1989), or the new enlightenment (*xin qimeng zhuyi*).[40]

The Sartre (or Existentialism) fever, like the new enlightenment, the nationwide quest for spiritual renewal, for meaning, was more than doused by the events of Tiananmen Square in 1989. If condemned not to be free to choose sociopolitically, people seemed to feel, they were at least free – more or less – to pursue happiness in getting rich first. After all, this seemed what Deng Xiaoping was promoting during his 1992 "Southern Tour."[41] For many, the fervent spiritual quest of the 1980s soon dissipated and maxims such as "existence precedes essence" provided some kind of philosophical justification for practical pursuits. Nonetheless, the interest in plays by Sartre, Camus, Ionesco, and other Existential or Theatre of the Absurd writers persisted in the 1990s:

in 1990, Harold Pinter's *Dumb Waiter* (*shengjiangji*) was mounted in Beijing, directed by Meng Jinghui. This was followed by other productions – 1991: Ionesco's *The Chairs*, *The Bald Soprano*, and Pinter's *The Lover*; 1993: Jean Genet's *The Balcony*; 1998: Beckett's *Waiting for Godot* and *Three Sisters Waiting for Godot*, a "mishmash" of Chekhov and Beckett; and Sartre's *No Exit*.[42]

Jean-Paul Sartre

The 1981 staging of Sartre's *Dirty Hands* (*Angzang de shou*) in Shanghai was quite a remarkable event. It was directed by Hu Weimin (1933–1989), a talented and passionate theatre artist who had suffered more than his share in the "dirty hands" of the sociopolitical life of modern China – six years of "reform through hard labor" during the "Anti-Rightest Movement" in the 1950s and several more years of involuntary menial labor during the Cultural Revolution (1966–1976).[43] It was an audacious undertaking for Hu at the time because this existentialist play could be (mis)construed as "anti-communist" and was not staged in a socialist state until 1968. The mere fact that this play was allowed to be staged in China at the time is ample evidence of how much more "liberal" the country had become in the short span of three or four years after the Cultural Revolution was over.[44]

Artistically, this play presented a challenge to Hu and his cast and crew too. It is a seven-act play with Act I and Act VII taking place in the "present time": one day in 1945, at Olga's house. When Olga asks Hugo to tell her "Everything. Everything. From the beginning," the play "flashes back" to the bulk of the story, Acts II to VI, events that happened back in 1943. As Hugo puts it,[45]

> It's an idiotic story, like all stories. If you look at it from a distance, everything holds together, more or less; but if you get up close to it, it busts apart. One action is over too quickly. It seems to happen almost spontaneously and you don't know whether you did it because you wanted to or because you couldn't hold it back.

Would the play's extensive use of flashback, a technique better fit for fiction or film, that unfolds the story live on stage, hold everything together for the Chinese, the average theatergoer in 1981, who had probably never heard of the term "flashback?"

The play, set in the fictional country of Illyria, is both political and philosophical in its thematic thrust and therefore presents a challenge too in both arts and politics. Hu Weimin read the play as a condemnation of violence directed at political rivals within one's own ranks, more particularly shocking because it happened within the Proletarian Party. However, Hu felt the Chinese should be able to understand this because what Lin Biao (1907–1971), Mao Zedong's handpicked successor, had attempted to do to hurt Mao back in 1971 was already a "fact" known to all Chinese.[46] What

Hu did not mention (and could not have done so) was how violence, mental as well as physical, had been directed at political rivals and comrades of suspected loyalty ever since the early days of the Communist Party's history, even during the difficult days of the Long March (1934–35), not to mention all the political campaigns since 1949 all the way to the Cultural Revolution (1966–1976) that had inflicted massive psychic wounds in the ranks of the Communist Party as well as on the body politic. This line, said by Hoederer, a hero character if viewed from the dominant political morality of China, said to Hugo in Act V, seems to be speaking directly to the Chinese audiences in 1981 too:[47]

> How you cling to your purity, young man! How afraid you are to soil your hands! All right, stay pure! What good will it do? Why did you join us? Purity is an idea for a yogi or a monk. You intellectuals and bourgeois anarchists use it as a pretext for doing nothing. To do nothing, to remain motionless, arms at your sides, wearing kid gloves. Well, *I have dirty hands. Right up to the elbows. I've plunged them in filth and blood. But what do you hope? Do you think you can govern innocently?*
> (*Italics mine*)

Indeed, the complex and nuanced portrayal of the main characters – i.e., Hugo, the 23-year-old assassin, Hoederer and Louis (both leading figures in the Proletarian Party), and Olga – would present a challenge for the Chinese theatre artists as well as the audiences who were used to simple, straightforward moral judgment. For Hu Weimin, the best way to act Sartre's characters is not to "act," but to get under their skin, as real blood and flesh individuals, and live and breathe like them, spiritually at least, despite the cultural and other differences. The actors could achieve this by coming from outside in (understanding the characters) and then from inside out (performing them on stage).

When audiences asked Lu Shichu, cast for the role of Olga, "Is Olga a 'good human' (*haoren*) or 'bad human' (*huairen*)?" Lu knew that they wanted moral clarity and certainty when reality was murkier and didn't always offer simple answers. Lu understood Olga as not only a loyal and diehard revolutionary who follows orders resolutely without ever questioning them but also a woman who has feelings for Hugo. The challenge for Lu was how to channel the "contradictions" in the character, the conflicted feelings on stage, especially in Act VII, which Hu Weimin decided to keep despite the views of some on his team. They wanted to cut or significantly condense the last act of the play because they saw Act VI as climax of the dramatic action, a climactic act hard to follow. For Lu Shichu, however, Act VII, which shifts the dramatic action back to the "present time" at Olga's House, is the real emotional climax of the play: Failing to persuade Hugo to rejoin the revolution, Olga finally lets go the "revolutionary" in her and gives full-throated expression to the "woman" that she is and her feelings for Hugo. As midnight arrives, as the motor sound outside announces the return of Louis and his assassins – to kill Hugo, to silence him, because he has been "compromised," Olga hands him her revolver and begs him to leave, but to no avail.[48] The 1981 Chinese adaptation ends with Olga, as channeled by Lu Shichu, screaming at Charles and Frantz, assassins coming in to kill Hugo per Louis' orders:

Get the hell out of here!

Her love, hitherto repressed for the cause of revolution, her despair, and the awakening of her human spirit, finally find their voice – albeit too late for Hugo, and perhaps for herself too.

Wang Hongsheng, in the role of Louis, did not want to present a one-dimensional, flat character either. He saw Louis, a ruthless political player who plots and would not hesitate to kill his political rivals, as a complex character too, who doesn't fit the usual, simplistic mode of "bad human" (*huairen*). Rather, Louis is a devoted revolutionary leader who believes in what he is doing is right, right for the Party and for the cause. It is a life-and-death struggle after all. Wang tried to "empathize" with the character in order to channel him credibly on the stage. To help Chinese audiences understand the character, however, Wang added some visible cues, such as nervousness in his mannerism, to suggest "flaws" in his character.[49]

To help present the "philosophical" existentialist theme of *Dirty Hands* Hu Weimin had the stage design wrapped in a basic color tone of black, white, and gray, the backdrop suggestive of eyes, teary and thoughtful eyes reminiscent of that pair of fading, bespectacled eyes in Fitzgerald's *The Great Gatsby* painted on a billboard over the valley of ashes, as if God were staring down upon the hustle and bustle of a moral wasteland.[50] Sartre's play, though, despite the cruelty, violence, and absurdity, still reasserts the dignity of individuals, of independent thinking, and of the meaning of choice. As a matter of fact, for the 1981 production Hu and his team introduced a female chorus who sing wordless lyrics to expand and give the story an epic heroic feel. When Hugo was killed, the sky was alit with the color of blazing red, rousing music, etc., to mark the fall of a hero, which some Chinese critics found problematic. They understood, though, that such an "uplifting" ending was needed for the average Chinese audiences and indeed for the country that had only recently awaken from the nightmare of the Cultural Revolution.

In 2004, Hu Xuehua, son of Hu Weimin, directed another adaptation of *Dirty Hands*. By this time in China, the dust of the Cultural Revolution had long settled although national psychic wounds, old and new (e.g., the 1989 Tiananmen Square), cannot be said to have healed. Hu Xuehua relocated the story from Eastern Europe near the end of WWII to a Middle Eastern country of the present day (one year before this production, President George W. Bush had organized a "coalition of the willing" to invade Iraq for alleged "weapons of mass destruction," among other things).[51] On the stage for this 2004 production is a colossal fiberglass hand, 7 meters tall and 4 meters wide, which forms "V" and other hand gestures as the plot unfolds, bending oppressively like a cage to enthrall the actors/characters or reaching out, like an open palm, to lift them up. Indeed This 2004 production seemed more an experiment in form than an expression of existential angst, as was much more the case when director's father was mounting the same play back in 1981.[52]

Other notable Sartre productions in China include *No Exit* (1944) and *The Victors* (*Morts sans sepulture*, 1946).[53] The first Chinese translation of *No Exit* was published in 1980, which attracted considerable critical attention, in part because of the line Joseph Garcin says to Inès Serrano and Estelle Rigault toward the end of the play: "Hell is – other people!"[54] In the 1980s, most Chinese critics interpreted the "hell is other people" line as a condemnation of twisted human relations in bourgeois and capitalist societies of the West.[55] By the 1990s, when the "socialist market economy with Chinese characteristics," a hybrid, mishmash of socialism and capitalism had been going on in China for more than a decade, it would be no longer possible to dismiss the twisted human relations experienced and embodied by Garcin, Estelle, and Inès (enclaved in the "drawing room" in Second Empire style, with a massive bronze ornament standing on the mantelpiece) as exclusively symptomatic of Western societies. When such relatively easy, politically expedient dismissal or indictment was not tenable any more, Chinese scholars began to dig deeper into the play's unrelenting existentialist probing of the relationships between self and others, etc. In 1998 (reproduced in 2013), Shanghai Drama Arts Center mounted a production of *No Exit* at its experimental theatre (*xiao juchang*), directed by Zhao Yi'ou, a recent graduate from Shanghai Theatre Academy. Zhao also played Garcin. In 2013 another production of *No Exit* was mounted, directed by a young female theatre artist who wanted to stage the play from a woman's angle, although it was not entirely clear what that meant, why she chose this particular Western play for production, and how it would speak to the human conditions in China today, socioculturally as well as psychologically.[56] Nonetheless, as Garcin says right before the curtain falls, "*Eh bien, continuons*" ("Well, well, let's get on with it.")[57]

Sartre's 1946 play *The Victors*, granted not the most important play even by Sartre's own estimate, saw a notable Chinese production in 1997 and two revivals in 2005 and 2014 respectively, all directed by the same theatre artist Zha Mingzhe. It is a play that challenges the Chinese understanding of hero and cowardice, war – themed drama/theatre, and, more than anything, Sartre's existentialist philosophy.[58]

Albert Camus

It is interesting to know that a few months after Sartre and Camus met for the first time in June 1943 at the opening of Sartre's *The Flies*, Sartre asked

Camus to play the role of Garcin for his new play *No Exit*. Although this arrangement did not work out, because of the loss of funding for the production, although Camus did not consider himself an existentialist, and although their friendship eventually ended because of some serious arguments, the kinship (albeit not the sameness) in their existentialist views of life's essential absurdity cannot be mistaken.[59] By the summer of 1943, Camus had already published *The Stranger* (1942) and *The Myth of Sisyphus* (1942) and had finished writing *Caligula* (1938), although it would not be performed until 1945. This play, a retelling of the story of Caligula (12 AD–41 AD), a young Roman emperor – i.e., how the death of one of his sisters Drusilla (16 AD–38 AD), rumored to be his lover, transformed him – somehow caught the attention of a group of young Chinese theatre artists about 60 years later in Beijing.[60]

What did the young theatre artists of the recently formed Unicorn Drama Society (*dujiaoshou jushe*) in 2001 see in this Camus play about a young emperor, who, upon discovery that men are mortal and unhappy, takes it upon himself to teach the people how to live honestly by wielding his absolute power to inflict abject indignity and horror upon them? Caligula's "discovery" that "men die; and they are not happy"[61] is not anything earthshattering or particularly enlightening. Many come to such unsettling knowledge of human existence early on, as early as in young adolescence. Likewise, whatever new knowledge Caligula gains toward the end of the play – that he is freed from "memories and illusion," that "nothing, *nothing* lasts," that he has chosen a wrong path "that leads to nothing,"[62] or that, as Camus, his creator, sums it up for him, "no man can save himself alone and one cannot be free by working against mankind,"[63] etc. – comes too late and at too steep a price for the people under the "rapturous power" of a selfish, sadistic ruler. In this, despite the "knowledge" or "understanding" he gains, Caligula is not unlike the many psychopathic serial killers who inflict violence and horror upon the innocent by following a personal logic of their own, their twisted truth. Indeed, one would be hard put to accept Camus' own verdict that Caligula's story is that of "high-minded type of suicide,"[64] for his is a story of massive homicide that results from giving any individual the absolute power. There is nothing "high minded" about Caligula. Of course, Caligula proves to be alive not just in "history" (as he shouts at curtain fall, "Into history, Caligula! Into history!" "I am still alive!"), not just as a mirror but also a living reality, over and again, East (including China) and West, from ancient times to present-day.

The director for this 2001 production, Kang Feng, a recent (1997) graduate of the Central Academy of Drama, said that he wanted to focus less on the philosophizing aspect of *Caligula* and more on how people respond and react when put under such absolute cruelty and violence: to bear it silently, numbly, indifferently, as many of the characters in the play do, or to rise up, rebel, and put an end to it. Nonetheless, almost out of an irresistible habit of culture, the young Chinese theatre artists still wanted to give the character of Caligula a positive spin. According to them, the real "moon" that Caligula wants, the impossible, is[65]

To make happiness possible in a world that lacks happiness;
To make justice possible in a world that lacks justice;
To make freedom possible in a world that lacks freedom;
To make love possible in a world that lacks love.

No matter how one wants to spin or philosophize about it, there is no getting around the basic fact that the way Caligula goes about making happiness, justice, freedom, and love possible is to rob the world of happiness, justice, freedom, and love.

Artistically, Kang Feng and his young drama kindred spirits wanted to return to the simple and minimalistic way of theatre, to return the spotlight on actors, on acting, instead of indulging in fancy stage design, multimedia, and other glamorous sound and lighting technologies that turn serious theatre into a MTV party.[66] They were professed followers of Jerzy Grotowski (1933–1999), his ideas of the "poor theatre" (*zhipu xiju*).[67]

The playbill and program for the production, staged at the little theatre of China Youth Arts Theatre, featured a scene of massive multitudes of people crossed out by a big bloody red X, with this pitch printed on it:

Unicorn-Impassioned Inaugural Production-French Writer Albert Camus Stunning Masterpiece-*Caligula*-Seen in History and Still Alive

According to Li Yumin, Chinese translator of the play published in the early 1980s, the audiences were apparently shaken by the performance: as they were leaving the theatre, their faces were written with a mix of excitement, thoughtfulness, and perplexity, struggling to make sense of the play. This, for Li Yumin, was the debut of Camus on the Chinese stage, which was long overdue, but finally arrived.[68]

In 2010, a troupe of German theatre artists, led by director Jette Steckel, staged a production of *Caligula* in Shanghai in the style of interactive (if not immersive) theatre. As audience members walked into the theatre, they were each asked to put their faces down against the screen of a big photocopy machine. The actor who played the role of Caligula, Kreibich Mirco, would then push the photocopy machine onto the stage and put up the scanned copies of audiences' faces on the walls. During the performance, actors/characters would intermingle with the audiences some of whom, randomly selected, puzzled, were dragged onto the stage to experience Caligula's tyranny as his subjects.[69] Lithunian theatre artists, led by director Vidas Bareikis, presented another production of Caligula at the 2016 Wuzhen Theatre Festival. It was performed in Lithunian with English and Chinese subtitles.[70]

In 2015, Cai Yiyun, a 2006 graduate of Shanghai Theatre Academy, staged another Chinese production of *Caligula*. According to Cai, Caligula had been a favorite character of hers since her college days, because for a long time, she had felt like an "outsider" to the world she lived in:[71]

> *Caligula* is a play that I love the most, and Caligula is a character that I love the most: I love him, pity him, and admire him. . . . I wanted to create a Caligula that is more than a label, but a "man" (*ren*), a man in capital letters (*daxie de ren*). . . .

The Caligula in Cai's production, however, is a robot with a TV or computer screen that plays prerecorded speeches to issue orders and express his thoughts – to signify the absolute power that the government, mass media, and technology, such as the Internet and smartphones, hold over our everyday life: we are so controlled and willingly enslaved; we don't know the truth, and we don't resist and fight back. The venue for this production was not a conventional theatre, but an upper floor of a flashy modern building where downstairs is a Hermès store, a French high fashion luxury goods brand that sells expensive lifestyle accessories, home furnishings, perfumery, jewelry, watches, etc. The irony of it all screams to be heard.

If *Caligula* that features a psychopathic hero seems an odd choice of Western play to mount on the Chinese stage, the 2008 (2011) adaptation of Camus' 1947 novel *The Plague* based on a deadly cholera epidemic that hit Oran (a coastal city in the northwest of Algeria) in 1849 would speak to the Chinse in a way as direct as it is uncanny. Although several years had lapsed since the 2002–2003 outbreak of Severe Acute Respiratory Syndrome (SARS) that wreaked havoc in southern China, it posed pressing existential questions to the government, local communities, and individuals, especially to how to respond when facing such a calamity. The central government largely failed the test during the SARS outbreak in part by its failure to appreciate the scope and intensity of the epidemic, but mostly through its foolhardy attempt to cover up and its refusal to share information with the World Health Organization in a timely quest for diagnosis and effective treatment.[72] A few courageous individuals – i.e., the Chinese equivalents of Dr. Bernard Rieux or Dr. Stockmann (Ibsen's *An Enemy of the People*), did rise to the occasion and answer the questions heroically. One such citizen hero was Jiang Yanyong (1931–), chief physician of the 301 Military Hospital in Beijing who publicized a cover-up of the SARS epidemic, thus forcing the hand of the central government in how to handle the public health crisis publicly; another was Zhong Nanshan (1936–), a pulmonologist credited with discovering the SARS coronavirus as well as capably managing the SARS outbreak in Guangdong province.[73] More pertinently for this discussion, as the epidemic wreaked havoc in a big part of the country, one well-known Chinese writer, Sun Ganlu, mused aloud publicly: What should you read when you are coughing? His answer is the Camus novel:[74]

> Camus discovers absurdity of the world through the plague whereas the fashionable discovers fashion during the plague.

What Sun jabs at, good-humoredly perhaps, is the fact that during the SARS epidemic many Chinese, especially young women, put their creativity to work and turn the mouth masks they had to wear into personal fashion statements.[75]

For Ye Junhua, director for the 2011 production, the story of the plaque is not all doom and gloom. He feels that on the theatre scene in China today there is simply too much cheap entertainment and too little serious thought-provoking drama. So Ye wants to mount a play that is not only a reflection of reality but also inspires the audiences to think and appreciate the simplicity and joy of life, to search for what is beautiful in human nature, and to teach people how to remain kind under the extreme circumstances of unrest, war, and disaster, and how to hold on to justice when besieged by collective absurdity.[76] To make the story work for the stage, Ye and his team of young theatre artists from the recently formed Simple Drama Workshop (*jiandan xiju gongfang*) tried to be faithful to the original in the basic story and structure, but made major changes in the ensemble of characters and character profiles. For example, Cottard, a small-time traveling salesman in wines and spirits in the original, who takes advantage of the crisis to make money by selling contraband cigarettes, etc., is further developed for this production to show both the good and bad sides of people when caught in such situations. To give more nuanced portrayal of characters, or rather to challenge the audiences' perception and complicate their experience in the theatre, Ye has one actor (Lin Sensen) to play the roles of five or six characters – e.g., M. Michel (an old man, concierge of the building where Dr. Rieux lives, the first victim of the plague); the prefect, Father Paneloux; Dr. Castel; Jean Tarrou; and Joseph Grand. Although, as indicated by the many comments posted at *douban* (Chinese equivalent of Rottom Tomatoes, etc.), such an adaptation endeavor (based on a classic novel) could not please everyone, whether those who have read the novel (in translation) or not, Ye's production has gone on to perform several times in different cities.

Eugène Ionesco

Another important French playwright whose plays have seen interesting Chinese adaptations is Eugène Ionesco (1909–1994). Whether the label "Theatre of the Absurd" can be accurately applied to Ionesco (or Samuel Beckett, Jean Genet, Harold Pinter, etc., for that matter), his sense of the world "devoid of purpose," of man "(c)ut off from his religious, metaphysical, and transcendental roots" and hence is "lost," "all his actions become senseless, absurd, useless,"[77] certainly speak to a generation of Chinese who had survived the Cultural Revolution, a period of modern Chinese history whacked by extreme absurdity. One of Ionesco's plays that saw Chinese productions, *Rhinoceros* (1959), was inspired in part by his experience in his native Romania – where he eyewitnessed fascism surging up in the days right before WWII. For example, one of his professors using his lectures to recruit students into the Iron Guard, an ultra-nationalist, anti-Semitic, and anti-communist movement in Romania from the late 1920s to the early 1940s.[78] What Ionesco said about how Romanians were caught up in the feverishly contagious far-right ideology and the pressure of mob mentality should eerily remind the Chinese of what happened during the Anti-Rightest Movement and the Cultural Revolution.[79]

However, for the Chinese appreciation of Ionesco to move from print to stage would take time. The first Chinese translation of *Rhnoceros* was published in 1980, which was followed by a published translation of *The Bald Sopreno* in 1981 and an upsurge of other translations and scholarship (translation of Western criticism as well as original research) on Ionesco.[80] By 2006, when *Rhnoceros* (*xiniu*) was staged by the National Theatre Company of China (*Zhongguo guojia huaju yuan*), directed by Ning Chunyan,[81] the endeavor seemed more an intellectual and philosophical exercise which provided an opportunity to experiment with different forms of theatric expressions. One of the notable features of this production was its use of ink and rice paper and such iconic Chinese culture elements as symbolic representation of Rhinoceros. Whether intended or not, this production's use of ink and rice paper, which played an outsized, ubiquitous role in the form of big character posters during the Cultural Revolution, seemed to suggest that "Rhinocerism" is as native to the Chinese culture, history, and people as it is anywhere else in the world. It is an ingenious way to explore the themes of conformity and mob mentality which, albeit universal, hit home acutely in the context of China.

For this 2006 production, when the first Rhinoceros appeared in Act I, it was represented by ink splashed onto the white background made of rice paper, signifying the first drop of evil darkness in the world of pure innocence. The second time the Rhinoceros appeared (Act II), it was represented by a "black cat" soaked in ink tossed onto stage and more ink splashed onto the white rice-paper background. Again, whether intended or not, the "black cat" symbol is loaded with meaning from culture to culture, signifying good or bad, auspicious or ominous, and could even be read as a subtle jab at this well-known maxim from Deng Xiaoping: "It doesn't matter whether a cat is white or black, as long as it catches mice." Close to the end of the play, when just about everyone in town, except for Bérenger, has succumbed to rhinoceritis, the rice-paper background is covered completely by black ink. As Ning, the director for this production, explains,[82]

> The pure white background (for the stage design) symbolizes the purity of the world in its original condition whereas the inky darkness symbolizes the world of Rhinoceros. Inky darkness gradually permeates the background and turns it into darkness as the world dims.

Even in the midst of such oppressive doom and gloom, however, there is a glimmer of hope, in the form of one clean person left, Bérenger. Whether that lone soldier could take back the Planet of Rhinoceros, so to speak, or rather, restore the world to its pre-fall pure, innocent state, is anybody's guess. Besides, even that pre-fall, Edenic world filled with "infant joy" is more a myth than reality belied by the young chimney sweepers' cry of " 'weep! 'weep! 'weep! 'weep!" and the little black boy's angst over his dark body and sunburned face we can hear from *Songs of Innocence* by William Blake (1757–1827).

The same year 2008 saw another Chinese production of Ionesco: *The Bald Soprano* (1950), directed by Meng Jinghui,[83] a "replica" of the original English setting, to ridicule the banality of the bourgeois class and life. It is not clear why Meng and his team choose this particular play for production. Have the Chinese, about a decade into the twenty-first century and indeed three decades into "Reform and Opening Up," having achieved the world's longest economic boom in recent memories, reached a state, as described by Ionesco in 1957, where "there is no more incentive to be wicked, and everyone is good" and people don't know what to do with their "goodness," "non-wickedness," "non-greed," and "ultimate neutrality?"[84] The answer is no, as can be borne out by the public outcry over the perceived absence of good Samaritans in the news just about every day.[85] Yet, for many, especially the newly rich, the feeling of being "bored stiff" and a sense of not knowing "what we are doing here on earth and how" could certainly hit home. At least, for the millions of Chinese who, since the end of the 1970s, have tried to learn English by toiling with countless dialogs and sentence drills from such well-known textbooks as English 900 and the Linguaphone English Course can certainly appreciate how Ionesco was inspired to write this first play of his when he was learning English with the Assimil method (e.g., *Anglais Sans Peine*, English Without Toil).[86]

A more interesting adaptation was mounted by the Shandong Province Spoken Drama Company in 2015,[87] which relocates the story to today's China under the Chinese title *Qie'ai* (Love You Forevermore). This much Sinicized production of the play opens with a couple in their 40s, Shi, sitting there watching CCTV evening news. The show begins at 7:00 p.m., exactly the same time that CCTV evening news program for the day gets on the air. The evening news segment for the performance lasts for 15 minutes. According to one theatergoer, five minutes into the news broadcast audience members begin to agitate: we are here to see a show, not to listen to the CCTV news broadcast. The CCTV news broadcast we can not only listen to at home but also see, and it is free! Despite the cacophony of protesting noise from the audiences, the actors "carry on" till the end of the 15-minute segment.

Then, the Shis begin to talk, delivering the first line of dialog for the performance. They keep chitchatting offhandedly of unrelated and nonsensical topics until they are joined by the Mas who, like the Martins in the original play, after exchanging a long string of "coincidences" crisscrossing their lives, establish the fact that they happen to be husband and wife. Nonsensical exchanges such as the following permeate the performance:[88]

> "You're a donkey!"
> "I mean you don't know the joy of being a donkey because you are not a donkey!"
> "*You* are a donkey?"
> "How can I make you understand? I mean how can you know the joy of being a donkey when you are not a donkey!?"
> "You are a mule!"

They keep rearranging their chairs over and again; the very air is heavy with boredom, indifference, and paranoia. Gradually, it becomes more than apparent that husband and wife, bedfellows that they are, have become strangers to each other despite the intimacy of sharing the same bed. Life drags on in its unavoidable circularity of meaningless daily routine. There is nothing of real meaning for them to talk about, to share, and to pursue together. The only way left for them to fill the deadly silence between them is sitting in front of TV and watching boring evening news, day after day, and rearranging the chairs.

Zhao Sanqiang, director of the production, says he approaches the play (or rather adaptation) as both realistic theatre and "The Theatre of the Absurd." For him, the play reflects the socioeconomic and emotive realities of China today, the disconnect, the indifference, and the angst despite the boom:

> Love has nothing to with status, money, age, and race. Love is free, is independent, is impassioned, and is dedication. Love is love. Love can't be absurd! Audiences can recognize their neighbors and themselves in the characters. Love is simple; love is complicated; love is a habit; love is unpredictable; love expects no return; love gives and experiences joy in giving . . . So we would like everyone to love a bit more; a bit deeper; a bit long lasting; hence *Qie'ai* (Love You Forevermore).

This rather upbeat reinterpretation of the play, or rather, the upbeat, romantic spirit in which the adaptation was mounted, feels quite a distance from the original Ionesco play, but moves closer to meeting the needs of the Chinese audiences. At least, this is how the production was received when performed for the graduating class of students at a Shandong university whose last lesson was "Marriage: Management and Creative Development." "We learn from *Qie'ai*," as one student summed up the wisdom they had gained from this unusual theatric experience, "that love is really simple":[89]

1   Be a good person;
2   Find a good person;
3   Love each other and cherish the love.

What would Ionesco say if and when he finds out that his 1950 play on the absurdity of life has gained some unambiguous moral clarity in its transcultural journey to the China of the twenty-first century and now serves as a negative example of how not to mess up the bliss of matrimony?

Ionesco's 1952 play *The Chairs*, which features two people, Old Man and Old Woman, sitting there and talking and not much more, also saw a Chinese production in 2014.[90] Unlike the couples in *The Bald Soprano*, Old Man and Old Woman in *The Chairs* are not so much disconnected or indifferent to each other as they are desperate. The promotional pitch from the 2014 production goes like this:

> Let's use disharmonious environment and illogical speech to let you experience an extraordinary mode of comedy. In this age of isolated commodification, what you think is impassioned speech may be no more than incoherent babbling. Angst, rage, joy, fear, misery, excitement, surprise . . . and love, every little detail is given different coloration. We represent despair on stage and convey hope in despair; we try to catch glimmers of meaning of existence on the fringe of meaningless life.

One can hope to catch glimmers of meaning in other productions of French plays too, such as *The Game of Love and Chance* by Pierre de Marivaux (1688–1763),[91] *Against a Small Wood* and *Theater without Animals* by Jean-Michel Ribes (1946–), *Rue de Babylone* by Jean-Marie Besset (1959–), *In the Solitude of Cotton Fields* by Bernard Marie Koltès (1948–1989), *The Balcony* by Jean Genet (1910–1986),[92] and *Far from Hagondange* (1975) and *Make Blue* (2000) by Jean-Paul Wenzel (1947–).

As can be expected, not all of these bold adaptation endeavors have met with positive reviews and good box office results. Trying to adapt any Western classic for the Chinese stage is an undertaking that would always carry risks. One would never know how the audiences would respond. The 2006 *jingju* adaptation of Hugo's *Les Miserables* would be another case in point. This was a production mounted by the National Academy of Chinese Theatre Arts (*Zhongguo xiqu xueyuan*), established in 1950 and dedicated to education in the art of *jingju*.[93] A collective endeavor by the academy's various departments, from writing to stage design, lighting to performance, this *jingju* adaptation turned out to be more controversial than anyone could have anticipated.[94]

The production team's goal was to be approved by those who are familiar with *Les Miserables*, to be understood by those who are not, and to present it as a *jingju* that gives a new reinterpretation of a Western classic.[95] It took the team two years – e.g., going through more than 20 drafts – before the production debuted at Beijing University as "Peking Opera of Classic Novel for Ordinary Audience" (*mingzhu jingju pingmin kan*). The challenge remains of how to Sinicize Western classics so that neither the quintessential spirit of the original play nor the artistic beauty of the traditional Chinese drama genre is lost.

In this 130-minute *jingju* adaptation of *Les Miserables*, Jean Valjean is cast as a *laosheng* (old man role, who speaks and sings with his real voice), Fantine as a *qingyi* (female leading role, typically righteous woman), Thénardier as a *chou* (male clown), and Madame Thénardier as a *caidan* (female clown). One of the performances for foreigners in Beijing – more than 500 from about 60 countries and international organizations – met with enthusiastic responses.[96] Before the performance, there was a short presentation and demonstration of the art of *jingju*, from masks to roles to stylized acting and music, to prepare the audiences on how to appreciate the *jingju* adaptation. For the foreign audiences, thoughtfully attuned prior to the show, the *laosheng* Jean Valjean comes across very Eastern (Chinese) thanks to the full-throated vibrancy of *jingju* (song, dance, costume, face-painting, etc.) yet does not lose his Western spirit and cultural identity. It was quite a different theatric experience, however, for many Chinese audience members. They felt that the actors spoke more like those in a spoken drama, their acting is reminiscent of Model Peking Opera, and their costumes feel neither French nor Chinese. Indeed, some complained that such a production loses both the beauty of the *jingju* and the spirit of the original story. Their displeasure ultimately shows itself in the poor box office results. Indeed, as the production team lamented, our new Peking opera *Les Miserables* was miserable indeed. The box office in Beijing didn't improve even when the ticket price was dropped to 10 yuan (RMB0, a fraction of the typical ticket price for such performances in China today, with added incentive of free copies of Chinese translation of the Hugo novel for the audiences.[97]

If the thirteenth-century Yuan *zaju The Orphan of Zhao* traveled to Europe in the eighteenth century via the agency of a Jesuit missionary (Joseph de Prémare) and an Enlightenment giant (Voltaire), more recently, Chinese have begun to take their dramatic creations to France out of their own volition – e.g., to perform at the Festival d'Avignon, the oldest extant festival in France and one of the world's greatest drama/theatre festivals.[98] In 2015, for example, four Chinese plays traveled to the festival. One of them is *Tiaoqiang* (Jumping Wall) that features a young monk who, still at the cusps of pubescent adolescence, enters the monastery, and experiences more than his share of hilarious encounters.[99] In 2016, another five Chinese drama productions were invited to perform at the festival.[100] One of them is *Zhuang Xiansheng* (Mr. Zhuang), inspired by the story of Zhuang Zhou (4 BC), one of the most important early Taoist philosophers: one day, Zhuang Zhou dreamed that he was a fluttering butterfly, and upon waking up, puzzled, he wondered whether it was Zhuang Zhou who had dreamed that he was a butterfly or it was the butterfly that had dreamed that he was Zhuang Zhou.[101] Although all of these visits and many more are not much more than teasers, to borrow the culinary figure of speech used in the title of this chapter, and do not amount to anything like the continuous "grand feast" of French classics in China since early twentieth century, they are valiant efforts to "repay," so to speak, in kind, and they do present a culturally enriching experience not only for the Chinese and the French but also for the world at large.

Notes

1 "Chinoiserie."
2 Voltaire, 175–80. See also Alfred Owen Aldridge, 141–47.
3 From there and then on, the story would continue to find new reincarnations – e.g., *Orphan of China* by Arthur Murphy in 1756, which also saw highly successful performances in England, which then traveled to the United States in 1767 and was performed at the Southwark Theatre in Philadelphia, Garrick's production, and all the way to a 2012 adaptation by James Fenton and produced by the Royal Shakespeare Company.
4 Voltaire, 179.
5 Melvyn Richter, 237.
6 "These three ways of writing correspond almost exactly to three different stages according to which one can consider men gathered into a nation. The depicting of objects is appropriate to a savage people; signs of words and of propositions, to a barbaric people, and the alphabet to civilized peoples" (Jean-Jacques Rousseau, 17).
7 This portion of the discussion draws from Shouhua Qi, 30–46.
8 This portion of the discussion draws from Chapter 1 of this book.
9 See Siyuan Liu; and Iizuka Yutori.
10 This asymmetrical attribution of importance and flow of cultural influence continues to this day, although it has been corrected to a significant extent as China continues to rise on the world stage and acquire much more power in socioeconomics, culture, and almost everything else. Just talk to a typical college-educated Chinese and drop these terms and names (at the risk of name dropping), and chances are that you will see a sparkle of recognition in his or her eyes: the French Revolution, Napoleon, the Louvre, the Eiffel Tower, Palace of Versailles, Arc de Triomphe, the Seine, Notre-Dame de Paris, Champs-Élysées, Molière, Racine, Diderot, Montesquieu, Voltaire, and Descartes. Rousseau, Balzac, Hugo, Flaubert, de Maupassant, Baudelaire, Monet, Cezanne, Degas, Sartre, Beckett, Foucault, Lacan, Derrida, etc.
11 See Xu Guanghua.
12 "*Qingchou jian.*" See also "*Gaonaiyi mingzuo*" (Classic Corneille Play)
13 See "*Xinbian jingju*" (New Peking Opera).
14 "*Changhe yuan*" (Happy Harmony Garden).
15 Jun Le.
16 "China | Festival Croisements 2013."
17 Xu Huanyan, "*Moli'ai xiju zhongguo*" (Cultural Factors) .
18 Xu Huanyan. "*Lun Gu Zhongyi*" (On Gu Zhongyi's). See also Xu Huanyan, *Moli'ai xiju yu ershi* (Moliere Comedy and Twentieth-Century).
19 "Battle of Shanghai."
20 "Ning Chunyan."
21 Wang Xiaoyi.
22 Guo Wenbo.
23 "*Falanxi xijuyuan*" (The Comédie-Française).
24 "2015 'Shanghai,'" Wang, Yan.
25 "*Faguo jutuan Beijing shangyan*" (French Drama troupe Performs).

26 As told in the 2009 Chinese film *Yaotiao shenshi* (*My Fair Gentleman*). See also Kay Li, 121–22.
27 "2015 *Guojia dajuyuan*" (2015 National Center of Performing Arts).
28 Yang Yang.
29 Bi Rang.
30 Jushi Bururen.
31 Zhang Liyun.
32 Pan Yu, "*Zhongfa lianhe dazao*" (Sino-French Joint Production).
33 "If You are the One."
34 "*Shao Sifan.*"
35 "'Dagongmei': Female Migrant Labourers."
36 Anne-Marie Brady, 94–5, and Gary Cox, 190–91.
37 Song Xuezhi, n.p.
38 Chen Zengrong and Han Xi.
39 Zhang Ming'ai; Liu Datao, "*Xin qimeng zhuyi*" (Translation and Introduction).
40 Duncan Hewitt.
41 "To Each According to His Abilities."
42 See Chapter 3 for more discussion of the sociopolitical context and the theatre/drama scenes in China around the events of 1989.
43 "Hu Weimin."
44 Hu Weimin, "*Angzang de shou daoyan zishu*" (*Dirty Hands* Director's Account); Chen Gongmin et al.
45 Jean-Paul Sartre, *Three Plays*, 17.
46 "Lin Biao."
47 Sartre, *Three Plays*, 121.
48 Ibid, 152.
49 Chen Gongmin et al.
50 F. Scott Fitzgerald, 23–4.
51 "Iraq War."
52 "*Shanghai huaju*" (Shanghai Spoken Drama).
53 Liu Datao, "*Chongdu jingdian*" (Reread Classic).
54 Jean-Paul Sartre, *No Exit and Three Other Plays*, 45.
55 Liu Datao, "*Chongdu jingdian*" (Reread Classic).
56 Pan Yu, "Shanghai fupai Jinbi" (Shanghai revives *No Exit*).
57 Jean Sartre, *No Exit and Three Other Plays*, 46.
58 See "*Si wu zangshen zhi di*" (*The Victors*).
59 Ronald Aronson, 9–22; Robert C. Solomon, 245.
60 "*Paiyan Kaligula*" (*Caligula* Director); Li Yumin.
61 Albert Camus, *The Collected Plays*, 10.
62 Camus, 63–6.
63 Albert Camus, *Caligula and Three Other Plays*, 186–89.
64 Jacob Golomb, 189.
65 "*Paiyan Kaligula*" (*Caligula* Director).
66 "*Jishu shidai*" (Performing in the Age of High-Tech).
67 Jerzy Grotowski, 15.
68 Li Yumin.
69 Chen Xihan.
70 "*Kaligula*" (*Caligula*).
71 Cai Yiyun; "*Jinwan women guanju*" (We Go See a Play Tonight).
72 "Severe Acute Respiratory Syndrome."
73 See "Jiang Yanyong" and "Zhong Nanshan."
74 "*Jiamiu mingzhu*" (Camus Classic Novel). See also Zhu Dake and "Sun Ganlu."
75 Zhou Xiang.
76 "*Jiamiu mingzhu*," Liu, Chang, and Liu Yu.

77 Martin Esslin, 23.
78 Anne Quinney, 41–2. For more about the Iron Guard, see Stanley G. Payne, 394.
79 Quoted in Quinney, 42.
80 Chen Jinfeng.
81 *"Ning Chunyan tan"* (Ning Chunyan Talks) and *"Faguo huangdan ju Xiniu"* (National Theatre Presents).
82 *"Ning Chunyan tan"* (Ning Chunyan Talks).
83 *"Tutou genü"* (*The Bald Soprano*)
84 Martin Esslin, 43.
85 John Sexton.
86 Eugène Ionesco and Jack Undank, 10–13.
87 *"Jingdian huangdan xiju"* (Classic Absurd Comedy).
88 Sun Congcong and Yang Liu.
89 *"Rensheng ruci jiannan"* (Life Is So Hard).
90 *"2014 'Juhai guanchao'"* (2014 'New Wave Theatre').
91 Ning Chunyan, *"Faguo wenhua dacan"* (French Culture Grand Feast).
92 *"Faguo huangdanpai daibiaozuo"* (French Classic Absurd Play).
93 *"Zhongguo xiqu xueyuan"* (National Academy of Chinese Theatre Arts).
94 Qiu Zhili.
95 A. Mang, *"Jingju Beicanshijie"* (Audiences Cool Reception) and Xu Ci.
96 A. Mang, *"Jingju yan Yuguo"* (Peking Opera Adaptation of Hugo).
97 *"Xiju de zhongguohua wenti"* (Sinification of Western Classics).
98 "Festival d'Avignon."
99 A. Jian.
100 Liu Qiong.
101 "Zhuangzi."

Bibliography

"2014 *'Juhai guanchao' huaju zhanyan ji Youneisiku huangdanpai xiju jingdian Yizi)"* (2014 'New Wave Theatre' Spoken Drama Festival Ionesco Classic Absurd Play The Chairs), October 24–25, 2014. www.228.com.cn/ticket-53221397.html.

"2015 *Guojia dajuyuan guoji xijuji: Bali beifang jutuan Moli'ai Guirenmi"* (2015 National Center of Performing Arts International Theatre Festival: Paris *Theatre des Bouffes du Nord* Presents Molière's *Bourgeois gentilhomme*). National Center of the Performing Arts, June 10–13, 2015. http://ticket.chncpa.org/product-1001443.html.

"2015 *'Shanghai guoji xiju jie' kaimu"* (2015 Shanghai International Comedy Festival Open), October 28, 2015. www.shanghai.gov.cn/nw2/nw2314/nw2315/nw31406/u21aw1070854.html.

Aldridge, Alfred Owen. "Voltaire and the Mirage of China," in *The Reemergence of World Literature: A Study of Asia and the West*. Newark, NJ: University of Delaware Press, 1986, 141–47.

Aronson, Ronald. *Camus and Sartre: The Story of a Friendship and the Quarrel that Ended It*. Chicago, IL: University of Chicago Press, 2005.

"Battle of Shanghai." https://en.wikipedia.org/wiki/Battle_of_Shanghai.

Bi, Rang. "*Renjunbujin hunran tiancheng: Kan Qudachenyi*" (Hilarious and Flawless: My View on *The Doctor In Spite of Himself*). November 22, 2013. www.cando360.com/ess/52028.html.

Brady, Anne-Marie. *Making the Foreign Serve China: Managing Foreigners in the People's Republic*. New York: Rowman & Littlefield Publishers, 2003.

Cai, Yiyun. "*Guanyu Jiamiu juzuo Kaligula de yanchu gousi*" (On Staging Camus Play *Caligula*), March 30, 2015. www.douban.com/note/491312606.

Camus, Albert. *Caligula and Three Other Plays*. Revised ed. Translated by Stuart Gilbert and Justin O'Brien. New York: Vintage, 1962.

———. *The Collected Plays of Albert Camus*. London: Hamish Hamilton, 1965.

"*Changhe yuan*" (Happy Harmony Garden). www.cnpoc.cn/channels/189.html.

Chen, Gongmin, et al. "*Yanyuan wu ren tan Angzang de shou*" (Five Actors on *Dirty Hands*). *Xiju yishu* (Theatre Arts) 2 (1981): 113–19.

Chen, Jinfeng. "*Jin ershi nian lai Youneisiku yanjiu zongshu*" (Ionesco Research in the Last Twenty Years: An Overview), October 20, 2014. http://f.ttwang.net/RoomFile/NewsShow.aspx?RoomId=9166&NewsId=9587.

Chen, Xihan. "*Huaju Kaligula shouyan*" (Spoken Drama *Caligula* Opens) June 14, 2010. www.xijucn.com/huaju/20100614/17722.html.

Chen, Zengrong. "*Huangdanpai xiju zai zhongguo de yijie yanjiu yu chuanbo*" (Translation, Research, and Reception of the Theatre of the Absurd in China). *Xiju wenxue* (Drama Literature) 5 (2010): 17–21.

"China | Festival Croisements 2013." http://culture360.asef.org/event/china-festival-croisements-2013.

"Chinoiserie." https://en.wikipedia.org/wiki/Chinoiserie.

Cox, Gary. *Existentialism and Excess: The Life and Times of Jean-Paul Sartre*. London: Bloomsbury Academic, 2016.

"'Dagongmei:' Female Migrant Labourers." *China Labor Bulletin*, June 3, 2004. www.clb.org.hk/en/content/dagongmei-female-migrant-labourers.

Esslin, Martin. *The Theatre of the Absurd*, 3rd ed. New York: Vintage, 2001.

"*Faguo huangdanju Xiniu guojia huajuyuan zhongguo shouyan*" (National Centre for the Performing Arts Presents First Performance of French Absurd Play *Rhnoceros* in China), May 16, 2015. www.youtube.com/watch?v=bT7ElOa5OwY.

"*Faguo huangdanpai daibiaozuo Rang Renei Yangtai juben langdu*" (French Classic Absurd Play Jean-Pierre Jeunet's *The Balcony* Staged Reading), April 19, 2016. http://blog.sina.com.cn/s/blog_6767e3c50102w6hk.html.

"*Faguo jutuan Beijing shangyan Moli'ai xiju Guiren mi: Shouru juanzhu zhongguo pinkun ertong*" (French Drama Troupe Performs Molière Comedy *Bourgeois gentilhomme*: Box Office Donated to Support Impoverished Chinese Children), June 4, 2011. http://news.ifeng.com/world/news/detail_2011_06/04/6822737_0.shtml.

"*Falanxi xijuyuan Wubingshenyin jingyan liangxiang: Jingdian laoju rengju pushi jiazhi*" (The Comédie-Française Presents Stunning Performance of *The Imaginary Invalid*: Old Classic Play Still Shines With Universal Value). National Center for the Performing Arts, October 27, 2011. www.chncpa.org/zxdt_331/zxdtlm/yczx_332/201608/t20160823_102559.shtml.

"Festival d'Avignon." https://en.wikipedia.org/wiki/Festival_d%27Avignon.

Fitzgerald, F. Scott. *The Great Gatsby*. New York: Scribner, 1925.

"*Gaonaiyi mingzuo gaibianju Qingchoujian tansuo jingju waixiao xinlu*" (Classic Corneille Play Adaptation Love Hate Sword Exploring New Way to Get Peking Opera Into International Market), June 8, 2009, *Sohu Yule* (Sohu Entertainment). http://yule.sohu.com/20090608/n264388669.shtml.

Golomb, Jacob. *In Search of Authenticity: Existentialism From Kierkegaard to Camus*. London and New York: Routledge, 2004.

Grotowski, Jerzy. *Towards a Poor Theatre*. New York: Routledge, 2002.

Guo, Wenbo. "*Xinban zhijing moli'ai: Gudian zhuzuo rongru chaoliu yuansu*" (New Edition of Don Juan Pay Tribute to Molière: Ancient Classic Injected With Trendy Elements). *Beijing Wenwang*, June 22, 2009. http://beijingww.qianlong.com/2061/2009/06/22/226@94389.htm.

Han, Xi. "*Huangdanpai xiju zai zhongguo*" (Theatre of the Absurd in China). *Foreign Literature*, no. 6 (2005): 99–103.

Hewitt, Duncan. *China: Getting Rich First: A Modern Social History*. Cambridge, UK: Pegasus, 2009.

Hu, Weimin. "*Angzang de shou daoyan zishu*" (*Dirty Hands* Director's Account). *Xiju yishu* (Theatre Arts) 2 (1981): 120–7.

"Hu Weimin." https://baike.baidu.com/item/%E8%83%A1%E4%BC%9F%E6%B0%91/5778294.

"If You Are the One." https://en.wikipedia.org/wiki/If_You_Are_the_One_(game_show).

Ionesco, Eugène, and Jack Undank. "The Tragedy of Language: How an English Primer Became My First Play." *The Tulane Drama Review* 4, no. 3 (March 1960): 10–13.

"Iraq War." https://en.wikipedia.org/wiki/Iraq_War.

"*Jiamiu mingzhu gaibian huaju Shuyi*" (Camus Classic Novel Adapted Play *The Plague*), June 28 to July 2, 2017. www.gewara.com/drama/347315562.

Jian, A. "*Sibu zhongguo zuopin jiang liangxiang jinnian faguo A'weiniweng xijujie*" (Four Chinese Plays Will Perform at this Year's Festival d'Avignon in France), July 5, 2015. http://news.xinhuanet.com/world/2015-07/05/c_1115818641.htm.

"Jiang Yanyong." https://en.wikipedia.org/wiki/Jiang_Yanyong.

"*Jingdian huangdan xiju Tutou genü zhongguo ban Qie'ai*" (Classic Absurd Comedy *The Bald Soprano* Chinese Edition Love You Forevermore). www.228.com.cn/ticket-63356591.html.

"*Jinwan women guanju: Jiumiu xiju Kaligula*" (We Go See a Play Tonight: Camus' Play *Caligula*), August 27, 2016. www.wenji8.com/p/2d3zdHR.html.

"*Jishu shidai de yanchu yu Kaligula*" (Performing in the Age of High-tech and *Caligula*), April 24, 2001. http://yule.sohu.com/61/34/earticle163123461.shtml.

Jun, Le. "*San chang jingju daxi yao ning mianfei kan*" (Three Peking Opera Big Productions Invite You to See Free of Charge). *Haixia doushi bao* (Strait Metropolis Paper), February 20, 2013. www.jingju.com/jingjuxinwen/yanchudongtai/2013-02-20/4281.html.

Jushi, Bururen. "*Zhonggui zhongju de Yichang xiju*" (A Comedy Well-wrought and Well Performed), November 24, 2013. www.cando360.com/ess/52033.html.

"*Kaligula*" (*Caligula*). Wuzhen Theatre Festival, October 18–21, 2016. http://2016.wuzhenfestival.com/newcn/ScheduleList2.aspx?classId=37&Id=1371&id2=4627.

Li, Kay. *Bernard Shaw's Bridges to Chinese Culture*. New York: Palgrave Macmillan, 2016.

Li, Yumin. "*Zuowei xijuren de Jiamiu*" (Camus as a Playwright). *Tribune of Social Sciences* 3 (2003): 64–8.

"Lin Biao." https://en.wikipedia.org/wiki/Lin_Biao.

Liu, Chang, and Liu, Yu. "*Haiguipai daoyan Ye Junhua tan huaju Shuyi beihou de gushi*" (Returnee Director Ye Junhua Tells Behind the Scene Story of Spoken Drama *The Plague*), August 13, 2012. www.xijucn.com/huaju/20120813/38957.html.

Liu, Datao. "*Chongdu jingdian: Sate de Jinbi*" (Reread Classic: Sartre's *No Exit* in China). *Journal of Hunan University of Science and Engineering* 11 (2011): 48–50.

———. "*Xin qimeng zhuyi yujing xia de Sate zai zhongguo de yijie*" (Translation and Introduction of Sartre in China in the Context of New Enlightenment). *Journal of Zunyi Normal College* 13, no. 6 (December 2011): 43–7, 51.

Liu, Qiong. "*Wubu zhongguo zuopin jiang liangxiang faguo A'weiniweng xijujie*" (Five Chinse Plays Will Perform at Festival d'Avignon in France), July 7, 2016. http://news.xinhuanet.com/2016-07/07/c_1119180543.htm.

Liu, Siyuan. "Adaptation as Appropriation: Staging Western Drama in the First Western-Style Theatres in Japan and China." *Theatre Journal* 59, no. 3. Theatre and Translation (October 2007): 411–29.

Mang, A. "*Jingju Beicanshijie gaibian guanzhong lengluo xiande hen beizhuang*" (Audiences Cool Reception of *Les Miserables* Peking Opera Adaptation Causes Misery), December 26, 2006. http://yule.sohu.com/20061226/n247267770.shtml.

———. "*Jingju yan Yuguo mingzhu Beicanshijie rang waiguo youren jiaohao*" (Peking opera Adaptation of Hugo Classic Novel *Les Miserables* Enthusiastically Received by Foreign Friends). March 27, 2006. http://yule.sohu.com/20060327/n242484283.shtml.

Ning, Chunyan. "*Faguo wenhua dacan: Yu faguo zongli he wenhua buzhang tan zhongfa xiju jiaoliu*" (French Culture Grand Feast: A Conversation With French Prime Minister and Minister of Culture on Sino-French Exchange in Drama/Theatre), January 8, 2010. www.cucp.com.cn/WebSites/CMDX/xwzx/mtyw/350.htm.

"Ning, Chunyang." http://by.sta.edu.cn/detail.aspx?id=32812.

"*Ning Chunyan tan Youneisiku huangdan xiju*" (Ning Chunyan Talks About Ionesco Absurd Plays), October 13, 2016. http://chuansong.me/n/964116851036.

"*Paiyan Kaligula daoyan chanshu*" (*Caligula* Director Talks About Staging the Play), April 24, 2001. http://yule.sohu.com/66/34/earticle163123466.shtml.

Pan, Yu. "*Shanghai fupai Jinbi: Jiemu houlang xiao juchang yundon*" (Shanghai revives *No Exit* to Draw the Curtain for "New Wave" Little Theatre Movement). *Oriental Morning Post*, February 20, 2013. http://ent.sina.com.cn/j/2013-02-20/09223859829.shtml.

———. "*Zhongfa lianhe dazao Moli'ai jingdian xiju Taitai xuetang*" (Sino-French Joint Production of Molière's Comedy *The School of Wives*). *Sohu yule*, September 2, 2014. http://yule.sohu.com/20140902/n403987887.shtml.

Payne, Stanley G. *A History of Fascism, 1914–1945*. Madison, WI: University of Wisconsin Press, 1995.

Qi, Shouhua. *Western Literature in China and the Translation of a Nation*. New York: Palgrave Macmillan, 2012.

"*Qingchoujian*." https://baike.baidu.com/item/%E6%83%85%E4%BB%87%E5%89%91.

Qiu, Zhili. "*Xin jingju Beicanshijie Shanghai yanchu zhongxihebi re zhengyi*" (New Peking opera *Les Miserables* Blending East and West Causes Controversy), April 14, 2006. http://yule.sohu.com/20060414/n242804103.shtml.

Quinney, Anne. "Excess and Identity: The Franco-Romanian Ionesco Combats Rhinoceritis." *South Central Review* 24, no. 3 (fall 2007): 36–52.

"*Rensheng ruci jiannan Qie'ai qiezhenxi*" (Life Is So Hard: Love Forevermore and Cherish Forevermore). Shandong Agricultural University, June 17, 2016. https://doc.sanwenba.com/p/130aiDD.html.

Richter, Melvyn. *The Political Theory of Montesquieu*. Cambridge: Cambridge University Press, Reissue edition, 1977.

Rousseau, Jean-Jacques. *On the Origin of Language*. Chicago, IL: University of Chicago Press; Reprint edition (1966, reprint 1986).

Sartre, Jean-Paul. *No Exit and Three Other Plays*. New York: Vintage International, 1989.

———. *Three Plays*. New York: Alfred A. Knopf, 1949.

"Severe Acute Respiratory Syndrome." https://en.wikipedia.org/wiki/Severe_acute_respiratory_syndrome.

Sexton, John. "Why Are There no Good Samaritans in China?" June 11, 2017. https://hotair.com/archives/2017/06/11/no-good-samaritans-china/.

"*Shanghai huaju jiang yan Sate mingju Angzang de shou*" (Shanghai Spoken Drama Stages Sartre Classic *Dirty Hands*). *Sohu yule*, August 4, 2004. http://yule.sohu.com/20040804/n221354788.shtml.

"*Shao Sifan xiju zuopin Juedui gaoji*" (Shao Sifan dramatic work *Absolutely Fashionable*). www.penghaotheatre.com/xijujieIns_show/327.html.

"*Si wu zangshen zhi di*" (*The Victors*). www.douban.com/location/drama/10864015/.

Solomon, Robert C. *From Rationalism to Existentialism: The Existentialists and Their Nineteenth Century Backgrounds*. Lanham, MD: Rowman & Littlefield, 2001.

Song, Xuezhi. "*Tanxun cunzai zhuyi zai zhongguo de 'cunzai' guiji*" (Tracing Existentialism's "Existence" Trajectory in China). *Zhonghua dushubao* (China Reading Weekly), March 30, 2005, n.p.

Sun, Congcong. "*Qie'ai shishui xiao juchang huaju shangye yunzuo*" (Love You Forevermore Tests the Water of Little Theatre Commercial Market), March 7, 2015. http://news.china.com.cn/live/2015-03/20/content_31909102.htm.

"Sun Ganlu." https://baike.baidu.com/item/%E5%AD%99%E7%94%98%E9%9C%B2.

"To Each According to His Abilities: Market Reforms Mean that China Is Becoming More Unequal." *The Economist*, May 31, 2001. www.economist.com/node/639652.

"*Tutou genü*" (The Bald Soprano). www.douban.com/location/drama/10863504/.

Voltaire. "To the Most Noble Duke of Richelieu," in *The Works of Voltaire*. Edited by De La Pacification, Vol. XV. New York: E. R. Dumont, 1901, 175–80.

Wang, Xiaoyi. "*Faguo xiju huicui kaizhou daxi Moli'ai jingdian mingzhu Tanghuang*" (French Drama Highlights Opening Performance Molière classic *Don Juan*), May 10, 2010, *Wangyi yule*. www.wangjiwang.com/Memorial/memorial_shc.aspx?id=13668.

Wang, Yan. "*Shoujie Shanghai guoji xiju jie shangyan Moli'ai zuopin Wubingshenyin*" (Inaugural Shanghai International Comedy Festival Features Molière Play *The Imaginary Invalid*), *Shanghai Wenyi*, October 30, 2015. www.shwenyi.com.cn/renda/2012shwl/n/node16470/u1ai6081433.html.

"*Xiju de zhongguohua wenti: Ping jingju ban Beicanshijie*" (Sinification of Western Classics: On Peking Opera Adaptation of *Les Miserables*), March 28, 2006. www.chinadaily.com.cn/hqylss/2006-03/28/content_553978.htm.

"*Xinbian jingju Qingchou jian*" (New Peking Opera Adaptation *Love and Hate Sword*). www.piaocn.com/yanchupiao/259.html.

Xu, Ci. "*Jingju ban Beicanshijie de zuida quedian shi gai diu le hun*" (The Biggest Flaw of Peking opera edition of *Les Miserables* is Its Soul Being Lost in the Adaptation), February 21, 2013. http://cul.china.com.cn/2013-02/21/content_5746199.htm.

Xu, Guanghua. "*Faguo wenxue zai zhongguo de yijie*" (Translation and Reception of French Literature in China (1894–1949)). *Zhongguo bijiao wenxue* (Chinese Comparative Literature), no. 4 (2001): 62–76.

Xu, Huanyan. "*Lun Gu Zhongyi dui faguo xiju de zhongguo gaibian*" (On Gu Zhongyi's Chinese Adaptations of French Plays). *Art Theory and Criticism*, no. 2 (2017): 143–50.

———. *Moli'ai xiju yu ershi shiji zhongguo huaju* (Molière Comedy and Twentieth-Century Chinese Spoken drama). Beijing: Beijing University Press, 2014.

———. "*Moli'ai xiju zhongguo wutai chuanbo de wenhua donyin*" (Cultural Factors in Reception of Molière Comedy on the Chinese Stage). *Art Theory and Criticism*, no. 6 (2013): 129–32.

Yang, Liu. "*Qie'ai*." November 6, 2015. http://blog.sina.com.cn/s/blog_626165550 102w2le.html.

Yang, Yang. "*Moli'ai mingju Qudachengyi yanchu jiazuo*" (Molière Classic *The Doctor In Spite of Himself* Performance Standing Room Only). *Jinghua shibao* (Jinghua Times), November 11, 2013. www.chinanews.com/cul/2013/11-18/5516311. shtml.

Yaotiao shenshi (*My Fair Gentleman*). https://baike.baidu.com/item/%E7%AA%88 %E7%AA%95%E7%BB%85%E5%A3%AB.

Yutori, Iizuka. "*Cong Dusike dao rexue yu relei: Rizhong liangguo zaoqi huaju jie dui yi bu faguo xiju de gaibian*" (From *La Tosca* to *Hot Blood* and *Hot Tears*: Early Spoken Drama Adaptation of a French Play in Japan and China). *Zhongguo xiandai wenxue yanjiu* (Modern Chinese Literature Studies) 02 (2007): 9–31.

Zhang, Liyun. "*Moli'ai jingdian xiju Taitai xuetang Shanghai shouyan*" (Molière Classic Comedy *The School of Wives* Opens in Shanghai), September 17, 2014. http://enjoy.eastday.com/e/20140917/u1a8345405.html.

Zhang, Ming'ai. "An Article Influences Chinese History." January 19, 2008. www. china.org.cn/2008-01/19/content_1240036.htm.

"*Zhongguo xiqu xueyuan*" (National Academy of Chinese Theatre Arts). www.nacta. edu.cn/.

"Zhong Nanshan." https://en.wikipedia.org/wiki/Zhong_Nanshan.

Zhou, Xiang. "*Kouzhao de fei dianxing meili*" (Mouth Masks' Surprising Beauty), June 4, 2003. http://news.eastday.com/epublish/gb/paper148/20030604/class0148 00013/hwz956919.htm.

Zhu, Dake. "*Jinian Jiamiu zhisi: Xixifu he Dong Yong de wenhua shenfen*" (Cultural Identities of Sisyphus and Dong Yong). *Zhongguo tushu pinglun* (China Book Review), no. 6 (2006), np. http://blog.sina.com.cn/s/blog_47147e9e010004ln.html.

"Zhuangzi." https://en.wikiquote.org/wiki/Zhuangzi.

Epilogue

To adapt is to make suitable to or fit for a specific use or situation. Adaptation, innate or involuntary, unconscious or deliberate, contributes to an organism or species' fitness and survival. For the Chinese in much of the modern times since its door was blasted open by Western Powers in the mid-1800s, adaptation to the "brave new world" was more forced than voluntary, and it was often a fitful and painful process. Through adaptation, however, China, or rather, the Chinese civilization, has not only survived but also become fitter and much stronger although much may have been lost in the process too.

Adaptation from another dramatic tradition (itself being polymorphous, fluid, and resistant to neat definitions), whether driven by necessity for survival or by a desire to break down walls and open up new vistas – to imagine anew, to recreate, to reclaim past glories real and imagined – has never been easy. This book, once again, is a study of transnational, transcultural, and translingual adaptations of Western classics for the Chinese stage – the complex dynamics between texts (dramatic and socio-historical), contexts (domestic and international), intertexts (Western classics and their Chinese reincarnations in *huaju* and various genres of traditional *xiqu*), and dominance and resistance (of culture and ideology) – across the rugged terrain of more than 100 years of modern Chinese history.

Comprehensive as it is, this book is not meant to be encyclopedic and exhaustive, having a chapter for each source culture of each Western classic of which there has been a Chinese adaptation. Because of space limits, important Western playwrights such as Henrik Ibsen, Eugene O'Neill, Tennessee Williams, Johann Wolfgang von Goethe, August Strindberg, and Luigi Pirandello, are "passed over" without receiving their well-deserved share of attention in this book.[1] Once again, although this book has a rather broad scope, it does not include adaptations of Western classics on the stages in Taiwan or Hong Kong.[2] They each have such a rich and vibrant history of adaptation endeavors shaped by their unique cultural identities, historical experiences, and socioeconomic conditions that only a full-length book study can hope to do justice to.

From the bold albeit amateur adaptations staged by young Chinese studying in Tokyo (1907) to the post-modern play mounted by Beijing People's Art Theatre (2007) to reimaging the rehearsing of *Black Slave's Cry to Heaven* 100 years before; from the publication of a special Ibsen issue by the iconoclastic *New Youth* magazine (1918) and the first staging of *A Doll's House* (1924) in Shanghai to a new adaptation mounted by Central Experimental Spoken Drama Theatre (1998) that has Nora following her Chinese husband to his ancestral home in the China of the 1930s, thus adding transcultural and interracial complications to the theme of gender equality; from the first translations of Shakespeare (1903) to more than 20 of the Bard's plays adapted into *jingju, kunju, yueju, yuju, chuanju, qinqiang, bangzi,* and other traditional *xiqu* genres as well as *huaju* to reimagining for the Chinese audiences today dramatic works by a galaxy of luminous playwrights, from Sophocles, Molière, Chekhov, Gogol, Ibsen, O'Neill, Wilde to Miller, Brecht, Beckett, Sartre, Camus, Ionesco, and many more – adaptations of Western classics have profoundly transformed the drama/theatre scene and experience[3] and, for that matter, the cultural life of modern China and will continue to do so years and decades into the future.

Indeed, as new history is being made every day, new studies will be conducted from new and refreshing perspectives. That is the only constant in the ongoing story of Western classics in China as Chinese drama/theatre artists not only mount their bold and creative works, original plays, and adaptations at home for the Chinese theatergoers but also take them to stages outside China to share with the world.

Notes

1 For the reception and adaptions of Goethe in China, see Terry Siu-Han Yip, Li Xia, and Antjie Budde.

For the reception and adaptations of Strindberg in China, see "Strindberg in China." Chen Nan; and "Strindberg's Miss Julie Singing in Beijing Opera in Shanghai."

For the reception and adaptations of Pirandello in China, see Gloria Davies.

2 For a quick overview of the reception and adaptations of Western drama in Taiwan and Hong Kong, see Alexa Alice Joubin and Thomas Y. T. Luk.

3 To get a sense of the drama/theatre scene of China today, see Meng Jinghui.

Bibliography

Budde, Antjie. "Faust's Spectacular Travels Through China: Recent Faust Productions and Their History," in *International Faust Studies: Adaptation, Reception, Translation*. Edited by Lorna Fitzsimmons. New York: Continuum, 2008, 177–204.

Chen, Nan. "Miss Julie' Wins Top Award at Drama Festival for Beijing Colleges." *China Daily*, November 09, 2017. www.chinadaily.com.cn/culture/2017-11/09/content_34315456.htm.

Davies, Gloria. "Pirandello: Searching for a People." September 4, 2012, Australian Center on China in the World. www.thechinastory.org/2012/09/searching-for-a-people/.

Joubin, Alexa Alice. "Western Influence on Asian Theatre: Taiwan." MIT Global Shakespeares, July 20, 2014. http://globalshakespeares.mit.edu/blog/2014/07/20/western-influence-on-asian-theatre-taiwan/.

Li, Xia. "Faust Made in China: Meng Jinghui and Shen Lin's Irreverent Socio-Cultural Deconstruction of Goethe's Iconic Masterpiece." *Neohelicon* 37, no. 2 (2010): 509–35.

Luk, Thomas Y. T. "Adaptations and Translations of Western Drama: A Socio-cultural Study of Hong Kong Repertory Company's Past Practices." LEWI Working Paper Series, David C. Lam Institute for East-West Studies Paper No. 50, 2006, Hong Kong Baptist University.

Meng, Jinghui. *I Love XXX: and Other Plays* (In Performance). Translated by Claire Conceison, Bay City, MI: Seagull Books, 2017.

"Strindberg in China." *China Daily*, May 26, 2005. www.china.org.cn/english/culture/129978.htm.

"Strindberg's *Miss Julie* Singing in Beijing Opera in Shanghai." *China Daily*, July 11, 2014. http://blog.chinadaily.com.cn/blog-1433447-21007.html.

Yip, Terry Siu-Han. "*Goethe in China: A Study of Reception and Influence*." Ph.D. Dissertation. University of Illinois at Urbana-Champaign, 1985.

Index

adaptation(s) i, vi, viii, x, xii, xiii–viii,
xx–ii, 1, 8–9, 11, 15–17, 19–23, 29,
32, 36–8, 40, 52, 58–66, 68–9, 70,
74–8, 81–6, 88–94, 98–9, 101, 104–5,
107, 109, 111–12, 118–21, 124–5,
127–8, 130, 135, 137, 139, 143–4,
148, 154–9, 165, 169, 170, 172–6,
178–9, 181, 183, 184–6
adaptation studies i, xvi, xx
adaptation (transcultural, translingual,
transnational) i, viii, x, xiv–vii, 1–2, 18,
22–3, 55, 66, 74, 85, 89, 123, 127–8,
144, 152, 154, 156–7, 174, 184–5
Aeschylus 5, 67–8, 75, 78, 81, 83;
Oresteia 69, 75, 81, 82
Antigone xx–ii, 68–9, 71, 75, 78–9, 81,
84–5; *see also* Sophocles
Aristophanes 5, 68, 82–3, 85;
Lysistrata 68
avant-garde 22, 25, 41–2, 45, 61, 64,
83, 119, 120

Bald Soprano, The 29, 44, 161, 163,
172, 174, 178, 180, 182; *see also*
Ionesco, Eugène
Beckett, Samuel xiii, 27, 29, 40–2, 46,
48–53, 58–9, 61–2, 66, 94, 123, 143,
155, 162–3, 170, 176, 185; *Endgame*
41–2, 52, 62, 65–6; *Three Sisters
Waiting for Godot* 65–6, 143, 163;
Waiting for Godot 21, 41–2, 44–6,
49–53, 60–1, 63–6, 94, 105, 143,
162–3
Beijing People's Art Theatre xiii, xiv–v,
xvii, 21, 25, 65, 78, 83, 107, 125,
139, 143, 149, 185
Black Slave's Cry to Heaven (*Heinu
yutian lu*) viii, xv, xvii, 1, 6, 11–12,
15–16, 18–20, 23, 26, 89, 185; *see also*
Spring Willow Society (*Chunliu she*)

Black Slave's Hate (*Heinu hen*) 16;
see also Black Slave's Cry to Heaven
Brecht, Bertolt xii–iv, xviii–xx, xxii,
27–42, 55, 57–60, 62–6, 102–3,
123, 147, 185; *The Caucasian
Chalk Circle* 30, 37, 62, 64; Epic
Theatre xii, xiii, 30–2, 38; *The Good
Person of Beijing* 38–40, 61, 63,
65; *The Good Person of Jiangnan*
28, 40, 63; *The Good Person of
Szechwan* 30, 38, 60, 66; *The Life
of Galileo* xiv, 28, 33–5, 37, 41–2,
55, 63–4; *Mother Courage and Her
Children* xiv, 32–3, 35, 58, 60, 62,
66; *Verfremdungseffekt* ("alienation
effect"; estrangement effect) xii,
xix–xx, xxii, 30, 32, 37, 40, 57, 62–3,
65, 133

Caligula 167–9, 177–81; *see also*
Ionesco, Eugène
Cao Yu 17–18, 44, 54–5, 57, 76, 93,
125–6, 136, 145, 148, 150–1
Caucasian Chalk Circle, The 30, 37, 62,
64; *see also* Brecht, Bertolt
Chekhov, Anton xviii–ix, 11, 25,
49–51, 103, 121–4, 136–44, 146–51,
163, 185; *The Cherry Orchard*
141–4, 146–8, 150–1; *The Seagull*
143–4, 146–7; *Three Sisters
Waiting for Godot* 65–6, 143,
163; *Uncle Vanya* 137–41, 143–4,
147–9, 151
Chen, Baichen xx–i, 125, 130
Chen, Yong 34, 37, 133
Cherry Orchard, The 141–4, 146–8,
150–1; *see also* Chekhov, Anton
chuanju (Sichuan opera) ix, xv, 66,
105, 185; *see also xiqu* (traditional
Chinese drama)

comedy 21, 41, 43, 58, 74, 80, 84, 87, 93, 109, 113–15, 124, 129, 136, 141–3, 148, 156–7, 159–61, 174, 176, 178–83

Crucible, The xvii, 29, 54–5, 58, 62; *see also* Miller, Arthur

Cry to Heaven (Yutian) xxiii, 16; *see also* Black Slave's Cry to Heaven (*Heinu yutian lu*)

Cultural Revolution xiii, xvii–viii, 21, 27–9, 34–6, 41, 54–5, 57–9, 61, 65–6, 68, 89–90, 112–13, 126–7, 129, 132, 137, 162–5, 170–1

Dai, Hongci 4, 8, 9

Death of a Salesman xiv, xvii, 29, 53, 55–6, 63, 93, 106–7; *see also* Miller, Arthur

Desire under the Elms 21, 29; *see also* O'Neill, Eugene

Dirty Hands 29, 162–3, 165, 177, 179–80, 182; *see also* Sartre, Jean-Paul

Doctor in Spite of Himself, The 124, 158–9, 178, 183; *see also* Molière

Doll's House, A xiii, xv, 90, 105, 111, 117, 119, 125, 137, 185; *see also* Ibsen, Henrik

Don Juan 3, 158–9, 179, 182; *see also* Molière

Dumas, Alexandre, fils viii, 1, 3, 11, 153–5; *La Dame aux Camilias* viii, 1, 11, 16, 29; *see also* Spring Willow Society (*Chunliu she*)

Emperor Jones, The 29, 56, 109; *see also* O'Neill, Eugene

Endgame 41–2, 52, 62, 65–6; *see also* Beckett, Samuel

Enemy of the People, An 17, 169; *see also* Ibsen, Henrik

Epic Theatre xii–iii, 30–2, 38; *see also* Brecht, Bertolt

Euripides 5, 67–8, 75, 83; *Medea* 68–9, 75–8, 84–5

existentialism 161–2, 179, 182; *see also* Sartre, Jean-Paul

experimentation xiv, 28, 69, 90; *see also* fidelity; hybridization; indigenization

expressionism x, xiii, xix, 21, 56, 59

fidelity xiv, xx, 15, 20, 68, 70, 89–90, 105; *see also* experimentation; hybridization; indigenization

"fourth wall" xi, xix, 37, 40, 132

Frog Experimental Theatre 44, 61, 64

Fujisawa Asajiro viii, 16

Glass Menagerie, The xxiii, 29; *see also* Williams, Tennessee

Gogol, Nikolai 123–4, 129–34, 136, 144–5, 147–50, 157, 185; *The Government Inspector* 123, 130–5, 137, 144, 146–51, 157; *see also If I Were for Real* (*Jiaru wo shi zheng de*)

Good Person of Beijing, The 38–40, 61, 63, 65; *see also* Brecht, Bertolt

Good Person of Jiangnan, The 28, 40, 63; *see also* Brecht, Bertolt

Good Person of Szechwan, The 30, 38, 60, 66; *see also* Brecht, Bertolt

Gorky, Maxim 122–4, 127–30, 144–5, 147, 149, 150–1; *The Lower Depths* (*Yedian*) 123, 127–9, 144, 147, 149–51

Government Inspector, The 123, 130–5, 137, 144, 146–51, 157; *see also* Gogol, Nikolai

Guo, Qihong 78, 81, 84; *see also* Luo, Jinlin

Hamlet xv, 3, 6, 7, 21, 87–8, 94–8, 102, 105, 115–16, 119–20, 142–3; *see also* Shakespeare, William

Hebei *bangzi* xv, 69, 75–8, 81–2, 84–5, 99, 185

hero tragedy 67, 75, 78, 83; *see also* tragedy; tragic hero

Hong, Shen ix, xix, 108–9, 110–11, 117, 121; *see also Emperor Jones, The*; O'Neill, Eugene

Hongo-Za Theatre viii, 16; *see also* Spring Willow Society (*Chunliu she*)

huaju (spoken drama) viii–ix, xiii–v, xvii, xxi–iii, 1, 9–10, 12, 16–20, 22, 25–6, 28, 33, 37, 39, 51, 62, 64, 66, 68–9, 84, 89, 102, 104, 118–19, 121, 128, 132, 135, 137, 143, 145–51, 177–80, 182–5

Huang, Zuolin xiv, 30, 31–7, 44–5, 58, 60, 62–6, 127–8, 149; *see also Life of Galileo, The*; *Mother Courage and Her Children*

Hu Shi xiii; *see also* Ibsenism

Hutcheon, Linda xvi, xx–xxi

hybridization xiv, 68, 70, 78, 90, 105; *see also* experimentation; fidelity; indigenization

I Am Seagull (*Woshi haiou*) 143, 146, 150; *see also* Chekhov, Anton
Ibsen, Henrik vi, xiii, xv, xvii–xxii, 11, 17, 27–9, 32–3, 37, 40, 58–9, 64, 88, 90, 102–3, 105, 111, 117, 119, 125, 136–7, 145–6, 149, 169, 184–5; *A Doll's House* xiii, xv, 90, 105, 111, 117, 119, 125, 137, 185; *An Enemy of the People* 17, 169; *Peter Gynt* 29, 37
Ibsenism xiii, 27; *see also* Ibsen, Henrik
If I Were for Real (*Jiaru wo shi zheng de*) 27, 33, 59, 64–5, 132, 151; *see also Government Inspector, The*
Imaginary Invalid, The 158–9, 179, 182; *see also* Molière
Importance of Being Earnest, The 108, 112–15; *see also* Wilde, Oscar
indigenization xiv, 68, 89, 99, 105; *see also* experimentation; fidelity; hybridization
interfusion of arts (*zonghexing, zongyixing*) x; *see also* intermultimodal/intermultimodality
intermultimodal/intermultimodality x, xxi
intertextual/intertextuality xvi, xx, 17, 29, 69, 131
Ionesco, Eugène 29, 44, 155, 161–3, 170–4; *The Bald Soprano* 29, 44, 161, 163, 172, 174, 178, 180, 182; *Caligula* 167, 168–9, 177–81; *Rhinoceros* 29, 44, 161–2, 170–2

Jiang, Qing (Madame Mao; Lan Ping) 21, 28, 57, 82, 112, 125–6, 132, 137
jingju (Peking opera; Beijing opera) vi, viii–ix, xii, xv, xviii–ix, 14, 16, 29, 37, 39, 52, 68–71, 73–5, 81, 83–5, 99, 105, 155–6, 159, 174–82, 185

King Lear xv, 87, 98–102, 116, 118–20; *see also* Shakespeare, William

La Dame aux Camilias viii, 1, 11, 16, 29; *see also* Dumas, Alexandre, fils
Lady Windermere's Fan 108–9, 111, 117, 121; *see also* Wilde, Oscar
Lao, She 55, 132, 136, 151
Li, Hongzhang 4, 31
Li, Shuchang 2–3, 8–9
Li, Shutong 11–12, 18, 21–3; *see also* Spring Willow Society (*Chunliu she*)
Liang, Qichao 13–14, 123, 153

Life of Galileo, The xiv, 28, 33–5, 37, 41–2, 55, 63–4; *see also* Brecht, Bertolt
Lin, Shu 8, 15, 18, 21, 87, 90, 153–5; *see also Black Slave's Cry to Heaven* (*Heinu yutian lu*)
Lin, Zhaohua 46, 49, 51–2, 61, 64–5, 83, 94–5, 98, 105, 115–16, 119–20, 142–3, 146, 148, 150
little theatre 6, 64, 168, 181–2
L'Orphelin de la Chine vii, 152–3; *see also Caucasian Chalk Circle, The; L'Orphelin de la Maison de Tchao; Orphan of Zhao, The*
L'Orphelin de la Maison de Tchao 74, 152; *see also Caucasian Chalk Circle, The; Orphan of Zhao, The*
Lower Depths, The (*Yedian*) 123, 127–9, 144, 147, 149–51; *see also* Gorky, Maxim
Lu, Jingruo 11, 18, 23, 154; *see also* Spring Willow Society (*Chunliu she*)
Luo, Jinlin 68–9, 75–8, 81, 83–4
Lyceum Theatre (*lanxin dajuyuan*) 6, 9
Lysistrata 68; *see also* Aristophanes

Macbeth 29, 71, 87, 102; *see also* Shakespeare, William
Major Barbara 103, 105–6, 115, 118–20; *see also* Shaw, Bernard
Mao, Zedong 28, 30, 32, 54, 61, 122, 126, 130, 145, 149, 162–3
Medea 68–9, 75–8, 84–5; *see also* Euripides
Mei, Langfang vii
Meng, Jinghui 44, 61, 64, 94, 105–6, 120, 163, 172, 185–6
Merchant of Venice, The 7, 29, 87–91, 102, 118; *see also* Shakespeare, William
Miller, Arthur xiii–iv, xvii–viii, 21, 27, 29, 53–9, 62–4, 93, 107, 185; *The Crucible* xvii, 29, 54–5, 58, 62; *Death of a Salesman* xiv, xvii, 29, 53, 55–6, 63, 93, 106–7
Miser, The 17, 29, 157–8; *see also* Molière
mission colleges (mission schools) 2, 5, 7–8
modernism x, 64
Molière 3, 17, 124, 155, 157–60, 176, 178–9, 181–3, 185; *The Doctor in Spite of Himself* 124, 158–9, 178, 183; *Don Juan* 3, 158–9, 179, 182;

The Imaginary Invalid 158–9, 179, 182; *The Miser* 17, 29, 157–8; *The School of Wives* 160, 181, 183
Mother Courage and Her Children xiv, 32–3, 35, 58, 60, 62, 66; *see also* Brecht, Bertolt
Mrs. Warren's Profession 8, 103–5, 107, 109, 115, 117, 119; *see also* Shaw, Bernard

New Youth, The xiii, xv, 103, 185
No Exit 29, 161, 163, 166–7, 177, 180–1; *see also* Sartre, Jean-Paul

Oedipus the King 68–9, 70, 73, 75, 83–5; *see also* Sophocles
O'Neill, Eugene xv, xviii, xix, xxii, 11, 17, 25, 29, 56, 82, 103, 109, 121, 125, 136, 184–5; *Desire under the Elms* 21, 29; *The Emperor Jones* 29, 56, 109
Opéra in Paris 2
Oresteia 69, 75, 81–2; *see also* Aeschylus
Orphan of Zhao, The xii, xix, xxi, 74, 152–4, 175; *see also Caucasian Chalk Circle, The*; *L'Orphelin de la Maison de Tchao*
Ostrovsky, Aleksandr 123–6, 144–5, 150–1; *The Storm* (*Daleiyu*) 123–6, 144, 147–8
Ouyang, Yuqian 11, 16, 18, 23, 154; *see also* Spring Willow Society (*Chunliu she*)

Peter Gynt 29, 37; *see also* Ibsen, Henrik
post-modernism xxi
Pu, Cunxin 50, 96–8, 102, 143

realism x, xxi, 21–2, 27–8, 37, 41–2, 58–9, 64, 123, 128, 142
reception theory xvi, xxi
Ren, Ming 21, 46–9, 61, 65
Rhinoceros 29, 44, 161–2, 170–2; *see also* Ionesco, Eugène
role types 32

Salome 17, 108, 111–12, 119, 121; *see also* Wilde, Oscar
Sanders, Julie xvi, xx, xxii
Sartre, Jean-Paul 29, 155, 161–6, 176–82, 185; *Dirty Hands* 29, 162–3, 165, 177, 179, 180, 182;

Endgame 41, 42, 52, 62, 65–6; *No Exit* 29, 161, 163, 166–7, 177, 180–1
School of Wives, The 160, 181, 183; *see also* Molière
Seagull, The 143–4, 146–7; *see also* Chekhov, Anton
Search for Spring Willow Society (*xunzhao chunliushe*) xv, 1, 18, 22–3, 25–6; *see also Black Slave's Cry to Heaven* (*Heinu yutian lu*); Spring Willow Society (*Chunliu she*)
Shakespeare, William (Old Man Sha; Old Man Shakespeare) ix, xiv–v, xix, xxi, xxiii, 3, 6–8, 11, 17, 30, 71, 73, 80, 86–99, 101–3, 115–16, 118–21, 131, 176, 185–6; *Hamlet* xv, 3, 6–7, 21, 87–8, 94–8, 102, 105, 115–16, 119–20, 142–3; *King Lear* xv, 87, 98–102, 116, 118–20; *Macbeth* 29, 71, 87, 102; *The Merchant of Venice* 7, 29, 87–91, 102, 118
Shaw, Bernard (Shaweng; Old Man Shaw) 89, 102–4, 106–8, 113, 115–21, 180; *Major Barbara* 103, 105–6, 115, 118–20; *Mrs. Warren's Profession* 8, 103–5, 107, 109, 115, 117, 119
shingek xviii, 11–12, 23, 26; *see also* Spring Willow Society (*Chunliu she*)
shinpa xvii–viii, xxii, 11, 16, 19, 23, 154; *see also* Spring Willow Society (*Chunliu she*)
Sophocles 5, 29, 67–9, 75, 78, 83, 185; *Antigone* xx–ii, 68–9, 71, 75, 78–9, 81, 84–5; *Oedipus the King* 68–9, 70, 73, 75, 83–5
Spring Willow Society (*Chunliu she*) viii, xii, xv, xvii–viii, xxi, 1, 7–12, 14–23, 25–6, 89, 112, 154–5; *see also Black Slave's Cry to Heaven* (*Heinu yutian lu*)
Stanislavski, Konstantin 27–8, 32, 35, 37, 58–9, 123, 127, 134, 137–9, 143, 147
St. John's University (*Shengyuehan*) 7–8, 10, 87
Storm, The (*Daleiyu*) 123–6, 144, 147–8; *see also* Ostrovsky, Aleksandr
stylization (*chengshixing*) x, xii
Sun, Weishi 131, 137, 146, 151
symbolic representation (*xunixing, xieyixing*) x–xi, 171

Theatre of the Absurd xiii, 29, 41–2, 63, 65–6, 94, 159, 162, 173, 179–80
Three Sisters Waiting for Godot 65–6, 143, 163; *see also* Lin, Zhaohua
Tian, Han 106, 111–12, 117
tragedy 34, 43, 67–75, 77–8, 81–5, 98, 102, 124, 143, 156–7, 180; *see also* hero tragedy; tragic hero
tragic hero 67, 69, 70, 83; *see also* hero tragedy; tragedy
translation studies xvi, xix–xx, xxii, 119

Uncle Vanya 137–44, 147–9, 151; *see also* Chekhov, Anton

Verfremdungseffekt ("alienation effect"; estrangement effect) xii, xix–xx, xxii, 30, 32, 37, 40, 57, 62–3, 65, 133

Waiting for Godot 21, 41–2, 44–6, 49–53, 60–1, 63–6, 94, 105, 143, 162–3; *see also* Beckett, Samuel
Wang, Xiaonong 13, 24, 25–6
Wang, Youyou 8–9, 104, 109
Wang, Zhichun 4, 9, 10
Wilde, Oscar xix, 17, 86, 107–9, 111–14, 117–21, 185; *The Importance of*

Being Earnest 108, 112–15; *Lady Windermere's Fan* 108–9, 111, 117, 121; *Salome* 17, 108, 111–12, 119, 121
Williams, Tennessee xviii, 29, 184

xiqu (traditional Chinese drama) viii–xv, xvii–xx, 1–2, 6, 8–9, 12, 14, 16, 28–30, 32, 37, 39–40, 43, 58, 66–70, 74–5, 77, 81, 84, 87, 89, 99, 104, 109, 111, 135, 156, 174, 178, 183–5; *see also chuanju* (Sichuan opera); Hebei *bangzi; jingju* (Peking opera; Beijing opera); *yueju* (*yue* opera)
Xu, Xiaozhong 37, 90

Ying, Ruocheng 54–5, 57–8, 62, 105–7, 115, 117, 119, 121
yueju (*yue* opera) ix, xv, xviii, 63, 66, 75, 105

Zeng, Jize 3, 8, 10, 87
Zeng, Xiaogu 11–12, 15, 18, 23; *see also* Spring Willow Society (*Chunliu she*)
Zhang, Deyi 3, 4, 8, 18
Zhang, Qihong 90, 116, 119, 121

Printed in Great Britain
by Amazon